# Nordic Childhoods and Early Education

## Philosophy, Research, Policy, and Practice in Denmark, Finland, Iceland, Norway, and Sweden

*A volume in*
International Perspectives on Educational Policy, Research, and Practice
*Series Editor:* Kathryn M. Borman, University of South Florida

## International Perspectives on Educational Policy, Research, and Practice

Kathryn M. Borman, *Series Editor*

# Nordic Childhoods and Early Education

**Philosophy, Research, Policy, and Practice in Denmark, Finland, Iceland, Norway, and Sweden**

*Edited by*

## Johanna Einarsdottir
## Judith T. Wagner

INFORMATION AGE
PUBLISHING

Greenwich, Connecticut 06830 • www.infoagepub.com

**Library of Congress Cataloging-in-Publication Data**

Nordic childhoods and early education : philosophy, research, policy, and practice in Denmark, Finland, Iceland, Norway, and Sweden / edited by Johanna Einarsdottir, Judith T. Wagner.
    p. cm. – (International perspectives on educational policy, research, and practice)
  Includes bibliographical references.
  ISBN 1-59311-350-1 (pbk.) – ISBN 1-59311-351-X (hardcover)
  1. Early childhood education–Scandinavia. 2. Children–Scandinavia. I. Johanna Einarsdottir. II. Wagner, Judith T. III. Series.
  LB1139.3.S34N67 2006
  372.210948–dc22

                                                                    2005034819

Printed in the United States of America

# CONTENTS

# PREFACE

**Bernard Spodek**
*University of Illinois*

Over the many years I have been in early childhood education I have traveled to many places abroad and observed many early childhood education programs in different countries. I always return from such visits having learned a great deal. Not only have I learned about programs of early childhood education in other countries, but also each time I gained a different perspective regarding early childhood education in my own country, the United States.

In my travels, I would see practices that often were different from the ones with which I was familiar. Often these practices reflected a culture that was different from my own. Sometimes the practices were consistent with those I believed were appropriate for young children. And sometimes those practices were different from what I considered to be appropriate.

Not only would I learn about what happens to young children beyond our borders, but it helped me see our own practices in a new light. I would become aware that what we do to and for young children is not "natural" but rather a cultural invention that was created over a long period of time. These experiences abroad would lead me to question what I had taken for granted in relation to the education of young children. As my experiences broadened I became aware that we as a society had selected a particular form of education for our young children and that we might easily have selected other forms of education.

A book such as this, descriptive of early childhood practices in other countries—in this case Nordic countries—can serve the same purpose as visits to early childhood programs abroad. In learning about Nordic childhood and Nordic early childhood education we can reflect anew upon practices in our own countries, comparing and contrasting them as we use our knowledge of foreign experiences to sharpen our observations of what we have at home.

Many of the same issues we face in America regarding childhood and childhood education are evident in Nordic countries. Issues relating to the nature of childhood, the purposes of early childhood education, and what is considered the "good life" for children are raised in Nordic countries, just as they are in the United States. The way these issues are framed and how they are responded to may be different, however. In America, for example, we place great value on human lives, both in our social and political practices. However, we seem less concerned as a society with the quality of these lives as do those in the Nordic countries. We value childhood, but often one is not sure that we appreciate the nature of childhood itself. Too often we value childhood as preparation for later life rather than as a valued stage of life in its own right. Discourse related to the rights of children often seems strange to us. Play as a natural activity of childhood is often downplayed in favor of play as a means to learning academics. When we learn how other nations and other cultures respond to these issues, they can help us become more thoughtful about how we respond to them.

Early childhood education is both an international phenomenon and a local phenomenon. The pioneers of early childhood education, Froebel, Montessori, MacMillan, Dewey, and others, created their innovative programs in various countries to respond to the children living in particular local conditions. The ideas that had power, however, moved well beyond their local beginnings. Programs like the kindergarten of Froebel, the nursery school of Macmillan, the Montessori "house of the child," the Progressive educational ideals of Dewey all began within a particular local context. But these ideas spread worldwide. They were adopted by countries throughout the world. In each case, however, these models of early childhood education were adapted to the particular conditions in the countries in which they were transplanted. As we understand our own conditions and those of other countries, we can accept the fact that each culture will adapt educational ideas differently and that no one adaptation is necessarily better than another. Yet understanding each adaptation and how early childhood education functions within each culture can help us to better judge what we see in our own country and our own culture. It can also help us see new possibilities regarding the education of our young children that might not be evident if we look only to our own.

We are indebted to Johanna Einarsdottir and Judith T. Wagner for making this book available to us. By having early childhood scholars from Nordic countries write their chapters in English and by collecting them into a single volume, they have given us access to thoughts and ideas about early childhood education in another part of the world that would not otherwise be available to those of us who read only English. They have also allowed us to glimpse the broad intellectual community in early childhood education that exists beyond our own country and our language borders. We can only hope that others will continue such efforts to expand our view of international early childhood education.

CHAPTER 1

# NORDIC IDEALS AS REFLECTED IN NORDIC CHILDHOODS AND EARLY EDUCATION

**Judith T. Wagner and Johanna Einarsdottir**

Nordic culture, research, and practice make unique and broadly illuminating contributions to contemporary understandings of children and childhood, early childhood education, public policy, and child advocacy (Wagner, 2003, 2004). The chapters in this book, each in its own measure, exemplify the traditions and qualities of Nordic scholarship in early childhood education. This introduction provides background information on the Nordic countries and their perspectives on childhood and early education. It also summarizes topics and themes covered in the following chapters.

As we began our work as coeditors of this book nearly 2 years ago, we considered several interesting questions: Why publish an English-language book about childhood and early education in the Nordic countries? Who will be the audience for such a book? What qualifies the two of us as editors, given that one (Einarsdottir) is from Iceland, geographically distant from the other Nordic countries, and the other (Wagner) is an American?

*Nordic Childhoods and Early Education*, pages 1–12
Copyright © 2006 by Information Age Publishing
All rights of reproduction in any form reserved.

In thinking about the first question, Why publish an English-language book about childhood and early education in the Nordic countries?, we agreed that traditional Nordic views on children and childhood provide an interesting backdrop for discussions about early childhood research, policy, and practice in contemporary Western societies and, perhaps, in other parts of the world as well. Therefore, an English-language book seemed in order as a vehicle for communicating with scholars, policymakers, and practitioners who are not fluent in Nordic languages and not yet acquainted with the cultural and philosophical underpinnings of daily life for Nordic children and their families. In spite of differences between Nordic countries, Nordic people proudly lay claim to a distinctive, shared ideology about children and childhood, including such cherished cornerstones as egalitarianism, emancipation, democracy, compromise, solidarity, and the concept of the "good childhood" (Wagner, 2003, 2004). These ideals reveal themselves as repeated themes in this book.

Highly respected scholars from five Nordic countries readily accepted our invitation to contribute chapters on an intriguing array of topics. We quickly realized that our potential audience includes early childhood researchers and teacher educators, as well as graduate students and advanced undergraduate students. In addition, we imagine that scholars interested in Nordic social welfare systems might want to know more about how welfare policies and the uniquely Nordic philosophy that undergirds them evidence themselves in Nordic childhoods, family life, and approaches to early education.

This book represents a growing trend throughout the European academic community, especially in countries with languages read and understood by relatively few people outside the region, to publish in English as a way to enhance scholarly communication and dialogue across national and linguistic boundaries. All of our authors, except Wagner, have a native tongue other than English. Throughout the process of bringing this book to fruition, we have worked together to find ways to say in English what each author intended to say and to capture subtleties of meaning that could easily be lost "in translation" from the Nordic to the American context. Along the way to clarifying and reclarifying words, sentences, paragraphs, and concepts, we have learned a great deal, not only about similarities and differences among the Nordic countries but also about our own views, beliefs, and blind spots.

This growing trend to communicate in English represents both the promise and the problems associated with globalization, especially for geographically small and sparsely populated countries like those in the Nordic region. Nordic people view their languages as integral to their cultural heritage, their present-day identity, and their continuing distinctiveness. They show great interest in the preservation of their languages within the context of globalization. Each year, for example, the Finnish people pay homage to their native tongue on April 9, Finnish Language Day. November 16 marks Icelandic Language Day, described within the context of globalization by the country's former Minister of Education:

> It is the day when we Icelanders reflect upon our uniqueness as mirrored in our language [as a] a symbol of our certainty that we have our own remarkable history and cultural heritage.... The river of information flowing toward us becomes ever broader, moves ever faster; and it is a river no one would think of damming. On the other hand, we must remind ourselves that the Icelandic tongue is the instrument with which we convey our knowledge and the national vigor behind it. It is our single most potent cultural tool. It shapes our endeavors in the world of information and gives our contribution to it a singular value. By cultivating the uniqueness of our language, we strengthen our role in an international society. (Bjarnason, 1996, authors' translation)

Nordic languages, then, are an instrument for the enrichment of Nordic culture and cultivation of thought; but other languages, especially English, increasingly serve as instruments for communicating with the non-Nordic world. The Nordic debate about language revolves around preserving native tongues while engaging intellectually with an increasingly English-speaking world. This debate fits into the larger discussion of preserving what is characteristically and uniquely Nordic, while simultaneously becoming part of a global society. As Strand notes in Chapter 4 with regard to early childhood issues, multiculturalism and internationalization may diminish attention to what is inherently national or local, while, at the same time, placing the spotlight on local and national conditions in ways that would not be possible without the movement toward globalization.

## BRIEF INTRODUCTION TO THE NORDIC COUNTRIES

The Nordic region, or *Norden*, includes five countries—Denmark (*Danmark*), Finland (*Suomi*), Iceland (*Island*), Norway (*Norge*), and Sweden (*Sverige*), as well as the regions and provinces of the Aaland Islands (*Åland*), Faroe Island (*Føroyar*), and Greenland (*Grønland*). Each Nordic country has its own language, but those of the three Scandinavian countries—Denmark, Norway, and Sweden—are similar enough to be mutually understood. Icelandic, a close relative to Old Norse, the original language of the region, has remained relatively unchanged through the centuries, while the Danish, Norwegian, and Swedish have undergone many changes, including simplification of grammar and adoption of words from other languages, especially German and English. The official language of Finland, Finnish, is a non-Germanic language with roots similar to the languages spoken in Hungary and Estonia.

The Nordic countries range in size from Denmark, with 43,000 square kilometers, to Sweden with 450, 000 square kilometers. The population sizes range from Iceland's 295,000 inhabitants to Sweden's 8.6 million.

The Nordic countries are grouped together, not only geographically but also through shared heritage, culture, values, and ideals. We undertake these discussions of national and regional traits with humility, caution, and respect. "The line between authentically lived distinctiveness and stereotype can be blurry, especially when an outsider" has a hand in drawing that line (Wagner, 2003, p. 17). Each Nordic nation is distinct from the others in important ways, perhaps more readily apparent to themselves than to outsiders. However, the Nordic countries also share widely held, commonly understood, and deeply cherished views about children and childhood (Wagner, 2003; Wagner, Camparo, Tsenkova, & Camparo, 2005). This, we claim, is the most compelling *raison d'etre* for this book, which offers its readers the opportunity to learn about these views and their expression in everyday home, school, and community life.

## NORDIC CHILDHOOD AND EARLY EDUCATION

What stands out about childhood and early education in the Nordic countries, especially in comparison to America and many other contemporary societies, is their social welfare and educational policies, and, even more, the extent to which these policies are actually realized in everyday practice—a clear indication of the high value Nordic people place on children and childhood. In Chapter 2 Kristjansson highlights the social welfare model as one of two central and distinguishing features of "Nordicness" and Nordic childhoods. At the core of the social welfare systems in all Nordic countries, he argues, is the unfaltering conviction that all citizens, including children, should enjoy a high quality of life and an equal standard of living, as well as social and personal well-being. This conviction is substantially represented in each Nordic nation's early childhood education policies as well. A recent United Nations report (2004) acknowledges the Scandinavian societies as the world's most equal, economically and between genders. Child and family policies are based on Nordic ideology and traditions, emphasizing democracy, equality, freedom and emancipation, solidarity through cooperation and compromise, and a general concept of the "good childhood," or what life should be like for all children (Wagner, 2003). These ideals appear, sometimes boldly and sometimes subtly, in each chapter.

## UNIFYING THEMES

Although each chapter author tackles a different topic, both general and characteristically Nordic themes appear again and again throughout this book. Among the general topics in contemporary early childhood discourse addressed in various chapters are (1) the significance of the cultural contexts; (2) the preservation of local distinctiveness amid rapid globalization; (3) the influence of postmodern ideas, in general, and various child-related post-modern theories, in particular; (4) change, especially as it relates to the role of child care in contemporary society and the relationship between preschool and compulsory education; (5) children's rights; (6) the role of play, especially in relation to academic achievement; (7) the importance of relationship-building between children and adults; (8) methods and ethics of childhood research, early childhood professional preparation, and ECE practice; and (9) the complementary and contradictory roles of government (national and local) and professionals as decision-makers for early childhood policy and practice.

Throughout this book, each of these contemporary topics is infused with "Nordicness"—a term coined by Kristjansson in Chapter 2—as the authors write about them from the characteristically Nordic foundations noted above. For example, both Strand in Chapter 4 and Einarsdottir in Chapter 7 discuss the significance of the cultural contexts in which children live and in which public and educational policies are animated. Both authors describe the ways national history and Nordic cultural values have influenced the development of preschool education. They also write about how imported ideas, such as those from Froebel and, more recently, Reggio Emilia and High/Scope, have been adapted for use in the Nordic context. Einarsdottir notes the Icelandic effort to find a balance between openness to outside ideas and the desire to sustain traditional Icelandic perspectives and practices. On the other hand, Strand suggests that early childhood theory and practice can sometimes become insulated and isolated. She notes that in Norway, for example, the circle of intellectual ideas may be somewhat closed off because of a "social game" promoting the views of a select group of already established authorities.

From the perspective of postmodern feminist theory, in Chapter 10 Taguchi focuses on the ways in which accepted theory and practice can be maintained or, alternatively, changed through a process of active reflection, multiple "readings" (or analyses from various theoretical frameworks), deconstruction, and ethical resistance. Lenz Taguchi also describes the ways in which ECE practice has been influenced by a succession of societal orientations and pedagogical theories. For instance, Nordic preschools arose from a perceived societal need to provide substitute maternal care and home-like environments because of "disadvantaged" children's circumstances and/or labor market demands for women in the workplace. However, as the author notes, the central role of "female nurturing" in early education is being challenged by poststructural feminist ideology and contemporary educational theory focusing on children as active investigators of the world, constructors of their own knowledge, and, essentially, creators of their own, individual "self." In Chapter 3 Johansson also comments on the diminishing influence of traditional female perspectives in early childhood teacher education due, in large measure, to long-standing male domination in the universities. In Chapter 11 Wagner further discusses structural and poststructural feminism, as well as theories of construction and deconstruction, as frames for contemporary Nordic ECE discourse and scholarship.

Nordic child-centeredness inspires several chapter authors regardless of their specific topics. Nordic people generally view childhood as important in its own right, not simply as a platform from which to become an adult. Among the practical exemplars of this viewpoint is that Nordic children typically begin formal school later than children in most other parts of the industrialized world, so they have both time and freedom during the early childhood years to play and to explore the world around them, unencumbered by excessive (according to Nordic calibrations) supervision and control by adults. As Broström points out in Chapter 9, Nordic people have traditionally taken children and their rights quite seriously; but, even here, the influence of globalization becomes evident in the current debate about children's rights to freedom and independence versus their right to protection from modern dangers, perceived and real. Broström also probes ethical questions that arise when adult researchers study children so thoroughly and so closely that we invade their privacy and subject their lives to interpretation from the only perspective of which we are capable— the *adult* perspective.

As many of our authors point out, children's right to free play has long been a core value in Nordic ECE. However, increasing emphasis on academic learning (which many Nordic scholars and practitioners view as an "invasion" from other countries) encroaches on both the value and the time for childhood play, as each Nordic country in turn produces national curriculum guidelines and restructures early childhood teacher preparation, often to more closely mirror professional preparation of elementary school teachers. Along these lines, in Chapter 8 Hakkarainen proposes the use of play to promote specific learning goals, such as literacy development, often through more purposeful adult participation in both spontaneous and planned, narrative-based play activities. However, he cautions against underestimating the value of play for its own sake and its developmental benefits.

Another nearly-universal right of Nordic childhood is access to preschool. However, both the pedagogy and the content of preschool are broadly debated throughout the Nordic countries. How much free play should there be? What is the appropriate balance between freedom and structure? What kinds of structured activities are appropriate at the preschool level? To what extent should preschool be valued in and of itself and to what extent should it be viewed as preparation for entry into compulsory school? What kinds of adult preplanning enhance program quality and what kinds of adult preplanning squelch spontaneity and creativity among the teachers and the children as well?

Although Nordic early childhood educators have traditionally (and often loudly) rejected formal schooling as the model for preschool, several authors point out that traditional distinctions between preschool and primary school are rapidly blurring as Nordic states publish preschool curriculum guidelines and make concerted efforts to create smooth, even "seamless," transitions between preschool and school. Some see these trends as a threat, perhaps to the very existence of ECE as a distinct field and preschool teaching as a distinct profession. However, others, like Pramling-Samuelsson in Chapter 5, suggest that, at least in the Swedish preschool class (a special class for children in the year prior to their entry into compulsory school, similar to the American kindergarten class), greater coordination between preschool and school is leading to more professional preschool classes in which teachers work more consciously and participate in more substantive planning as they consider how they and the children will spend their days together.

As preschools have changed, often in the direction of becoming more school-like under the influence of new curriculum guidelines, so too has the professional preparation of preschool teachers throughout the Nordic countries. Traditionally, Nordic preschool teacher education has been conducted in separate colleges or seminaries, emphasizing theories and practical applications that were quite different from the course of study for primary-grade teachers. However, as Johansson illustrates in Chapter 3, the trend in Sweden, for example, is to minimize differences in the preparation of preschool teachers and school teachers, while other countries, like Finland and Iceland, struggle to maintain preschool teacher preparation as a distinct, but equal, course of study and Denmark combines preschool teacher education with social work, after-school care, and elder care. Johansson argues that potential threats to Nordic early childhood knowledge and tradition exist in all five Nordic countries. Although this theme of potential threat appears repeatedly throughout the book, some authors contend that many of the cherished preschool traditions will survive, even if in a somewhat altered state.

## DIFFERENCES IN TERMINOLOGY OFTEN REFLECT
## DIFFERENCES IN IDEOLOGY

Nordic early childhood discourse includes terms that are fundamental to Nordic philosophy and ideology, yet difficult to capture fully in translation, especially for an American audience. For instance, in America *preschool* (literally *before school*) is a superordinate term encompassing all kinds of out-of-home care prior to the start of compulsory education. However, Nordic people use different terms and for different reasons. For instance, Icelandic people use *playschool* as the general term for all group care for children under the compulsory school-start age. This represents more than a simple difference in terminology. The term *playschool* emphasizes the central role of play in Icelandic early childhood philosophy and practice. Similarly, Danes use the term *kindergarten*—literally *children's garden*—to refer to group care settings for children younger than compulsory school age. When they speak English, many Danes carefully avoid the word *preschool* because of their staunch belief that group care for children younger than age 6 should not be *school*-like and should not base its existence on being *pre* anything (Wagner, 2004).

Definitional differences are far easier to explain than conceptual differences. For instance, non-Nordic readers may be puzzled by Nordic distinctions between such terms as development and learning, care and teaching, or care and education (Wagner, 2003). In Chapter 6 Niikko illustrates how the terms *care, caring,* and *all-round care* represent fundamental and different concepts in Finnish early childhood education discourse. Further illustrating Nordic distinctions between terms that might be used interchangeably in America, Danish preschool teachers often protest being referred to as *teachers,* arguing adamantly that they do not *teach* children. Rather, they *care* for them. Here they are not referring to custodial care, as is often the case in American discourse about care, but rather to a widely shared and perhaps idealized Danish view of interactions between children—as active constructors of their own being through self-directed activity—and the adults who *care* for them, but do not *teach* them, by focusing on their needs, developing strong relationships with them, and engaging them in a democratic, egalitarian classroom community. Interestingly, the term *care,* as Danes use it, is ideologically consistent, in several fundamental ways, with American use of *education,* as in "developmentally appropriate *education*" for young children. "Therefore, Americans could easily be confused when a Danish pædagog (who does not want to be called a "preschool *teacher*") argues that she does not *teach* the children anything" (Wagner, 2003, p. 17). As Einarsdottir points out in Chapter 7, some Icelandic playschool teachers also draw a clear line between the concept of teaching and care, equating *teaching* with formal, whole-group instruction, which they view as inappropriate at the preschool level.

In what could seem like splitting linguistic hairs to an American reader unfamiliar with Nordic perspectives, Nordic ECE scholars and practitioners carefully distinguish between various terms and concepts, placing high importance on what may seem to outsiders as subtle differences. For instance, Broström (2003) defined three different, but overlapping, dimensions of child care: *need care, upbringing care,* and *teaching care.* According to Broström, these distinctions are difficult to explain in English. In simplistic terms, however, need care refers to supporting children in order to help them fulfill their wishes, needs, and intentions. Need care requires the adult to see each child as a person, with rights and responsibilities, and to provide boundaries for children as necessary to protect their health and safety as they actively explore the world and express their autonomy. Upbringing care is a general societal concept referring to the professional's role in helping children acquire normative standards, attitudes, and behaviors necessary for full functioning in a democracy. Teaching care refers to supporting children as they construct academic and social knowledge and skills.

These distinctions in terms and in the larger philosophical and ideological contexts they represent frame Nordic notions about childhood and early education, as well as current debates about the role and purposes of preschool in contemporary Nordic society. Such distinctions appear in the foreground in some chapters and in the background in others, since they are generally taken for granted as shared values and shared understandings when Nordic ECE scholars and practitioners communicate with one another.

## NORDIC INSPIRATIONS: CHAPTER SUMMARIES

Both from the perspective of an insider (Einarsdottir) and an outsider (Wagner), we find that Nordic ideals, theories, and practices have inspired our work with children, families, and teachers over many years. Together with the other authors in this book, we continue to explore Nordic traditions, policies, and values as frames for further understanding a variety of contemporary early childhood issues, such as those examined in the chapters that follow.

In Chapter 2, "The Making of Nordic Childhoods," Kristjansson describes two distinctive features of Nordicness and Nordic childhoods, namely, a pervasive and strong child-centeredness and the Nordic welfare state. Together, these features have contributed to the Nordic countries' international reputation for their ambitious and progressive child and family policies. The author traces the roots of contemporary child-centeredness and the welfare state back to the cultural history of the region and describes how these distinctive features influence contemporary life for Nordic children.

In Chapter 3 Johansson traces trends in Nordic early childhood education from the autonomous kindergarten movement, controlled by preschool teachers who were trained in specialized preschool teacher seminaries, to today's situation where preschool teachers have lost their dominant influence on the field and where professional preparation programs are no longer specific to early education. Based on these trends, Johansson presents a possible future scenario in which the professional position of preschool teacher may no longer exist, bringing to an end Nordic preschool teachers' long struggle for recognition of a set of transnational, maternalistic, and feministic values that started in Germany in 1850.

In Chapter 4 Strand points to the complex relations between common knowledge and beliefs in Norwegian ECE and ongoing social negotiations about Norwegianness. Based on her research, she suggests that the "social game" of Norwegian early childhood education is fundamentally about demarcating the field from other social fields and about generating a collective belief in the game. However, she argues that, because the early childhood field is fluctuating and marginalized and because the traditional conception of Norwegianness is also being challenged today, belief in the game itself seems threatened.

In Chapter 5, Ingrid Pramling Samuelsson focuses on the transition from preschool to elementary school in Sweden at three different levels: (1) the official level, as represented by public policy and official documents; (2) the scientific level, including findings from recent studies and the specific problems that have surfaced in recent research; and (3) the practical level, including suggestions for further integrating preschool and school through a research-grounded approach called developmental pedagogy.

In Chapter 6, entitled "Finnish Daycare: Caring, Education, and Instruction," Niikko takes a holistic look at Finnish societal, educational, and pedagogical characteristics and issues as they relate to the broader Nordic context. Focusing on universal social and educational services for Finnish children and families, the author examines unique features of daycare pedagogy in her country. She describes its multiprofessional approach to early childhood education, detailing important distinctions in terms and the larger Finnish and Nordic concepts they represent. She also explores the problems and the opportunities associated with the trend toward increasing pedagogical connections between daycare and school.

In Chapter 7, "Between Two Traditions, Between Two Continents: Early Childhood Education in Iceland," Einarsdottir describes the various contexts in which early childhood education occurs in her country and examines both distinct features and current dilemmas facing the Icelandic preschool. She notes frictions in Icelandic preschools that can be regarded as a conflict between long-standing cultural views and newer international trends, as Icelandic early childhood educators try to balance openness to outside ideas with reverence for traditional Icelandic perspectives and practices.

In Chapter 8 Hakkarainen analyzes the status of play in Nordic ECE programs and expresses particular concern about underestimation of the developmental potential of play in Finland. Too often, Hakkarainen argues, early educators and policymakers focus on play's role in cognitive development and the learning of facts, thereby underestimating and undervaluing the actual benefits of play. Proposing that a narrative-learning approach should be used in play contexts, the author provides illustrations from three different experimental programs: (1) a problem-solving situation in which two girls negotiate with an adult, (2) an example of literacy learning imbedded in play, and (3) a play world shared by adults and children aiming at particular educational goals and outcomes.

According to Brostrom in Chapter 9, entitled "Children's Perspectives on Their Childhood Experiences," progressive early childhood educators have criticized the view of children as objects and have argued that children should be seen as participants and active subjects with their own rights and responsibilities. In some periods, Brostrom says, this progressive approach has been too anti-authoritarian and overly child-centered. However, in recent years, influenced by the shift from modern to postmodern life, a more moderate version has prevailed. The author presents three interrelated theoretical frameworks, which can be seen as a context for growing interest in children's perspectives in education and research. These three frameworks are (1) childhood sociology, (2) childhood psychology, and (3) children as participants.

In Chapter 10, "Reconceptualizing Early Childhood Education: Challenging Taken-for-Granted Ideas," Lenz Taguchi questions the notion that there is, or ever could be, a single successful and appropriate learning theory for postmodern early childhood education. Instead, she suggests a reconceptualized poststructuralist, theoretically multidimensional, and inclusionary approach. The recommended approach incorporates an "ethic of resistance," using deconstruction as a tool for analyzing children's work and play. Drawing on two examples, the author shows what such reconceptualizations can be all about in everyday preschool practice. The first example illustrates a deconstruction process among the preschool teachers and the second example illustrates deconstructive learning processes among children.

In the final chapter, Wagner responds to the ideas presented by the other authors and reflects on her personal experiences and scholarly work in the Nordic countries, especially Denmark, during the last 18 years. Her essay concludes with an appeal to non-Nordic early childhood educators, researchers, and policymakers, especially in America, to think about the ways in which any society might be strengthened by adopting the ideals and values central to the Nordic concept of the "good childhood."

## REFERENCES

Bjarnason, B. (1996). *Dagur íslenskrar tungu* [Day of the Icelandic language]. Speech delivered on the first Icelandic Language Day, November 16, 1996. Retrieved February 21, 2001, from http://mrn.stj.is

Broström, S. (2003). Unity of care, teaching and upbringing: A theoretical contribution towards a new paradigm in early childhood education. In M. E. Lohmander (Ed.), *Researching early childhood: Care, play and learning curricula for early childhood education* (pp. 21–39). Göteborg: Göteborg University.

United Nations. (2004). *Human development report 2004: Cultural liberty in today's diverse world.* New York: United Nations Development Program.

Wagner, J. T. (2003). Introduction: International perspectives and Nordic contributions. In S. Broström & J. T. Wagner (Eds.), *Early childhood education in five Nordic countries: Perspectives on the transition from preschool to school* (pp. 11–25). Arhus, Denmark: Systime Academic Press.

Wagner, J. T. (2004). Fishing naked: Nordic early childhood philosophy, policy, and practice. *Young Children, 59*(5), 56–62.

Wagner, J. T., Camparo, L. B., Tsenkova, V., & Camparo, J. C. (2005). *Peer preferences and social status of Denmark's minority and majority children: En god barndom.* Manuscript submitted for publication.

CHAPTER 2

# THE MAKING
# OF NORDIC CHILDHOODS

**Baldur Kristjansson**
*Iceland University of Education*

This chapter describes and analyzes how it is to grow up as a young child in contemporary *Norden*, or more precisely, in the nation states of Denmark, Finland, Iceland, Norway, and Sweden. I focus on two cultural aspects: Nordic child centeredness and the Nordic welfare state. Building on the axiom that the present is born out of the past, I also try to identify some of the historical roots of these cultural dimensions.

The first aspect is what I call *Nordic child-centeredness*. In public everyday life, it manifests itself in that childhood-related issues are, and have long been, particularly prevalent within Nordic social and political discourse (Therborn, 1993). The most recent manifestation of this child-centeredness is the institution of the *Ombudsman for Children* system, introduced in Norway in 1981, and adopted by the other Nordic countries (except for Finland) in the mid-1990s. The Ombudsman for Children is a commissioner with statutory rights and duties to promote and protect the rights and interests of children and young people, first and foremost at the national level, but also internationally, as these rights are expressed in leg-

*Nordic Childhoods and Early Education*, pages 13–42
Copyright © 2006 by Information Age Publishing
All rights of reproduction in any form reserved.

islation and international conventions, such as the *United Nations Convention on the Rights of the Child* (ENOC, 2005). Norway publishes its Ombudsman for Children website in Norwegian and English, while Sweden publishes its website in its native tongue, English, and a few other languages. These websites provide extensive links to other international organizations and agencies, especially throughout Europe, further underscoring Sweden's and Norway's ambition to get out the message globally.

The second aspect relates to welfare policies developed by the Nordic nations, often referred to as the *Nordic welfare state* or *model* (Esping-Andersen, 1990, 1999; Hicks & Kenworthy, 2003; Vogel, 2000) and the family policies that are based on it (Arves-Parès, 1995; Tauberman, 1995).[1] I describe this model in greater detail in a later section. Here it suffices to say that among its distinguishing features is the vision of an egalitarian society, where all citizens enjoy equally high standards of living, as well as social and personal well-being.

Within the realm of family policy, the strong emphasis on social equality is manifested in diverse political measures aimed at enhancing gender equality within the family, and, in families with children, between the parents. These measures have, according to a recent United Nations report (2004), earned the Scandinavian societies the distinction of being recognized as the world's most equal, economically and between the genders.

## VARIATIONS IN NORDIC CHILDHOOD AND FAMILY POLICIES

Several indicators point to the appropriateness of selecting Nordic child centeredness and the Nordic welfare state as the frameworks for describing and analyzing what it is like to grow up in the Nordic countries. These indicators include research, such as the studies mentioned above, and international statistics, suggesting that these two factors can serve as defining features of Nordic childhoods. However, we must proceed with caution. Except for Therborn's unique study on children's rights from an international perspective (1993), none of the studies cited above on welfare-state models and family policies or other studies known by this author allow for simultaneous comparisons of *all* Nordic countries, *vis-à-vis* other Western nations. Furthermore, the studies cited above are heavily slanted toward Sweden. Sweden is represented in all of the studies, while Iceland is included in none of them. This skew is not without its reasons. First, it reflects the fact that Sweden is not only the largest Nordic country, but also, for a long time, the most affluent. In addition, Sweden also has a long tradition of ambitious and inventive family policy, the groundwork for which was laid in the early 1930s by the internationally renowned economists and social democrats, Alva and Gunnar Myrdal (1934).

Through the years, the Swedish family welfare system has received much international praise (Cohen, Moss, Petrie, & Wallace, 2004; Haas, 1996; Kamerman, 1991). However, a few warnings have been sounded as well, most notably from Popenoe (1988, 1991), who claimed that the strong Swedish focus on gender equality and dual parental employment were undermining the traditional nuclear family and related family values. To cite Popenoe (1988), and the title of his book, these modern trends were "disturbing the nest." What Popenoe did not take into account, however, is that the nuclear family, as it is classically understood in the United States and many other Westernized countries, has never been a fully embraced norm in Sweden or in the other Nordic cultures (Gaunt, 1996; Lassbo, 1999). Furthermore, its definition is less strict in the Nordic countries than in the Anglo-Saxon world, reflecting the fact that traditionally the "marriage family" has been less dominant in the Nordic countries than in most other Western societies (e.g., Gaunt, 1996). This issue is addressed further in a later section.

The overrepresentation of Sweden in Nordic research also raises some methodological issues. For instance, is not there a risk that the Swedish overrepresentation leads to analogous overgeneralizations, in that Swedish childhood conditions will be taken as applying to the entire Norden? And, in the case of Iceland, for which we have little research to build on regarding Nordic child centeredness or the Nordic welfare state, can we be sure that Icelandic childhood conditions fit at all within the Nordic framework?

As for the first question, a data compilation for the nations of the European Union (Ditch, Barnes, & Bradshaw, 1996) showed that the three Nordic EU members, Denmark, Finland, and Sweden, form a strikingly homogeneous cluster when it comes to public expenditures to compensate parents for child-related costs, ranging between 71.8% and 76.5%, with Finland in the lead. Even more importantly, their expenditures exceed by a large margin those of other EU nations, such as Belgium, which takes fourth place, with 61.5%. A comparative analysis of a similar kind by Olafsson (1999), based exclusively on the Nordic countries, showed Norway fully on par with the Nordic EU members.

*Quantitative* aspects of family policy, such as monetary expenditures, hint at the scope and the general direction of family policy ambitions; but to really comprehend family policies, we also need information about their *qualitative* aspects, such as the social norms, traditions, and values underlying the social practices themselves. Unfortunately, such information is limited or has not yet been systematized in Sweden or in the other Nordic countries. However, there are some strong indications that the Swedish social democratic tradition is, to a greater extent than in the other Nordic countries, outspokenly positive toward political measures intended to have immediate impact on the inner life of the family (e.g., Hedborg, 1995; Tauberman, 1995). However, these social policies are not without controversy in Sweden; they have their strong vocal critics. For example, some argue that these social policies carry an undertone of "we know what is best for you" (e.g., Kågeson & Lidmark, 2002), where the "we" is the government and the "you" is the parent. To support this claim, critics cite the lack of daycare alternatives. Parents must accept the prevailing public daycare and preschools for their young children because alternatives are neither deemed necessary nor made available by those in power.

Beginning in 1994, the Finnish adopted a policy that seems to be diametrically opposed to the Swedish policies described previously. The Finnish policy builds upon a child leave/benefits system that gives parents with small children the opportunity and economic possibility to choose how to arrange for their children's care for their first 3 years, including the possibility of one parent's taking care of the child in their own home. The underlying rationale is that parents with young children are entitled to a child benefit corresponding to, approximately, what it otherwise would cost the state to provide high-quality daycare for the child (Viitala, 1995).

Now we come back to the question about Iceland: Do Icelandic childhoods fit comfortably within the cluster of Nordic childhoods with regard to the cultural aspects in focus here, namely child centeredness and the Nordic welfare model? Hardly, if one is to judge from available research. For instance, Iceland is clearly an outlier from the Nordic cluster with respect to the percentage of gross national product (GNP) used for public support of families with children. In 1996–1997 public support to families with children was 2.35% of the GNP (Olafsson, 1999). This amount was equivalent to only 60% of the corresponding support in the other four Nordic countries, which ranged between 3.53–3.91% of their GNP, with Finland at the top. Furthermore, Eydal and Olafsson (2003) claimed that Iceland had no formalized, coherent policy for families with children before 1990. It was not until 1997 that the Icelandic parliament agreed that there was a need for a formal family policy (Juliusdottir, 2001). Interestingly, it appears that the Icelandic welfare model is gradually moving away from its Nordic roots, toward a more liberal (in the classical meaning) variant, resembling that of Australia and New Zealand (Olafsson, 1999), where family and child benefits are income-tested and kept to a minimum. On the other hand, however, the percentage of Icelandic children under 5 years of age who attend public daycare centers is among the highest in *Norden* (NOSOCO, 2004).

Succumbing to the realities that Sweden is not only the biggest of the Nordic nations but also (arguably, however) represented as the archetype of the Nordic welfare model, and also to the fact that it is by far the most thoroughly documented with respect to the topics of this chapter (Ree-gård, 2001), it is not only justified but unavoidable to give Sweden more attention than the other Nordic countries. Similarly, it is unavoidable that Iceland's deviations from the rest of Norden place it outside the framework of this discussion.

## NORDIC CHILD-CENTEREDNESS

Corporal punishment is as humiliating for him who gives it as for him who receives it; it is ineffective besides. Neither shame nor physical pain have any other effect than a hardening one. (Key, 1900)

If I were to name the year when the public discourse that I have chosen to name *Nordic child-centeredness* took off, it would be 1900. At that time Ellen Key, a Swedish teacher and philanthropist, published a much-celebrated book, *The Century of the Child* (in Swedish, *Barnets århundrade*). The book was almost immediately translated into many languages and became one of the most discussed books of its time. Until this day, it still has an impact in the Scandinavian countries, as indicated by the book's republication in 1996, with the Norwegian child researcher, O. Stafseng, as publisher. In the book, Key made an emphatic plea for the new 20th century to be devoted to the betterment of children's conditions, a more child-centered pedagogy, and upbringing where the children's own perspectives and interests were to be the guideposts for children's education.

Key eloquently argued against the authoritarian and insensitive upbringing of her time. Instead, Key noted, upbringing should be democratic, giving children a say, and, thus, contribute to creation of a better society. Many of Key's ideas about children's rights have had a lasting impact and have been adapted as children's legal rights, not only in Scandinavia but internationally as well. One example is Key's radical proposal that children should have the right to divorce their parents, which has recently been ratified in Norway.[2]

It may be argued that the historical timing for Key's *Century of Childhood* could not have been better. As latecomers into the industrial era, Denmark, Norway, and Sweden were still in the middle of an intense transformation from poor, peasant cultures into industrial, urban nation-states with rapidly strengthening economies (Hoffman, 1997). (At this time, Finland was still a part of Russia and Iceland was a Danish colony.) As had been the case in most of Western Europe over a century earlier, rapid urbanization brought with it social displacement *en masse*, not least among young people and families with children, resulting in widespread poverty and misery among those groups. In the wake of these changes came considerable social unrest. As a consequence, the well-established and influential bourgeoisie and a burgeoning middle class, to which Ellen Key belonged along with a growing number of child professionals, was gravely concerned (Hultqvist, 1990; Ohrlander, 1992). Without a doubt, Key's message inspired the bourgeoisie and growing middle class, including many teachers, to action.

Although hard to verify, it is very likely that Key's writings caught the attention of a group of jurists and civil servants of different ranks from the three Scandinavian nations (Denmark, Sweden, and Norway), who already in 1872 had launched an ambitious and internationally unprecedented project to harmonize their public policies, including legislation on children's rights. These efforts consisted of collaboration in the drafting of new laws, as well as frequent, institutionalized cross-national juristic exchange. According to Therborn, these efforts toward harmonizing policy eventually rendered the "Nordic family as the tightest [family of all Western nations]" (1993, p. 246) with regard to their public policy and legal systems of thought, traditions, and ideologies.

The firmest empirical support for Nordic child-centeredness as being stronger or more pervasive than in other Western nations comes from Therborn's (1993) comparative study of the development of children's rights in Western democracies, where twenty-one nations were involved, including the Scandinavian countries, Southern and Western Europe, North America, Australia, and New Zealand. The study was a part of a larger research project in which the participating nations were divided into, roughly speaking, four clusters or "families of nations," namely (1) The Anglo-American Common Law countries, originally emanating from the British Empire; (2) the Romanistic family of Southern, mainly Catholic, Europe; (3) the Germanic family, consisting of the German speaking countries; and (4) the Nordic family. As illustrated in Table 2.1 (adapted from Therborn, 1993, p. 256), children's rights legislation is grouped into three categories. The table shows that for each category of children's rights, Norway figures as a pioneer, alone or accompanied by either Denmark or Sweden.

Keeping in mind that Therborn's analysis was based on 21 Western societies, it seems safe to conclude that, within the legal areas covered by the study, the Nordic countries stand out in their endeavors to protect children's rights. The timeline shown in the table's far-left column indicates, furthermore, that the Nordic countries, spearheaded by Norway, play a pioneering role in initiating such laws, as illustrated by Norway's status as the only nation so far to adopt a law on children's rights to divorce their parents, as suggested almost a century earlier by Ellen Key, the avant garde advocate of children's rights.

**Table 2.1.    The Development of Children's Rights in 21 Western Nations (Adapted from Therborn, 1993, p. 256)[a]**

| Rights | Rights, in more detail | First two clusters to fully implement (within paranthe-ses: partial implementation) | Time of implementation |
|---|---|---|---|
| **Children's rights for a child-centered family** | Explicit legal formulation of equal parental obliga-tions and of the best inter-est of the child as a paramount principle (e.g., in custody litigations). | **1st cluster:** Norway, Sweden | By 1918 |
| | | **2nd cluster:** *Denmark, Finland,* England, N. Zealand, Scotland, (US) | By World War II |
| **Equal rights for all children** | Equality between children of married and nonmarried parents with regard to both paternity and inheritance. | **1st cluster:** *Norway, (Sweden)* | By 1918 |
| | | **2nd cluster:** *Denmark, (Finland)* | By World War II |
| **Children's rights to integrity** | 1. Legal prohibition of corporal punishment by parents and other custodians | **1st cluster:** *Norway, Sweden* | By 1980 |
| | | **2nd cluster:** *Denmark, Finland,* Austria | By 1990 |
| | 2. Children's right to divorce their parents.[b] | **Only nation:** *Norway* | By 1990 |

[a] With kind permission from the author.
[b] Although Norway was first to ratify both laws, it was Sweden who first prohibited corporal punishment.

As with any lawmaking, legislation aimed at protecting the rights of chil-dren *vis-à-vis* adult society is only a first step. If any earnestness lies behind the effort, the establishment of an effective system of law enforcement at different levels of society must follow. The institution of a special authority, *Ombudsman for Children,* first introduced in Norway in 1981 and adopted by the other Nordic countries in the mid-1990s, can be seen in this light.[3] In addition to ensuring that children's legal rights and interests are respected at state and municipal levels, the Ombudsman for Children is expected to (1) be on the watch for local and global trends that might threaten chil-dren's rights and interests, (2) initiate research to promote children's interests, (3) monitor legislative propositions and analyze their conse-quences for children, (4) inform the general public about children's rights and interests, and (5) promote children's interests in a wider, international context. However, if one is to judge from official documents and public information, the Norwegian and Swedish Child Ombudsman offices are far more comprehensive than those in the other Nordic countries (BO, Nor-way, 2005; BO, Sweden, 2005).

In the new millennium new offices are being established around Eastern and Western Europe. Notably, among the large Western European nations, only England and Italy are missing from the lists of countries working to establish an office of Children's Ombudsman. An examination of the website of the European Network of Ombudsmen for Children (ENOK, 2005) reveals that the Nordic offices, in particular those of Norway and Sweden, enjoy markedly higher status within their countries and governmental systems, as indicated by levels of state funding, staff numbers, and degrees of autonomy within the public administration.

## THE WIDER LANDSCAPE OF NORDIC CHILD-CENTEREDNESS

Inquiries into Nordic child-centeredness consistently show that childhood is highly valued by the Nordic peoples. But the question has to be raised about whether this phenomenon is so unique. I propose an answer of "no but yes." Sound judgment tells us that *invariably* every culture must take childhood seriously and foster cultural values to ensure that children are appreciated and cherished; otherwise, the culture would degenerate in due time and cease to exist. What, however, is culturally *variable*, due to differing social and material conditions and historical circumstances, is how and in what social contexts these sentiments are expressed (Heywood, 2001). In the Nordic countries such manifestations are part of the public discourse, arguably to a greater extent than in other parts of the world, and a significant aspect of discourse in the private sphere as well.

But the issue is far more complicated than that. I argue that childhood may be valued on the basis of two loosely related perspectives. The first I call the perspective of *prospective value*, since it focuses on the significance of childhood on the basis of its future value for society; its significance for the individual child him- or herself; or, today, especially in the third world, as a future asset for the family and a security for aging parents (e.g., Stearns, 1989). The child-like features of the childhood period are not so much appreciated for their own sake, but rather on the basis of what they will likely develop into in adulthood. This orientation toward childhood is characterized by attitudes that are more pragmatic than emotional. And, due to its prospective orientation and a representation of childhood as a transitory phase, it is seen as legitimate, even desirable, to "fiddle with the clock of childhood," thereby trying to accelerate the tempo in which children acquire adult-like skills (e.g., Elkind, 1981).

Although the relative strength of this prospective perspective surely varies across cultures and historical epochs, it is, by necessity, universal, since it paves the way for cultural continuity. However, I argue that modern society's strong reliance on education and strivings for maximization of resources, including human resources, have brought this perspective into the forefront as never before, leading to increasing pressures by policy-makers to introduce formal education and training to children at an ever younger age (Kristjansson, 2001). Although the Nordic countries lag far behind most other Western societies when it comes to academically ori-ented programs for young children below compulsory school age, the increasing pressure by policymakers to introduce formal instruction to younger children has an increasing impact on the social discourse on early childhood education in many countries, including the Nordic coun-tries (e.g., Dahlberg & Taguchi, 1994).

I call the second perspective on the value of childhood the perspective of *here and now*. Like its prospective counterpart, it is universal, not so much at society's macro level, but, rather, at its micro level. Its universality rests on the assumption that positive sentiments toward children for their own sake—ranging from love and affection to enjoyment and amusement over children—are ingrained in healthy human nature. Theoretically, this per-spective finds support in research based on attachment psychology, accord-ing to which positive affective feelings and active interest in the child are instrumental in establishing intimate human bonds and in promoting secure attachment (Bowlby, 1978). Further support for the inherent qual-ity of this perspective comes from ethological research, suggesting that attachment-promoting social interactions between infants and caregivers are strikingly similar all over the world, and that some typically baby-like features and expressions, irrespective of culture, tend to produce feelings of caring, affection, and enjoyment in adults of both sexes (e.g., Alley, 1981; Lorenz, 1943).

In contrast to the pragmatism of the prospective perspective, the here-and-now perspective romanticizes childhood, valuing children and child-hood for their own sake. The here-and-now perspective includes a strong tendency to regard attributes typically associated with childhood, such as playfulness, fantasy, and childish naivety, in positive terms. Consequently, according to the here-and-now perspective, child-initiated activities, such as all forms of children's play, are seen as naturally healthy and conducive to optimal development, and are, therefore, given ample time and space by adults. In this respect, interaction with peers and peer-play activities are viewed as developmentally important and equal to or better than instruc-tion from adults, at least for very young children.

According to the here-and-now perspective, the childhood period car-ries an intrinsic value and is no more transitory than other life phases. Con-sequently, children should not be rushed through it. The perspective of here and now can be epitomized in the following way: "Children should be allowed to be children as long as they need to."

As already argued, the here-and-now perspective is especially applicable at society's *micro* level, in adult–child social interactions. However, that is far from a guarantee that the here-and-now perspective plays any important role in social and political discourse at society's *macro* level. The difference is significant, since at the micro level, it is children as *individuals* who are valued; while at the more abstract and complex macro level, the focus is on childhood as *a generalized abstraction* (e.g., as an age cohort or a generation). It is in this macro sense that I claim that the Nordic societies excel; that is, in the vitality and vividness of the public discourse on childhood and in the policies arising from this discourse.

As stated above, the sort of public child-centeredness found in the Nordic countries bears witness to a positive appraisal of childhood in its own right. Let me finish this section with some complementary observations closer to the everyday contexts of young Nordic children, including their schools, daycare or preschools, and their homes.

Perhaps the most significant indicator of Nordic child-centeredness is the late entry of Nordic children into formal, compulsory education in comparison to most other countries. Another indicator is that compulsory schools in all Nordic countries place very little emphasis on individually differentiating performance grades (or marks) during the first school years. However, Iceland is a notable exception in this respect: since the early 1990s, the school starting age has been set at 6 years, and there are ongoing plans to lower it to 5 years, by transforming 5-year-olds' preschool year into a more academic experience, with strong undertones of formal education. Furthermore, Icelandic children are subject to graded school tests from early school age.

In contrast, compulsory school-start in Denmark, Finland, and Sweden remains at 7 years, or is flexible; that is, parents have the right to a say in determining when their children are mature enough to start school. In Denmark, for example, it is not uncommon for educated middle-class families, in particular, to choose to postpone their children's school-start by a year, or until they feel that their children are "school ready." However, increasing numbers of Danish 6-year-olds are enrolled in noncompulsory school-preparatory kindergarten classes, *børnehaveklasse.*

Since the early 1990s, a similar development has been taking place in Sweden, where the majority of Swedish 6-year-olds are now enrolled in "zero grades," which are noncompulsory, academically oriented classes, typically located in elementary school buildings and often taught by elementary-certified teachers. Although the Nordic countries, except Finland, seem to be gradually moving toward earlier school start, the Nordics are, generally speaking, cautious in taking such steps, engaging pedagogical expertise in the decision-making process or in making the transition between school and preschool as smooth as possible (e.g., Dahlberg & Taguchi, 1994; Kjøller & Bengtson, 1992).

When considering formal school-start in *Norden,* one needs to take into account that the overwhelming majority of older preschool-age children are enrolled in public daycare or preschool programs. The pedagogical ambitions and sophistication of these programs vary greatly within and between the countries. Unfortunately, to my knowledge, no comprehensive analysis has been undertaken recently regarding the relative weight of play (defined as child-initiated activities) versus school-like or adult-instructed activities in Nordic daycare centers. However, an analysis undertaken by me (Kristjansson, 2001) based on data from a study of the everyday life of 87 Nordic 5-year-olds and their dual-earner families, carried out in 1987–88, found that in the children's daycare centers, daily schedules were heavily dominated by more or less obviously child-initiated peer activities, in the form of either indoor or outdoor play activities. Only a small fraction of the teacher-structured activities were explicitly school preparatory, such as efforts to teach the children the alphabet or numbers or how to write their names. More common teacher-organized activities were, for example, daily storytelling or occasional visits to museums or learning about nature outside. By and large, it was as if the Nordic daycare centers had a hidden agenda aimed at giving the children a relaxed, loosely structured day while in their out-of-home care (Kristjansson, 2001). As for Denmark, relaxed time structures in the daycare institutions, with abundant opportunities for child-initiated activities and playing with peers, seems still to be the norm (Ellegaard, 2005).

This Nordic study (Kristjansson, 2001) also included interviews with the 5-year-olds' parents, where they were asked to describe the everyday family life and their children's social interactions during an entire ordinary day at home. The analysis of the interview transcripts presented a general picture of time-pressed Nordic dual-earner families eagerly trying to make the most out of their family time, but also of parents that went to great lengths not to pressure their children more than was absolutely necessary. Thus, in many families, especially families with middle-class backgrounds, mornings were tailored to give the children the time they needed for doing what was expected of them and what the children themselves wanted to do, at their own tempo, such as playing with a sibling, painting, browsing through a picture book, or watching a video film. To ensure that the morning preparations went smoothly, it was not uncommon that the parents developed playful strategies to keep their children content. These strategies could be based on ritualized games involving the child and one parent, on humorous fantasy play,[4] or on devising *win–win* games, such as who can run fastest to the daycare, the boy or his time-pressed father on his way to work (Kristjansson, 2001). Overall, these few examples offered a picture of busy but child-centered parents, intent on giving their children enjoyable child-hoods and, as circumstances permitted, allowing them to "be the children they are."

## THE NORDIC WELFARE MODEL

A requirement for children's psychological well-being and social welfare is a healthy and well-functioning family. Therefore, almost by definition, childhood policies and family policies are inseparable. Yet, in the Nordic countries the two policies are separable in that they have partially different historical and ideological backgrounds. In the preceding section we saw that the child-centered policies of the Nordic countries were linked to late modernization, and that the betterment of children's general conditions was, to a great extent, a middle-class project. The Nordic family policies, on the other hand, are usually seen as a logical implementation of a sociopolitical scheme of higher rank, intimately associated with the ideology of social democracy. Consequently, it is often referred to as the social democratic welfare model—or on a more technical note, as "the social democratic world of welfare capitalism" (Esping-Andersen, 1999)—while the Nordics themselves prefer the name *Nordic (or Scandinavian) welfare model.* There is no use in contesting that this model has, to a great extent, become a social democratic project; but its historical legacy goes further back than that particular ideology, and it is already reflected in the coordination of Nordic social policies, which commenced in the late 19th century (Therborn, 1993). Further support comes from Baldwin (1990), who traces its origins to the conservative ideas of social solidarity usually associated with Northern Germany and the Bismarck era, which in the late 19th and early 20th centuries exerted a particularly strong influence on Denmark, and to a somewhat lesser extent on Sweden.

One such feature, the very *modus operandi* of the Nordic welfare model, that I claim has more to do with cultural tradition than with political ideology and is more or less strongly shared among the Nordic cultures, is an endeavor to reach social consensus on issues with conflict-evoking potential by creating forums for dialog and consultations where representatives of differing interests are to meet and explain their positions. To a stranger, not socialized into this way of settling things, such sessions may seem too many and too lengthy. However, once decisions are made through this process, all parties are likely to feel a commitment to live up to them.

Within the Nordic welfare model, such consensus efforts lie behind many sociopolitical reforms. For example, the government might invite the most powerful interest groups in society, typically representatives for employers and labor unions, for consultations, or promote the establishment of more informal contacts. Irrespective of form, however, the state plays a proactive and facilitative role in trying to reach constructive agreements.

This mode of working through issues that, if not solved, might weaken the integrity of society have reached their highest level of refinement within the Swedish welfare model[5] (Swenson, 2002), although, even in Sweden, it has become weaker in more recent years. Swenson's (1989) examination of summaries from such consultation meetings and interviews with senior representatives of the employers' confederation revealed that the Swedish daycare reform of the 1960s, which brought an explosive expansion of public, institutionalized daycare, was *not,* contrary to popular belief, initiated by the social democratic government or the labor union, but instead by the conservative employers' confederation. At the time, the Swedish economy was blooming as never before, with a serious labor shortage as a result. The solution, proposed by the employers' union, was an expansion of public daycare services to enable mothers to join the workforce. While illustrating the significance of the consensus-seeking tradition in Swedish/Nordic society, with tangible consequences for children and their families, this example also reveals a nondogmatic and *down-to-earth* mentality, which is sometimes seen as a Nordic cultural trait. Thus, for instance, the Nordics have a reputation of dislike for authoritarian prescripts, either from church or kings (Olafsson, 1999), a lesson they may have learned through the generations from having to rely on themselves and their creativity to survive with scarce resources and sometimes adverse conditions (Gaunt, 1996).

The political scheme of the Nordic welfare model is founded on the egalitarian vision of a society where every citizen has the right to a *good quality of life,* irrespective of his or her gender, social or family background, or physical and mental abilities. Furthermore, for this vision to become reality, it is seen as essential that the state powers play an active, mediating role.

Two aspects contributing to the uniqueness of the Nordic welfare model deserve special attention, since they have ramifications for the everyday lives for most Nordic children. The first aspect relates to the Nordic definition of "good," as in the "good quality of life" to which all citizens have a right in an egalitarian society, as explained above. This signifies that members of society are seen as entitled to public benefits and services of generous and high standards. For families with young children, a good quality of life includes access to subsidized daycare of high quality. More young children, per capita, attend daycare institutions full time in Denmark than in any other country, followed by Sweden, Iceland, and Norway (Harms, 2005). In Denmark 72.5% of 1-year-olds and 96.4% of 5-year-olds attended public daycare in 2002. The corresponding figures for Sweden were 45.3% of 1-year-olds and 92.9% of 5-year olds and for Iceland 49.2% of 1-year-olds and 91.5% of 5-year-olds (*Norden i tal,* 2003). As for Nordic public daycare, it appears that quantity accompanies quality, at least for the Swedish day-care system, which has been subject to some international attention and comparison. Repeatedly, these studies have proposed Swedish daycare as exemplary, for such attributes as (1) striking a sound balance between school preparatory education and activities promoting social development (Cohen et al., 2004); (2) good availability and high educational level of the staff (OECD, 2001); and (3) the personnel's respectful attitudes toward children, allowing "the children to be children instead of being trained to be adults" (Ekman, 1999). Finally, Linda Haas (1996) arrived at similar conclusions in her analysis of Swedish family policy as a whole, illustrated, for example, by the practice of adapting the opening hours of daycare services to parents' work schedules.

Although there are some distinctive inter-Nordic differences in the quality of daycare, similarities prevail across the Nordic countries within key areas (e.g., Eydal, 2004). Thus, for example, similar high standards have been established for the physical environment of daycare facilities. In addition, the required educational level for preschool teachers is high, generally at university level. As a rule, only licensed preschool teachers are in the highest positions and are responsible for the programs in the daycare groups. However, in each Nordic country, daycare centers also employ other staff members with lower qualifications. Notably, even these less qualified personnel are required to have some courses in psychology and children's general needs.

The Nordic welfare state models are the world's most comprehensive and resource- demanding,[6] their financing, correspondingly, requiring very high tax levels. Although criticized by some, heavy taxation is reasonably well accepted, or at least tolerated, for two reasons. The first reason is practical. Due to the system's general nature, many individuals get in return what they pay for through heavy taxation. For example, parents with young children are well aware of the benefits they reap from the system. The second reason is ideological. The social democratic vision of equality and solidarity is firmly rooted, especially in Sweden, Denmark, and Norway (in the named order).

Comparative research on welfare states tends to be too econocentric in the sense that it limits itself to different aspects of resource redistribution and its financing of sociomaterial benefits and services. Such a perspective misses a key aspect of the Nordic welfare state model, which is the high political priority given to *social inclusion,* according to which it is seen as every citizen's right to participate in society in a meaningful manner, each after his or her premises, mainly by doing productive work (Björnberg, 1995). It is argued that having a paying job is instrumental for personal welfare and for sustaining a sound society (Korpi, 2001; Vogel, 2000).[7] Accordingly, it is seen as a high-priority governmental obligation to secure a well-functioning labor market through directed incentives and legislation. Since the inception of the social democratic period in Scandinavia, the Nordic countries have enjoyed significantly higher employment rates than elsewhere in Western Europe.

The emphasis on social inclusion is one reason for the priority given to *gender equality* in the Nordic countries, in particular on women's and mothers' rights to work, or perhaps more adequately put, on their rights to share the breadwinner and parental roles with their partners on equal terms. Public statistics on Nordic gender-based employment rates from 1999 indicate that the Nordic welfare states have been highly successful to this end; thus, for Nordic women and men in the age range of 25–54 years (i.e., when they are most likely to have young children), employment rates for women ranged from 86–97% (with Finland and Sweden, respectively, as the extreme points) of the rates for men (Kristjansson, 2001, pp. 87–88). Note that these numbers say nothing about working hours. However, full- or near full-time employment for women is the most common arrangement in most of the Nordic countries. Given the high rate of daycare attendance for young children, these numbers should not come as a surprise. But there are other contributing circumstances as well, such as ambitious legislative measures aimed at reconciling work and family life, for which the Nordic countries are envied by many Western nations (Tauberman, 1995), and ways of organizing family life, with cultural historical roots that are specific to the Nordic countries (Gaunt, 1996). We take a closer look at these aspects of Nordic childhoods after the next section.

## NORDIC FAMILY POLICIES

The line of argument in this chapter has been that the child centeredness so prevalent in the Nordic countries (especially in Sweden and Norway), as well as some salient aspects of the Nordic welfare model, are most adequately understood as a part of a Nordic cultural heritage and social democratic policies. But in the same manner as Nordic child centeredness tends to bring up the name of one person, Ellen Key, so the Nordic welfare model is intimately linked to the internationally celebrated Swedish couple, Alva and Gunnar Myrdal. During much of their active lives, they figured as the chief ideologists of the Scandinavian social democratic movement.[8] In 1934 the Myrdals published the book, *The Demographical Crisis* (in Swedish, *Kris i befolkningsfrågan*), in which they offered a long-term road map and a sociopolitical rationale for a high-profile and proactive family policy, firmly embedded within a more comprehensive welfare-state program. Its reception was enthusiastic in both Sweden and Denmark, although the global depression of the 1930s, followed by World War II, stood in the way of materializing its most radical and ambitious reform proposals, such as universally subsidized public daycare (Stokholm Banke, 2001). It was not until the 1960s, when both Denmark and Sweden experienced their greatest economic boom, that the time was ripe for a grand-scale expansion of public institutionalized daycare (Florin & Nilsson, 2003), which is commonly seen as one of the greatest achievements of Nordic family welfare policies.

At first glance, the topic of the Myrdals' book may not appear to be immediately linked to family policy as a state concern, and even less so to the development of public daycare. But what was of major concern to the Myrdals and Swedish politicians at that time were sinking fertility rates, which were perceived as a threat of catastrophic dimensions to Sweden's future as a welfare state. Their thesis was that modern industrial society, through its very way of functioning, was marginalizing women and mothers, leaving them, in the words of the Myrdals, "entrapped and isolated in their homes," while their partners were busy participating in social and economic life. The line of reasoning went approximately like this: For the family, the arrival of industrial society meant that the primarily household-based economy of the preindustrial period was being replaced with a paternal, *one-income* organization of family life, with women being clear losers in that they were being deprived of the traditional economic functions, which they had carried out all through history along with caring for their children. The Myrdals argued that for women and young wives the prospect of staying at home with little else to do than serve their husbands and tend to their common children was not a sufficient life fulfillment, and was, viewed in a cultural-historical and political perspective, disturbingly unfair, and meant ultimately a hazard to the general well-being of the whole family system, in particular to the mothers and their children. To support their claims, the Myrdals referred to a study in which researchers compared health indicators for rural and urban families with children. The Myrdals' argument boiled down to the fact that, in modern society, there is a fundamental conflict between the family and the labor market, between being a parent, particularly being a mother, and being a breadwinner. This conflict, then, renders families with children especially vulnerable. Consequently, it was the welfare state's most urgent obligation to alleviate this inherent tension by making maternal employment a feasible option. The most urgent step to be taken in this direction was, according to the Myrdals, the installation of generally available public daycare of the highest quality, where children would be cared for by committed professionals.

## SOME GLIMPSES INTO MODERN NORDIC FAMILY LIFE AND ITS HISTORICAL ROOTS

So far, the reader has been given only fragmentary glimpses into how everyday life can be for ordinary families with young children in the Nordic welfare states, at least those living in modern, urban settings. Needless to say, all sorts of variations, both within and between the countries, prohibit any detailed characterizations. However, we have seen that the dual-income lifestyle prevails in all the Nordic countries, and likewise we may conclude that many families with children are pressed for time. Thus, in a study of Swedish families with preschool children, Kihlblom (1991) found that parents' biggest everyday concern was lack of time with their children. This concern even outranked, for example, their economic concerns. However, as already noted, the Scandinavian welfare systems have gone to great lengths to reconcile work and parenthood. Affordable, high-quality daycare benefiting parents with young children is one such measure. And for parents and school-age children, after-school care is also readily available, especially in larger towns and cities (Statistical Yearbook of Sweden, 2004). For the past two decades or so, concerted efforts have been made in each of the Scandinavian countries, encompassing the state, employers, and labor unions (Arve-Parès, 1995) to create family-friendly workplaces. Most notably, these efforts have led to the institution of flexible work hours, enabling parents in two-income families to optimize their time use, and to spend the time thus saved together with their children (Kristjansson, 2001). Along the way, it has become increasingly clear that the predominant lifestyle of Nordic families with children does not conform well with the sort of one-income nuclear family philosophy that the Myrdals were so wary of. The *family-structural aspects* deviate even more from that philosophy.

If one looks over the entire age interval of childhood, 0–17 years, most Nordic children grow up with their married parents. This is very clearly the case in Finland, followed by Denmark, with 64% and 63% of all children, respectively, living with their married parents. For Iceland, however, the picture is very different; only 54% live in such families (Norden i tal, 2003). Although informative, figures like these are based on a single point in time, 2001, and consequently are like a still photograph of what, from the children's point of view, is a journey starting at birth and ending at their 18th birthday. During this "journey" it is not unlikely that they have experienced more than one family situation (see below).

According to Jensen (1999), the *concubinage family*,[9] as a childhood arena, is especially common in the Nordic countries, although this is clearly not the prevailing family pattern. Unlike what seems to be the norm in other parts of Europe, the Nordic concubinage family is typically associated with early parenthood. These circumstances are reflected in the rates of premarital childbirths, which are not nearly as high in Europe as in the Nordic countries. In Denmark, Norway, and Sweden approximately 50% of children are born to unmarried women and in Iceland the number soars above 60%. It is only in Finland, where the premarital birthrate is approximately 30%, that these numbers are more in keeping with European norms, placing Finland among the cluster of nations, Austria, France, and Belgium, closest to *Norden* in this respect (Jensen, 1999).

I claim that it is fruitful to conceive of the concubinage family as a more or less extended period of "intimate relationship experiment" for young people and, particularly in *Norden,* for young parents, before they decide whether to take on the more binding and formal obligations of marriage. The possible outcomes of this experiment are essentially three: (1) a dissolution, or, from a child perspective, a separation; (2) a mutual confirmation through marriage of love that was already there during the concubinage, and of a willingness to share future commitments; or (3) a permanentizing of the concubinage situation.

It follows from these considerations that the concubinage family should be significantly less stable than the marriage family. That this is so has been repeatedly confirmed in a number of studies, international and Nordic (e.g., Jensen, 1999). The relatively strong presence of Nordic concubinage families with children should furthermore indicate a certain overrepresentation of *single mother families* in these countries, for the simple reason that a family breakup almost inevitably leads to single motherhood for shorter or longer periods.

Available Nordic statistics show that single-mother families are most common in Iceland, with 26%, whereas it lies evenly at 20% in the other Nordic countries (*Norden i tal,* 2003). The high rate of Icelandic single mothers may be linked to the fact that Icelandic mothers are the youngest in *Norden,* with the rate of teenage mothers standing at 4.6% of all births—almost three times the rates in Sweden and Denmark. For Iceland this means that teenage parenthood is a part of the culture. Judging from their age, the young parents are just in their initial phase of a concubinage relationship when their baby is born; they are either still in school or have only unskilled, low-paying jobs. Due to an almost nonexistent public rental market, the young parents often have to live in one of their parents' homes (Icelandic homes are often spacious), and, depending on the circumstances, may receive anything from minimal to substantial economic or practical help from the new grandparents. When relationships of this type do break up, which is often the case, they are unlikely to leave as deep traces—emotionally, economically, or socially—with the child and others involved as would separations in longer-lasting concubinage families or divorces of marriage families.

In the Nordic countries, it seems that the marriage family is gradually giving way to other, less stable forms of family life. Indeed, it is a global trend that can be traced to myriad converging trends underlying social modernization (e.g., Kristjansson, 2001); but it is generally agreed upon that it started in the Scandinavian countries, mainly Sweden (e.g., Popenoe, 1991), where the Myrdals' writings, as early as in the early 1930s, was a major catalyst.

Table 2.2 indicates the decline of the Nordic marriage family over three decades, by weighing marriage rates and divorce rates against each other. Note that the figures are based on marital statistics only, and thus do not cover concubinage relationships. Therefore, the real scope of family break-ups is greater than indicated in the table.

**Table 2.2.  The Marriage-to-Divorce Ratio in the Nordic Countries (Adjusted Ratios Italicized)[a,b]**

| Year | Denmark | | Finland | | Iceland | | Norway | | Sweden | |
|------|---------|------|---------|------|---------|------|---------|------|---------|------|
| 1999 | 6,6:2,5 | *2,6:1* | 4,7:2,7 | *1,7:1* | 5,6:1,7 | *3,3:1* | 5,3:2,1 | *2,5:1* | 4,0:2,4 | *1,7:1* |
| 1961–70 | 8,2:1,5 | *5,5:1* | 8,2:1,1 | *7,5:1* | 8,0:1,0 | *8,0:1* | 7,1:0,7 | *10,2:1* | 6,9:1,3 | *5,3:1* |

[a] Marriage rates are shown to the left o of the colon sign [:], divorce rates to the right.
[b] *Nordisk statistisk årsbok* (Nordic statistical yearbook) 1991; *Nordisk statistisk årsbok* 2000.

These figures are not confined to families with children. It is, however, unlikely that the ratios, *per se,* are significantly biased. According to Dencik and Lauterbach (2001, 2002), *both* marriage and divorce rates are higher for parents with young children.

The table depicts Sweden as least oriented toward the marriage family, with Finland as second. On the other end of the spectrum, Denmark has the highest marriage rate. Since Sweden scores lowest on marriage, and has (together with Finland) the lowest marriage-to-divorce ratio, it is tempting to probe deeper into relevant Swedish statistics. According to Andersson's (1996) analysis of demographic data from 1995, three in four Swedish children (0–17 years) lived in unbroken families at that point in time. Once again, however, reservations need to be made against such a "frozen" picture of an 18-year-long childhood in constant motion. According to the same source, the divorce rate for families with children is sharply on the rise. Thus, the annual divorce rate for families with children was 1.8% in 1990; in 1995 it had increased to 2.5%. This signifies a 40% increase in only 5 years.

Although exact forecasts cannot be made because, among other factors, the concubinage families do not show in the general family statistics, it is nevertheless tempting to try to get some idea of how many Swedish children born in 1995 will, at the end of their childhood period, have experienced parental divorce. If an estimate is made on the basis of 1995's divorce rate of 2.5%, and this is multiplied by 18 years, then by 2013 approximately 45% of all children will have experienced at least one family breakup.

Findings from a longitudinal study of the family history of two Danish cohorts,[10] one from 1981 and the other from 1995, provide unique insights into the vicissitudes of family life for Danish children, and, presumably, to

some extent for children in other Nordic countries as well (Dencik & Lauterbach 2001, 2002). During their first year, 92% of the 1981 cohort lived
with both of their parents. Eight years later 76% did so; but at 17 the rate
was down to 63%.

Unlike the 1981 cohort, members of the 1995 cohort are still in their
childhood period. As a consequence, comprehensive comparisons of the
two cohorts cannot be made at this point. So far, however, Dencik and
Lauterbach's comparative analysis of the two cohorts' provide some interesting indications. For example, only a negligible decline of two-parent
families—that is, of marriage and concubinage families put together—is
detectable between the two cohorts when the children are between 0–1
years (92–90.4%). However, there is a dramatic increase in concubinage
families among the 1995 cohort. Thus, 38.3% of them were born into such
families, as compared to 26.7% of the 1981 cohort (Dencik & Lauterbach,
2002). The relative change is 43%. However, during the 1- to 4-year age
interval, the difference leveled out somewhat, in that more parents of the
1995 cohort married during this period than did parents of children in
the 1981 cohort during the same age interval. Yet, the differences
remained highly significant: 17.5% versus 23.1%. Subtle as they may seem,
these differences in family types are a clear indicator of a less stable family
life in the future for many Danish children in the 1995 cohort. This assertion is partly based on research confirming such relationships (see above),
but also on a separate analysis, carried out by Dencik and Lauterbach, of
the 1981 cohort. There, the researchers found that the likelihood of a
family breakup was 25% greater for the children born to concubinage
families than to those born into marriage families. Furthermore, the children of the concubinage families were twice as likely, at the end of their
childhood period, to have had a highly "turbulent family history," defined
as having experienced four or more different family types, with the likelihood being 11.3%, in contrast to 5.2% for the group of children born to
married parents.

A detailed discussion of the extent to which these family arrangements
are a product of the Nordic welfare-state politics or can be traced to a background in the cultural history of *Norden* is beyond the scope of this chapter.
However, in the following section, I describe some striking historical analo-
gies between the present and the past.

## NORDIC FAMILIES:
## THE PRESENT MIRRORED IN THE PAST

Inspired by the dictum that the present, at every point in time, is a historical arena where the past constantly surfaces, it is meaningful, albeit fraught

with epistemological and methodological difficulties, to try to unveil some of the linkages between the past and present of Nordic family life. Can we, for example, find some of the "unorthodox" (from a Western European point of view) Nordic family patterns of today, as discussed in the preceding section, in the Nordic past? Implicitly, I have already answered that question in the affirmative. Let me elaborate, assisted by a few historically oriented family researchers.

David Gaunt (1996) started his impressive study of the history of Nordic family life with three sets of comparative statistics from 15 European nations, dating from the turn of the 19th century. These statistics all support the image of Nordic family life as less oriented toward the institution of marriage. The first set shows that the annual marriage rates were significantly lower in *Norden* than on the European continent, ranging from 3.3 to 4.2% in the *Norden* (with Iceland representing the lowest rate) and from 5.4 to 5.7% in Europe (Gaunt, 1996). The second set of statistics gauging the marriage rates in the two regions showed that, while 13 to 17% of 45- to 49-year-old women in selected European countries had never married, the rate in Iceland was a spectacular 29% (p. 16). Finally, the third set of statistics, showing the mean age of marriage in selected European countries, revealed that the mean age of marriage was highest in Sweden at 26.4 years, as compared to 23.6 in Italy and 23.7 in France, to take but two examples.

Gaunt (1996, pp. 79–84) also presented data about unmarried or lone mothers and their illegitimate or premarriage children. Beginning during the first half of the 18th century, the numbers of unmarried mothers started to increase, although there were significant regional differences within *Norden*. Coincidence or not, unmarried or lone mothers were more common in the Northern parts of Denmark, Norway, and Sweden, and in the richer regions. Before this time, premarital childbirths were seen as a grave moral problem and were met with punishment and humiliation, but gradually the phenomenon became increasingly tolerated and much more common. From this time onward, it was redefined as a social and economic problem, rather than a moral problem, for the counties that were obliged to give food and shelter to the lone mothers and their children. Considering that this was a period of explosive population increase, those problems posed a big challenge. In some regions during the 19th century, lone motherhood gained endemic proportions. In 1820, for example, more than 20% of all childbirths in an East Norwegian community were illegitimate or premarital. And approximately 40% of all brides were pregnant at their wedding.

In his study of life in an Eastern Swedish community at the start of the 19th century, Carlsson (1977) found similar figures. Furthermore, Carlsson concluded that almost all of the young mothers eventually got married and did not suffer any lasting stigmatization. Carlsson remarked that illegiti-mate children were, as a rule, no social catastrophe for their mothers.

With increased urbanization, these patterns were carried over to the growing cities. By 1864 in one district of Stockholm, one out of four chil-dren was born in a premarital relationship, and every third family was, prior to marriage, a concubinage family (Gaunt, 1996).

The concept of family life contains many more dimensions than have been treated in this section. One such dimension, discussed in an earlier section, is *gender relationships*. The Myrdals gave gender relationships, and in particular the lack of gender equality, primacy in their diagnosis of the ailing Swedish welfare state of the 1930s. Ever since, women's and mothers' rights to social participation on equal footing with men has been a recur-ring theme in the political discourse of *Norden*. It has led to the definition of the family as a focus for the creation of a more gender-equal society. Therefore, the question to be asked here is this: Are there any circum-stances in the past that can be associated with the centrality of the gender equality discourse of today and the high level of equality that Nordic women seem to enjoy (e.g., Arve-Parès, 1995), and, in fact, the recent inter-national nomination of the Nordic countries as the most equal societies in the world (United Nations, 2004)?

Two or three circumstances of traditional *Norden* are particularly likely to have made Nordic women and mothers "socially strong" and influential, more so than in most other parts of Western Europe. The first is funda-mental in Gaunt's (1996) interpretation of traditional family life in *Norden*, namely, the harsh conditions of living in most parts of the region. Short summers, capricious climates, low-yielding crops, and infertile soil in many places required small, flexible, and often hard-working family units (at least during the light and warmer season)—a far cry from the big, stem-like families of warmer climates. Furthermore, scarce resources often demanded that the husbands go fishing or hunting, sometimes with their older sons, after harvest time or during low season in household-related production. Consequently, women were needed not only as caregivers to their children, but also in the day-to-day household production. Taking care of the household during their husband's absences for fishing and hunting gave them autonomy and a say-so in family matters.

A second historical circumstance allowed for the maintenance of Nordic women's strong social position through the centuries. Feudalism, with its hierarchical and authoritarian power structures, penetrated most of West-ern Europe. This sociopolitical force relied on a patriarchal family system, where inheritance and power went, by default, from father to son (Gies & Gies, 1987), thereby disenfranchising women. However, feudalism never got into the deeper layers of the Nordic cultures (Therborn, 1993).

Women's relatively strong social position in the Nordic countries is further explained by another factor linked to feudalism, or rather, to its relative absence in the Nordic region. The church held a relatively weak position in *Norden* and faced difficulties in reaching out with its message to ordinary people. The church's efforts were usually made in allegiance with the feudal kings, and as such, its preachings contained, among other things, the message that mothers' and women's position within the family and in society was, by nature, lower than their husbands'. Such religious dogmas had difficulty getting through the reality filters of everyday, laymen's culture in the Nordic countries. This was, according to Gaunt (1996), one reason why the Nordics resisted for a very long time the notion of marriage as a churchly, religious institution.

We have now painted some of the historical background to socially strong and relatively autonomous women and mothers, which may explain why premarital motherhood was, if not accepted, then at least tolerated to a greater extent than in other parts of Europe. This autonomy may also explain why young, unmarried women became economically active and an important part of the general labor force in the late 19th century at the dawn of the industrial epoch in *Norden.* This, in turn, gave them some political influence (Florin & Nilsson, 2003). It is not unlikely that it was from these women, the parent generation of Alva and Gunnar Myrdal, that they got their ideas and ideals of women's and mothers' active role in society.

The past has met the present.

## THE FUTURE DIRECTIONS OF NORDIC CHILDHOODS: CONCLUDING REMARKS

The future is no longer what it used to be. (Dencik & Lauterbach, 2002)

The aim of this chapter has been to portray how it is to grow up as a young child in the contemporary *Norden,* on the basis of two sociocultural circumstances, epitomized by pervasive child-centeredness and the Nordic social welfare model politics, which have been proposed as defining aspects of Nordic childhoods. I contend, however, that along the way, we have unearthed an additional aspect, namely deep-rooted traditions of specifically Nordic family life patterns, whose common denominator has been greater gender equality than has been the case in most other Western cultures. These patterns, I argue, facilitated the institution of the welfare model of the Nordic countries, especially the Scandinavian countries.

Throughout this chapter, I have referred to past conditions and historical processes to give the reader a deepening perspective on the present. What gives additional weight to such an approach is that it purports to indicate likely future scenarios, in our case regarding the future directions of Nordic childhoods. The value of such future insights is extremely high, since children are, by virtue of their very existence, the link from the past and present to the future. Children are, in other words, the inheritors of the accumulated cultural capital of their native cultures and the harbingers of what will be, first and foremost, for their national cultures, but also, to a lesser or a greater degree, for the cultural regions in which they grow up— in this case, *Norden*. Thus, for the sake of cultural continuity, everyone has a vested interest in the future.

As claimed in the *Dencik* quote above, albeit rather cryptically, "The future is no longer what it used to be." I argue, however, that the validity of this claim is based on the fundamental fact that, due to accelerating social change, contemporary people are faced with too many new realities, challenges and problems for which they do not have answers. As a consequence, an unknown and "different" future is perceived as threatening. Therefore, because our children's future will surely be different from what we know, we almost necessarily find the future somewhat threatening, and consequently, a source of pessimism.

Generally speaking, the people of *Norden* are very conscious about their Nordicness and proud of the societies they have built. Despite their relatively small sizes, the Nordic countries enjoy the highest general welfare in the world as measured by public health, technology, education, employment, and quality of public service. This pride encompasses, to a great extent, the high-profile child and family policies that were developed during the 20th century and that have continued into the new millennium. For several reasons, however, pessimism is quite widespread about the future of these policies. For the most part, it is linked to doubts about the future of the Nordic welfare model as a whole, where many international economists and political scientists (some of them Nordic) have forecast its demise sooner rather than later. Almost invariably, the roots of the problems have been traced to increasing *international interdependence* and *globalization*. The general line of reasoning has gone like this: The Nordic countries base their advanced general welfare systems on high-cost employer- and business-financed labor insurance and high-income tax systems. (For instance, Denmark and Sweden have the world's highest income taxes.) In an ever more globalized world with free movement of labor, capital, and businesses, the Nordic countries will lose jobs and businesses, and therefore, much-needed tax revenues, to countries with lower wages, fewer labor insurance requirements, and more favorable tax policies. This predicted development would bring an end to the Nordic welfare state model as something distinctly different from the rest of Europe in terms of generality and generosity; or in the wording of Mikko Kautto (2001), the Nordic welfare state would be subject to a "Europeanization."

Ultimately the fate of Nordic childhoods (as far as the welfare aspect is concerned) would be the same.

But has this pessimistic scenario materialized? No, it has not (Kautto, 2001), at least not yet. In the wake of the state financial crises in Finland and Sweden during the 1990s, only minor structural adjustments were made to these countries' respective welfare systems, and the general levels of child and family benefits have returned to their pre-crisis levels (Hiilamo, 2002).

So, have the pessimists then been proven wrong? The first round may have gone to the optimists but there are more rounds to come. However, it is possible that the pessimists may have underestimated the importance of other economic growth-enhancing factors, which speak for the Nordic welfare states, namely a long tradition of active labor market politics, high levels of professional education, and infrastructures that promote labor flexibility, with generous access to quality daycare, as only a few examples.

According to Meidner (2004), one of the foremost architects of the Swedish welfare model, all post-industrial societies face a built-in dilemma, which is already burdening the Nordic welfare state model and may force its downward adjustment. Economic growth no longer necessarily leads to corresponding growth in the labor force. Businesses can thrive even in times of increasing social marginalization, which very much runs counter to the social solidarity ideal inherent in the Nordic welfare state model. Thus, the self-regulating relationship between high labor incomes and state tax revenues is impaired.

So, on the basis of this limited analysis, what is the best guess about the future of Nordic childhoods as far as the welfare state is concerned? The answers here are rather tentative, based on the information above, as well as unsystematic, personal observations, rather than on research or statistics, which, to my knowledge, are not available. The guess is that the structural features of childhood politics and family support systems will remain largely unchanged for a long time, but that parents will have to pay more out of their own pockets for all but the core services, such as preschool or daycare. The likelihood of a permanent "Europeanization" of the Nordic childhood and family politics is very small. Yet, the possibility should not be dismissed entirely, given that the issue has been brought up in a variety of contexts, including the Swedish EU referendum and the more recent EMU referendum, where some prominent members of nearly all political parties warned against that possibility. However, as for now, there are no signs that Nordic childhoods are being "Europeanized"; on the contrary, the Nordic childhood and family welfare models seem to evoke more praise and envy than disapproval within the EU.

An additional reason for the likely maintenance or possibly even a strengthening of the public services for families with children in the Nordic countries, at least in those countries that are lagging behind the others, most notably Norway and Iceland, relates to traditional Nordic family values, where it is seen as normal for even young mothers to be active in the labor force.

The presumed future of Nordic child-centeredness has not been touched on yet. The continuing development and fortifying of the Ombudsman for Children systems (with Finland most recently joining the other Nordic countries) indicate that the individual rights of children will be very much in focus in the years to come. As suggested by Therborn (1993), the increased emphasis on children's rights may be seen as a logical extension of individualism as a social modernization trend. As such, there is no reason to expect its diminishing importance in the near future.

Focusing rather exclusively on the two features described here as defining aspects of Nordic childhoods—namely, child-centeredness and the Nordic welfare state—it is my conclusion that Nordic childhoods are relatively well and thriving. We must keep in mind, however, that Nordic childhoods, both in the present and in the future, exist as a mental category rather than a concrete object. Therefore, the children of the Nordic countries need to be taught about or otherwise made aware of their Nordicness. The responsibility for this aspect of cultural transmission rests with adults and the education system.

Let us return briefly to the study on the everyday lives of 87 5-year-old Nordic children (Kristjansson, 2002), since it is relevant here. An analysis of the interview transcripts with the parents and the preschool teachers did not yield a single reference to the concept of Norden or any of its possible derivatives, such as telling children about their Nordic roots or describing aspects of their cultural heritage shared with neighboring countries, or telling them about fellow Nordic children or about events or places in some other Nordic country. Thus, it appeared that adult efforts to create anything resembling a Nordic awareness or identity in children at this age were absent. In contrast, the material was rich with examples of introducing children to their own country's cultural heritage, be it learning about the mythology of their cultures, the language, historical events, nature, or cultural artifacts. It is worth noting that adult instruction about these national cultural phenomena most often took place in the children's preschool settings rather than at home.

This modest analysis indicating the absence of adult effort to instill "Nordic identity" among 5-year-olds is not to say that it will not take place when these children are older. In fact, learning about Nordic heritage and identity starts as early as the first grade in compulsory school, and, when the children are older quite often include visits to selected friend-classes in another Nordic country. But the analysis can serve as a healthy reminder that, after all, the *Norden* consists of several separate, self-contained cultures.

## NOTES

1. There is a well-established tradition of using the term "Nordic welfare model" in singular form, as shall be respected here. I claim, however, that this is unfortunate, since it gives the impression that the model is identical, both in its underlying philosophy and in its implementation, across the Nordic region. All the Nordic countries subscribe to its general principles (see below) and its overarching goals, but their *realizations* do vary, due to such factors as country-specific economic realities and varying social and political traditions. Conversely, there is no tradition for using the term "family policies" exclusively in singular form. Consequently, I shall take the liberty to use the term in plural form when referring to the family policies of two or more Nordic countries at the same time. In other cases I use the singular form.

2. The interested reader can find an online edition of Key's book, based on the English translation, on http://www.socsci.kun.nl/ped/whp/histeduc/ellenkey/, or search for other Web material about her through any search engine.

3. The exception is Finland, where the (semi-public) Mannerheim Institute has a similar, but a more low-profile function than the official child ombudsman authorities in Norway and Sweden, in particular.

4. Such as a dad managing to let his tired and morning-drowsy 5-year-old daughter "disappear," while still in bed, by pushing her belly button, only to "reappear" downstairs in the kitchen a few minutes later, all smiling and fully dressed to the parents' "big surprise."

5. Perhaps that is why the Swedish may have the most telling word for this kind of politics, "samförståndspolitik" or "politics of mutual understanding."

6. For comparative analyses of Western welfare nations, see Esping-Andersen, 1990, 1999; Hicks & Kenworthy, 2003; and Schut et al., 2001.

7. From another point of view, it may be argued that the very ambitious, state-financed Nordic welfare programs would collapse if it were not for the generally high employment rates.

8. Alva Myrdal won the Nobel Peace Prize in 1982; Gunnar Myrdal won the Nobel Prize in Economics in 1974.

9. That is, a family with children in which the parents are unmarried.

10. Based on the *Børnedatabasen i Danmarks Statistik* ("The Child Database," Denmark Statistics).

## REFERENCES

Alley, T. R. (1981). Headshape and the perception of cuteness. *Developmental Psychology, 17,* 650–654.

Andersson, G. (1996): *Risken för skilsmässa ökar* [Increasing divorce risk]. Välfärdsbulletinen, 1. Stockholm: SCB.

Arve-Parès, B. (Ed.). (1995). *Building family welfare: Report from a Nordic seminar on families, gender and welfare policy.* Stockholm: Norstedts Tryckeri.

Baldwin, P. 1990. *The politics of social solidarity: Class bases of the European welfare state 1875–1975.* Cambridge, UK: Cambridge University Press.

Björnberg, U. (1995). Services for social integration—the Scandinavian approach. In B. Arve-Parès (Ed.), *Reconciling work and family life—a challenge for Europe* (pp. 57–60). Stockholm: Norstedts Tryckeri.

*BO, Norway* [Ombudsman for children, Norway]. Retrieved March 3, 2005, from http://tinyurl.com/3skbl

*BO, Sweden* [Ombudsman for children, Sweden]. Retrieved March 3, 2005, from http://tinyurl.com/5vhvv

Bowlby, J. (1978). *Attachment and loss: Attachment.* Harmondsworth, UK: Penguin Education.

Cohen, B., Moss, P., Petrie, P., & Wallace, J. (2004). *A new deal for children? Re-forming education and care in England, Scotland and Sweden.* Bristol, UK: The Policy Press.

Dahlberg, G., & Taguchi, L. (1994). *Förskola och skola—om två traditioner och om visionen om en mötesplats* [Preschool and school—on two traditions and the vision of a meeting point]. Stockholm: HLS Förlag.

Dencik, L., & Lauterbach, J. (2002) Mor og far and mor og hendes nye partner: Om børns familier og familieskift gennem opvæksten i senmoderniteten. In M. Hermansen & A. Poulsen (Eds.), *Samfundets børn* [Society's children] (pp. 75–126). Århus: Forlaget Klim.

Ditch, J., Barnes, H., & Bradshaw (Eds.). (1996): *A synthesis of national family policies in 1995.* York, UK: European Observatory on National Family Policies, Commision of the European Communities.

Elkind, D. (1981). *The hurried child: Growing up too fast too soon.* Reading, MA: Addison-Wesley.

Ellegaard, T. (2005). *Et godt børnehavebarn? Daginstitutionens kompetencekrav og hvordan børn med forskellig social baggrund håndterer dem* [The competence demands of the daycare institution and how children with different social backgrounds handle them]. Doctoral dissertation, Roskilde Universitetscenter.

ENOC (2005). Retrieved March 3, 2005, from http://www.ombudsnet.org

Esping-Andersen, G. (1990). *The three worlds of welfare capitalism.* Princeton, NJ: Princeton University Press.

Eydal, G. (2004, November). *Structural features of the Nordic daycare systems—a comparison.* Paper presented at a Congress of the University of Iceland and the Icelandic Ombudsman for Children.

Eydal, G., & Olafsson, S. (2003). *Social and family policy: The case of Iceland.* Third report for the project Welfare Policy and Employment in the Context of Family Change.

Florin, C., & Nilsson, B. (2003). *"Något som liknar en oblodig revolution..." Jämställdhetens politisering under 1960- och 70-talen.* ["Something resembling an unbloody revolution..." The politicization of gender equality during the 1960s and the 1970s]. Umeå: Umeå universitet.

Gaunt, D. (1996). *Familjeliv i Norden* [Family life in the Norden]. Södertälje: Gidlunds.

Gies, F., & Gies, J. (1987). *Marriage and the family life in the middle ages.* New York: Harper & Row.

Haas, L. L. (1992). *Equal parenthood and social policy: A study of parental leave in Sweden.* Albany: State University of New York Press.

Harms, T. (2005). *The day at home and away: How sixteen Danish five-year olds spend their time: An empirical, theoretical and methodological analysis*. Doctoral dissertation, Roskilde Universitetscenter.

Heywood, C. (2001). *A history of childhood: Children and childhood in the west from medieval to modern times*. Oxford, UK: Polity.

Hicks, A., & Kenworthy, L. (2003). Varieties of welfare capitalism. *Socio-Economic Review, 1*(1), 27–61.

Hiilamo, H. (2002). The *rise and fall of Nordic family policy? Historical development and changes during the 1990s in Sweden and Finland* (Stakes, Research Report No. 125). Saarijärvi: Gummerus.

Hultqvist, K. (1990). *Förskolebarnet: En konstruktion för gemensskapen och den individuella frigörelsen* [The preschool child: A construction for gemeinschaft and individual emancipation]. Stockholm: Symposion.

Jensen, A.-M. (1999). Børn i den skandinaviske samboerfamilie. In L. Dencik & P. S. Jørgensen (Eds.), *Børn og familie i det postmoderne samfund* (pp. 342–366). Copenhagen: Hans Reitzels Forlag.

Júlíusdóttir, S. (2001) *Fjölskyldur við aldahvörf Reykjavík* [Families at the turn of the century]. Reykjavík: Háskólaútgáfan

Kågeson, P., & Lidmark, A.-M. (2002, July 8). Partitoppen kallsinnig mot småbarnen [The social democratic power elite indifferent to young children]. *Dagens Nyheter* [Swedish newspaper].

Kamerman, S. B. (1991). Child care policies and programs: An International Overview. *Journal of Social Issues, 4*(2), 179–196.

Kautto, M. (2001). *Diversity among welfare states—comparative studies on welfare state adjustment in Nordic countries*. Helsinki: Stakes.

Key, E. (1900). *Barnets århundrade* [The century of the child]. Stockholm: Albert Bonniers Förlag.

Kihlblom, U. (1991). *Barns utveckling och mödrars arbete* [Child development and maternal employment]. Stockholm: Almqvist & Wiksell.

Kjøller, E., & Bengtson, U. 1992). *Skola, förskola, daghem för 6-åringar* [School, preschool, day-care for six-year-olds]. Stockholm: Brevskolan.

Korpi, W. (2001). Class, gender, and inequality: The role of welfare states. In M. Kohli & M. Novak (Eds.), *Will Europe work?* (pp. 52–72). London: Routledge.

Kristjansson, B. (2001). *Barndomen och den sociala moderniseringen: Om att växa upp i Norden på tröskeln till ett nytt millennium* [Childhood and social modernization: On growing up in the Nordic countries at the dawn of the new millennium]. Stockholm: HLS Förlag.

Kristjansson, B. (2002). På spaning efter det 'nordiska' och 'nordbarnet' [Searching for the Nordic and the 'Nordchild']. *Barn, 3,* 47–71.

Lorenz, K. Z. (1943). The innate forms of possible Experinece. *Zeitschrift fürTierpsychologie, 5,* 233–409.

Meidner, R. (2004, April 9). Socialdemokraterna och tillväxten: Om välfärdssamhällets framtid [The social democratic party and economic growth: On the future of the welfare state]. SR [Swedish Radio].

Myrdal, A., & Myrdal, G. (1934). *Kris i befolkningsfrågan* [The demographical crisis]. Stockholm: Bonniers.

*Norden i tal 2003* [Norden in numbers 2003]. Copenhagen: Nordic Council of Ministers.

*Nordisk statistisk årsbok 1991* [Statistical yearbook 1991]. Copenhagen: Nordic Council of Ministers.

*Nordisk statistisk årsbok 2000* [Statistical yearbook 2000]. Copenhagen: Nordic Council of Ministers.

Ohrlander, K. (1992). *I barnens och nationens intresse: Socialliberal reformpolitik 1903–1930* [In the children's and the nation's interest: A social-liberal reform politics 1903–1930]. Stockholm: Almqvist & Wiksell International.

Olafsson, S. (1999). *Íslenska leiðin: Almannatryggingar og velferð í fjöljóðlegum samanburði* [The Icelandic way: Social security and welfare in a multinational comparison]. Reykjavík: Tryggingastofnun ríkisins.

Organisation for Economic Cooperation and Development (OECD). (2001). *Starting strong: Early childhood education and care.* Paris: Author.

Popenoe, D. (1988). *Disturbing the nest: Family change and decline in modern societies.* Berlin: Aldine de Gruyter

Popenoe, D. (1991). Family decline in the Swedish welfare state. *The Public Interest, 102,* 65–77.

Reegård, S (2001, March). *The American model and the Nordic labour market.* Paper presented at the Nordic Alternative Seminar, Stockholm.

*Statistical yearbook of Sweden 2004.* Örebro: SCB.

Stearns, P. N. (1989). Historical trends in intergenerational contacts. *Journal of Children in Contemporary Society, 20,* 21–32.

Swenson, P. (1989). *Fair shares: Unions, pay, and politics in Sweden and West Germany.* Ithica: Cornell University Press.

Swenson, P. (2002). *Capitalists against markets: The making of labor markets and welfare states in the United States and Sweden.* New York: Oxford University Press.

Tauberman, A.-C. (1995). Swedish family policy: Main steps and present concerns. In B. Arve-Parès (Ed.), *Building family welfare: Report from a Nordic Seminar on families, gender and welfare Policy* (p. 23–26). Stockholm: Norstedts Tryckeri.

Therborn, G. (1993). The politics of childhood: The rights of children in modern times. In F. G. Castles (Eds.), *Families of nations: Patterns of public policy in Western democracies* (pp. 241–291). Aldershot: Dartmouth.

United Nations. (2004). *Human development report 2004: Cultural liberty in today's diverse world.* New York: United Nations Development Program.

Vogel, J. (2000, October). *Welfare production models and income structure: A comparative and longitudinal perspective.* A paper presented at the Rich and Poor conference of Working Group 6, International Sociological Association, Berlin.

CHAPTER 3

# WILL THERE BE ANY PRESCHOOL TEACHERS IN THE FUTURE?

## A Comment on Recent Teacher-Education Reforms in Sweden

**Jan-Erik Johansson**
*Oslo University College, Norway*

Nordic approaches to preschool-teacher preparation have rich traditions, with distinctive philosophical and methodological underpinnings. Until recently, professional preparation for preschool teachers in all Nordic countries differed in important ways from professional preparation for elementary-school teachers and for social workers. However, reform movements during the last 10 to 15 years in both Denmark and Sweden have brought dramatic changes in the structure and the content of teacher education, and mark the end of a separate and distinctive education for preschool teachers in both countries.

*Nordic Childhoods and Early Education*, pages 43–69
Copyright © 2006 by Information Age Publishing
All rights of reproduction in any form reserved.

In Denmark in 1992 professional preparation programs for preschool teachers, child social workers, and after-school teachers were unified into one general education for social educators, who often adamantly object to being called by the general term, "teacher." The fact that social educators and school teachers typically object to being confused with one another reflects the differing philosophies and professional practices of their respective specialties (Broström & Wagner, 2003).

Nearly a decade later in 2000, Sweden merged almost all teacher education into one general model, divided into two certificate paths, one for "early-years" teachers working with children between the ages of 1 and 12 and the other for "later-years" teachers working with ages 12–19 in secondary and upper secondary school. With few exceptions, separate preparation for teachers working with preschool children became a thing of the past.

Given these changes in the design of preschool teacher education in the two countries, preschool teaching might disappear as a well-defined professional competence, at least in Denmark and Sweden. Are preschool teachers witnessing the end of their specialty in terms of both practical and theoretical knowledge?

It is hard to predict the effects of the reforms in Denmark and Sweden, but the present models no longer guarantee a focus on the preschool experience as distinctive and unique. The explicit professional development of preschool staff will no longer take place during their education, but will begin when they start to work in preschools as teachers. Whether this will result in a loss of general professional quality is hard to say, but the preschool teacher profession has definitely lost its direct influence on the education of preschool teachers in Denmark and Sweden. Preschool teacher unions are still strong in both countries, but not in terms of controlling the education of preschool teachers as a specific, well-defined path toward preschool education.

As a consequence, the Nordic preschool model—with its German roots in Froebel's kindergarten and in the German bourgeois women's movement—is directly threatened. Among the important traits in this model are the focus on (1) care instead of school subjects, (2) aesthetics and creative arts instead of analytical facts, (3) a thematic approach instead of a school subject matter organization of the curriculum, and (4) a nonconfessional ecumenical orientation, where corporal punishment is not allowed. The model also involves a focus on play in many respects, together with an interest in the group of children, not just the individual child. The home and women were the ideological foundation of this model, developed by Henriette Schrader-Breymann in Berlin during the 1880s (Allen, 1991). Schrader-Breymann coined the then-radical concept of "intellectual motherhood [geistigen Mütterlichkeit]" to describe the new role of women outside the family. The Nordic preschool model developed inside the philanthropic sector, organized by women, without much support from established and male structures like schools, colleges and universities, or state bureaucracy.

The potential for erosion or even disappearance of preschool teaching as a distinct profession and, along with it, the loss of the group's knowledge base is most evident in Denmark and Sweden (Johansson, 2004); but there are also indications of problems in Finland and Norway, where there is a growing trend to allow untrained and semi-skilled preschool staff to perform tasks and responsibilities previously under the purview of professional preschool teachers. Preschool teaching in Iceland seems to be in a similar position.

In this chapter, I briefly outline the development of early childhood teacher education in Denmark, Iceland, Finland, Norway, and Sweden. Then I present results of a small study of the Swedish teacher-education reform as it has developed at Gothenburg University. I conclude with some tentative answers, based primarily on the Swedish experience, to questions posed at the beginning of this chapter about the future of preschool teaching as a profession.

## EARLY CHILDHOOD TEACHER EDUCATION IN THE NORDIC COUNTRIES

In the Nordic countries[1] the majority of mothers with preschool-age children work or study outside the home. Therefore, many children enter full-day care as early as their first birthday. Throughout the Nordic region, with the exception of Denmark, most mothers stay at home until the child is 1 year old because of state-financed maternal leave support systems. Norway and Finland have *cash benefit systems,* with economic support for families not using preschool institutions, which means that fewer children enter preschool before 3 years of age. The majority of children in Nordic countries are in full-day programs by the time they are age 3. Denmark, Finland, and Sweden also have special programs for children in the year before they start compulsory school. A main purpose of these programs is to prepare children for primary school. In Denmark, Finland, and Sweden, children begin primary school at age 7. In Iceland and Norway, children begin compulsory education at age 6.

As a part of the bourgeois female movement in Europe and with roots in the German Froebel movement, preschool teacher education started in Finland, Denmark, and Sweden at the end of the 19th century. In Norway preschool teacher education first started in 1935 and in Iceland in 1946. Historically, preschool teacher education programs in Sweden, Norway, Denmark, and Finland emphasized the Nordic Froebel tradition (Hatje,

1999), which was less prevalent in Iceland, where Swedish influence was mixed with American.

**Table 3.1.   Children in Day Care as Percent of Age Group, 2003**

| Age | Denmark | Finland | Iceland | Norway | Sweden |
|---|---|---|---|---|---|
| 0 years | 9.4 | 1.4 | 7.8 | 2.0 | 0.0 |
| 1 years | 72.4 | 27.5 | 54.7 | 29.8 | 44.6 |
| 2 years | 84.3 | 43.9 | 89.2 | 50.6 | 86.9 |
| 3 years | 91.1 | 62.3 | 93.3 | 76.6 | 90.9 |
| 4 years | 93.5 | 68.5 | 94.0 | 84.2 | 85.7 |
| 5 years | 97.3 | 73.0 | 92.9 | 86.5 | 96.9 |

*Note:* Denmark day-care includes after-school arrangements. Finland, Iceland, and Norway 2002 data. Source: *The Nordic Countries in Figures 2003.* Copenhagen: Nordic Council of Ministers.

Until the middle of the 20th century when more and more Nordic children began attending preschool, preschool teachers themselves largely controlled their field. Preschool teachers ruled preschool teacher education and preschool pedagogy. The influence of the state was minimal. Since 1970, however, the direct power of preschool teachers and preschool teacher educators to control the preschool and the preschool teacher training has been gradually eroding throughout the Nordic region. Over the last three decades, governmental departments and town councils have taken an increasingly more decisive and controlling role in determining both the structure and the content of educational programs for children, as well as for professional development programs for teachers at all levels. More and more, the development of knowledge in the field of early childhood, elementary, and secondary education has become the exclusive purview of government-supported colleges and universities, with little input from practitioners. Both the structure and the content of secondary teacher education and daily instructional practice seem to have achieved privileged and influential status, starting to edge out or compromise both philosophy and pedagogy traditionally associated with early childhood and elementary education. For instance, in Sweden preschool teachers no longer have unions of their own. The reforms in teacher education in Denmark and Sweden are one of the latest instances of this process.

In the Nordic countries, preschool teachers have traditionally worked with children between the ages of 1 and 6 or 7 years, depending on the entry age for compulsory school in each country. Until recently, very few infants below 1 year of age attended preschools, and preschool teachers worked mainly with children ages 3–6. Semi-skilled and unskilled staff have more often been working with preschool children under age 3.

Early on, the training of preschool teachers was 2 years or shorter and the colleges required only lower secondary education as a prerequisite. However, from the 1970s through the recent reforms, to be detailed later, preschool teacher education in most Nordic countries required 3 years of formal, postsecondary education. Preschool teacher education programs typically included preparation for various kinds of work with children prior to their entry into compulsory school, including half-day preschool, full-day preschool or daycare, and special "school preparation" classes in Denmark, Finland, and Sweden (similar to "kindergarten" in America) for children during the year before they enter first grade in compulsory school.

Although each Nordic country had its own "flavor" in preschool teacher education, perhaps with the greatest similarity between Denmark and Sweden, common themes were also evident in early childhood teacher preparation throughout the region. In addition to Nordic versions of Froebelian philosophy and methodology, Nordic preschool teacher education tended to be decidedly child-centered, oriented toward play, homelike, and nonacademic. Teacher preparation programs were deeply infused with Nordic ideals of democracy and emancipation for young children, as well as with Nordic concepts of the "good childhood" (Broström & Wagner, 2003).

Those who completed preschool teacher education programs, called "educated preschool teachers," have been viewed as the most professional members of the preschool staff. In all five Nordic countries, preschools have traditionally employed both educated teachers and unskilled or semi-skilled staff. Semi-skilled staff, with brief, upper-secondary level training, has typically worked in infant-care centers or as assistants in preschool settings.

Across the Nordic countries, unskilled and semi-skilled workers make up one-third to two-thirds of the total preschool staff, while educated preschool teachers comprise the remaining portion. The highest standards for teacher preparation can be found in Denmark and Sweden, where the majority of staff are educated preschool teachers. However, given recent changes in preschool teacher education, combined with governmental guidelines for preschool programs throughout the region, we might expect a general erosion of standards rather than a widespread movement toward the higher standards historically exemplified in Denmark and Sweden.

Leisure-time or after-school programs are most prevalent in Denmark and Sweden. Norway has adopted a less sophisticated model and its after-school programs employ a very high proportion of untrained personnel. The after-school movement has its historical roots in Denmark, where it became more closely aligned, philosophically and pedagogically, with preschool practices than with elementary or secondary-school practices. Only

Denmark and Sweden have had specific professional preparation programs for after-school teachers. In Denmark, however, there are also many less advanced after-school programs with bigger groups of schoolchildren and semi-skilled or untrained staff.

The higher education systems in the Nordic countries have many common traits, but they are not identical. One commonality is that universities have research and doctoral programs in traditional university disciplines, which colleges seldom have. Colleges have professional programs mainly for elementary teachers, preschool teachers, or nurses and perhaps undergraduate courses in some other subjects. There are also technical universities and other high-status professional programs at the university level. Teachers in elementary school and preschool were traditionally trained in separate colleges recruiting pupils from the lower secondary school level. Secondary school teachers in general have always been trained in university disciplines.

The greatest distance between colleges and universities is found in Denmark. In Sweden there are different models. For example, there is a high degree of integration in some universities, where all teacher education is organized by university departments out of a traditional discipline model. However, this model is not universal in Swedish teacher-education colleges.

## Denmark

While some decidedly Nordic commonalities exist, each of the five Nordic countries employs a preschool teacher education model that differs from the others in several significant respects. In Denmark, for example, the preferences of local welfare and social service authorities prevailed in preschool teacher reform efforts, perhaps because most preschool teachers worked in the social services sector (where preschools and after-school programs are organized) rather than in the formal education sector along with elementary schools. Danish preschools, daycare centers, and after-school programs are administered by social services and social welfare authorities, not by education authorities, which are responsible for compulsory schooling (Gytz Olesen, 2005). The only exception is the special classes, called *børnehaveklasser*, for children in the year prior to compulsory school entry. These classes for 6-year-olds are administered by the education authorities.

The reforms in Danish teacher education initiated in 1992 created a unified $3\frac{1}{2}$-year-long preparation program for "social educators" across settings and age groups. The training of staff for preschools and after-school programs was included in this new program at the colleges for social educators. The three professions have had a common labor market for a long time. They now form a new unified profession with strong borders delimiting them from elementary school teachers. In spite of this clear boundary between social educators and elementary teachers, however, the elimination of distinctions between preschool teacher, child social worker, and after-school teacher may have profound effects upon the way each previously separate career path will be viewed from within the profession, as well as from the broader social and political perspective.

This new, combined profession is quite general in nature, and the preparation program incorporates few specific connections, theoretical or practical, to various components of any of the three professions. The social educator curriculum emphasizes the development of general educational competence in working with children, youth, and adults, but also with social and psychological problems and the disabled. The curriculum does not focus on educational practice in preschools or after-school programs. The colleges are members of regional Centers for Higher Education, together with other professional programs like teachers' colleges and nursing schools (Gytz Olesen, 2005).

How to work with children in preschool settings, once a central feature of preschool teacher preparation, is barely addressed in the new program. Social education students must complete practicum experiences, but there is no requirement that any of these experiences must be in preschool. The focus is on general knowledge, not the educational context of preschools. The specific knowledge of preschool teachers seems to have been lost in the common curriculum.

## Finland

The Finnish early childhood education system is, in many ways, the most traditional of all five Nordic countries. A traditional and separate preschool teacher education remains. This professional preparation program is 3 years long and is now offered at the university level. Prior to 1995, preschool teacher education was offered at separate preschool teacher colleges.

Finish preschool teachers typically work in preschool or daycare centers, normally with children between 3 and 6 years old. However, in preschool and daycare centers, educated preschool teachers make up only 20% of the workforce, while 10% are social workers. The remaining 70% of the workforce has vocational training at the upper secondary school level. Finnish children enter the formal education system at age 6 in a kindergarten class under the auspices of the school administration. In Finland, institutions for children below 6 years of age operate under the auspices of the social services sector. The state has shown very limited interest in after-school programs.

## Iceland

In Iceland the whole preschool system has been reformed with full day care. Preschool teacher training is 3 years long and has been offered at the university level since 1998. Preschool teachers and school teachers are educated in the same institutions, but their education is quite different.

In Iceland, preschools are part of the school system, but preschools have a national curriculum of their own. Children begin compulsory school when they are 6 years old. An after-school program is available (Einarsdottir, 2003). Preschool teaching is still a separate profession in Iceland, and preschool professional knowledge seems to be in a stable state in comparison with Sweden and Denmark. Both the preschool and the teacher education are part of the educational authorities at both the national and local level. Approximately 30% of the staff in Iceland's preschools are educated preschool teachers.

## Norway

In Norway the essence of the Nordic preschool tradition remains largely intact, but even there threats to the tradition may be just around the corner. Preschool teacher education requires 3 years of study in college. However, each college has its own structure and local application of the national curriculum for the education of preschool teachers. This flexibility may ultimately weaken the foundation of traditional early childhood education. For example, the colleges may organize their courses in a more traditional, comprehensive preschool teacher education framework, or in a more academic disciplinary format, with a weaker connection to the preschool tradition.

In the typical Norwegian preschool, educated preschool teachers are a minority, as they are in Finland and Iceland. Educated preschool teachers often serve as leaders and work together with two untrained assistants, who do most of the daily, hands-on work with the children while the educated preschool teacher attends meetings and completes administrative tasks.

Both locally and at the national level, the Norwegian preschool is a part of the social care system. Children start compulsory school at age 6, and educated preschool teachers are also qualified to work in the first grade of elementary school.

Educated preschool teachers may earn certification to teach at the elementary level by taking an additional 1-year course of study, which trains preschool teachers to teach in elementary schools. Since there is no teacher education for after-school programs in Norway, some preschool teachers also work in this field, but without any special preparation.

In Norway the preschool has lost the 6-year-old children to elementary school, and in debate today more school knowledge is demanded for grade 1. Some say that there has been too much play. The legislation on preschools is about to change and the importance of preschool teachers might be reduced.

## Sweden

In Sweden traditional preschool teacher preparation has been subsumed by the university, the academic disciplines, and the conventional wisdom of secondary teacher preparation. The reform, as it has been implemented in Sweden from the year 2000, now means that the university perspective on teacher education dominates, even though there are differences between universities and colleges, since every teacher education program is developed and controlled locally. The state department of education has almost no influence, and there is no national curriculum for teacher education, only one page of official regulations. The new "early-years" teacher education requires $3\frac{1}{2}$ years of study and qualifies candidates for work in preschool, after-school programs, or elementary school with children up to 12 years of age. The comprehensive, professional education of preschool teachers, which was later combined with preparation programs for teachers in after-school programs, no longer exists.

The Swedish preschool system has recently become part of the Swedish public education system. Among the other four Nordic countries, only Iceland has also integrated preschool into the public education system. Wages and working conditions are better at the elementary school level than at the preschool level, so many Swedish student teachers and preschool teachers have moved away from preschool and after-school careers and toward elementary school teaching.

## A Nordic Comparison

In summary, then, there are growing differences among the Nordic countries in terms of how each country educates its preschool teachers. The traditional education of preschool teachers remains largely intact in Finland and Iceland, and to a somewhat lesser extent, in Norway. In Finland, Iceland, and Norway preschool teachers still complete separate, university-level professional preparation programs. They work in preschool institutions with preschool children; at 20 to 30% they constitute a minority of the overall preschool staff.

However, more dramatic changes in the direction of preschool teacher education are evident in Denmark and Sweden. The trend in Danish education for social educators is decidedly in the direction of general social

work, with no relationship to teacher education for elementary school. In
Sweden teacher education is becoming more general and more academic,
obviously leaving traditional preschool knowledge behind.

Regardless of the relative stability of traditional approaches in Finland,
Iceland, and Norway and the more obvious losses of tradition in Denmark
and Sweden, however, potential threats to Nordic early childhood knowledge and traditions can be seen in all five countries. Will preschool teaching continue as a separate profession in the Nordic countries or will lines
between preschool teaching and other professions continue to blur, as they
already have in Denmark and Sweden? Will the traditional preschool
knowledge base continue to erode or simply be dismissed in favor of
knowledge in academic disciplines? Will the preparation of preschool
teachers resemble more and more the preparation of social workers, elementary teachers, or secondary teachers? A closer look at recent teacher
education reforms in Sweden may shed light on these questions.

**Table 3.2.   Present Status of Early Childhood Teacher Education
in Denmark, Iceland, Finland, Norway, and Sweden**

|  | *Denmark* | *Finland* | *Iceland* | *Norway* | *Sweden* |
|---|---|---|---|---|---|
| *Name of education* | Social education college | Department of Child Education | Preschool teacher education | Preschool teacher education | Teacher education |
| *Affiliation* | — | University | University | — | University |
|  | College | — | — | College | College |
| *Certificate* | Social educator | Preschool teacher | Preschool teacher | Preschool teacher | Early-years teacher |
| *Workplace* | Preschool | Preschool | Preschool | Preschool | Preschool |
|  | After-school | — | — | After-school | After-school |
|  | — | — | — | Elementary school | Elementary school |
|  | Child social work | — | — | — | — |

## REFORM OF TEACHER EDUCATION IN SWEDEN

Until recently Swedish preschool teacher education was organized as a comprehensive university-level professional program, sharing many common
courses with preparation programs for teachers who planned to work in
after-school or leisure-time programs. Professional preparation programs for
elementary school teachers were organized in the same type of comprehen-

sive teacher's college model. However, the preparation of secondary teachers (with pupils between 13 and 16 years old) and upper secondary teachers (pupils from 16 to 19) has traditionally been quite different in content and format than that of preschool and elementary teachers in Sweden. Unlike programs for preschool and elementary teachers, preparation programs for secondary and upper secondary levels have focused on academic disciplines represented in the curriculum (like mathematics, science, French, German, English, social science, and Swedish) rather than on pedagogical concerns or developmental characteristics of the students to be taught.

Recent reforms in Swedish teacher education have consolidated the training of teachers at all levels, from preschool through upper secondary, as well as specialty area teachers, such as after-school, music, or handicraft teachers. These reforms have not simply brought changes to the curriculum for teacher preparation at each level, but also they have led to changes within both the comprehensive college model and the university disciplinary model of teacher education. The new model is a kind of hybrid between a comprehensive teachers college model, as was previously used for preschool and elementary teacher education, and a university discipline model, as was used for secondary and upper secondary teacher preparation.

The new model for early-years teachers is organized more like an academic discipline model than before in the sense that there is no continuous practice teaching in any subject from the beginning to the end of teacher education, but the teaching is course delimited in time and takes place during one semester, or perhaps two. On the other hand, university discipline-based programs for secondary school teachers now include a newly created, foundation course in "general education" for all kinds of teachers. The national curriculum for the new teacher education gives every college or university the full freedom to decide which kinds of teacher education courses to offer. First there was no demand of specific knowledge in any field for the "early-years" students, but in 2005, knowledge in how to teach reading, writing, and arithmetic was added to the national curriculum. The "later-years" teachers are still required to study defined combinations of academic disciplines. As a consequence, no teacher education has to have courses on early-years preparation or any other specific field whatsoever aiming at preparing early-years teachers. The university ideology focusing on disciplinary knowledge clearly provides the overarching framework for teacher preparation at all levels (Johansson, 2004).

## Background to the Swedish Reform

Sweden's recent teacher education reforms began in 1997 with the creation of a statewide committee. Several studies had criticized Sweden's existing elementary and secondary teacher training programs, citing lack of relevance, as well as lack of integration between theory, pedagogy, and student teaching assignments in relation to the realities of these teachers' future work (Carlgren, 1996; Englund, 1996; Gran, 1995). This criticism was leveled against the education of school teachers, not preschool teachers. The committee presented a white paper (Utbildnings- och kulturdepartementet, 1999) to the Swedish parliament, and a government bill was presented in spring 2000 (Utbildnings- och kulturdepartementet, 2000). During the fall of 2000, the parliament decided on the new approach to teacher education in which the preparation of teachers across all grade levels, preschool through secondary, was to be combined into a more general preparation program to replace the age- and stage-specific programs that had existed previously. The new model was to be implemented nationwide beginning July 2001. The aim was to establish a general framework for Swedish teacher education. There was also a wish to recruit more student teachers to mathematics and science in secondary school, where the lack of teachers was alarming. The idea was to attract young people to the teaching profession, and then stimulate them to choose science during their teacher education. Another aspect of the plan was to connect the education of preschool teachers and teachers for after-school programs with elementary school teacher education, since the three fields have become more interrelated because of the significant expansion of preschool and after-school programs in Sweden during the last decades of the 20th century.

Although the state has articulated a framework for integrating teacher education programs across all levels from preschool through upper secondary and including preparation of teachers for after-school programs, Swedish universities and colleges have considerable freedom to implement the reforms as they see fit within the framework. For example, preparation programs for early-years teachers, who typically work in preschool settings, have very few mandates from the state. Among the mandates is that early-years teacher preparation programs must be $3\frac{1}{2}$ years long.

## Three Models of Teacher Education in Sweden

The two approaches to teacher preparation—the comprehensive pre-reform model typically used for the preparation of preschool and elementary teachers, and the academic disciplinary model used for the preparation of secondary teachers—are clearly different. The two approaches have different historical backgrounds and different theoretical underpinnings. Preschool teacher education in Sweden developed as part of the German Froebel movement, which was located practically and philosophically inside the bourgeois female movement. The Froebel movement incorporated ideals from the 1848 German revolution, uniting the Froebelian pedagogy with radical ideology (Allen, 1991).

Pre-reform elementary education programs developed out of the introduction of compulsory elementary school in Sweden in 1842, but took definite form at the end of the 19th century when the school starting age was designated to be 7. Elementary school was controlled by the Protestant state and church and influenced by German models of elementary school. The main content included reading, writing, and arithmetic, together with catechism, religious education, and subjects supporting the nation and the royal family. Women almost exclusively taught the younger school children, while men took over the higher grades in elementary school. Until the 1930s elementary teachers for the first two grades in elementary school had a very short, comprehensive training but teachers for grades 3 to 6 had a 4-year comprehensive education at secondary school level. Since the 1960s a number of reforms have promoted the development of elementary teacher education in Sweden, but the comprehensive model remained until the present reform.

Secondary teacher education programs had their roots in the old university system, and took a modern form in the beginning of the 20th century when secondary school teachers had to study some education (half a semester) and also attend school practicum for a year in order to be certified as secondary school teachers. This means that Sweden has had three distinctly different models: one model for the preschool and after-school programs, a second for elementary school, and a third for secondary school.

Pre-reform teacher education programs, at least at the preschool and elementary levels, were structured in such a way as to create at least the possibility for close communication and collaboration between the different components of teacher training, including coursework and student teaching. Preschool teachers themselves were among the most influential voices in the pre-reform preschool teacher's colleges. Sometimes they were even described as "mother hens" because of their close and controlling relationship to the students in preschool teacher preparation programs. These days, however, fewer working preschool teachers are active as teacher educators. One reason is the transformation from the comprehensive model of teacher education meant that teacher educators had low wages and many weekly hours to teach, almost equivalent to a secondary school. When wages began to increase and the direct teaching load per week was reduced, fewer teachers were needed in general since these changes took place within the very same economical frames. The direct teaching load per week was also reduced. Second, there has been a redistribution of the resources, which means that other disciplinary fields like creative arts, social science, and science have gained and education and preschool education have lost resources. This means that the proportion of preschool staff with preschool education working in the institutions has been reduced the last decades. Another problem is that preschool teachers from earlier on lack academic credentials, which means that they have not been members of the high-status groups in the Swedish reforms of the higher education that started in 1976. This is changing slowly. Today all new teachers must earn a bachelor's degree that is equivalent to a bachelor's degree in any other field. There is a growing group of competent preschool teachers with doctoral degrees, but few positions have been available in teacher education programs.

## A CASE IN POINT: GOTHENBURG'S EARLY-YEARS TEACHER PREPARATION PROGRAM

Teacher education programs vary considerably from institution to institution throughout Sweden. Each university is free to develop its own local plan in accordance with the faculty's understanding of the government bill from 2000 (Utbildnings- och kulturdepartementet, 2000) and their view of what the teaching profession needs. Student teachers have considerable freedom to choose among the locally determined core courses and special courses.

The early years teacher education at Gothenburg University (Figure 3.1) is only one of many ways to implement the reform. The following paragraphs are based on plans from Gothenburg University (Utbildnings- och forskningsnämnden för lärarutbildning, 2003), discussions with teachers and administrators at the university, and on the government bill behind the reform (Utbildnings- och kulturdepartementet, 2000).

The program consists of three different modules that are mandatory but the content and structure is defined locally: *General education* courses (three semesters with 10 weeks of student teaching), *Core courses* (two semesters with 10 weeks of student teaching); and *Specialized courses* (one semester without student teaching). Every student has to take the General education courses, and can choose two Core courses, or one Core course and two specialized courses.

G.E.    General education module
C.C.    Core course
Sp1     Special course 1
Sp2     Special course 2

Figure 3.1.

According to the government bill (Utbildnings- och kulturdepartemen-tet, 2000), the General education module consists of professional knowl-edge common for all teachers, and multidisciplinary knowledge. Core courses are based on school subjects or groups of subjects, multidisci-plinary studies, thematic studies, or competencies that are specific for teachers. It can also be the teaching of a subject or group of subjects for a certain age group. Specialized courses may give deeper, wider, or newer perspectives on previous knowledge from other courses. They might also focus school subjects, academic disciplines, or the teaching profession.

The first module, *General education*, is required for all students. It is a 1½-year module that may be divided into different courses as at Gothenburg University, as illustrated in Figure 3.1. The General education module includes content considered universal for all teaching professions, chosen locally by each university or college. This module should also examine gen-eral topics in preschool and compulsory-school education through multi-disciplinary study. The idea is to support the professional, vocational relevance of student teaching and school subject content in courses.

The second module, *Core courses* for the teaching profession, is a 1-year course of study in one discipline or a group of disciplines. Each university or college may define its own set of core courses. In Gothenburg, for exam-ple, six Core courses were included in the early-years teacher education program during 2002. These Core courses, each combining two or more academic or aesthetic disciplines, were the following at Gothenburg Uni-versity during the year 2002. Each of them, except "Children's social envi-ronment, learning and development," focused on subject matter to be taught in preschool or school.

1. Children's social environment, learning, and development
2. Culture and language for the early years
3. Learning and information technology
4. Man, nature, and society for the early years
5. Nature and mathematics in the world of the child
6. Creative arts for the early years

The third module, which includes specialized courses, consists of half-year courses of study in any university discipline or a specially designed cur-riculum. The underlying idea is to support student teachers' future profes-sional development. The rational behind this part of the teacher education program is also to provide a balance between the General Education foun-dation every teacher gets in the first module and the individual student teacher's choice of one discipline or group of disciplines selected from the Core courses. Interestingly, the specialized courses of study do not require student teaching of any kind. Instead, future teachers select the specialized courses to provide the knowledge and skill they themselves think they will need to continue their professional development as they begin their careers in preschool, elementary, or secondary teaching.

I will comment on parts of the reform that were operative during the year 2002; that is, the first time two of the Core course modules were taught. At this time the third module of the reform, the specialized courses, was not yet implemented. The University of Gothenburg's new early-years teacher education program illustrates differences between teacher education programs as they existed prior to the reforms and the new approach. For instance, Gothenburg's formerly comprehensive teacher education curriculum for preschool teachers was transformed into an early-years teacher preparation program with three distinct modules with separate courses controlled by several academic departments, such as education, English, and biology. The preparation program leads to certification to teach early years, that is, ages 1–12 in preschool, after-school programs, and elementary school.

## Module 1—General Education

The *General Education* module, required of students preparing to teach at all levels, is a joint venture between the department of education and various other university departments. As was the case in other Swedish universities, faculty members in some academic departments at Gothenburg viewed this module as problematic because it took time away from what they perceived as the more important business of disciplinary study, which, prior to the reform, was the backbone of secondary teacher preparation. This criticism reflects an orientation toward what is—or is perceived to be—most important for secondary teachers even though the module is for students preparing to teach at all levels, preschool through secondary. However, faculty in the academic disciplines are not the only ones who criticize the module. For example, faculty from the former colleges for preschool teachers—who now work in the post-reform combined teacher education programs—also question the module, not because it siphons time from academic disciplines, but rather, because, in their view, it lacks relevance and applicability. These instructors, who still focus on preparation of early-years teachers, tend to have a more vocational and practical point of view than do faculty from the traditional academic disciplines.

## Module 2—Core Courses

Gothenburg's program does not include any core courses focusing on applied, vocational issues students in the early-years program will face when they begin their practical work as student teachers in preschool, elementary, and after-school settings. Because the coursework itself does not include application of theoretical knowledge or attention to practical issues, student teachers are left to their own devices to integrate the knowledge and experiences they got in bits and pieces during their courses and, hopefully, to craft these bits and pieces into professional competence needed for their work in preschool, kindergarten, and after-school programs, which still exist today, even though there might be changes in the future.

## Student Teaching

Another basic goal of the reform is help students make connections between academic, theoretical knowledge and their hands-on fieldwork experience in ways that will ultimately lead to sound practical knowledge and competence. Toward this goal, Gothenburg has reorganized its approach to student teaching and supervision during the school practicum, which takes place during the general education courses (module 1) and the core courses. Unfortunately this part of the reforms seems to be hard to implement, at least in Gothenburg. Previously, student teachers were assigned to an individual classroom, where they were supervised by a single teacher in the role of practicum supervisor and visited regularly by instructors from their teacher education program. Since the reform, however, a whole school or even an entire local school district becomes the practicum fieldwork site for a student teacher. A group of teachers in the area are supposed to supervise the student teacher. One desired outcome behind this new approach is to give student teachers access to a greater variety of perspectives and methods than they got when they were assigned to only one supervising teacher. Now they are, in principle at least, able to see many teachers and classes from preschool to upper secondary school.

Another change, which seems contradictory to the overall goal of helping students make connections between theory and practice, is that instructors from the teacher education program no longer visit student teachers during their practicum. The elimination of this long-standing practice deprives students of regular opportunities to discuss their practicum experiences in situ with their college instructors. Proponents of this new approach note that it provides a more flexible framework for student teaching and gives them ready access to the expertise of several experienced teachers, not just the one assigned as their supervisor.

Inherent in this flexible approach are some obvious pitfalls. For instance, the new approach relies on local authorities to organize the student teaching in a good way. Still five years after the reform, there is no general agreement on how to finance and organize student teaching and supervision. It is clear that some student teachers will be able to use these student teaching experiences to integrate theory and experience into practical knowledge, which is the aim of the reform, while others will not.

As stated previously, the reform aimed at increasing the number of highly qualified teaching professionals for both preschool and the compulsory school system. A particular goal was to recruit more secondary science and mathematics teachers. To meet these goals, teacher education programs like Gothenburg's design coursework in education, the teaching of different subjects, and practical areas as fields of scientific inquiry and research, rather than primarily as vocational training, as was the case in many pre-reform teacher education programs. In addition, the generalist approach in the first general education module and in the core courses for the early-years teachers provides the foundation for teaching at any grade level for the years 1–12 and also for teaching tasks outside preschool and school.

Instead of having to decide for sure upon entry, students have flexibility to choose courses and emphasis areas as they go along. An additional benefit of this new approach is that teacher education programs, with their new emphasis on academics and scientific inquiry, have the potential to better prepare students for further graduate study in master's or doctoral degree programs. However, it remains to be seen whether all these choice points will lead to a conglomeration of loosely connected courses or a coherent, well-articulated course of study through which students gain both the academic and practical knowledge they need to successfully enter the teaching profession at the level of their preference.

## A CLOSER LOOK AT TWO OF GOTHENBURG UNIVERSITY'S CORE COURSES

As part of a small case study (Johansson, 2004), I evaluated two year-long core courses from Gothenburg's 2002 teacher education program. Consistent with the results of another recently published study (Högskoleverket, 2005), my study revealed some problems that might be intrinsic to Sweden's new teacher training approach. As the principle investigator, I followed two groups of teacher-preparation program students during their second and third semesters, including 52 students in the *Learning and Development* core course and 30 students in the *Creative Arts* course.

My aim was to outline the focus of the new teacher education according to students, teachers, and administrators, since the new program aimed at a general knowledge regardless of the age of the children and the content to be taught. I conducted informal, conversational interviews with the students in groups. Students also completed questionnaires. I also interviewed instructors and program administrators involved in the two core courses, using informal protocols. One goal was to get an impression of the participants' backgrounds and subjective orientations toward teaching. A starting point for my interviews was my effort to discover whether the new approach to teacher education effectively handled the integration of preschool, after-school programs, and elementary school into a unified, generalist course of study or whether important components could be lost in the translation to the new approach. I also tried to get information about the students' backgrounds, which turned out to be quite traditional. Many of them had been working in schools or in caring professions, and many of were inclined to work with children.

My analysis indicated that the content of the two courses bore little relationship to the reality of the students' future careers as teachers, calling the appropriateness and the long-term value of the courses into question. According to many administrators, teachers, and students who participated in the study, the content and primary goals of these courses differed significantly from traditional teaching in preschool and school. For instance, students were expected to apply their knowledge outside the traditional school context and also to prepare for doctoral studies. These interviews suggested that specific preparation for working with children under 3 years of age, as well as preparation for teaching reading and writing at the primary level, were deemphasized or missing from these courses.

In addition to interviews, questionnaires, and informal contacts with students, faculty, and administration, I had access to results of local evaluations of the courses made by the teacher educators themselves. I found that the teaching was generally of acceptable quality with no indication of any serious problems. Of course, as with almost any teaching situation, the evaluations included some minor complaints from students, such as a preference for content other than what was covered in the class and questions about how the instructor evaluated student work.

As I examined the two courses carefully, interesting paradoxes emerged. For instance, the content of the Creative Arts course was something of an enigma, with both characteristics of the university's disciplinary structure and somewhat incongruous characteristics of the more practical pre-reform approach to teacher education. Although this was not an academic, theoretical, or scientific course, it did, in several ways, exemplify the disciplinary university model, with its emphasis on separate disciplines like music, drama, dance, painting, and other visual and creative arts. At the same time, this course had traits of the pre-reform music teacher education, with a focus on the practical sides of being a creative arts teacher. However, the course lacked focus on teaching children in preschool or elementary school, where the creative arts often are used both as subjects to be experienced and as tools for teaching other subjects.

## Creative Arts for the Early Years

The School of Musical Education, a former college for music teachers and not a traditional university department, organized the course. The faculty of the School of Musical Education are subject matter experts and are known as capable teachers. As they developed the creative arts course, they used the disciplinary discourse of the university, rather than the more practical discourse of the former music teacher preparation college. They emphasized the importance of exposing children to high-quality aesthetic and creative experiences, focusing course content almost exclusively on the characteristics of the aesthetic and creative experiences, with little or no emphasis on the characteristics of the children. Paradoxically, in spite of the disciplinary discourse in the development of the course, the course as it was implemented was rather weak in terms of theoretical content and research methodology. This suggests that the School of Musical Education faculty were talking like a university department as they marked disciplinary boundaries between traditional preschool or elementary school teacher education and the core Creative Arts course.

At the same time, both the content and the instructional methodology employed in the course had strong practical implications. However, this practical focus was not based on insights or critical reflections on the pre-reform education of preschool and elementary teachers. The predominant theme seemed to be that the creative arts are essential at all levels of education, from preschool onward. Yet, the course made no attempt to make connections with the content or teaching methods of either the preschool or the elementary school. It was as if proclaiming the inherent value of the creative arts and focusing on practical knowledge in many of the discrete visual, performing, and creative arts would be enough to ensure that future teachers would be able to create high-quality aesthetic and creative environments wherever they wound up teaching.

## Children's Social Environment, Learning, and Development

The second course, Children's social environment, learning and development, was quite different from the *Creative Arts* course. My analysis of this second course revealed a different, but still familiar problem. The Creative Arts course lacked relevance to the practical aspects of a preschool or elementary school teacher's work and was also rather weak theoretically and scientifically. However, this course presented the opposite problem. Even though this course required five consecutive full weeks of fieldwork in a preschool or elementary school, students consistently said the course was too theoretical. This course included theory and research methods, as well as a written essay for the examination. It introduced the "sociocognitive perspective" on learning through, for instance, the sociocultural theory of Russian psychologist Lev Vygotsky.

Why, then, did students in this second course view it as too theoretical even though the course also included a strong practical component? Was it that the course instructors did not help the students make connections between the theories they examined in class and their fieldwork experiences? Perhaps. But another possibility is that many of the teachers these students met in their practicum placements did not agree with the "modern" sociocultural approach. Instead, they held to the popular theorists of the previous generations, such as Jean Piaget and Erik Homburger Erikson, whose works were influential in Sweden's preschool reform movement of the 1970s.

This seems to be an instance of what teacher educators sometimes describe as the "vicious circle," where "radical" and modern teacher education comes into direct contact with "conservative" teachers in the field. I wonder, though, if most preschool teachers would agree that they are conservatives, even if they do not quickly adopt the latest educational theories.

Teacher educators need to focus serious attention to the problem of this vicious circle because its very existence will undoubtedly create problems for students in courses like the one under discussion here. It is ironic that one of today's problematic theories, that of Piaget, was introduced with all good intentions about 30 years ago, sometimes by today's followers of Vygotsky. Thirty years ago in Sweden, Jean Piaget was the much-heralded solution to the problem of that era: the outdated and long-dominant developmental studies of Arnold Gesell. This, then, is a case of the vicious cycle revisited generation after generation.

## The Early-Years Teacher

There is a growing cooperation in schools and preschools between preschool teachers, staff for after-school programs, and elementary school teachers into what might in the future evolve into a new unified position of "primary grades teacher" for children age 5–10. Most core courses in a general sense included discussion of this integration of preschool and school; but no specific core course focused on the emerging educational context for children where the after-school program of today could become an integral part of a full-day elementary school program in the future. An unintended consequence of Gothenburg's emphasis on 5- to 10-year-olds seems to be a very limited interest in children under 3 years of age. Hence, the whole idea of the early year's period as starting with 1-year-olds seems to be lost in this developing emphasis upon the integration of later preschool and primary grades.

The credential is designed to prepare candidates for work with older preschool and kindergarten children in the year prior to compulsory school entry, as well as with children in grades 1 to 3 in elementary school. It seems inevitable that this combined training will have at least two significant outcomes that may, ultimately, lead to an amalgamation of preschool, kindergarten, and primary grades from the perspective of the children's experience in these programs. First, the combined training program will inevitably reduce the level of teachers' knowledge about developmental differences as children grow from preschool to early middle childhood. Second, the combined professional preparation program will likely result in greater similarity of teaching methods across preschool, kindergarten, and primary grades than has been the case in the past.

## THE SWEDISH TEACHER EDUCATION REFORM—
## SUCCESS OR FAILURE?

First I question the relationship between academic studies and practical experience. Next, I explore the question of whether the end is near for preschool teacher education in Sweden. And, finally, I comment briefly on the comprehensive teacher education in relation to the discipline-based academic approach.

### The Power of School Experiences

The Swedish reform agenda has many goals. One of the most important is development of a strong theoretical and practical relationship between teacher education courses and the preschool or school practicum. The basic idea is that theoretical knowledge will interact with practical experience and result in practical knowledge and competence. However, findings from the case study described above (Johansson, 2004) indicate a significant lack of communication and interaction between university instruction at Gothenburg University and student teaching practicum experiences in preschool and school practica. There is limited consistency between the content of university courses and the students' actual tasks and experiences in the field.

In general, the students in my study appreciated the practical parts of their training, but they frequently referred to a weak or missing connection between the theoretical coursework at the university and their student teaching experiences, especially with regard to the practical knowledge required of teachers in preschool and school settings.

Based on this case study and a recent evaluation of the reform (Högskoleverket, 2005), then, the basic idea behind the reform—namely, the integration of theory and practice—appears to be at risk and, in fact, may never be fully realized. One reason is that the only postreform channel between the theoretical and the practical is the individual student (as is the case in Gothenburg), who is now responsible for the interaction between teacher education coursework and the practicum. This lack of strong and direct lines of communication and coordination between university faculty and student teaching supervisors in the field increases the risk that the local practical knowledge individual student teachers encounter will only maintain that student's private knowledge, but will not enhance the student's ability to apply theoretical knowledge examined in their academic courses as they meet the realities of daily work with children in preschools, after-school programs, or primary grades.

Work from several decades ago remains astonishingly relevant to today's debates about teacher education. For instance, Lortie (1975) argued that most teacher education has only a limited impact on its students and is seldom powerful enough to transform the private worlds of students into collective, professional knowledge. For instance, Lortie pointed out that students in teacher education programs rarely transform their childhood school experiences—as an *"apprentice of observation"*—into a more collective, professional knowledge.

The "apprenticeship of observation" concept centers on the reality that most of us have already attended school for thousands of hours for more than a dozen years before we enter our teacher preparation programs. This background leads us to believe that we already know a great deal about teaching and what is required for one to become a good teacher. This is a mistake, since children never go "backstage," to use Erwin Goffman's (1959) expression. Pupils very seldom have the opportunity to observe and experience what teachers say and do when they not are teaching in the classroom. Therefore, most teacher thinking probably goes unnoticed by their pupils. Perhaps it is the same in teacher education. Lortie (1975) found that students in teacher education programs preferred practical experiences to their coursework at the teacher's college. Through his work we can trace back several decades the problems of coordination and interaction between teacher training institutions and the field.

In the new Swedish model for teacher education, the student is the maker of her or his future because of the numerous choice points in the university curriculum and because student teachers now observe and participate in a much wider spectrum of daily educational practice than was the case when they were assigned to only one classroom with one supervising teacher. However, a major problem exists, as evidenced by the case study in Gothenburg: the connection between theory and practice remains as weak as the coordination and communication between the university and the practicum sites. Student teachers are left to integrate the realms of theory and practice for themselves, correctly or incorrectly, logically or illogically.

The Swedish reform, then, merely reproduces in a new structure the long-existing problem of insufficient integration in teacher education. The concept of freedom of choice in course selection and credential paths has been introduced in a somewhat market-like fashion, perhaps focusing more on attracting more students than on informing them in advance about the intellectual, academic, and professional attributes of the programs they are considering. The consequence might well be that teacher education will no longer be a true professional preparation program, but rather a general, academic deprofessionalized course of study.

## A New Primary School Teacher

Generally, there was rather strong interest in teaching older preschool children as a professional path among the students I met in Gothenburg. However, these students had decidedly less interest in working with younger preschool children, such as infants and toddlers. Most student teachers choose practicum assignments in preschools with children over age 4, or elementary schools. Few chose practica with children between 1 and 3 years of age. Interestingly, the two core courses I evaluated in my study were both viewed as weak in both theoretical knowledge and practical experiences about younger preschool children.

It seems, then, that the new teacher education model in Sweden may have given birth to an early-years certificate emphasizing ages 5–10, which, in turn, may bring about a new kind of primary school for ages 5–10. It seems as if preschool teachers today are migrating from work with younger children and moving instead toward the elementary school, where teachers are better paid and have better working conditions. In the reformed teacher education programs I have studied, this pattern emerges early on, with students choosing courses that will prepare them to work with older preschoolers through primary-grade children rather than with the birth to 3 age group. One explanation for this phenomenon is that students do not receive simple and straightforward information about which courses to choose for their preferred career path or about the consequences of choosing one set of courses over another. For instance, at Gothenburg six core courses focused on work in preschool and elementary school, but there was no guidance in course selection or sequencing after the first core course. Students are informed only that they must choose any two special-ized courses or one more core course.

Perhaps because Gothenburg's program is firmly rooted in the traditional, disciplinary academic model for preparing secondary teachers, post-reform teacher education seems to have few easy or obvious choices of courses aim-ing directly at work in preschools or elementary schools, professional fields that have no traditional place inside the Swedish university system.

## Practical Experience and Knowledge Development

Not only have working preschool teachers lost a considerable part of their influence in teacher preparation programs, but also, their voices have been diluted as practicum supervisors, since this responsibility is now spread thin across an entire school's teaching staff or even across an entire school district. Prior to the reform, preschool teachers had a more direct role in the reproduction of the preschool ideology and practice as they supervised preschool practicum students one by one. In earlier times, pre-school teachers spent hours observing and evaluating student teachers. but now preschool teachers have a more general but limited role in the repro-duction of the preschool ideology and practice during the preschool practicum.

The pre-reform education focused on teacher socialization, and perhaps there sometimes was a too heavy interest in the characteristics of a good teacher. On the other hand, pre-reform education also fostered an elite echelon among preschool teachers who developed the preschool ideology and practice. The question for the future is how the reform will address both teachers' socialization and ongoing professional development needs.

As a result of the reforms, today's preschool teacher education seems to have been turned away from its historical connections with the European bourgeois women's movement in favor of male-dominated university struc-tures. The reform model features decidedly weaker connections between teacher education programs and "the field," defined as existing preschools and elementary schools. Regardless of the good intentions in the reform, this might mean that the school practicum will gain importance and influ-ence, while the academic coursework at the university will have an even more limited influence on students. The results from the evaluation of two core courses in Gothenburg suggest that students still prefer student teach-ing and that they have less appreciation for their academic coursework.

The profile of the preschool teaching profession will most likely change in Sweden. First, it is clear that separate and distinct preschool teacher education is a thing of the past at most universities and colleges. As a result of the reform, many teachers will be educated in a $3\frac{1}{2}$-year course of study, which likely will produce academic generalists with limited preschool and elementary classroom experience prior to graduation, even if that is not the intention of the reform. Of this 3½-year course of study, only a small portion, if any at all, will be devoted exclusively to preparation for work at the preschool level. Furthermore, because the new teacher education programs have so many choice points, each student will, in essence, develop his or her own individual course of study. This will mean that every applicant for a preschool teaching position will have to be evaluated individually, since the content of each preparation program will vary considerably.

These developments are not limited to Sweden. A similar process began nearly 10 years earlier in Denmark with the integration of preparation programs for preschool teachers, child social workers, and after-school teachers into a generalist program for social educators who are, supposedly, prepared to work with clients from birth to grave. In both Finland and Norway, preschool teaching as an important and distinct profession is at risk, since more and more of the daily work in preschools is now being done by unskilled and semi-skilled workers without benefit of university-level professional preparation. Iceland seems to be in the same situation.

Who will care for the youngest children in the Nordic countries in the coming decades? Professionals specializing in the early years, or nice, but uneducated people whose main qualification is that they enjoy working with children? Unless we reform the reforms, the answer seems obvious and inevitable.

## NOTE

1.    Five countries make up the Nordic region. These include Denmark with Greenland and the Faroe Islands; Finland and the Åland Islands; Iceland, Norway, and Sweden. The total population of the Nordic region is approximately 25 million inhabitants.

## REFERENCES

Allen, A. T. (1991). *Feminism and motherhood in Germany 1800–1914*. New Brunswick, NJ: Rutgers University Press.

Broström, S., & Wagner, J.T. (Eds.) (2003). *Early childhood education in five Nordic countries: Perspectives on the transition from preschool to school*. Århus: Systime.

Carlgren, I. (1996). Lärarutbildning som yrkesutbildning. In Utbildningsdepartementet (Ed.), *Lärarutbildning i förändring* (DsU 1996:16, Bilaga 2) [Teacher education in change] (pp. 111–155). Stockholm: Utbildningsdepartementet.

Einarsdottir, J. (2003). Charting a smooth course: Transition from playschool to primary school in Iceland. In S. Broström & J. T. Wagner (Eds.), *Early childhood education in five Nordic countries: Perspectives on the transition from preschool to school* (pp. 101–127). Århus: Systime.

Englund, T. (1996). Strategisk utvärdering av grundskollärarutbildningen. In Högskoleverket (Ed.), *Grundskollärarutbildningen 1995: En utvärdering* (Högskoleverkets rapportserie 1996:1 R) [Teacher education for compulsory school in 1995: An evaluation] (pp. 16–82). Stockholm: Högskoleverket.

Goffman, E. (1959). *The presentation of self in everyday life.* New York: Doubleday.

Gran, B. (1995). *Professionella lärare: Lärarförbundets utvärdering av grundskollärarutbildningen.* [Professional teachers: The teachers' union evaluation of teacher education for compulsory school]. Stockholm: Lärarförbundet.

Gytz Olesen, S. (2005). *Rekruttering og reproduktion: Om praktikker og italesættelser i pædagoguddannelsen* [Recruitment and reproduction: On practice and rhetoric in the education of social educators]. Unpublished manuscript, København: Københavns Universitet, Institut for Filosofi, Pædagogik og Retorik.

Hatje, A. K. (1999). *Från treklang till triangeldrama: Barnträdgården som ett kvinnligt samhällsprojekt under 1880–1940-talen* [From harmony to conflict: The kindergarten as a female societal project during the 1880s to the 1940s]. Lund: Historiska media.

Högskoleverket (2005). *Utvärdering av den nya lärarutbildningen vid svenska universitet och högskolor: Del 1: Reformuppföljning och kvalitetsbedömning* [Evaluation of the new teacher education at Swedish universities and colleges: Part I: Reform evaluation and quality assessment]. Stockholm: Högskoleverket.

Johansson, J.-E. (2004). *Lärare för yngre åldrar: Konstnär, forskare eller praktiker? Utvärdering av två inriktningar i den nya lärarutbildningen i Göteborg* [The early years teacher: Artist, researcher or practitioner: Evaluation of to components in the new teacher education in Gothenburg]. Göteborg: Göteborgs universitet, Utbildnings- och forskningsnämnden för lärarutbildning.

Lortie, D. (1975). *Schoolteacher: A sociological study.* Chicago: University of Chicago Press.

Utbildnings- och forskningsnämnden för lärarutbildning (2003). *Lärarprogrammet 120–220 poäng: En förnyad lärarutbildning vid Göteborgs universitet 2003–2004* (2003-03-07). [The teacher education program 120–220 credit points: The new teacher education at Gothenburg University]. Göteborg: Göteborgs universitet, Utbildnings- och forskningsnämnden för lärarutbildning.

Utbildnings- och kulturdepartementet (1999). *Att lära och leda: En lärarutbildning för samverkan och utveckling* (Lärarutbildningskommitténs slutbetänkande SOU 1999:63) [To be teacher and a leader: A teacher education for co-operation and development]. Stockholm: Utbildnings- och kulturdepartementet.

Utbildnings- och kulturdepartementet (2000). *En förnyad lärarutbildning* (proposition 1999/2000:135) [A reformed teacher education: Government bill]. Stockholm: Utbildnings- och kulturdepartementet.

# CHAPTER 4

# THE SOCIAL GAME OF EARLY CHILDHOOD EDUCATION

## The Case of Norway

**Torill Strand**
*University of Bergen, Norway*

### INTRODUCTION

Several studies have revealed that childcare institutions, such as pre-schools and daycare centers, may be a good starting point for understanding a society, since early childhood education is closely related to nation-building, local culture, and social values (Baker, 2001; Hayden, 2000; Tobin, Wu, & Davidson, 1989; Wollons, 2000). In light of this perspective, I discuss the results of my research project on the social constructions of educational beliefs in Norway. One purpose of the study was to elucidate the ways in which the epistemology, or common knowledge and beliefs, within early childhood education is part of a continual negotiation about "Norwegianness."

The title of the project, The Epistemology of Early Childhood Education, refers to the educational beliefs that are constructed, reconstructed, and justified through social practices and representations within the field.

*Nordic Childhoods and Early Education*, pages 71–99
Copyright © 2006 by Information Age Publishing
All rights of reproduction in any form reserved.

The project focuses on how knowledge and beliefs are generated and validated. In other words, it is not the subject matter and problems of early childhood education that are primarily in focus here, but rather the social processes that construct, reconstruct, and justify the unique terrain of educational beliefs and sets of arguments we refer to collectively as early childhood education. We can say, therefore, that the project is a sociological elucidation of the social formation and validation of Norwegian early childhood education.

To establish the framework of the discussion, I begin by looking at the current situation in Norway. I show how Norwegian early childhood education represents both an extension of and a sharp demarcation from ECE in other parts of Europe. I also point out how Norwegian ECE is part of the welfare state and how Norwegian preschool teachers' training has continuously been a part of social democratic reforms aimed at improving the entire school system, even up to the university level.

Having described this framework, I then discuss some of the results from the following four phases of my research project: Canonized Beliefs, Prophesies, Oppositions, and Collective Myths and Fables. Finally, under the heading "Virtual Beliefs," I discuss whether the project has succeeded in shedding light on the complex relations between the epistemology of early childhood education and the ongoing social negotiations about Norwegianness.

## THE NORWEGIAN PRESCHOOL

Norway is a sparsely populated, social democratic country on the outskirts of Europe, where the nationalist mission has been vital since long before Norway became an independent national state in 1905. The central features of a social democracy, as practiced in Norway and other Nordic countries, are freedom, equality, and solidarity. Freedom encompasses freedom from poverty and oppression, as well as opportunities for personal development and creative self-expressions. Equality refers to equal rights and obligations for everyone, independent of social background, sex, religion, or ethnicity. Solidarity includes international solidarity, as well as solidarity with the next generation.

Norwegians, numbering 4.5 million, enjoy a relatively high standard of living and education. In Norway, the public school system is viewed as an important tool for nation-building, constructing identity, and equalizing social differences. In the Norwegian way of thinking, then, the preschool is, at once, both the goal and the means of realizing the full potential of an ideal social democracy—a social democratic utopia. As a realized idea, the Norwegian preschool protects the good Norwegian childhood, while, at the same time, serving as a means for building and developing the welfare state. The preschool's special characteristics encompass the children's well-being and the symbolic values of childhood, as well as consideration of the total economic and cultural capital of the nation.

## Building a Nation

Preschool is not a legal right for Norwegian children. In fact, no more than 63.5% of all children between the ages 1–5 attend preschool (Statistics Norway, 2001b). The state partially funds both public and private preschools, which exist in equal numbers in Norway. The state curriculum and associated guidelines published in 1997 regulate and standardize the curriculum. Public financing and curriculum regulation are two key indicators that the Norwegian preschool is inscribed within the welfare state. It must be pointed out, however, that the notion of "welfare state" is not unambiguous, uncontroversial, or static (Pierson & Castles, 2000). Nevertheless, we can say that one of the premises of the welfare state is that the state, or the government, has particular responsibility for the material or social welfare of its population, whether it is about protecting against poverty, or ensuring the health, education, and social participation of its citizens (Pierson, 1991).

In 1999 the Organization for Economic Corporation and Development (OECD) claimed that one of the key characteristics of the Norwegian Early Childhood Education and Care policy is that it both justifies and reproduces the clear and strong notion of the "good, Norwegian childhood." Norwegian children must be protected from adult oversupervision and control, be allowed to play unhampered in nature, and to choose freely their own activities. Consequently, the children's own culture, free play, and friendship have a high status. The preschool is seen as a meeting place and a forum for children, an environment for growth and development that protects the good Norwegian childhood rather than a place where children are prepared for later phases of life. However, since Norwegian preschool is based so decidedly, explicitly, and emphatically on Norwegian values and behavior, the OECD recommended that Norwegian preschools develop a more tolerant environment based on sets of values and an educational framework that can be acknowledged both by ethnic Norwegians and by Norwegian families from other ethnocultural backgrounds.

...it seemed to us that Norway was at that stage of becoming a multi-ethnic society when the majority may see the minority as a problem or a challenge, or both, to be helped and integrated but also to some extent controlled and shaped. While the minority ethnic population itself has not the confidence or security to assert itself and make its voice heard. The result tends to be a one-way process—"what can we do for them?", "how can they participate in our Norwegian society?"…rather than a process of dialogue and mutual change. (OECD, 1999, p. 25)

Daycare institutions have existed in Norwegian cities since the turn of the 20th century. Initially daycare centers were rather widespread geographically, but some preschools also arose simultaneously. The daycare centers were a local, Norwegian version of philanthropic child-saving projects, popular throughout Western Europe at that time. The preschools mirrored a Norwegian version of Frobelian pedagogy. However, the Norwegian preschool as we know it today is a relatively young institution with weak bonds remaining to the original European heritage. Once the imported ideas encountered Norwegian culture and values, they were immediately "corrected" and transformed, creating a clear and lasting demarcation between the European and the Norwegian ECE (Korsvold, 1998; Myhre, 1988; Rudberg, 1983). One example is the preschool teacher training program, which by no way—according to the principal— could be "translated into Norwegian conditions" (Grundth-Pedersem. 1960, p. 90). Contrary, the training of Norwegian preschool teachers established in the 1930s "had to be based on Norwegian values and traditions" (Berg, 1990, p. 35).

The very first daycare institutions were solely urban phenomena, and there was a clear distinction between daycare centers and Frobelian preschools. Daycare centers were for working-class children of the poor eastern part of the city of Oslo, and Frobelian preschools were for the middle-class children of the affluent west side. The division not only marked a social class difference and the great divide between the living conditions of the east and west, but also a divide between different childcare ideologies. The rationale behind the childcare institutions was primarily that poor children needed to be looked after. In other words, the childcare institutions were meant to "…prevent the damage the children could suffer by being left alone or thwart the damnation that loitering, begging, and mingling with the outcasts of society will necessarily lead to" (Grude, 1987, p. 26). The rationale behind the preschools was, however, neither custodial care nor protection from social needs or poverty; but rather, preschools were established as a supplement to the upbringing of the affluent homes (Myhre, 1988).

The distinctions between daycare and preschool lingered as daycare institutions were established in other parts of Norway during the rebuilding of the country after World War II. The "child protection millions" from the Norwegian state and donations from the Swedish Red Cross funded daycare centers and preschools in devastated Norwegian cities and villages

(Grude, 1987; Korsvold, 1998). The country was now to be rebuilt and Norwegian children were to be assured of good living conditions.

Nevertheless, it was not before the great exodus of mothers from the homes during the 1970s, inspired by the Woman's Liberation Movement, that the expansion of preschools in rural areas accelerated. The Day Care Act of 1975 established that daycare institutions for children below compulsory school age should be called "preschool." They should be educationally oriented and led by qualified preschool teachers. These new provisions erased, at least to some degree, established divisions between daycare and preschool.

Social changes in recent decades have contributed to an explosion in the number of preschools and several shifts in the debate about children, childhood, and the social mission of early childhood education (Borge, 1998; Myhre, 1994). The slogan of the 1970s was "build preschools now." In the 1980s the slogan was the "good childhood;" and in the 1990s, it was "quality in preschools." The 1970s introduced wide acceptance of new family constellations, such as working mothers and single parents. These changes gave rise to debates about the construction, regulation, and financing of preschools. New family constellations also brought with them changes in children's lifestyle and daily routine, which became a focus of discussion during the 1980s. This was the decade of the child.

A new Children's Act in 1981 and the establishment of an Ombudsman for Children signaled the government's administrative takeover of the Norwegian childhood, or at least its attempt to manage portions of it. The preschool debate was no longer about the speed of expansion or forms of management, but, rather, about the conditions of childhood. The question was whether preschool was more of a constructed ghetto than a window toward life. In the beginning of the 1990s, therefore, the content of early childhood education was high on Norway's political and social agenda. The government initiated a "common effort for quality" by investing in early childhood research, revitalizing preschool teachers' training, and raising the qualifications of assistant teachers. The educational mission of the preschools, contrary to the social mission of the institutions, was now to become more visible, the educational content invigorated, and early childhood education policy brought closer into line with compulsory school policy, such as public regulation of the curriculum and an extension of teacher training requirements (Strand, 1996).

Current public documents define the Norwegian preschool as an "educationally oriented" enterprise that must provide children with "...solid opportunities for development and activity in close understanding and collaboration with the children's homes" (Act No. 19 of 5 May 1995 on Day Care Institutions, § 1). The intention is that there should be high-quality care for all children at a price that does not exclude young families with a weak family economy (Ministry of Children and Family Affairs, 1998). The National Curriculum—the Framework Plan—describes the quality standards:

> A good daycare institution should provide the children the freedom to manage their everyday lives themselves within limits to which they can relate, based on their age and stage of development. The good daycare institution should not have a rigid program but be flexible in its planning and pave the way for good experiences. (Ministry of Children and Family Affairs, 1995, p. 11)

In spite of the noble intentions in the quality standards, however, the majority of preschool personnel lack formal qualifications, since only one out of three employees is a trained teacher. These differences in the quality expectations and teacher preparation have created a situation where preschool personnel often feel under siege. This may be one of the reasons why Norwegian preschool teachers frequently "take a stand against the primary-school teachers, against mothers at home, but also against women they work with, i.e., assistants and apprentices" (Korsvold, 1997, p. 226).

## Teacher Training

Norwegian preschool teacher training has been largely characterized by an oral tradition, as well as by a strong female presence and bonding. The first educational institutions for preschool teacher preparation, established during the 1930s, were small private schools in which the director had strong influence. The instructors considered their "...students as future comrades in arms and incited them to battle for the preschool." This created "...a common culture, a common set of values, with common goals and common understanding in this group of professionals" (Balke, 2002, p.18). In this manner, early childhood education became closely associated with and defined by a handful of Norwegian women with shared visions and a zealous engagement.

Another trend in the early preschool teacher education was "cultivating and controlling motherhood" (Korsvold, 1997, p. 238), a goal that was expressed through a curriculum that reflected certain middle class ideals. For example, in one teacher education institution, this type of "cultivation" went all the way down to the practical level, with "...instructions about what the students should wear, how to stub a cigarette, and how to brew, pour and drink a cup of tea..." (Korsvold, 1997, p. 239). There were, of course, many critical voices against these small, private teacher-training programs. Among the criticisms were that the programs qualified their graduates for "stiff-legged teaching" rather than for meeting the needs of the children, that only "girls from affluent families were able to attend," and that the principal "personally selected her students" (Bøe, 1988, p. 32).

Nevertheless, it was not until the 1970s that the state took over responsibility for educating preschool teachers. At that time preschool teacher training was integrated into public educational colleges and became equal to the training of elementary school teachers, both in terms of admission qualifications and length of study. These new educational colleges were given a threefold task: First, to prepare the students for teaching, second to "promote professional ethics," and finally to "perform action research" (Lærerutdanningsloven No 49, § 19). The National Curriculum defined the contents of the new, 3-year teacher training program as "curriculum theory," "school subjects," and "practice." The aim was "...to provide an overall professional basis for creating a rich and inspiring environment for preschool children" (Lærerutdanningsrådet, 1971, p. 5).

A new wave of reform hit the country during the 1990s. With the slogan "lifelong learning," the social democrats reformed all of the Norwegian educational system from preschool through high school. The preschool became more interconnected with the school. The school age was lowered from 7 years to 6 years, and qualified preschool teachers were allowed to teach in primary schools. The educational colleges became an integrated part of other professional studies in large, new university colleges. In 1995 the Act of Norwegian Universities and Colleges replaced the Act of Teacher Training from 1969. A new common curriculum (Ministry of Church, Education and Research, 1995) established that a Norwegian teacher "...should be a resource for children and youngsters in the learning process and has to ensure their freedom and choice" (p. 3). The preschool teacher training program remained 3 years, but its content was changed to "curriculum theory and practice," "school subjects," and "specialization." The aim was to develop "an intuitive capability in their daily work with children and knowledge through a reflected perspective about their vocation" (p. 39).

After a rapid expansion, preschool teacher training programs are now available in 19 university colleges spread all over Norway. Each year, over 2,000 candidates graduate, of whom around 8% are men (Statistics Norway, 2001a). Following the "Quality Reform"—a new and comprehensive reform meant to internationalize Norwegian higher education—a new national curriculum was implemented in 2003 (Ministry of Education and Research, 2003). The new preschool teacher training qualifies candidates for a bachelor's degree in Early Childhood Education, which, among other things, aims at providing an international perspective on preschool and the role of preschool teachers. In addition to providing an international frame of reference, students within the new program are encouraged to do part of their studies abroad. In this way, the new program "...shall qualify the student for active participation in [national and international] debates about and the development of the good preschool education for all children in current and future society" (Ministry of Education and Research, 2003, p. 12).

In short, we can say that the Norwegian preschool, actualized as it is conceived, would become both the aim and the means within a social democratic utopia. As an accomplished idea, the preschool should foster the "good Norwegian childhood," while being a means of building and developing the welfare state. This vision of preschools as they should be justifies the need for professional preparation for preschool teachers. At the same time, preschool teacher preparation is part of a system of Norwegian universities and colleges that is meant to produce economic and cultural capital. These trends show that preschool education is now increasingly creating closer bonds to national and international academic institutions. To put it succinctly, the most important element in teacher training is no longer practical training, but, rather, internationalization. Preschool teachers' most important qualifications are not cultivating and controlling motherhood as in the past, but, rather, research-based education. The fundamental aim for teacher training is no longer to provide a basis for "creating an inspiring environment" for children, but, rather, to qualify future teachers for "active participation in the debate."

These trends raise the question of whether the production of knowledge in teacher training can be understood independently from the broader social context in which national and cultural capital is continually defined and redefined. This inspires me again to ask whether my research project, focusing on social constructions of educational beliefs, has been able to reveal the ways in which the epistemology of ECE is embedded in the social negotiations of Norwegianness. What follows is a description of the study and a discussion of findings from each of the four sections of the study: Canonized Beliefs, Prophesies, Oppositions, and Collective Myths and Fables.

## A SOCIOLOGICAL STUDY ON EDUCATIONAL BELIEFS

The title of the project—the Epistemology of Early Childhood Education—points to the beliefs generated, upheld, and legitimized through social practices and representations in the field of early childhood education. In what ways does this epistemology occur? How is it preserved, and how is it justified? In other words, it is not the themes and problems of early childhood education that are primarily in focus here, but rather the social processes that generate, uphold, and justify the unique topology of early childhood education.

In planning this project, several issues had to be illuminated. First, I wanted to reveal the characteristics of early childhood education. Second, I wanted the possibility to capture the dynamic, complex, and perhaps paradoxical character of the social constructions of knowledge. Moreover, I wanted to investigate how various social agents, institutions, and interests are integral parts of a continuous construction and reconstruction of the epistemology of early childhood education. Third, the project had to include a systematic reflection on my own role as researcher. (The methodology for a self-reflexive sociology, referring to a sociology objectifying the researchers own practice as a knowing subject, is discussed in detail in other publications, including Strand [2001, in press].)

The research is based on the French sociologist Pierre Bourdieu's cultural sociology. For Bourdieu (1977, 1990, 2000), a social field is generated and upheld through the common interests of social agents and institutions. At the same time, the field itself produces this interest. The social field can be seen, on the one hand, as a *magnetic field*—a social field of forces—that influences the participants. On the other hand, as a *game* in which the aim is to win the rights to set the rules and the opportunity to decide what, in fact, is at stake. Taking the fact that the field is constituted and maintained by various agents' common interest in early childhood education, this common interest generates a magnetic effect—a social force—that keeps the field together. The social game, then, is about the right to decide the rules concerning how early childhood education should be defined, as well as the right to define what is at stake (Bourdieu, 1996).

The four phases of the project illuminate the social bases and norms of justification for early childhood education. The first phase is a construction of the field. The second phase is a more nuanced description of the established epistemology. The third phase is the deconstruction of this description. The fourth phase is a reconstruction through a more systematic investigation of the reliability and the validity of the project's results. I will introduce the empirical basis and present some of the results from each of the study's phases: Canonized Beliefs, Prophesies, Oppositions, and Collective Myths and Fables.

## Canonized Beliefs

Where and how do preschool teachers and those who prepare them in the colleges for their professions collectively construct their epistemology of ECE? In the first phase of the project, I created the social space in which the epistemology of early childhood education is constructed, conserved, and justified. I started with Bourdieu's assumption that there is a dialectic relationship between the field and the epistemology that the field acknowledges, that is, that the field recognizes and reproduces the very same epistemology that is the foundation of the field's existence. I collected all the mandatory reading lists on curriculum theory from all teacher-training programs in Norway during 2 years of study. These readings, then, collectively represented the current knowledge to which ECE laid claim. To the extent that these lists were authorized texts, since the faculty and/or the field sanctioned them, they can be seen as "canonized." In fact, these texts were canonized in 1994–1995 by the faculty and 6,000 students in 18 teacher colleges, and in 1999–2000 by 7,500 students in 19 teacher colleges.

These reading lists, seen as representing the canonized, or authorized, beliefs, provide access to the social production and distribution of early childhood beliefs. Therefore, I transferred the information from the reading lists to a database, and categorized them according to year of study and educational institution, number of students, the title of the books or articles and their topics, number of pages of obligatory reading, writer's name, writer's institutional affiliation, and sex. This categorization narrowed down the field and drew a topographical map of the social production and distribution of the relevant epistemology. Generally, most of the literature was written by Norwegian college teachers, among whom were a few more women than men. In other words, very little material was imported from other research areas and only a small part of the literature was written by preschool teachers. Few foreign textbooks were included, except for some Scandinavian selections.

In short, the first phase narrowed down the field to the literature used in all the preschool teacher-training programs in the country in 1994–1995 and 1999–2000. The reading lists suggested that mostly Norwegian authors, affiliated with one of the teacher training programs, produced the vast majority of the literature. Judging by this overview, it seemed as if there was a border between a rather localized field of Norwegian early childhood education and other fields of knowledge. Although there was a widespread exchange of curriculum literature between the Norwegian colleges, the reading lists included very few selections from other national or international academic circles.

In short, the first phase of my project confirmed Bourdieu's assumption about the dialectic relationship between the field and the epistemology the field acknowledges, that is, that the field itself produces and reproduces the same epistemology that is the basis for its existence. The textbooks read by preschool teachers during their preparation programs were mostly written by the faculty within these Norwegian programs. There are very few texts written by authors situated in external fields of knowledge.

## Prophecies

In the second phase of the study, my goal was to gather more information about the epistemology of ECE by interviewing the "prophets," that is, the authors read by most students. The assumption was that the authors of the most widespread textbooks, the prophets, were in possession of what is considered valuable knowledge. In other words, the prophets were not interesting to me as individuals, but, rather, as social agents who verbalize, and thus bring into focus, the symbolic capital of the field (i.e., the socially recognized beliefs and practices generated by the field), motivating the agents to invest their time, honor, and life in the social game of Norwegian ECE (Bourdieu, 1991a, 1991b).

Early childhood education has traditionally been defined by and justified through women's sociopolitical engagement. As a field, ECE represents a professionalization of a typically feminine nurturing role. Overall, authorship of the reading lists was almost evenly divided between men and women, and only three women were among the seven most read authors.

All of the most-read authors were affiliated with teacher training institutions. Two of the women writers declined to participate in the project, so I was able to interview only four men and one woman. These five were willing to participate despite the fact that the project's design and the nature of the material made it difficult to ensure their anonymity.

The interviews aimed at getting the informants' own descriptions of the current Norwegian ECE, the changes in the field, and their utopian visions of this particular field of knowledge. The intention was to present a more nuanced picture of (1) the position of the field of ECE in comparison with a larger field of educational knowledge and beliefs, (2) social positions and positionings within the field, and (3) the production, reproduction, and justification of the field's symbolic capital.

*The Social Position of the Field.*   It is not surprising that this research confirms the field's relatively weak position compared to other fields of knowledge. There are three signs: (1) the lack of autonomous strategies for justification, (2) the relatively widespread influence of external forms of hierarchy, and (3) the power of the negative sanctions or positive incitements applied to preserve orthodox practices. In the paragraphs below, I clarify what I mean by these three signs of ECE's relatively weak social position.

By "autonomous strategies of justification," I mean that an epistemology is judged by some internal standards, originated by and original to the field itself. However, as evidenced by the five popular authors whose texts were widely read by students in teacher preparation programs across Norway, ECE lacks such autonomous strategies. For example, three of the five prophets immediately and categorically rejected the term "early childhood education" as a description of their field of study. One author claimed to know nothing about early childhood education. She said her knowledge was primarily about *children's play*. The other two authors said their focus was on children before school age, but not necessarily about preschool. They preferred to justify their research as an epistemology on and for small children, not as an epistemology of ECE itself.

As to the influence of external forms of hierarchy, all the prophets, except one, disclosed that their professional background was from another academic field, not ECE. They said that their current professional interests relating to ECE were primarily a product of fields of knowledge other than early childhood education, such as organizational theory, psychology, and didactics. This suggests that four of the five prophets were importing their ideas from other disciplines and discourses into the epistemology of ECE. These prophets' professional status exudes authority; but, according to them, not the authority of ECE knowledge itself, but, rather, the authority of other, more reputable disciplines and discourses. In other words, the field imports symbolic capital, not directly through syllabus literature written by external authors, but circuitously by acknowledging the authorship of external logics of practices. Such an indirect import indicates that the field adopts external forms of hierarchy. Consequently, the field easily allows external fields of knowledge to define, classify, and validate ECE knowledge.

The third sign of the field's weak position is the power of the negative sanctions and the positive incitements in enforcing the preservation of orthodox practices. The more threatened, the more important it is to keep the field together by inducing conformity. For example, one of the prophets constantly tried to excuse, explain, and almost defend what he himself regarded as an unorthodox professional stance. He believed that Norwegian preschool education must focus more on conveying core knowledge to preschool children: "...it is something that one has to put into words. And I am in fact not afraid to say so." And when one of the interviewees spontaneously interrupted herself, straightened her back, spread her arms, and burst out, "Oh, I just love the Scandinavian preschool!" is an example of a positive incitement. In other words, the positive incitements and the negative sanctions of the field can seem quite powerful.

*Positions and Positionings.* As mentioned earlier, the social position of the prophets is mediated through a dual system of differences: on the one hand, through a comprehensive social structure, or as Bourdieu said the "universe of positionings" and on the other hand, through the "social game of the field." The "universe of social positionings" thus denotes the social structures of the social field of ECE, determining the limits and possibilities of the activities in the field. The "social game of the field" denotes the social practices and negotiations among agents and institutions, aiming at gaining or losing symbolic capital. When the interviewee announced that she just *loves* the Scandinavian preschool, the statement may have been a sign of her social position allowing her to give such a statement. Moreover, the statement itself was part of the social game she was playing, allowing her to gain even more symbolic and social capital, and thus strengthening her social position.

With regard to the universe of positionings, the social field of ECE resembles a magnetic field, or a field of social forces, having both attractive and repulsive effects. In other words, social agents possessing the specific kind of symbolic capital highly recognized by the field of ECE may be attracted, while agents possessing a different type of symbolic capital—a symbolic capital highly recognized within other social fields—may be repelled. Each agent's social position, both within the field of ECE and in relation to other social fields, will thus determine how their representations and practices both reflect and are affected by these contradictory forces. However, in order to avoid a social determinism, it becomes important to consider the other system of difference, that is, how the social game of the field creates a field of possibilities.

How can social agents, like our prophets, exploit ECE as "a field of possibilities"? During an interview, one prophet, for example, claimed, "At the risk of being accused of blasphemy," preschool education needs "to pay more attention to the content."

Another prophet chose to leave her career as a criminologist to do research on children's play instead. Each of them acquired a position and then contributed to the agenda. The first one thought perhaps that he had expanded the borders of the field a little, when 25 years ago he introduced a new topic: content-oriented didactics. The second person believed that her writings had revitalized a topic that was central in the beginning of the Froebel kindergartens. Both have contributed to the field in ways that have strengthened their own positions in that same field and, at the same time, provided justification for their further research on their topics. In other words, all the agents in the field—including our prophets—participate in a game that, on the one hand, provides opportunities for precisely their own brand of research, and, on the other hand, continues to define and preserve the game itself.

The interviews with the prophets revealed great differences between them, both in their professional biographies and in their research interests. The only thing they seemed to have in common, at least at first glance, was a collective rejection of "schooling," referring to formal, compulsory education. These prophets, then, justified the epistemology of early childhood education through a rebellious, child-centered rejection of traditional schooling. They clearly drew a demarcation line between themselves and the notion of formal education; but beyond this, they did not share alliances, even to the ECE, given that four of five claimed that ECE was not their primary field of research. Overall, we may say that the differences between the prophets were more striking than their similarities. Yet, by virtue of their positions and their work, they were all participants in the same social game. In other words, the game itself can be seen as their alliance. These prophets, thus, meet in a common belief—or confidence in—the social game of the field, which may indicate that the belief in the game itself is the foundation of the game.

*The Field's Production, Reproduction, and Justification of Symbolic Capital.*   It is this collective belief in the game that justifies the agents' desires, or, rather, the belief in the game becomes the agents' professional drive. (Social agents in ECE include our prophets and the college instructors who select their texts and, ultimately, the students who read them.) The agents believe in the game and use the game as a call to participate in the social play of early childhood education. The strength of the agent's belief in the ECE game, however, determines his or her level of investment in the game. The prophets, for example, have made great investments, including their research work and their publications. Their professional biographies revealed the symbolic capital that has been their ticket, first to enter the social game of ECE and next to gain prophet status as a player in the field.

Professional visions, or utopian ideas, create a driving force behind scholarly research. The five prophets had completely different professional utopias. For example, one of them envisioned more flexible and "user-friendly" preschools in the future. For him, the "horror vision"—or anti-utopian scenario—was a deprofessionalization in which teachers become administrators. Another prophet envisioned a higher status for preschool teachers and that preschool would acquire "official status as part of the education system." The third hoped to see the preschool employees become more open to children's curiosity and thirst for knowledge. The fourth believed that preschools should contribute more directly to enculturation processes: "We must offer some 'nutrition,' something to grow on." Only one of the five was concerned directly with the field of educational research. His vision was of further professional development for ECE, "I hope that early childhood education is further developed and strengthened, and that one can have more cooperation and collaboration among different academic circles. I do hope so. It is very important. It can be very fruitful for all parties."

Bourdieu pointed out that central agents rarely speak directly about the game. More often, external or peripheral agents are the ones who comment on the game and thus can point out the collective values and interests that are at stake. By virtue of their central positions and their strong influence, the prophets can surely be identified as "central agents." Predictably, as we might have expected from Bourdieu, none of them spoke of the game during the interviews. The prophets' professional engagements grew out of very different interests, including an interest in children, the profession, the role of preschools, social development, and educational research. What values and interests for ECE were really at stake here? The interviews revealed little about that, as the prophets were silent about the game itself, as well as about their individual and collective roles in it.

## Oppositions

The third phase of the project was based on the assumption that, unlike prophets, opponents can contribute with a perspective on the game as a game. From their position, they have a more distanced view on both the game and the collective interests and positionings that define, and are defined by, the game.

I interviewed three opponents. All were authors of books included in the reading lists, but their books were not widely read. The opponents were all women, willing to participate with full name, and quite happy to be labeled as "opponents" within the framework of this project. What they had in common was extensive knowledge about ECE as a field, since all were trained preschool teachers, held a higher degree in education, and were now tenured faculty at university colleges affiliated with a program for early childhood education. In addition, they all had solid research experience. Nevertheless, their research did not register among the "widely read" works on the reading lists. Consequently, these authors occupied peripheral positions, in contrast to the positions of the prophets.

I based my interviews with the opponents on the protocol I had used with the prophets. My intention was to reveal the opponents' descriptions of early childhood education and to find out how their professional biographies, aspirations, and utopias compared to those of the prophets. The goal was to give a more diverse picture of the social game within early childhood education. From these interviews, three major themes arose about the game: (1) order of the field; (2) characteristic themes, or configurations, of the field; and (3) existence of the field.

*The Order of the Field.*   The interviews of the prophets described Norwegian early childhood education as an uncertain place because it attracts and welcomes agents with wide variation in symbolic capital, dispositions, and professional ambitions. The prophets were neither particularly concerned with preserving or defending an established order within the field. On the contrary, their interviews revealed little or no interest in defining, defending, and controlling the borders of the field. The prophets seemed to have a few shared ideas about tickets of entry into the ECE game or rules for playing it, but beyond that, they had little to say about how the field should be defined, maintained, or contained. However, my conversations with the opponents gave a more nuanced picture. Like the prophets, the opponents spoke about the uncertainty within ECE. They noted that the field of ECE knowledge has a weak position, is elastic, and in a flux. However, the opponents pointed more explicitly to the legitimacy of the game itself, acknowledging that the game cannot be seen separately from its rules of participation and the agents who are given the authority to define and approve these rules.

The first opponent believed that master's degree programs in early childhood education give legitimacy to the field. Her reason was that a master's program produces, preserves, and justifies some myths, which, in turn, become the foundation of and potential for ECE as a distinct field of knowledge. (Here the term "myth" refers to familiar stories with recurring themes, often embodying cultural ideals.) For example, this opponent spoke of the myth about the "preschool child," living a distinct phase of life—with its own culture and unencumbered free play—with a high intrinsic value, which should be protected and recognized on its own premises.

In addition to the opponent's notions about the myth of the preschool child, for example, as fundamental to the preservation and justification of ECE knowledge, the interview also revealed this opponent's concern that "the idea of a preschool is marginal," and, therefore, the field is endangered. In 1998, the Norwegian government had implemented a cash benefit for parents who stay home with their children under the age of 3. Simultaneously, the government lowered the school age from 7 to 6. Consequently, the Norwegian preschool became only for children between the ages of 3 and 5. As a result, she claimed, the significance of preschool as an institution was diminished, as was its cultural capital. Thus, this opponent feared that preschool teacher-training programs would soon be co-opted into professional preparation programs for compulsory school teachers.

Another opponent viewed current Norwegian preschools as ghettos where "we fence the children in" and prevent them from experiencing a natural childhood. According to this opponent, the problem was that traditional early childhood education is based on "Norwegianness" and justified through a scholastic way of thinking, which is rather disrespectful toward the children's own experience and forms of knowledge. When this kind of knowledge and beliefs has a monopoly, a real danger arises for undermining or discounting other, perhaps non-Norwegian, knowledge, beliefs, values, and ways of being.

This opponent's vision was to develop a pedagogy based on the children's lived experience, local culture, and traditions. Paradoxically, she indicated that such pedagogy is capable of incorporating both that which is specific to the children's own contexts and that which is universal. Therefore, she held that her idealized pedagogy becomes more international and allows the children to transcend national borders. In short, she called for an educational program that pays more attention to human values, spiritual dimensions, and practical forms of knowledge.

The third opponent was more concerned with the training of preschool teachers. She argued that a specific female harmonizing and nonreflective attitude toward family-oriented nurturing logic mars early childhood education. According to her, the problem arises from a "traditional pedagogy of the womb," grounded in family-oriented and nurturing logic. This means that custodial care of the child is perceived as more important than future-oriented upbringing and education. This traditional "pedagogy of the womb" is, according to this opponent, too introverted and harmonizing, thereby capable of endangering the field from within. This danger consists of a collective, and typically unconscious, consensus to disregard or trivialize disagreements among early childhood educators in service of shared values "of the womb." This opponent called for teacher preparation programs to develop more conscious and conscientious ethical and political reflections on ECE practices and the beliefs that underlie them. From this, the next generation of preschool teachers might unveil the pedagogy of the womb. In short, this opponent called for "masses of questions and a consciousness about diversities."

To summarize the three opponents' views about the entrance ticket and the rules for the game, then, the first believed that early childhood education becomes legitimate when there is a higher degree, such as a master's, in the field of study. The second opponent believed that the Norwegian monopoly on knowledge included in teacher education programs results from scholastic traditions and strong commitments to ideas associated with "Norwegianness." The third stated that early childhood education is based on a consensus-oriented "nurturing logic," which she called the "pedagogy of the womb."

If we accept the opponents' narratives at face value, we could draw the conclusion that successful entry into and mastering of the social game of Norwegian ECE are achieved through higher education, scholastic knowledge, feminine nurturing, and a shared conception of Norwegian values and ways of being. However, if we read these narratives in light of the prophets' narratives, we discover that the opponents pointed more explicitly to the social order of the field, acknowledging that the social game of ECE cannot be seen separately from its rules of participation and the agents who are given the authority to define and approve these rules. Consequently, the opponents—in the role as agents on the edge of the field—appear as guardians. The social negotiations about the order of the field should therefore not be read independently from the negotiations about legitimate visions and divisions of the field, including, for example, its characteristic themes and configurations.

*The Characteristic Themes of the Field.*   When the field of early childhood education is an uncertain, elastic, and fluctuating field, negotiations about legitimate visions and divisions can come across as paradoxical, changing, and complex. In light of Bourdieu's cultural sociology, however, we can see a kind of pattern in these negotiations. From the perspective of the opponents, for example: (1) the field allows external agents to define and categorize valid knowledge; (2) the history of the field is present in its characteristic themes; (3) the field's characteristic themes must be seen in light of the material production of educational beliefs; and (4) the field's characteristic themes should be read in relation to the social recognition of these beliefs.

Already in the second phase of the project, it became clear how the field allows external agents to define and validate knowledge. This is a sign that the field lacks autonomous strategies for justification, and thus widely incorporates external ways of hierarchical classifications. Both prophets and opponents interpreted this delegation of self-definitional power as a sign of the field's weak position in relation to other fields of knowledge. Although the first opponent wanted to move the power of definition closer to the field, she, in a sense, also showed this tendency when she argued for transferring the definition of legitimate visions and divisions to the rituals of higher education. She believed that master's degree programs produce "authorized knowledge about what early childhood education is." Or, as she said later in the interview, "It is the master's program that has produced a label: here we have a field of knowledge called early childhood education." In other words, she held that the master's program authorizes legitimate visions and divisions within the epistemology of early childhood education. The curriculum of the master's program, then, may legitimize the goal and content of the epistemology and thus contribute to the demarcation of early childhood education as a relatively autonomous field of knowledge.

Another opponent pointed to the field's history. When she was asked to characterize Norwegian early childhood education, she named several traditions within Scandinavian ECE. Thereafter, she used most of the interview to problematize the relation between tradition and innovation, and argued that teacher training should make the students more aware of the close connection between pedagogy and politics. She explained, "We are talking about a female-dominated education, which has been largely formed by men. The pedagogy of the womb is quite an accurate description because there is a very close connection between mother and children and women's happiness in life." This opponent's opposition can thus be seen as an example of how current negotiations about legitimate visions and divisions are historically inscribed in—and should be read in relation to—traditional ECE discourses, such as the philanthropic child-saving project, as a legitimate place for women's sociopolitical engagement.

Bourdieu's cultural sociology also takes into consideration that our epistemologies are generated in relation to the material world. In this project, this means that the main themes of the field are generated, preserved, and justified in relation to material conditions, such as the authors', the publishers', and the institutions' investments in economic capital. To what extent was the reading material in the course syllabi produced, preserved, and justified by economic considerations of any or all of the players?

Another example is the opponent who believed that preschools "fence the children in." She related her views on Norwegian early childhood education to concrete material manifestations, such as buildings, books, and national borders. Her opposition was about wanting "to tear down the walls," promote practical knowledge, and go beyond national borders.

Another issue is that the characteristic themes of and educational beliefs within the field cannot be seen separately from the social recognition of these beliefs. In a stable field of knowledge, the social positions of the agents will be in agreement with their positionings. This means that if the social field of Norwegian ECE had been stable, the social positions of the various agents would be in agreement with the beliefs they uphold. However, since the Norwegian field of ECE is uncertain, elastic, and fluctuating, the social positions did not necessarily correspond with the positionings. Thus, the social recognition of legitimate themes and beliefs within early childhood education remain uncertain. Consequently, as the field is in constant flux, it is difficult to say whether the visions of the prophets actually receive as much validity as their social position would indicate. Neither do we know whether the opponents' educational beliefs and arguments achieve a greater or lesser degree of recognition than their peripheral position would indicate. Nevertheless, since the opponents, as intellectuals, are in possession of a relatively large amount of cultural capital, and, at the same time, as former preschool teachers affiliated with preschool teacher-training programs own a big share of ECE capital, it is not unreasonable to assume that they, to a relatively large extent, influence the epistemology of ECE.

*The Existence of the Field.*  The opponents' opposition had a remarkable common denominator. All three on their own accord problematized the future existence of the field. This indicates clearly that the game is not only about the characteristic themes of early childhood education, but also about the belief in the game. The opponents' distrust may be due to their peripheral position and may point to a lack of interest, or investment, in the game. However, it may also indicate that the opponents were deliberately using the interviews to comment on the elasticity of the field or the fact that Norwegian early childhood education is an uncertain field of knowledge.

As already mentioned, the first opponent believed that the field of ECE knowledge was on its way out. The reason was that preschool is a marginal social institution, and Norwegian preschool teacher training programs will soon become integrated into professional preparation programs for elementary school teachers. Another opponent believed that the field of knowledge was threatened from within because of its harmonizing, feminine, nurturing logic, which tends to ignore professional disagreements. Without professional conflicts, the field lacks a potential for development and renovation. A third opponent expressed clear distrust of scholastic forms of knowledge, as well as institutionalized pedagogy.

As mentioned before, there is a dialectic relation between the social production of the common *belief in the game* and the *characteristic themes*—or thematic configuration—of the field. On the one hand, the agents' investments in the field—to some extent arising from a belief in the game—determine, in large measure, the field's production, reproduction, and justification of its symbolic and cultural capital, which in turn influence the social production of a common belief in the game. On the other hand, the thematic configuration of ECE creates a field of possible social positions and positionings. In short, the belief in the game—materialized as the agents' desire—is a product of the dialectic relation between the field's characteristic themes and the social production of the common belief in the game. As an example, the prophets' beliefs in the social game of Norwegian ECE made them invest in and therefore gain a social position in the field. Next, as their books and articles exploring characteristic themes and educational beliefs within ECE were given prophetic status, the prophets' beliefs in the social game of Norwegian ECE were strengthened. However, when the opponents described an *alternative* configuration of themes and educational beliefs and claimed to have dystopian visions about the future, they were not only expressing a lack of confidence in the game, but also were challenging the game's legitimacy. Thus, the opponents questioned the very existence of the field. Overall, the opponents' arguments force us to analyze critically whether the social field we call ECE remains a potentially vigorous or dying field of knowledge.

## COLLECTIVE MYTHS AND FABLES

The aim of the fourth phase of the project was to verify its preliminary results by gathering information about the informants' perceptions of this study, as well as their descriptions of Norwegian early childhood education as a field of knowledge. Therefore, all the informants, both prophets and opponents, were invited to a group interview, organized as an exploring focus group (Fern, 2001), in which creative processes become a central feature. The goal was to reveal different perspectives, possible conflicts, and epistemological variety to be used as the basis for developing questions to further probe the project design, theoretical underpinnings, methods, and findings. From the beginning, the participants were fully aware of the premises of the study, as well as my preliminary description of the epistemology. The group interview was organized as five conversations about "the concept of early childhood education," "the notion of epistemology," "the unpleasant research," "the pleasant myths," and "utopias and professional aspirations." Each of these conversations lasted 20 minutes, and there were clear breaks between conversations.

The focus group interviews yielded rich material, which, in combination with the data from the first three phases of the project, allowed a number of sophisticated analyses that can reveal and problematize the social formation and validation of beliefs surrounding Norwegian early childhood education. However, since the central question here is whether the social field is a vigorous field of knowledge, only the following three points will be discussed: (1) the relation between doxa and episteme as defined below, (2) the concept of early childhood education, and (3) collective myths and fables.

*Doxa and Episteme.*   The project evokes problematization of the relationship between doxa and episteme, or the relationship between that which is taken for granted (often below the level of conscious awareness and unspoken) and that which is explicitly verbalized. Of foremost concern here is the socially produced basis and norms of validity of early childhood education, including the visions and divisions that the field acknowledges.

In the first part of the project, I used topics from syllabi and reading lists from preschool teacher colleges as a basis for defining the characteristic themes of early childhood education. In the second phase of the project, I related these characteristics to the prophets' professional biographies and visions. In the third phase, I interviewed opponents, those who oppose the field's traditional ways of determining and justifying what constitutes valid knowledge in ECE. Data from these three different phases provide information about social negotiations about the thematic configuration, since the material reveals a number of different epistemological position and positionings. At the same time, the data reveal various levels in the discourse, and, thus, the relationship between the doxic and the epistemic: Canonized beliefs apparently represent topics in the preschool teacher training. The prophecies mirror the prophets' professional interests. While the opponents' oppositions point to the ways in which visions on early childhood education cannot be separated from the doxic, defined as hidden assumptions as well as collective myths and fables.

Conversation in the focus groups confirmed the relationship between the epistemic and doxic culture of ECE. When we discussed what could be relevant, valuable, and valid knowledge in ECE, the group agreed that knowledge is connected to a traditional feminine nurturing logic. One example is how student teachers often plan their work in the preschool according to the way in which they would care for their own children. However, ECE textbooks focus on universally accepted and explicitly conceptualized theories. According to the participants, this theoretical knowledge is a valuable part of teacher education. However, the problem is that the theoretical literature may disregard the doxic character of early childhood education, that is, how educational beliefs are closely related to, and cannot be seen independently from, socioculturally generated values, representations, and logics of practice.

*The Concept of "Early Childhood Education."* As mentioned, many of the informants immediately and categorically rejected the term "early childhood education" as a description of their research interests. Instead, they preferred terms like "play pedagogy" or "the education and upbringing of children before school age." The informants' rejection of the term "early childhood education" can be interpreted as both a product of and a condition for the negotiations about the power to define and authorize the epistemology of ECE. The negotiations do not concern only the order of the field, but also the right to authorize that order.

To discuss the notion "early childhood education" with the focus group, I began with a diversion by introducing the circus as a metaphor for the field. I invited the participants to imagine ECE's field of knowledge as a colorful circus, an arena with a variety of performers—jugglers, magicians, a band, some clowns, trapeze artists, popcorn-sellers, acrobats, and maybe a lion tamer. Here there is constant activity, both in the ring, high up under the roof, on the bleachers, and just outside the tent. The lights, the colors, the smells, and the music are continuously changing, depending on what is happening in the ring. The circus performers, the members of the band, and the tamed animals come in, perform, and leave the stage to make room for new acts. Some of what is happening can be inspiring, some is breathtaking, some is funny, and some is so mundane as to become almost boring.

Immediately, one participant confirmed the metaphor, "Yes, they are the ones that create knowledge together!" Another informant was somewhat more reserved: "I feel that those who have created something within this field are those who had a very special contribution to make." The contributor may have been an anthropologist, a psychologist, or a philosopher, "...but the educationalist, whoever that may be, is difficult to find." (Here, the term "educationalist" refers to a person whose only focus is pure pedagogy, since Norwegian universities offer "pure" bachelor's, master's, and

PhDs in education.) The third participant rejected the metaphor, "In the circus I assume that all the actors are capable of something. They come with a specialized competence to perform. However, within ECE—whether it is within the preschool or preschool teacher training—I imagine that we rather create something together." Overall, the focus group questioned the validity of the circus metaphor, but recognized "the circus tent": There is a professional field of knowledge, but the position and role of the educationalists are problematic. However, the participants could not agree on how practices within the field are to be described. In addition, it was difficult for them to identify targets for the production of knowledge: "The audience is very small in this circus." The field is like a "church, where we applaud and boo each other."

*Common Beliefs.*   If the field of ECE knowledge can be compared to a church or a congregation in which its members mostly applaud and boo at each other, then it is pertinent to ask what keeps the congregation together and what attracts some agents and repels others. In other words, is it possible to identify the congregation's common "belief," that is, the socially produced "facts" that construct, reconstruct, and justify the epistemology? I have called these beliefs collective myths and fables.

The focus group confirmed that "belief," manifested as collective myths, constitutes the premises of the field's existence. Moreover, the participants were concerned with how the myths, and those who create them, achieve disciplinary power. Next, the focus group pointed out how collective creation of myths could reinforce some marginalization processes affecting the field. Shared allegiance to a collectively created myth can threaten the field of knowledge from within, as when, for instance, the myth of ECE as "mothering" leads to the collective, nurturing, and harmonizing way of ignoring professional disagreements. However, as the field's existence is threatened, it becomes vital to preserve these collective allegiances. In other words, the more the external threats, the greater the need to keep together by ignoring internal professional disagreements.

As examples of collective myths, the focus group mentioned the following: preschool is good for children; preschool teachers have a "calling" to the profession; the most qualified faculty within teacher training colleges are the preschool teachers themselves; practical training is the most important part of the teacher training programs; and there is such a thing as "preschool children." However, my project discloses that the fundamental myth of early childhood education is more related to the social negotiations about the "good Norwegian childhood," referring to the social negotiation about Norwegianness. This does not mean that the focus group's views were insignificant. However, what the focus group described as common myths I would rather describe as fables inscribed in the creation of the collective myths because the existence of the field is not primarily justified through collective fables about the preschool, the preschool teachers, or the faculty within the teacher training programs. The epistemology of early childhood education in Norway is, rather, based on, and justified through, the social negotiations about national culture, identity, and values.

Nevertheless, the focus group may have a point that the creation of myths has a disciplinary power. As one informant said, "Once one identifies oneself with the field, and this area of brotherhood, or rather sisterhood, one is very, very, very loyal. There is a deep sense of solidarity." Therefore, the focus group interviews confirmed the extended use of incitements and negative sanctions to preserve orthodox practices and forms of representations.

A third element is how collective creation of myths or fables intensifies when the field is marginalized. The focus group suggested that myths and fables could be used as a type of collective pledge of allegiance, or mantra, constantly repeated when the world becomes uncertain. For example, in the 1990s a familiar mantra in ECE was "quality in preschools."

In this way, the myths and fables contribute to a provisional reproduction of the ECE practices and forms of representation that were earlier acknowledged and recognized by preschool teachers as valid (Bourdieu, 1977, 2000). However, the problem is that unquestioned allegiance to traditional myths and fables will threaten the field from within. A communal commitment to hidden myths may prevent an explicit and critical examination of those myths and fables, and thus hinder a revitalization of the epistemology of early childhood education.

## VIRTUAL BELIEFS?

In short, we may say that ECE epistemology is constructed, reconstructed, and justified in relation to the logic of practice and material arrangements acknowledged by the Norwegian educational and welfare discourses. As such, the epistemology of early childhood education is related to the ongoing social negotiations about "Norwegianness." In addition, the field—marginalized and fluctuating as it is—is an uncertain place. The uncertainty is not only about the entrance ticket or about the rules of the game, but also apparently about the stakes, and, thus, the belief in the game itself. In other words, it seems as if the collective myths and fables produce the game and later threaten the field's autonomy and social status. For instance, the shared fable that there is such a thing as the "preschool child" substantiates the myth about the "good Norwegian childhood." This fable and myth, then, produce the game of caring for the "preschool child" and support the myth that the best way to do that is to protect children's own free time and give them access to free play in nature. The Norwegian pre-school child should therefore be protected from "schooling," meaning oversupervision and control. This very myth about the "good Norwegian childhood" is therefore enforcing an invisible, traditional, harmonizing pedagogy of "mothering," which is threatening the field's autonomy and social status.

## The Logic of Practice

Here the "primacy of practical reason" (Bourdieu, 2000) has been taken into consideration. Bourdieu's cultural sociology does not describe knowledge in traditional terms of exact knowledge, but rather as "habitus," or a set of dispositions that generate our culturally based judgments and logic of practice.

> The principles embodied in this way are placed beyond the grasp of consciousness, and hence cannot be touched by voluntary, deliberated transformation, cannot even be made explicit; nothing seems more ineffable, more incommunicable, more inimitable, and, therefore more precious, than the values ... achieved by the hidden persuasion of an implicit pedagogy, capable of instilling a whole cosmology, an ethic, a metaphysic, a political philosophy, through injunctions as significant as "stand up straight" or "don't hold your knife in your left hand." (Bourdieu, 1977, p. 94)

The acquisition of habitus occurs through the body and social experiences, not just through the intellect, or verbalized conscious learning (Bourdieu, 1977, 1990, 2000). This means that the epistemology of early childhood education as social practice and representations will reflect the social and material arrangements in which they are inscribed. As such, the epistemology becomes, on the one hand, the result of the field's history, and on the other hand, a kind of logic of practice, which has the potential to actively interfere and rewrite that history (Bourdieu, 1996, 2000). It is therefore tempting to ask whether the field's particular logic of practice can function as conserving or expansive when Norwegian preschool teacher training—and thus the social production and justification of the epistemology of early childhood education—is caught between tradition and innovation, preschool and university colleges, vocation and academia.

As a marginalized and threatened field, Norwegian early childhood education is an uncertain place as its borders, topics, and collective production of myths and fables are challenged. The National Curriculum points out that the preschool teacher's most important qualification is no longer transmitted through a "cultivating and controlling motherhood," but rather through "research-based teaching." The most important element in preschool teacher training is no longer "practical learning," but, rather, "internationalization." The aim is no longer preparing student teachers "to create an inspiring environment for growth," but, rather, qualifying them for "active participation in the debate." This means that the curriculum no longer recognizes the traditional logic in terms of motherhood, the pre-school's daily routine, and the good Norwegian childhood. Now, a new logic connected to research, internationalization, and professional debate provides legitimacy. However, the question is whether the new curriculum can be read as a measure of drastic change in a fluctuating field of knowl-edge. Will completely different agents and institutions eventually dominate the field? Will new topics be introduced? And will the collective myths and fables themselves change radically? In general, it is pertinent to ask whether the changes within the Norwegian field of early childhood educa-tion may also indicate a great upheaval in our understanding of "Norwe-gianness."

## Epistemic Transformations?

When the Norwegian field of early childhood education is a marginal-ized and fluctuating field of knowledge, it not only creates uncertainty about the entrance tickets for and rules of the game, but it also creates con-fusion about the stakes. Thus, the very belief in the game is threatened.

This research reveals several trends and patterns. First, Norwegian early childhood education is no longer justified through the preschool itself, but, rather, through the programs for preschool teacher training at the university colleges. The recognition of early childhood educational beliefs, therefore, takes place within tangential or external fields of knowledge rather than within internal preschool and childcare discourse. Moreover, there are clear indications of increasing efforts toward internationaliza-tion, both of Norwegian research and of Norwegian higher education. This means that the national and the local are, to some degree, pushed aside to make room for the international and the global, while, at the same time, the trend toward international recognition helps fortify and call attention to the local. In other words, increased globalization is instrumen-tal in intensifying local and national negotiations about identity, in turn making these social negotiations about identity particularly vulnerable because living in an era of constant change calls for multiple identities that are able to cope with these continual transformations. This includes the "Norwegianness" within early childhood education.

A third trend, as the OECD (1999) also pointed out, is that the Norwe-gian society is changing gradually from a homogenous ethnic society to an increasingly multicultural community. However, since Norwegian early childhood education is justified through the cultivation of the "good Norwegian childhood," it contributes to the preservation of "Norwegianness." At the same time, such conservatism is challenged by the multicultural. In other words, what seem to be at stake are the collective myths and fables produced by the game. These are the very same myths and fables that help justify and consolidate the relative autonomy of the field of ECE. Nevertheless, it may still be too soon to conclude whether the field is dying or still vital. Or whether the epistemology of Norwegian early childhood education will be undermined or transformed.

## REFERENCES

*Act No. 7 of 8 April 1981 relating to children and parents (Children Act)*. Retrieved September 21, 2004, from http://www.ub.uio.no/ujur/ulovdata/lov-19810408-007-eng.pdf

*Act No. 19 of 5 May 1995 on day care institutions (Day Care Act)*. Retrieved September 21, 2004, from http://www.ub.uio.no/ujur/ulovdata/lov-19950505-019-eng.pdf

Baker, B. (2001). *In perpetual motion: Theories of power, educational history, and the child*. New York: Peter Lang.

Balke, E. (2002). *"Vi kom sent, men vi kom godt!" Inger Grundt Pedersen og kampen for barnehagelærerutdanningen* ["We arrived late, but for the sake of the good." Inger Grundt Pedersen in the social struggle for preschool teacher's training]. HiO-rapport 2002 no 25. Oslo: Høgskolen i Oslo.

Berg, T. S. (1990). Pedagogiske linjer gjennom 40 år i førskolelærerutdanningen: Viktige utredningsarbeider på veien frem [Educational trends through 40 years of preschool teacher education: Important challenges towards a new era]. In U. Bleken (Ed.), *Barnet viste veien: Festskrift til Eva Balke* [The child shows the way: Special publication in honor of Eva Balke] (pp. 35–50). Oslo: Barnevernsakademiet i Oslo.

Borge, A. I. H. (1998). *Barnets verd og barnehagens verdier: En kunnskapsanalyse* [The Child's worth and the social values of the preschool A report on knowledge]. Oslo: Statens institutt for folkehelse.

Bøe, A. (1988). *Førskolelærerutdanning i Norge: Framvekst og utvikling fram til 1973* [Preschool teacher's training in Norway: Appearance and growth until 1973]. Unpublished master's thesis, University of Bergen, Norway.

Bourdieu, P. (1977). *Outline of a theory of practice*. Cambridge, UK: Cambridge University Press.

Bourdieu, P. (1990). *The logic of practice*. Stanford, CA: Stanford University Press.

Bourdieu, P. (1991a). *Language and symbolic power*. Cambridge, MA: Harvard University Press.

Bourdieu, P. (1991b). *The political ontology of Martin Heidegger*. Stanford, CA: Stanford University Press.

Bourdieu, P. (1996). *The rules of art: Genesis and structure of the literary field*. Stanford, CA: Stanford University Press.

Bourdieu, P. (2000). *Pascalian meditations*. Stanford, CA: Stanford University Press.

Fern, E. F. (2001). *Advanced focus group research*. London: Sage.

Grude, T. (1987). Det begynte med barneasylene [It originated with the child care institutions]. In E. R. Tømmerbakke & P. Miljeteig-Olsen (Eds.), *Fra asyl til barnehage: Barnehager i Norge i 150 år* [From child care institutions to preschools: 150 years of preschools in Norway] (pp. 23–62). Oslo: Universitetsforlaget.

Grundt-Pedersen, I. (1960) *Barnevernsakademiet i Oslo gjennom 25 år* [Oslo College of Preschool Teachers Education through 25 Years]. Oslo: Tanum.

Hayden, J. (Ed.) (2000). *Landscapes in early childhood education: Cross-national perspectives on empowerment—A guide for the new millennium.* New York: Peter Lang.

Korsvold, T. (1997). *Profesjonalisert barndom. Statlige intensjoner og kvinnelig praksis på barnehagens arena 1945–1990* [Institutionalized childhood: The state and maternal practices in the preschools 1045–1990]. Nr. 20 i Skriftserie fra Historisk Institutt. Trondheim: NTNU.

Lærerutdanningsloven. No. 49 [Law on teacher education No. 49] (1973). In *Norges Lover 1687–1990* [The Norwegian acts 1687–1990] (pp. 1737–1742). Oslo: Grøndahl.

Lærerutdanningsrådet. (1971). *Rammeplan for førskolelærerutdanning* [Framework plan for preschool teacher's rraining]. Oslo: Universitetsforlaget.

Ministry of Children and Family Affairs. (1995). *Framework plan for daycare institutions—a brief presentation.* Retrieved September 21, 2004, from http://odin.dep .no/bfd/engelsk/regelverk/rikspolitiske/004005-990083/index-dok000-b-f-a.html

Ministry of Children and Family Affairs. (1998). *OECD—thematic review of early childhood education and care policy. Background Report from Norway.* Oslo: Ministry of Children and Family Affairs.

Ministry of Church, Education and Research. (1995). *Framework plan for preschool teacher's education.* Oslo: Ministry of Church, Education and Research.

Ministry of Education and Research. (2003). *Framework plan for preschool teacher's education.* Retrieved September 22, 2004, from ttp://odin.dep.no/filarkiv/217217/Rammepl.Foerskole.vasket.BM_opprettet_0704_ny.pd

Myhre, J. E. (1994). *Barndom i storbyen: Oppvekst i Oslo i velferdsstatens epoke* [Urban Childhood: Growing up in Oslo during the Epoch of the Welfare State]. Oslo: Universitetsforlaget.

OECD (1999). *Early childhood education and care policy in Norway. OECD country note, June 1999.* Retrieved July 3, 2003, from http://www1.oecd.org/els/education/ecec/docs.htm

Pierson, C. (1991). *Beyond the welfare state? The new political economy and welfare.* University Park: Pennsylvania State University Press.

Pierson, C. & Castles, F. G. (Eds.). (2000). *The welfare state reader.* Cambridge, UK: Polity Press.

Rudberg, M. (1983). *Dydige, sterke, lykkelige barn. Ideer om oppdragelse i borgerlig tradisjon* [Virtuos, strong, happy children. Educational beliefs within the Bourgoise tradition]. Oslo: Universitetsforlaget.

Statistics Norway (2001a). *Aktuell utdanningsstatistikk 6/2001* [Current Statistics on Education 6/2001]. Retrieved September 14, 2004, from http://www.ssb.no/emner/04/utdanning_as/200106/au_200106.pdf

Statistics Norway (2001b). *Barnehagestatistikk.* [Statistics on preschools]. Retrieved September 14, 2004, from http://www.ssb.no/aarbok/fig/f-040210-181.html

Strand, T. (1996). *Ethos og læreplanen: Hvordan forstå og bruke Rammeplan for barne-hagen* [The ethos of a curriculum. How to understand and use the Framework Plan]. Oslo: Ad Notam Gyldendal

Strand, T. (2001). Paradoxes in Pierre Bourdieu's practice of theory. *Nordisk Peda-gogik, 21*(3) 197–213.

Strand, T. (in press). Beyond what is given as givens: Promises and threats of self-reflexive research. *Australian Journal of Early Childhood Research.*

Tobin, J. J., Wu, D.Y. H., & Davidson, D. H. (1989). *Preschool in three cultures: Japan, China, and the United States.* New Haven, CT: Yale University Press.

Wollons, R. (Ed.). (2000). *Kindergarten and cultures: The global diffusion of an idea.* New Haven, CT: Yale University Press.

CHAPTER 5

# TEACHING AND LEARNING IN PRESCHOOL AND THE FIRST YEARS OF ELEMENTARY SCHOOL IN SWEDEN

**Ingrid Pramling Samuelsson**
*Göteborg University*

The transition from preschool to school is not only interesting and important in its own right, but also transition-related questions necessarily touch on a variety of broader social, political, and educational issues. With a focus on teaching and learning, this chapter discusses the transition from preschool to elementary school in Sweden at three different levels: (1) the official level, as represented by public policy and official documents; (2) the scientific level, including findings from recent studies and the specific problems that have surfaced in recent research; and (3) the practical level, including suggestions for further integrating preschool and school through developmental pedagogy, an approach grounded in research.

---

*Nordic Childhoods and Early Education*, pages 101–131
Copyright © 2006 by Information Age Publishing
All rights of reproduction in any form reserved.

I argue from the perspective of the child, in accordance with both contemporary developmental and educational theories (Pramling Samuelsson & Asplund Carlsson, 2003; Sommer, 2003a, 2003b; Valsiner, 1990) and their applications in contemporary curriculum and instructional practices. The central tenet of the perspective of the child is that children are driven by their interests and direct involvement with the world around them, including people and objects. Children are intentional; they create meaning; and they are socially competent even from their earliest years. From the perspective of the child, then, early childhood programs, both at preschool and elementary levels, must take these basic characteristics of children into consideration. In concert, the perspective of the child incorporates a view of the teacher as someone who listens, guides, supports, challenges, and focuses children's attention on learning opportunities and outcomes.

## TRANSITION FROM PRESCHOOL TO SCHOOL: THE OFFICIAL LEVEL

In Sweden, as in most other countries, preschool and elementary school differ in their origins, traditions, and central concerns. Historically, development and play have been the central concerns of preschool, in contrast to teaching and learning as the central focus of elementary education. In addition, distinctions existed between preschool and daycare. Preschool, formerly referred to as "kindergarten" in Sweden, was typically only 3 hours a day for 5- and 6-year-olds. Daycare was open all day and children from 6 months to 6 years stayed for as long as their parents needed care for them. Guidelines existed for either preschool or daycare, and those that did exist focused mainly on child–adult ratios, physical space, health promotion, and the like. However, recent decades have brought significant changes in early childhood policy and practice. Notably, both policy and, to a somewhat lesser extent, actual practice have minimized differences between preschool and daycare provisions, as well as between preschool and early primary grades.

During the 1960s questions arose about the appropriate starting age for compulsory schooling and about coordination between preschool and the primary grades. In the late 1960s, the Swedish government appointed a committee, called "Barnstugeutredning," to investigate the content and structure of the preschool. In 1975 parliament enacted the committee's recommendations into law, declaring that all 6-year-old children have the right to a preparatory year in preschool, funded by the state. Other important aspects of the committee's recommendations were incorporated into the new law as well. Importantly, Jean Piaget's, Erik Homburger Erikson's, and George Herbert Mead's theories were now acknowledged as the foundation for early childhood pedagogy, thereby bringing children's thinking, interactions with others, and ways of learning and knowing center stage in preschool and primary settings (SOU, 1972).

The adoption of new terminology reflected other important changes. All programs for children before compulsory school start were now referred to as "preschool," rather than as "kindergarten" or "daycare," both of which had previously been decidedly nonacademic or "non-school-like." Use of the umbrella term *preschool* (i.e., before *school*) signaled an intentional shift in philosophy, at least on the part of the committee and parliament, about the purpose of childcare provisions before compulsory school start and about the purposes of both preschool and elementary school. The Department of Social Health and Welfare eliminated differences in guidelines for preschool and daycare. Now the only distinction between the two provisions for children before school age was to be their hours of operation. Daycare facilities were, by definition, to be open early enough in the morning and late enough in the afternoon to accommodate working parents.

Another change was the requirement that qualified preschool teachers should have the responsibility for work with all children between 1 and 6 years of age regardless of the type of preschool setting. Previous regulations had required trained preschool teachers in childcare settings with children age 4 and older, but persons with lesser qualifications, called "nursery nurses," could work with children in infant and toddler groups.

To summarize, then, the new law enacted in 1975, based on recommendations by a committee appointed in the late 1960s to study both the structure and the content of various childcare provisions, represented several milestones in Swedish early childhood education. Notably, children acquired the universal right to a year of preschool education prior to the start of compulsory schooling. Children themselves became the centerpiece of early childhood programs, regardless of type, as theorists, researchers, and practitioners gained greater understanding of children's ways of learning and knowing, as well as of the importance of their experiences and their interactions with people and objects in their environments. Historical quality differences between preschool and daycare began to crumble, as equal guidelines were established for the two program types. In addition, the new law established that all children between 1 and 6 years of age, regardless of the program type, should be in the care of qualified preschool teachers. In Sweden, qualified preschool teachers have at least 3½ years of university education, while nursery-nurses have a lesser educational requirement of a 2-year senior high school course.

In 1987 the first national guidelines for preschool in Sweden appeared (Socialstyrelsen, 1987), followed in 1998 by guidelines for before- and after-school programs for school children (Socialstyrelsen, 1988). Shortly thereafter supplementary texts about specific issues for the staff in preschool were also published (e.g., Kärrby, 1990; Pramling, 1993; Socialstyrelsen, 1990).

At the beginning of the 1980s another new committee appointed by the government reported its findings concerning the transition from preschool to school (SOU, 1985). More precisely, the committee's task was to generate suggestions for eliminating the gap between preschool and primary school and ensuring a continuum between the two levels of education. The committee presented three alternatives: (1) keeping things as they were, (2) lowering the school entry age from 7 to 6, or (3) creating a more flexible school start. The parliament selected the third alternative and introduced "flexible school start" in 1991. Parents now had the right to determine whether their 6-year-old children would attend preschool or kindergarten classes (called *forskoleklass*, or preschool class, in Sweden) located in the elementary school. School entry tests measuring children's maturity were not to be used anymore. The underlying assumptions here were that every new kindergarten class should incorporate the best of both preschool and primary educational practice and, therefore, be well prepared to meet every child who arrived at its door (SOU, 1994). Most parents chose not to send their children to elementary school at age 6, opting instead to leave them in kindergarten for the year and let them start primary school at age 7, as had been the custom in Sweden.

Around this time, similar ideas about incorporating the best from two traditions of schooling were instituted in other Nordic countries, including Denmark and Norway; but, as was the case in Sweden, they were neither universally popular among parents nor without criticism from educators. For instance, Norwegian Peter Haug (1996) claimed that this and other reforms were based on false beliefs and inspired by political motivations to achieve consensus, rather than by pedagogy grounded in sound theory or research. A close reading of the official state texts reveals underlying intentions and hope that preschool, with its more open approach, would influence school in a positive way.

Additional reforms were enacted throughout the 1990's. New theories about learning and knowledge articulated in the Swedish Government Official Report (SOU, 1992), based largely on work by experts and researchers from the field, ultimately led to a new national curriculum for compulsory school (Ministry of Education and Science in Sweden, 1994). A few years later, the national curriculum was revised to include both kindergarten classes (i.e., special classes for 6-year-olds in elementary schools) and before- and after-school programs, called leisure-time activities in Sweden (Ministry of Education and Science in Sweden, 1998a). In 1996 the Ministry of Education took over the responsibility for preschool, which had previously operated under the auspices of the Ministry of Health and Social Affairs. Only 2 years later Sweden had its first national curriculum for preschool, that is, for children age 1–5 years (Ministry of Education and Science in Sweden, 1998b). The Swedish curriculum for preschool (1–5 years) and for the compulsory school, kindergarten, and after-school center (6–16 years) appear as two 16-page documents. These documents state the values and perspectives of learning and knowledge formation for preschool, compulsory school, kindergarten, and after-school programs. In addition, the documents articulate the goals for preschool, as well as both goals and expected learning outcomes for school. The documents, which are similar in structure, present rather general directions for teachers, including the intention that teachers should evaluate their practice (i.e., the activities they provide), *not* the children's achievements (Oberheumer, 2004).

In 2003 the local authorities claimed to have sufficient preschool spaces for all children from 1 to 5 years of age, and a new reform was launched. The reform, called "max-taxa," instituted a maximum fee (about 100 euro) per month for the first child, with decreasing fees for each additional child from the same family, regardless of time spent in preschool. Prior to 2003, parents paid fees according to their income. In addition to instituting the new fee schedule, however, the reform also works toward equality and the child's right to be in preschool even if one parent is home on parental leave or is unemployed. The reform gives children the right to a minimum of 3 hours' education per day, free of charge, from the age of 4. Essentially, then, access to preschool has been transformed from a right for parents of 1- to 5-year-old children to now a shared right for parents and children.

Approximately 84% of Swedish children attend preschool from their second year of life (Skolverket, 2003b). The most recent preschool proposition (Regeringens proposition, 2004), called Quality in Preschool, establishes preschool as a part of the Swedish education system, and recommends that preschools employ more personnel and offer further in-service training for teachers on such topics as multiculturalism and gender issues. Furthermore, the new reform establishes the right for foreign children to get support in learning both their primary language and Swedish and requires that preschools conduct annual program quality reviews.

The most innovative part of the proposition was that the Preschool Minister organized a large survey, asking children about their opinions of their preschool. Results indicated that children generally loved their preschool, especially playing with their friends!

In summary, then, the trend in Sweden during the last 30 years has been toward viewing preschool more and more as an entitlement for both parents and children, and, more and more, as a part of the public education system. These developments bring with them the obligation to more carefully and systematically scrutinize teaching and learning practices in both preschool and elementary school.

## Preschool and School Curricula and Collaboration

Curricula for preschool and elementary school (Ministry of Education and Science in Sweden, 1998a, 1998b) are quite similar in form and content. Both have an introduction describing fundamental values and tasks of preschool and school. Both clearly reflect social-cultural perspectives influenced by theorists such as Lev Vygotsky (1978) and phenomenographic-inspired theories such as the theory of variation (Marton & Booth, 1997; Pramling, 1994), as well as pedagogical practices associated with these perspectives. Both curricula feature the concept and practice of democracy as a bridge between preschool and school.

Democracy has traditionally been emphasized throughout the Swedish education system. From preschool onward, Swedish educators introduce children to democratic principles through daily experience, as well as through age-appropriate instruction. In its evaluation of preschools in 12 different countries, the Organization for Economic Cooperation and Development (OECD; 2001) noted observations of democratic practices with even the youngest children in Sweden. A typical example of democracy in action at the preschool level in Sweden might be to give children opportunities to make choices about how they will spend their time. For instance, it is typical in Swedish practice for children to be able to decide most of the day whether they prefer to be indoors or outdoors. As further examples, Swedish preschool children often discuss with their teachers what topic or theme they would like to work on, which toys they would like to buy, and how they would like to celebrate a special occasion. At the very heart of the reform and contemporary educational practices is the notion that adults must really listen to children and meet them in their thinking and feelings, so that each and every one feels accepted and respected.

Since 1996 the question of democracy has also been of concern to the Government in its "development plan for preschool, school, and adult education," which stresses that (1) every person is of equal value and should be given the same opportunities, (2) a continuous dialogue with parents is important, and (3) the whole school system should reflect multiculturalism. There is also a warning against too much focus on the single child's learning, since that can easily lead to segregation in society due to lack of understanding of other's points of view (Regeringens skrivelse, 1996/97).

Since the demographics in Sweden have changed dramatically during the last 30 years, multicultural questions are very important. About 20% of all children in school have at least one parent that speaks another language other than Swedish. In the two largest cities, immigrants constitute about one-third of the population. In Malmö, the third largest city, 50% of the preschool children are bilingual. The curriculum says: "The internationalization of Swedish society imposes high demands on people's ability to live with and understand values in cultural diversity. The preschool is a social and cultural meeting place, which can reinforce this and prepare children for life in an increasingly internationalized community" (Ministry of Education, 1998b, p. 9).

Both preschool and elementary-school curricula set forth similar goals and both charge educators with responsibility for ensuring that children attain these goals. However, neither curriculum is highly prescriptive. Rather, both provide a framework that leaves considerable room for teacher- and child-choice about specific content and approaches to learning and instruction.

The preschool curriculum includes 23 goals reflecting Swedish cultural values and norms, as well as skill development objectives and outcomes relevant to helping children make sense of the world. These goals complement goals for elementary and secondary education in Sweden. For example the preschool curriculum states that "the preschool should strive to ensure that all children develop their ability to discover, reflect on and work out their positions on different ethical dilemmas and fundamental questions of life in daily reality" (Ministry of Education and Science in Sweden, 1998b, p. 11) and "the preschool should try to ensure that children develop their ability to accept responsibility for their own actions and for the environment of the preschool" (p. 15). This means that children should accept responsibility for the environment, inside as well as outside. With support from their teachers, children are responsible for how the preschool environment looks and how clean it is. They are responsible for taking proper care of the toys and tending the gardens. The preschool curriculum also includes goals for cooperation with family members and preparation for meeting school expectations by the time children enter kindergarten class at age 6.

The preschool curriculum encourages preschool teachers and other preschool staff members to serve on cooperative teams with kindergarten, primary-grade, and leisure-time teachers. Under the heading, "Cooperation with School," the document reads in translation:

The work team should:

Exchange knowledge and experiences with the staff of the kindergarten class, the school and leisure-time center and cooperate with them, as well as

Together with the staff in the kindergarten class, the school and leisure-time center, pay due attention to each child's need for stimulation and support. (Ministry of Education and Science in Sweden, 1998b, p. 16)

The underlying aims of the preschool curriculum are lifelong learning, relatively new to the Swedish educational agenda; smooth transitions from preschool to school; and the creation of rich, stimulating learning environments throughout the entire Swedish education system. As noted earlier, another fundamental aim is to instill democratic ideals, primarily by creating democratic classrooms for children of all ages.

In today's discourse, cooperation and collaboration are central features in democratic early childhood environments. The goal is to promote cooperation and collaboration between children and adults, as well as between children and their peers. However, analysis of official texts, such as guidelines and curricula, reveals interesting changes in perspectives on cooperation and collaboration for children. In the 1960s, for instance, the prevailing wisdom was that children should not be expected to collaborate until they are mature enough, probably after the first few years of compulsory schooling. In the 1970s collaboration between children of all ages was perceived as a great benefit to psychological well-being. In the 1980s the perspective became more sociological in that preschool and school were considered to be the center of all kinds of collaboration for all children in society, sharing this role with libraries, youth organizations, culture, and working life (Williams, Sheridan, & Pramling Samuelsson, 2001). By the 1990s collaboration had become the source of democracy in two interrelated respects: collaboration was expected to promote participation in democracy and, thereby, to promote learning about democracy. According to this view, children will develop democratic values and an understanding of the world around them by interacting, communicating, and sharing. From this perspective, collaboration and interaction are preconditions for democracy, as well as for developing the skills and knowledge children are supposed to gain through education (Williams et al., 2001).

Contemporary theory and philosophy promote the notion that preschool and school should be joyful, meaningful, and secure for children, who should be taken seriously as participants with influence. However, education must still promote knowledge and skill development in the academic content areas, including art, music, and drama, as well as such skills as cooperation, communication, critical thinking, flexibility, and learning to learn (Council for Cultural Co-operation, 1996). Education should involve substantial contact with the surrounding society so as to remain relevant to the contexts in which children live outside school.

In summary, then, various school reforms during the last 30 years, with a view toward continuity across the entire education system, have attempted to bring preschool and elementary school closer together in terms of their philosophy, goals, and theoretical orientations, as well as their approaches to teaching and learning as inextricably interactive processes. But have preschool and elementary school really changed? Are they more similar now than in the past? What does research tell us about the gap or the continuity between these two levels of education in Sweden?

## TRANSITION FROM PRESCHOOL TO SCHOOL: THE SCIENTIFIC LEVEL

During the last 30 years in Sweden, considerable resources have been put to the question of the transition from preschool to school (Roos, 1994). Most of this funding has gone toward the development of practical projects and programs to improve coordination between preschool and school before, during, and after children make the transition. Some funding has also gone toward scholarly research on transitions. A review of results from local and national transition studies (Pramling Samuelsson & Mauritzson, 1997) revealed four major themes:

1. The need for shared educational theories, goals, and perspectives.
2. A general trend toward dominance of the elementary school over the preschool in setting agendas for cooperation.
3. Teachers' views that collaboration is extremely time-consuming.
4. Efforts to promote collaboration and coordination between preschool and school typically begin at the level of organizational structure rather than at the level of pedagogy. For instance, transition projects often create an organizational structure, such as a visit by preschoolers and their teachers to the neighborhood elementary school, rather than with a serious look at similarities and differences between teaching methods or children's perspectives in the two institutions.

This study of transition research clearly showed that preschool and elementary school still have different perspectives on children, their learning, and the teacher's role. However, this review of the research literature also indicated that teachers were at least aware of the need to find common ground. Together, these findings indicate that school reform documents are ahead of reality in terms of a shared foundation and consistent views about children and their learning.

Research findings repeatedly showed that elementary schools dictated conditions for preschool to school transition work. For example, according to one study by the Swedish Board of Education (Skolverket, 2001), preschool became organized more like school with lessons and breaks. Also the content was influenced by school, with extended work on literacy, for example. Similar phenomena have been documented in studies on leisure-time programs (analogous in many ways to before- and after-school programs in America). Leisure-time teachers consistently allowed elementary teachers to dictate curriculum and practices from the perspective of the school setting rather than from the perspective of the leisure-time setting (Gustafsson, 2003). However, only a few Swedish studies have tackled the question of why preschool and leisure-time teachers fall prey to the power of elementary teachers. For instance, Hansen (1999) studied the intersection between these two professions and their respective professional cultures, noting that preschool teachers and school teachers have different conceptions of their professional identity, depending on what tradition they belong to. For example, the elementary school teacher typically views her function as a mediator in children's learning, while the preschool teacher typically sees herself mainly as a model for the child. Broström, Hermandsen, Krogh-Jespersen and Sommer (2002) found similar differences between Danish leisure-time teachers and primary school teachers.

The term "development work" refers to efforts to create (develop) new programs, projects, or approaches. It was not surprising that teachers consistently viewed development work on preschool to school transitions as time consuming. Development work of any kind is characteristically time consuming and often completed in addition to teachers' usual responsibilities. However, a more interesting question, not often addressed in the studies reviewed, is whether teachers believed transition work to be worth the time they spent to develop new transition projects or programs, something teachers have different opinions about (Broström & Wagner, 2003). Furthermore, it was not surprising that most transition work started with structural changes rather than changes in philosophy or pedagogy, given that human nature typically leads us to start with circumstances outside ourselves, like the organization.

Several recent studies have shed light on the themes and questions that emerged in the review of the literature on transition work (Pramling Samuelsson & Mauritzson, 1997). For instance, Davidsson (2002) followed four teams of preschool and school teachers from two different schools as they tried to combine their kindergarten and primary-grade classes and to integrate their practices for 6- and 7-year-olds. In each case, as preschool teachers and school teachers explored ways to improve cooperation and coordination, they decided to begin with circle time. Interestingly, circle time was the most structured time in the preschool day, so it was a comfortable beginning point for the school teachers, whose approach was typically more structured than the approach of most preschool teachers. As discussions continued about the "content" of circle time, however, differences between preschool teachers and school teachers became more apparent. Central differences included their perspectives on knowledge and their views on the teacher's role during circle time. Should circle time be used to teach knowledge and facts, as the elementary teachers preferred, or should it be for developing social skills, as preschool teachers believed? Should the teacher be the one to decide which topic to discuss, as elementary teachers suggested, or should they let children come up with their own ideas, as preschool teachers suggested? How far they came in the process of addressing these questions differed from team to team.

As preschool and school teachers continued to work together to create a joint program aimed at smoother transitions from preschool to school, other differences between them emerged. For instance, school teachers often spoke in dichotomous terms, referring to children as mature or immature, while preschool teachers tended to speak of children's competence, resourcefulness, and capacities for learning. However, preschool teachers and school teachers began to create more consistent and shared perspectives as they grappled with a concrete situation—how to use the dramatic play shop in their shared program. A shared perspective was not established until the teachers had worked together in concrete situations, such as discussing how "the shop" could be used as the beginning of collaboration as well as for the traditional educational purposes. Before they were able to work out a joint program between preschool and school, the staff had to reach a consensus on what a child is and what learning in these age groups means. Importantly, throughout their working time together, the team members clearly believed that their groups included representatives of two distinct professions: preschool teaching and elementary school teaching.

In spite of some areas of consensus that developed as the preschool teachers and teachers worked together, differences between them remained apparent. The two groups differed in several fundamental ways—ranging from their views on children's learning and the teacher's role, to the function of play and desired characteristics of adult–child interactions in preschool and school settings. As Davidsson (2002) noted, successful collaboration between preschool teachers and teachers seemed to require three arenas: one for the teacher, one for the preschool teacher, and a third shared space. The title of Davidsson's thesis stands as a striking metaphor for the entire challenge of integrating preschool and school: "Between the Sofa and the Teacher's Desk." In these few words, Davidsson captures the essential informality of Swedish preschools, with her reference to the snuggly sofa, and the more formal school environment, with her reference to the teacher's desk.

The Swedish National Agency for Education has monitored the development of kindergarten, as well as the integration of preschool, kindergarten, leisure-time activities, and school (Skolverket, 2001). The original intentions expressed in official reform documents clearly stated that both preschool and elementary school were to provide a child-centered environment emphasizing play and creativity over the traditional subject-centered and time-scheduled school syllabus. In other words, the intention was that preschool traditions would influence the subject-centered and time-scheduled school syllabus. However, in the Swedish National Agency for Education's report (Skolverket, 2001), it was already clear that the influence has been in the opposite direction. Time in preschool has become more structured, with lessons and breaks as in school, and the content has also become more school-like.

According to the report, the central intention of the reform as expressed in official documents—namely, that play and creativity should be the main focus of both preschool and school—remains largely unrealized except in a few individual cases. The report pointed to a lack of necessary conditions for full realization of the reforms, both on the community level and on the professional level. For instance, the report noted that the local government and school headmasters had only a vague understanding of the reform, and were, therefore, unprepared to provide systematic leadership toward reform goals. However, the report also included some signs of progress in individual cases, especially in kindergarten classes. Many teachers in kindergarten (the special classes for children in the year prior to their entry in compulsory school) seemed to fully understand the new code. They were both willing and able to implement the reforms; but, all too often, their efforts were thwarted by elementary school teachers and school administrators.

The report acknowledged some overall progress over the last 20 years, noting that elementary school has slowly but noticeably moved toward more openness and more child-centered practice, both of which represent a shift toward traditional preschool practice and away from some of the most content-centered aspects of traditional elementary school practice.

The Swedish National Agency for Education recently published a report on integration and collaboration between preschool, school, and leisure-time activities (Skolverket, 2003a). Focusing on adult collaboration and avenues for fully utilizing the professional competence of all members of collaborative teams, the report described three different models of collaboration: concurrence, consideration, and companionship. Teams included preschool teachers, kindergarten class teachers, primary grade teachers, and after-school or leisure-time teachers working together to develop a coordinated literacy program from preschool through the primary grades.

On the team representing the concurrence model, power became central as team members fought to preserve their own positions and perspectives. Here, the school teacher had the power to decide about the content and learning outcomes in reading and writing, while other team members were left simply to concur with the more powerful team member. Team members from preschool, kindergarten, and leisure-time had to figure out how to incorporate the elementary-school literacy model into their programs.

A team representing the consideration model focused on teamwork, or at least the appearance of teamwork, as a basis for change. However, this approach often results in a kind of superficial harmony wherein participants continue to do what they have always done rather than challenging one another's points of view or bringing out into the open their underlying differences of opinion. There is little open dissent, but also little progress. The literacy team that represented this model had little open disagreement and relatively little progress in terms of changes in their teaching behaviors, but all team members did, at least, focus consistently on the children's best interest. While this did not result in immediate progress, it may have paved the way for future child-centered discussions.

Finally, teams representing the companionship model tried to find a common understanding of children and the part each program can play in literacy development. They searched for mutually acceptable policy to guide their work. Here, teams were better able to take advantage of the skills and talents of each team member and build upon the concepts they had in common, rather than simply protecting their own turf, as in the concurrence model, or maintaining the status quo, as in the consideration model.

In the various types of development work involving preschool, kindergarten class, primary grades, and leisure-time programs, several patterns or themes emerge. For instance, some teams seemed to assume that the elementary school teacher had the knowledge and experience necessary to teach children to read and write. While preschool teachers on the team often seemed to accept the elementary teacher's approach to literacy and perhaps even indicated that they would adopt some of the elementary teacher's methods, in daily practice, preschool teachers often continued working with the children the way they always had. This can be seen as a kind of silent resistance on the part of the preschool teacher.

Another pattern emerged in which both preschool teachers and primary-grade teachers agreed that preschool is best viewed as a time of preparation for later schooling. They agreed that it is appropriate for preschool teachers to simply wait for elementary teachers to teach reading and writing once the children have matured sufficiently.

Representing a third pattern, some teams focused on interactions among children and between adults and children as an important pathway for developing reading and writing skills. Teams working from this perspective viewed literacy in a more holistic way as it relates to children's overall learning and development. These teams recognized that children needed both support and challenges from preschool throughout the elementary grades.

In summary, then, the Swedish National Agency for Education's study of integration and collaboration between preschool, school, and leisure-time activities (Skolverket, 2003a) identified three distinct approaches to collaboration and several patterns and themes that emerged as the teams worked together. Interestingly, the way individual team members worked on the collaboration projects often mirrored the way they worked with children in their classrooms. Among the most evident conclusions of the study was that preschool, kindergarten class, elementary-grade, and lei- sure-time teachers cannot develop a complementary approach to develop- ing literacy activities for children until they establish common goals and directions for their work.

Still another crossroad in the land between preschool and primary school is teachers' perceptions of teaching. Germeten (2001) distin- guished four discourses in teaching as expressed by the teachers them- selves: (1) teaching as disseminating knowledge, (2) teaching as arranging or organizing the classroom, (3) teaching as motivating or provoking inter- est, and (4) teaching as a "meeting" between grown-ups and children, and also between children and their peers as they learn from each other. These discourses should be viewed in the light of contemporary research about young children's learning. Prevailing views about the central goals and pur- poses of early childhood education include:

1. Supporting and challenging children (Siraj-Blatchford, 1999). Here the teacher's mission is to make children feel secure enough to dare to try new and different tasks, problems, and situations.

2. Providing experiences for children (Pramling, 1990, 1994, 1996). Here the teacher seeks to provide children with new or different experiences, opening opportunities for them to encounter knowl- edge and phenomena differently, thereby awakening new thoughts.

3. Directing children's awareness toward the learning objective (Alex- andersson, 1994; Marton & Booth, 1997). Here the teacher focuses on making aspects of the world around the child more transparent and visible.

4. Communicating and interacting with children (Pramling Samuels- son & Asplund Carlsson, 2003; Säljö, 2000). Here the teacher orga- nizes the classroom in such a way as to maximize communication.

5. Creating intersubjective meetings (Johansson, 2003). Here the teacher must see each child as a subject (not as an object) with his or her own experience, intentions, and rights to be listened to.

The Swedish preschool curriculum defines teaching as "a conscious action in the direction toward a goal." This definition represents an amal- gam of the prevailing views outlined above.

Research, then, suggests that, while some progress toward reform is tak- ing place in Sweden, old traditions weigh heavily on the process, especially with regard to cooperation between preschool and primary school (Göte- borgs Stadskansli, 2003; Skolverket, 2004). Preschool teachers and primary teachers often hold vastly different views about children, as well as about teaching and learning. These differing views are strongly rooted in old structures and established traditions, which influence their ways of thinking and acting. Both in terms of structure and practice, the kindergarten class for 6-year-olds may represent an opportunity for closing the gap between school teachers and preschool teachers (Myndigheten för skolutveckling, 2004).

In the following section, I present a perspective that could help teachers from both preschool and primary levels overcome their traditional differences and construct a common approach to children's learning. Previous evaluations show that this approach not only promotes children's learning and literacy development (Johansson, Klerfelt, & Pramling, 1997), but also gives them confidence to speak up for themselves in primary school (Kullberg, Pramling, Williams, & Graneld, 1996).

## THE PRACTICAL LEVEL: THE CONCEPT OF THE "PLAYING-LEARNING" CHILD AND PEDAGOGY

Is it possible to integrate preschool and elementary school or, at least, to ensure that continuity between the two levels of education? I think so, but certain core elements require attention if such progress is to be realized. To achieve integration between preschool and primary school—a consistent goal in official Sweden reform documents, but, according to research, still unrealized in most settings—the most fundamental challenge may be establishing a common perspective on children, about what learning means and what children are supposed to learn during preschool and the primary grades.

What, then, is a child? A child is born into a culture with certain values and ways of acting and behaving that are, most often, taken for granted (Rogoff, 2003). The way a society thinks about its children affects its opinions about their capabilities and skills. For example, if a society views children simply as immature versions of the adults they will become, then learning is seen primarily as an internal process relying mostly on maturation. If we think in this way, then what do we need professional teachers for?

Although we often hear maturation-based ideas expressed directly and indirectly by early childhood educators, probably more often by preschool teachers than school teachers, such maturational views are largely out of favor in contemporary developmental science. Most contemporary theories of children's learning and development have adopted a sociocultural perspective, in which children's experiences are central (Olson & Torrance, 1996; Säljö, 2000; Sommer, 2003a, 2003b). Constructivists regard children as individuals with vast resources to both influence and be influenced by their environments. From this perspective, children are active participants in the construction of their own childhoods, largely through interaction with others. This view of children requires a totally different perspective on children's learning and opportunities for development than the perspective of maturationists. Constructivists see children as rich and active and interactive with the environment and their teachers. This, then, provides a new framework for thinking about what learning ought to be about in preschool and the primary grades, as well as what the teacher's role should be.

Besides taking notice of contemporary learning theories as they approach their daily practical work, it is also important for teachers to think of creativity as the core of learning, whatever the learning objective is meant to be (Next Generation Forum, 1999). Here, I am not talking about creativity as teachers often think of it within the limited context of painting and drawing and dramatizing. Rather, I am taking about *creativity as creation*, the central process through which children make (construct) sense and meaning from their experiences in preschool and school, as well as from their experiences outside of school. This means that creativity is as important in mathematics (Doverborg & Pramling Samuelsson, 1999b, 2001) and science (Pramling & Pramling Samuelsson, 2001) as in writing and drawing (Gustafsson & Mellgren, 2000).

Coming to terms with traditional and contemporary conceptions of play and learning is another prerequisite to progress toward reform in early childhood education. Just as learning theories have largely changed in recent times, so too have theories about play. According to contemporary theories, both play and learning are about creating meaning; and, in that sense, they are the same. Research clearly shows that play is as influenced by teachers and the surrounding world as is learning. Both play and learning in preschool and school settings require give-and-take in the interaction between the teachers and the children, as well as between the children themselves (Hutt, Taylor, & Hutt, 1989; Sylva, Roy, & Painter, 1980; Williams et al., 2001).

Adults often speak about learning and play as fundamentally different phenomena. Play is fun. Play is something children choose to do. On the other hand, adults speak of learning as something that can be fun or can be hard work. In school settings adults typically decide what is important for children to learn, as well as when and how they will learn it. How consistent is this adult view with prevailing theories about children's cognitive development and learning? How consistent is this view with children's own understandings of play and learning? Lilian Katz and Sylvia Chard (1989) provided insight into these questions, showing that the names children give to their activities in preschool and school are largely dependent upon the expectations and vocabulary of the adults around them. From the young child's perspective, then, there is no inherent difference between play and learning unless the adults around them communicate a difference through their words, actions, and expectations.

Children do not, on their own, differentiate between play and learning in their early years. They like to play and they like to learn. They are playful learners. They are learners who play. A study by Maria Johansson (2004) revealed how children themselves integrate play and learning. In the study, school-age children talked about play and learning in similar ways. They described both play and learning as an enjoyable activity, and they indicated that play and learning are linked together in ways that transcend adult distinctions between the two. For example, Ebba, 8 years and 11 months, said: "Well, I don't know how to explain it, if you think what you work with is fun, it could be play... handwriting I like a lot ... and then it seems like play." Anton, 9 years and 3 months, said: "I'm not sure... you understand better... if you learned about a new game you didn't understand when you were younger, but when you grow older you do." Hence our terms "the playing-learning child" and "playing-learning pedagogy."

In his book *The Ambiguity of Play*, Brian Sutton-Smith (1997) described play as central to the human experience throughout the entire lifespan. He argued that play is a form of mental feedback for human development. He also referred to Stephen Jay Gould's (1996) theory of evolution, where Gould argued that differences and variations are the keys to biological development. According to Gould, variability characterizes biological development, not precision and adaptation, as Darwin once claimed. This variability represents the innumerable opportunities for development and learning within young children. According to Sutton-Smith, a rich play environment capitalizes upon the human capacity for variability and actively engages children's developing minds in ways that best enable learning processes, opportunities, and potentials.

Studies of play reveal that children create themes as they play together (Mauritzson, 2003; Sawyer, 1997). That means that the content or focus of play is constructed among and between the children themselves. The play involves a subject, a topic, something to communicate about. Communication is the center of play; that is, children communicate about something (an object, an event), but they also spontaneously produce the scene through meta-communication, or thinking and talking aloud about how and what they are communicating. They talk about what they are going to do or say as they go along. (For example, a child might say to a playmate in the pretend shop, "No, when I say 'May I help you?' you say, 'I can't find the potatoes,' and then Martin can say, '....'") In this way the *act* of talking about acting becomes visible. Play necessarily involves talking and thinking, but it can also involve higher-order metacognition and metacommunication, especially when teachers help children focus attention on what they are doing, what they are saying, and what they are learning as they play (Pramling, 1990, 1994, 1996).

There seems to be a parallel between children's spontaneous ways of acting in play and the approach to learning developed in our research group—an approach now called developmental pedagogy (Pramling Samuelsson & Asplund Carlsson, 2003). The title "developmental pedagogy" should be seen in the light of education related to children's development. This means that the experiences children have in preschool, in close relation with their earlier experiences, influence their learning and development. Learning and development become two sides of the same coin, since the ontological base is that the subject (the child) and the surrounding world are not separated, but closely related to each other. When children incorporate aspects of their surroundings, the world becomes a part of the children. Each child's understanding of the world also becomes a part of the child's developing personality. Knowledge is, then, deeply personal— existing in a world where people experience or create meaning in many different ways. In "child development" the child's inner drive is more of a figure, while the environment is the background. In "developmental pedagogy," it is the internal relation between the child and the world around him or her that is the figure. A child's way of acting, thinking, and communicating is always dependent on both earlier experiences and how the child perceives his or her particular settings, tasks, questions, interactions, and experiences. This means that the learning becomes central, noting here that learning includes learning objectives and goals (the visions or intentions), the process of learning itself, and the products that result from the process.

For example, a teacher might be working toward a goal expressed in the curriculum that the child should learn to use symbols, such as alphabet letters, for communicating within a given culture. The teacher arranges activities and experiences for the children to engage with letters in various teacher-initiated tasks, as well as in their play. As the children engage with alphabet letters through these teacher-initiated activities and through spontaneous play, they are engaged in the process of learning. Finally, one day or another, the teacher wants to see what the child has learned, that is, to evaluate the outcome of the activities and experiences she arranged. One child has now started to scribble; another has begun to write the letters in the alphabet, putting them in long rows; and another has begun to put letters into words, writing them the way they sound even if this is not a conventional spelling. Learning, then, includes both the objective (learning to manage the shared symbol system of the culture), the activity (in this example, both what the teacher plans and the related activities children initiate on their own, especially in play), and the results (in this example, how they represent letters in their writing).

## DEVELOPMENTAL PEDAGOGY

Developmental pedagogy focuses on both children's learning and teacher strategies for creating learning opportunities. Integrating play and learning is one such strategy (Johansson & Pramling Samuelsson, in press). Developmental pedagogy shares another similarity with play besides the one discussed above—the role of variation in children's learning. Marton (1999) argued that the less we know about what the children's future will look like, the more they need to experience variation in their daily lives during childhood. Marton did not argue for variation simply for variation's sake or for maximum variation in every situation, but, rather, for variation over repetition in their early childhood experience. Bowden and Marton (1998) noted, however, that even variation must have some traces of the familiar, the routine, the repetitive, in order to capture and capitalize upon the power of children's previous experience as the backdrop for new experiences. They described learning as a question of preparing children for what is unknown (the future) by using what is known (present knowledge).

> The kind of learning we are interested in is learning which implies that the learner develops capabilities for seeing or experiencing situations or phenomena in certain ways. For every kind of situation and phenomenon it is possible to identify a limited number of distinctively different ways in which the situation or that phenomenon can be experienced. The differences between different ways of seeing a particular phenomenon (or a particular class of situation) can be understood in terms of critical aspects that defined the phenomenon (or situation) as experienced. For each phenomenon there is a limited number of critical aspects that can be discerned and focused on simultaneously. So differences in how the phenomenon is experienced reflect differences in what critical aspects are discerned and focused on simultaneously. (p. 24)

It has been said that it is impossible to take a bath in the same river twice (Herakleitos 1997 [500 B.C.]), since a body of water is always moving. This idea is also applicable to children and learning. A child is never in the same learning situation twice. As time goes by, both the child and the situation change. A child discerns something in every situation, and this discernment springs from the experience of variation. Or, in other words, a child cannot discern what does not vary (Marton, Runesson & Tsui, 2004). This phenomenon relates to a classical question in learning psychology: transfer. However, Bowden and Marton (1998) argued that transference naturally and necessarily occurs in every learning situation and that no true learning takes place without transference. One can never replicate precisely the situation in which a child learned something for the first time. Therefore, both the child and the situation will differ in some ways, perhaps minor, perhaps important. This turns the question of transference into a question of learning and begs this question: What is it the child has learned that makes it possible for him or her to handle the next step in learning, which, by definition, is a new situation, a variation of what has been previously known or experienced?

From the perspective of childhood learning presented here, all educational experiences are important for the learning process, regardless of the level of schooling, preschool or elementary school. Each educational experience, in turn, has the capacity to contribute to the ways in which the child experiences the next educational experience and how the child makes sense of this task, problem, situation, or communication and the next, regardless of whether we as teachers perceive the learning as correct or incorrect, good or bad. This leads to the question of whether a theoretical approach to learning, with the features presented here, can help teachers from both preschool and elementary school realize that they have to take a step toward something slightly challenging, something different in their teaching approach if they are to challenge children's learning. But just what is the change, the variation, required by this theoretical approach?

## Variation as a Central Feature in Developmental Pedagogy[1]

According to Marton and Pang (2003), *discernment, contemporaneousness,* and *variation* are critical aspects of learning. Marton (1999) described a British study by John Fazey in which children practiced throwing a ball into a basket. One group of children practiced in only one way, with the same ball and from the same distance to the basket. The other group's practice sessions were characterized by variation. They used balls of different weights and sizes. The distance and the angle to the basket also varied. Results showed that the children in the group with greater variation had much greater skill development in throwing toward a specific target than did children in the group with just the variation that every child create by "nature."

Findings from this study suggest that learning derived, in part, from distinguishing between the act of throwing, in general, and the act of throwing toward a target, in particular. Children's learning also derived, in part, from becoming simultaneously aware of variations in the experience of throwing the ball from different angles and different distances. To become skilled in throwing a ball at a target means to simultaneously be aware of and take various aspects of the experience into consideration, something constituted in the child with or without reflection.

Lindahl and Pramling Samuelsson (2002) described how a child named Wataru developed his ability to make objects spin. A teacher showed him how to make a plastic ring spin. He became fascinated and showed with his whole body that he also wanted to master this skill. In his mind he formed an idea of what is required to make an object spin. He spent days searching for objects suitable for this action. He chose plastic rings of different sizes, thicker wooden rings and trays with a round shape. He distinguished the critical aspects of objects necessary for spinning, realizing that objects must be similar in certain critical properties that allow them to spin. However, he also realized that "spinable" objects could still vary along other dimensions. He did not select objects randomly or by trial and error, but rather he deliberately selected a variety of objects, developing his skill in spinning and his understanding of the task's requirements as he went along. Here an individual child produced variation by choosing different objects for the act of spinning.

In the same article, Lindahl and Pramling Samuelsson (2002) described how a group of toddlers used their own bodies to produce variation as they went down a slide. They constructed variations on the concept and experience of sliding—going down this way one time and that way another time. They also worked together to create different approaches to sliding. In this example, both the individuals and the group produced the variation.

How can teachers become more aware of how children themselves produce variation during the school-start age from 4–6 years? And how can teachers become more skillful in utilizing variation as a teaching tool—novel territory for both preschool and elementary school teachers?

Valsiner (1989) pointed out how variations arise from many different sources and circumstances during childhood. For instance, adults in early childhood environments may vary their ways of interacting with ("meeting with," as Nordic people say) a child even in situations that are more or less similar. They may do this purposefully to create variation, or they may do it inadvertently. Valsiner also showed that the same person acts in different ways toward the child even when the situation is familiar or frequently recurring. For example, an early childhood teacher may allow the child to take a book outside one day but not the next. Similarly, variation appears away from school. Perhaps the mother says it is OK for books to go outside, but the father says no. Then the grandmother, who often looks after the child, thinks the child can take certain books outside but not others. Still another time the mother is tired and says no to the child's request, but the father, who has noticed that the mother usually allows the child to play with the books outside, becomes ambivalent and lets the child play outside with the books occasionally.

At first blush, it may seem that so much variation would confuse children. However, Valsiner claimed this is not so; rather, the opposite—because of exposure to variation, children develop by seeing the opportunities and being willing to try out new ways and by pushing their limits.

When observing children as they try to solve different kinds of tasks, researchers note that children seem to vary their strategies spontaneously. Both the children's spontaneous learning strategies and their experiences vary—in their immediate physical environment as well as in their interactions with people. On the other hand, just as children invoke variation naturally and spontaneously when they try to solve cognitive challenges and learn new skills, they also tend to use repetition as a learning tool, especially when they are trying to master a physical skill or when they are simply fascinated by a phenomenon. When left to their own devices, then, children seem to use both variation and repetition in service of their own learning goals and their engagement in activities that hold meaning for them.

Both similarity and variation are fundamental to several critical aspects of cognitive development in childhood, including the ability to distinguish one learning objective or phenomenon from others, which, in turn, is fundamental to the categorization process. For example, for a young child to be able to understand the concept of flowers, rather than simply to name a single flower as a flower, it is necessary for the child to experience a variety of flowers. Through experiencing variation they become able to distinguish the essential features that constitute what we call a flower. However, it is not sufficient simply for children to simply experience a variety of flowers. They also need to experience that flowers differ from other plants, such as trees, shrubs, and grass. Gradually children become able to understand the concept that flowers come in many different varieties, each with its own critical distinguishing features. This enables them to distinguish a rose from other flowers and eventually to distinguish one variety of rose from another.

Certainly this applies to other dimensions of school content as well. To be able to learn an important principle, rule, or value at preschool or at elementary school, it has to have personal meaning, which can be induced by using the rule in different situations (the rule being constant). It also has to be clear that this rule can have different meanings (variation) to different people. Finally this rule must have critical features that distinguish it from other rules. For example, the principle of every child's right to equality is an important one in Sweden. For this abstract principle to make sense to children, it must be discussed in many different contexts and negotiated in a variety of real-life situations before this cultural value will have a deeper meaning for the children.

The mutual benefit of both repetition (the familiar) and variety (the novel) are well-known and well-accepted aspects of the Sweden preschool tradition. Both repetition and variation are broadly used in daily preschool work (Doverborg & Pramling, 1988). When working with the theme of apples, for example, children sing songs about apples, read stories about apples, buy apples from the market, bake apple pie, talk about apples, and draw pictures of apples (Johansson & Gustafsson, 1992). The focus on apples is the constant, the repetition. The ways of experiencing apples is what varies.

However, from a pedagogical perspective, the starting point for the teacher has not been with the value of variation as an instructional strategy, but, rather, with the fact that children learn best by *experiencing with all their senses. Learning through the senses* is important in itself and has contributed to children's experiencing variation in preschool settings—as an essential component in children's learning. However, this is not the kind of variation my colleagues and I advocate as an approach to learning in preschool and primary school. The kind of variation we advocate defines learning as the *variety of ways* in which *one child* produces variation, the *variety of ways* in which *a group of children* think about one and the same phenomenon, the same problem or concept.

In our view, the variety of ways in which a child thinks about a single phenomenon, problem, or content is itself the content of the teaching process (Doverborg & Pramling, 1995; Doverborg & Pramling Samuelsson, 1999a, 1999b, 2000; Pramling, 1990, 1994). In other words, the teacher uses variation as a strategy to make particular knowledge, skills, ideas, and phenomena visible to the children. As they think in *various* ways about a topic or phenomenon, they become able to recognize variations within the topic or phenomenon, different meanings that may be derived from it.

A study by Doverborg and Pramling Samuelsson (1999a) revealed how preschool teachers incorporate the notion of variation into everyday experiences. For instance, a teacher gave the children half an apple at lunchtime for several days, asking them one by one how they would like to cut their apple. The children eagerly engaged in discussion about various ways of cutting the apple and how many pieces might result from different cutting procedures. As they cut the apples, they continued to discuss the process and the results. Afterward the teacher asked them to draw a picture to illustrate how they cut their apple and how many pieces resulted. Once again the various ways children solved the problem became visible and the focus of discussion with their peers. In this way they could follow their own ways of solving the apple cutting problem over time and also become increasingly aware of their own way of solving the problem in relation to their peers' ways of solving the same problem.

Pramling and Mårdsjö (1994) provided further examples of how to make the variety of ways of thinking about an experience highly visible in preschool settings. For instance, when preschool children were working with the theme "the development of society," teachers asked them to think about and illustrate how they thought people lived from the time they dwelled in caves to the modern housing structures of today. A burning debate erupted among the children as they discussed (and sometimes argued about) their ideas (see also Pramling Samuelsson & Mårdsjö, 1997). For instance, one child proclaimed that people lived in "snow houses," while another argued that people lived in grass huts.

Results of this study indicated that children who experienced this conscious exposure to variation gained deeper understanding of the development of society as represented through their dwellings than did children in a reference group. The reference group experienced an instructional approach featuring more traditional, action-based learning, where children's understandings are thought to derive from their doing. For example, children in the variation group were more advanced in their understanding of the relationship between people's innovation and the development of society. This difference was attributable to the fact that these children had the opportunity to express their ideas and that the variation in their expressed ideas became the content of the educational process. Their own thinking became visible to them, giving rise to new and more advanced opportunities for reflection (Pramling, 1996). These results indicate more advanced meta-cognitive abilities than many theories would suggest for preschoolers. The reason for the unique results may be that very few studies of meta-cognition have focused on children's everyday experience in preschool (NSIN Research Matters, 2001). Instead, most previous studies of meta-cognition among very young children has involved tests in unfamiliar settings (Wellman, Cross, & Watson, 2001).

In our study (Pramling & Mårdsjö, 1994) the children's understanding of society as a cultural phenomenon was superior to that shown by children in other preschools that were similar in many ways, but differed in the instructional approach (Pramling, 1994). By consciously using variety and variation as the centerpiece of teaching and learning, teachers challenged the children's "taken for granted" ways of thinking and understanding and led them to question both the material they were studying and their ways of thinking about this material. Individual children could think about their own ways of thinking within the context of what they had learned about other children's ideas and perspectives.

In summary, "developmental pedagogy" is a specific perspective on learning, where the child's perspective takes center stage and where the child is envisioned as one who plays and learns, hence the term the "playing-learning child." But the approach also features variation as a tool for fostering learning and development (for more theoretical features, see Pramling Samuelsson & Asplund Carlsson, 2003).

Conscientious use of variety and variation as learning strategies, then, has proven to be highly effective among children (Pramling 1990, 1994). In addition, this pedagogy of variation has proven to be effective among teachers as well (Pramling Samuelsson, Johansson, Davidsson, & Fors, 2000). Here we could see how teachers changed over time. In the beginning teacheres tended to take an adult's perspective, expressing their need to tell children what they themselves think about life's questions. As time passed, they began to tell children that there are multiple ways to think about any issue or question. At this stage, teachers began to provide a kind of "smorgasbord" from which children were supposed to choose. In the end, however, teachers began to think of teaching as a question of helping children create meaning by changing and developing their perceptions.

## TEACHING AND LEARNING FROM THE EARLY YEARS

The pedagogical challenge for both preschool and elementary-grade teachers is to create opportunities for children to see, experience, and comprehend what teachers want them to learn, the content around them, and to approach this challenge in various ways and through a variety of ways of thinking. This leads to the question of what children should learn at the ages around the school start. Here we see long-standing and well-entrenched differences between preschool and elementary school in Sweden. Preschools have traditionally framed their learning objectives in terms of broad content areas and themes, such as social competence, relationship building with peers and adults, and the development of self-reliance (Pramling Samuelsson, 2003), while elementary schools focus on specific academic subjects, such as mathematics and writing. At the preschool level, psychological development has been a central focus. This is, of course, important for all children; but I believe preschool must also include other learning objectives, objectives that are more consistent with and more valued at the beginning of primary school. In order to achieve coordination and coherence between preschool and elementary school and, thereby, create smooth transitions for children at the school-start age, preschool and elementary school must share at least some of the same learning objectives—or, at least, recognize common aspects of skills or knowledge to be developed at both levels of education. This means that social skills, traditionally valued more highly at the preschool level than at the elementary level, must attain a higher status in elementary settings, just as learning the fundamentals of mathematical knowledge must become more valued in preschool settings. This does not mean to lower the traditional emphasis on learning to count from elementary school to preschool, but, rather, to help preschool children think and reflect on basic notions for mathematics in the world around them (Doverborg & Pramling Samuelsson, 1999b). For example, the surrounding world provides many and varied encounters with numbers and shapes and other basic mathematical "content" that preschool teachers can capitalize on during everyday activities. The surrounding world also provides countless opportunities to encounter symbol systems, such as alphabet letters, and to gain facility with the form and meaning of language.

It must be noted here that the Swedish preschool curriculum emphasizes culturally *normative values and skills* (e.g., ability to cooperate, take the initiative, communicate, take responsibility, reflect, be flexible and creative), as well as *understanding of oneself and different aspects of the surrounding world* (Ministry of Education and Science in Sweden, 1998b). Preschools need to attend to these normative values and skills, again thoughtfully and conscientiously taking advantage of the lessons of everyday experiences in the surrounding environment, just as they should do to promote learning objectives valued in primary grades.

The state curriculum also points to the importance of developing creativity in all children, as emphasized by the Next Generation Forum (1999). This suggests that both preschool and elementary school must ensure development of creativity, as well as mastery of traditional academic and social knowledge and skills. Focusing on the development of creativity will, inevitably, broaden both the use and the value of variation in children's ways of thinking, knowing, and representing what they know.

In summary, then, we can see that Swedish public policy clearly favors the integration of preschool and school into a unified whole. However, research studies show that many challenges remain before the goal of integration can be achieved. Challenges for future collaboration between preschool and school include (1) making sense of new theories (I have suggested one direction for doing this), (2) developing curricula that cross traditional boundaries between preschool and school, and (3) developing a new pedagogy that is neither traditional preschool nor status-quo elementary school.

To make real progress other matters beyond the scope of this chapter must be considered as well. For instance, formative and summative evaluation should be an integral part of all preschool and school integration projects. However, on a broader scale, the most difficult challenge will be changing teachers', parents' and policymakers' attitudes about schooling and helping them see children as playing-learning children with the competence to become skillful learners if we have trust in them—and if we have well-educated teachers who can support and challenge them from their first day in preschool and every day thereafter.

## NOTE

1.   Pedagogy here means the content and the approach to teaching and learning in preschool.

## REFERENCES

Alexandersson, M. (1994). *Metod och medvetande* [Method and awareness]. Göteborg: Acta Universitatis Gothenburgensis.

Broström, S., Hermandsen, M., Krogh-Jespersen, K., & Sommer, M. (2002). *En god start—det fælles grundlag [A good start—The shared bases]*. Århus: Klim.

Broström, S., & Wagner, J. (Eds.). (2003). *Early childhood education in five Nordic Countries. Perspectives on the transition from preschool to school*. Århus: Systime A/S.

Bowden, J., & Marton, F. (1998). *The university of learning: Beyond quality and competence*. London: Cogan Page.

Council for Cultural Co-operation. (1996). Strasbourg: Council of Europe Education Committee.

Davidsson, B. (2002). *Mellan soffan och katedern. Om förskollärares och grundskollärares arbete med att åstadkomma en integration av förskola och skola* [Between the sofa and the desk: About preschool and school teachers' efforts in their work with integration between preschool and school]. Göteborg: Acta Universitatis Gothenburgensis.

Doverborg, E., & Pramling, I. (1988). *Temaarbete: Lärarens metodik och barns förståelse* [Working with themes: Teachers' methods and children's understanding]. Stockholm: Utbildningsförlaget.

Doverborg, E., & Pramling, I. (1995). *Mångfaldens pedagogiska möjligheter: Att arbeta med att utveckla barns förståelse för sin omvärld* [Pedagogical possibilities of diversity: To work with the developing of children's understanding of the world around them]. Stockholm: Utbildningsförlaget.

Doverborg, E. & Pramling Samuelsson, I. (1999a). Apple cutting and creativity as a mathematical beginning. *Kindergarten Education: Theory, Research and Practice, 4*(2), 87–103.

Doverborg, E., & Pramling Samuelsson, I. (1999b). *Förskolebarn i matematikens värld* [Preschool children in the world of matematics]. Stockholm: Liber.

Doverborg, E., & Pramling Samuelsson, I. (2001). Children's experience of shape in space. *For the learning of mathematics, 21*(3), 32–38.

Doverborg, E., & Pramling, I. Doverborg, E., & Pramling Samuelsson, I. (2000). To develop young children's conception of numbers. *Early Child Development and Care, 162*, 81–107.

Germeten, S. (2001). *Grenser for undervisning? Frihet og kontroll i 6-års klassen* [Limits for teaching? Freedom and control in the class for six year olds]. Stockholm: HLS förlag.

Göteborgs Stadskansli [Göteborg City Council]. (2003). *Kvalitetsredovisning avseende år 2002—för utbildningsområdet i Göteborgs kommun* [Quality account for the year 2002—for the area of education in Göteborg]. Göteborgs Stadskansli: Enheten för Välfärd och Utbildning. Drn 222/03.

Gould, S. J. (1996). *Full house: The spread of excellence from Plato to Darwin*. New York: Harmony Press.

Gustafsson, J. (2003). *Integration som text, diskursiv och social praktik: En policyetnografisk fallstudie av mötet mellan skolan och förskoleklassen* [Integration as text, discursive and social practice: A policy ethnographic case study of the encounter between school and the kindergarten] (Göteborg Studies in Educational Sciences 199). Göteborg: Acta Universitatis Gothoburgensis.

Gustafsson, K., & Mellgren, E. (2000). *En studie om barns skrivlärande* [A study about children's writing] (Report 2000:8.) Göteborgs Universitet: Institutionen för Pedagogik och Didaktik.

Hansen, M. (1999). *Yrkeskulturer i möt: Läraren, fritidspedagen och samverkan* [A meeting between cultures of profession: The teacher, the leisure time pedagogue and cooperation]. Göteborg: Acta Universitatis Gothoburgensis.

Haug, P. (1996). *Barnehage på skule: Evaluering av kjernetilbod og skolefritidsordning for 6-åringar* [Preschool and school: Evaluation of basic supply and the order of leisure time activities]. Trondheim: Norsk Centre for Barnforskning.

Herakleitos. (1997). *Fragment.* (H. Rehnberg & H. Ruin, trans.) Lund: Propexus. (Original work. 500 B.C.)

Hutt, S., Taylor, S., & Hutt, C. (1989). *Play, exploration and learning: A natural history of the preschool.* London: Routledge.

Johansson, E. (2003). *Möten för lärande: Pedagogisk verksamhet för de yngsta barnen i förskolan* [Encounters for learning: Pedagogical activities for the youngest children in preschool]. Stockholm: Skolverket.

Johansson, M. (2004). *Barns syn på lek och lärande i skolans praktik* [Children's view on play and learning in the the school context]. Göteborgs universitet: Institutionen för pedagogik och didaktik.

Johansson, J. E., & Gustafsson, B. (1992). *Intressecentrum och tema—en hundraårig historia. [Center of interest and themes—a one hundred years old history]* (Videotape). Göteborgs universitet: Institutionen för pedagogik.

Johansson, J. E., Klerfelt, A., & Pramling, I. (1997, March). *Att skriva och lösa problem i grundskolans tre första årskurser: Uppföljning av en försöksverksamhet i förskolan* [To write and solve problems during the three first years of elementary school: A follow-up study of an experimental work in preschool]. Paper presented at the annual conference of Nordisk Förening för Pedagogisk Forskning, Göteborg, Sweden.

Johansson, E., & Pramling Samuelsson, I. (in press). Play and learning—inseparable dimensions in preschool practice. *Early Child Development and Care.*

Kärrby, G. (1990). *De äldre barnen i förskolan—inlärning och utveckling* [The older children in preschool—learning and development]. Stockholm: Liber.

Katz, L., & Chard, S. (1989). *Engaging children's minds: The project approach.* Norwood, NJ: Ablex.

Kullberg, B., Pramling, I., & Williams Graneld, P. (1996). *Möjligheter eller hinder till lärande. Fjorton nybörjarelevs erfarenheter* [Opportunities or obstacles for learning. The experiences of fourteen beginners] (Report No. 12). Göteborgs Universitet: Institutionen för Metodik.

Lindahl, M., & Pramling Samuelsson, I. (2002). Imitation and variation: Toddlers' strategies for learning. *Scandinavan Journal of Educational Research, 46*(1), 25–45.

Marton, F. (1999, August). *Variatio est mater studiorum.* Paper presented at the invited address at the 8th European Conference for Learning and Instruction, Göteborg.

Marton, F., & Booth, S. (1997). *Learning and Awareness.* Hillsdale, NJ: Erlbaum.

Marton, F., Dahlgren, L.-O., Svensson, L., & Säljö, R. (1977). *Inlärning och omvärld-suppfattning* [Learning and the conceptions of reality]. Stockholm: Almqvist & Wiksell.

Marton, F., & Pang, M.-F. (2003). *Two faces of variation.* Invited address at the 8th European Conference for Learning and Instruction, Göteborg.

Marton, F., Runesson, U., & Tsui, A. B. M. (2004). The space of learning. In F. Marton & A.B.M. Tsui (Eds.), *Classroom discourse and the space of learning* (pp. 3–40). Mahwah, NJ: Erlbaum.

Mauritzson, U. (2003). *Barns perspektivtagande—hur barn lär sig ge och ta mening i interaktion* [Children's theories of others' minds—how children learn to share meenings in interaction]. Unpublished lic. theses at Institutionen för pedagogik och didaktik, Göteborgs universitet.

Ministry of Education and Science in Sweden. (1994). *Lpo 94. Läroplan för det obligatoriska skolväsendet* [Curriculum for compulsory school]. Stockholm: Utbildningsdepartementet.

Ministry of Education and Science in Sweden (1998a). *Curriculum for the compulsory school, the pre-school class and the after school centre. Lpo 94.* Stockholm: Fritzes.

Ministry of Education and Science in Sweden. (1998b). *Curriculum for pre-school. Lpfö 98.* Stockholm: Fritzes.

Myndigheten för skolutveckling [The Swedish National Agency for School Improvement] (2004) *Att bygga broar: Rapportering av regeringsuppdrag integration förskola, förskoleklass, grundskola och fritidshem. Slutrapport* [Building bridges: Report on the Government commission to integrate the preschool, the kindergarten, the elementary school and the the leisure time center]. Stockholm: Myndigheten för skolutveckling.

Next Generation Forum (1999). *Towards a creative society. Annual report 1999.* Billund: Author.

*NSIN Research Matters.* (2001). Learning about learning enhances performance. Issue 13.

Oberheumer, P. (2004, July). *International perspectives on early childhood curricula.* Paper presented at OMEP's World Congress—One World: Many Childhoods, Melbourn, Australia.

OECD. (2001). *Starting strong: Early childhood education and care.* Paris: Author.

Olson, D. R., & Torrance, N. (1996). *Handbook of education and human development: New models of learning, teaching and schooling.* Oxford: Basil Blackwell.

Pramling, I. (1990). *Learning to learn: A study of Swedish preschool children.* New York: Springer Verlag.

Pramling, I. (1993). *Barnomsorg för de yngsta: En forskningsöversikt* [Child care for the youngest]. Stockholm: Fritzes.

Pramling, I. (1994). *Kunnandets grunde: Försök med en fenomenografisk ansats för att utveckla barns sätt att uppfatta sin omvärld* [The foundations of knowing: Test of a phenomenographic effort to develop children's ways of understanding their surrounding world]. Göteborg: Acta Universitetis Gothenburgensis.

Pramling, I. (1996). Understanding and empowering the child as a learner. In D. Olson & N. Torrance (Eds.), *Handbook of education and human development: New models of learning, teaching and schooling* (pp. 565-590). Oxford, UK: Basil Blackwell.

Pramling, I., & Mårdsjö, A-C. (1994). *Att utveckla kunnandets grunder. Illustration av ett arbetssätt i förskolan Rapport nr 7.* [Developing the foundations of knowing. Illustration of a way of working in preschool. Report No. 7]. Göteborgs universitet: Institutionen för metodik i lärarutbildningen.

Pramling, N., & Pramling Samuelsson, I. (2001). "It is floating 'cause there is a hole." A young child experience of natural science. *Early Years, 21*(2), 139–149.

Pramling Samuelsson, I. (2003). Allt hör ihop i barnets värld [Everything belong together in the child's world]. *Pedagogiska Magasinet. Tema "Kunskap utan gränser", 2,* 14–19.

Pramling Samuelsson, I., & Asplund Carlsson, M. (2003). *Det lekande lärande barnet—i en utvecklingspedagogisk teori* [The learning, playing child—in a developmental pedagogic theory]. Stockholm: Liber.

Pramling Samuelsson, I., Johansson, E., Davidsson, B., & Fors, B. (2000). Student teachers' and preschool children's questions about life: A phenomenographic approach to learning. *European Early Childhood Educational Research Journal, 8*(2), 5–22.

Pramling Samuelsson, I., & Mårdsjö, A.-C. (1997). *Grundläggande färdigheter och färdigheters grundläggande* [Basic abilities and the foundation of abilities]. Lund: Studentlitteratur.

Pramling Samuelsson, I., & Mauritzson, U. (1997). *Att lära som sexåring* [To learn at six]. Skolverkets monografiserie. Stockholm: Skolverket.

Regeringen proposition [Proposition from the Government] (2004/05:11) *Kvalitet i förskolan* [Quality in preschool]. http://www.regeringen.se/utbildning

Regeringens skrivelse [Written communication from the Government] (1996/97:112) *Utvecklingsplan för förskola, skola och vuxenutbildning.* Stockholm: Regeringens tryckexpedition.

Rogoff, B. (2003). *The cultural nature of human development.* New York: Oxford University Press.

Roos, G. (1994). *Kommunerna och det pedagogiska utvecklingsarbetet inom barnomsorgen. Omfattning, inriktning och villkor* [The municipals and the pedagogical development work within child care. Range, direction and conditions]. Uppsala: Acta Universitatis Upsaliensis.

Sawyer, R. K. (1997). *Pretend play as improvision. Conversation in the kindergarten classroom.* Mahwah, NJ: Erlbaum.

Siraj-Blatchford, I. (1999). Early childhood pedagogy: Practice, principles and research. In P. Mortimore (Ed.), *Understanding pedagogy and its impact on learning* (pp. 20–25). London: Paul Chapman.

Skolverket [The Swedish National Agency for Education]. (2001). *Att bygga en ny skolform för 6-åringarna: Om integrationen förskoleklass, grundskola och fritidshem* [Building a new school form for the six years old: About the integration between the kindergarten,, elementary school and leisure time centers]. Stockholm: Fritzes.

Skolverket [The Swedish National Agency for Education]. (2003a). *Antologi: Lagarbete och tidig läs- och skrivutveckling* [Anthology: Teamwork and the development of early reading and writing] . Stockholm: Fritzes.

Skolverket [The Swedish National Agency for Education]. (2003b). *Uppföljning av reformen max-taxa, allmän förskola, mm.* [Follow-up of the reform "max-taxa," compulsory school etc.] Skolverkets rapport till Utbildningsdepartementet.

Skolverket. (2004). *Förskola i brytningstider. Nationell utvärdering av förskolan* [Preschool during changes in time. National evaluation of preschool]. Stockholm: Fritzes.

Socialstyrelsen [National Board of Health and Welfare]. (1987:3). *Pedagogiskt program för förskolan* [Pedagogic program for preschool]. Stockholm: Allmänna förlaget.

Socialstyrelsen [National Board of Health and Welfare]. (1988). *Pedagogiskt program för fritidshem* [Pedagogic program for leisure time centers]. Stockholm: Allmänna förlaget.

Socialstyrelsen. (1990). *Att lära i förskolan: Innehåll och arbetssätt för de äldre barnen i förskolan* [Learning in preschool: Content and ways of working for the older children in preschool]. Stockholm: Allmänna förlaget.

Sommer, D. (2003a). *Barndomspsykologi* [Childhood psychology]. København: Hans Reitzels Forlag.

Sommer, D. (2003b). *Barndomspsykologiske facetter* [Childhood psychological facets]. Århus: Systime Academic.

SOU [Swedish Government Official Reports]. (1972:26) *Förskolan Del I. Betänkande utgivet av 1968 års barnstugeutredning* [Preschool part I. Report from 1968 years' "Barnstugeutredning"]. Stockholm: Socialdepartementet.

SOU. (1985). *Förskola—skola. Betänkande av Förskola-skola-kommittén* [Preschool—school. Report from "Förskola-skola-kommittén"]. Stockholm: Allmänna förlaget.

SOU. (1992). *Skola för bildning: Huvudbetänkande för Läroplanskommittén* [A school for education: Main report from "Läroplanskommittén"]. Stockholm: Utbildningsdepartementet.

SOU. (1994). *Grunden för ett livslångt lärande. En barnmogen skola. Betänkande av Utredningen om förlängd skolgång* [The foundation for a life long learning. A child mature school. Report from the evaluation of an extended schooling. Stockholm: Fritzes.

Sutton-Smith, B. (1997). *The ambiguity of play.* London: Harvard University Press.

Sylva, K., Roy, C., & Painter, M. (1980). *Child watching at playgroup and nursery school.* London: Graut McIntyre.

Säljö, R. (2000). *Lärande i praktiken: Ett sociokulturellt perspektiv* [Learning in practice: A sociocultural perspective]. Stockholm: Prisma.

Valsiner, J. (1989). Collective co-ordination of progressive empowerment. In L. Winegar (Ed.), *Social interaction and the development of children's understanding* (pp. 7–20). Norwood, NJ: Ablex.

Valsiner, J. (1990). *Culture and the development of children's action.* New York: Wiley.

Vygotsky, L. S. (1978). *Mind in society: The development of higher psychological processes.* Cambridge, MA: Harvard University Press.

Wellman, H. M., Cross, D., & Watson, J. (2001). Meta-analysis of theory-of-mind development: The truth about alse belief. *Child Development, 72*(3), 655–684

Williams, P., Sheridan, S., & Pramling Samuelsson, I. (2001). *Barns samlärande—en forskningsöversikt* [Children working together—a research overview]. Stockholm: Fritzes.

CHAPTER 6

# FINNISH DAYCARE

## Caring, Education, and Instruction

**Anneli Niikko**
*University of Joensuu*

In current educational discourse, children are looked upon as active, capable, and resourceful, even though their lives are highly dependent upon decisions made by adults. To grow and develop, children need love, care, concern, and instruction. Adults must respond to these needs in one way or another.

In Finland's past, most children grew up in agricultural communities, where parents and grandparents both looked after them and expected them to work from the earliest ages. Children were taken care of in the context of daily agricultural work. They received attention as necessary and feasible under the circumstances. As Finland began to industrialize in the 1960s (Alestalo, 1986; Kortteinen, 1982), parents started to demand that society arrange daycare for their children. Publicly funded daycare commenced in Finland during the 1970s as support grew for daycare provisions to allow parents to work outside the home. Later, increasing attention was paid to "education" as a shared activity between families and public day-

*Nordic Childhoods and Early Education,* pages 133–158
Copyright © 2006 by Information Age Publishing
All rights of reproduction in any form reserved.

care. However, "education" in the Finnish early childhood context was (and still is) synonymous with "upbringing," a more overarching construct than "education," as the term is used in some other parts of the world to refer primarily to academic learning. The term "early childhood education" entered Finnish discourse in the 1980s.

In Finland, early education refers to all-around support for the care, growth, development, and learning of the child. "Daycare" is an administrative term embedded within early childhood education. Daycare is a service for all children below school-start age, and also for older children who need morning and/or afternoon and/or evening and/or night care. The number of hours children spend in daycare varies but may not exceed 10 consecutive hours in a day.

In Finland the term "preschool" as an administrative and pedagogical term refers to programs serving only 6-year-olds during the year preceding their entry into compulsory education. Preschools can be located in daycare or public school facilities. The duration of preschool education has been fixed at 700 hours per year. Preschool has been available as long as daycare, but it gained legal status only recently at the beginning of this millennium as a separate learning environment. According to the basic Education Act (Perusopetuslaki, 1998) and other official documents (Opetushallitus, 2000; Sosiaali- ja terveysministeriö, 2002), preschool is part of Finish early childhood education, but preschool has an independent status between daycare and primary school. Special curricular principles were drawn up to guide the pedagogical work in preschools (Opetushallitus, 2000). The primary task of preschool is to guarantee all 6-year-olds equal opportunities for learning.

By the beginning of the current millennium, the scope of daycare and preschool had broadened and is now referred to as "early childhood education service." In the Finnish context, "early childhood education" is a pedagogical term, whereas the term "early childhood education service" implies that children are viewed as clients of services in the same way as adults are. The term "early childhood education services" also reflects the view that daycare, preschool, and primary school should be viewed as a continuum of services, rather than as separate entities.

In this chapter, I discuss public daycare from the viewpoint of both society and the daycare center. I address the following questions: What is the significance of daycare in contemporary Finnish society? What are the goals and tasks of daycare? In what ways have daycare and early childhood education changed, both statutorily and functionally, in the 30 years during which daycare, early childhood education, and preschool have developed in Finland? What are the roles and positions of the early education personnel in modern Finland? I will use Uri Brofenbrenner's theory of social ecology as a structural framework because the daycare system can be appropriately viewed as a part of a multilayered and complex social web including micro, meso, exo and macro levels, operating together to form a system, as Bronfenbrenner defined the term. Each level provides a unique, yet interrelated, perspective from which to observe daycare: from the point of view of society (macro), of parents' work outside the home (exo), of children (micro), of daycare center, and of the family (meso) (Brofenbrenner, 1979; Huttunen, 1984; Välimäki, 1998).

The chapter focuses on three interrelated aspects of early childhood education in Finland. Although these aspects—care, caring, and "all-around care"—are difficult to define or differentiate in English, the fundamental concepts embodied in these terms are central in Finnish Early Childhood Education (ECE) discourse. The concepts can be viewed as mutually complementary dimensions of caregiving in early childhood education and daycare, with each of them manifesting itself on many levels in daycare situations. "All-around care" is the umbrella term Finnish preschool teachers use for these aspects of early childhood education. All-around care here refers to the individual and collective work by educators aiming at securing the child's well-being and good life. All-aound care includes the ethical dimension of education, too. In all-round care the object is to promote and ensure the child's physical, social, emotional, and cognitive development. The aims also include language development, as well as ethical and moral development.

The term "care" in the Finnish ECE context refers to those aspects of caregiving that focus on daily routines, such as eating, cleanliness, toileting, and basic safety. The term "caring" refers to attitudes and to taking notice, being interested in children, and to reciprocity between adults and children and among children themselves.

Recent studies on Finnish ECE have investigated the meanings of daycare and preschool from the viewpoints of professionals, parents, and children. Also researchers have investigated the various aspects of daycare and preschool in Finland, including the forms of all-around care, care, and caring, as well as education and instruction. Puroila (2002) considered both care and education in daycare centers. Alasuutari (2003) studied parents' views on the responsibilities of home and daycare centers for the education of children younger than compulsory school age. Niikko (2003) researched student teachers' perceptions of upbringing and education. Havu (2000) explored conceptual changes in preschool children in an instructional context.

## DAYCARE AS A SOCIAL SERVICE IN THE
## NORDIC CONTEXT

Like many other aspects of daily life, daycare in Finland reflects the country's close ties to its Nordic heritage, as well as to modern Nordic beliefs and practices. Nordic people tend to believe strongly in democracy and human equality. Universality is a central goal of the Nordic welfare states, in which governments take extensive responsibility for ensuring the general well-being, security, and equality of all citizens, regardless of age, sex, or ethnic background. This emphasis on equality and universality sets the Nordic countries apart from the rest of the European countries. These Nordic concepts of well-being and equality are viewed as woman-friendly (Välimäki, 1998) because, together, they enable women to become part of the workforce without stigma and because childcare responsibilities are, rightly, to be shared by mothers, fathers, communities, and the state.

The provision of universal services leading toward greater equality among all citizens is a chief characteristic of modern welfare states. Among the critical roles of the welfare state in a post-industrialized country like Finland is to solve the question of child care by providing public daycare for children before they reach the age of compulsory education. The provision of public child care has, in many ways, made it easier for women to work outside the home. About 73% of married or cohabiting Finnish women with children under the age of 7 are employed (Ministry of Social Affairs and Health, 2000; Tilastokeskus, 2004). The Act on Children's Day Care (Laki lasten päivähoidosta, 1973) defined daycare as a social service for all those who needed it. From its inception, daycare was to be so organized as to give a suitable and continuous place for a child's care and education at the times of the day when working parents needed it.

Prior to 1973 provision of public daycare was voluntary for municipalities throughout Finland. However, with the passage of the Act on Children's Day Care in 1973, each municipality became responsible for arranging and funding daycare provisions in cooperation with the state. Daycare was broadly defined as care for children in a daycare center, in family daycare in the home, or in some form of adult-supervised play at the playground. Over time, the term "daycare center" came to mean a place for children between birth and 6 years of age. This usage is consistent with the term in many other parts of the world. However, "family daycare" in Finland refers to systematic and controlled care in the family home by a member of the child's immediate family. Family daycare is an official, legally defined system. Municipalities usually offer family daycare to families who have children less than 3 years of age. Municipal authorities check on family daycare homes to be sure they are appropriate. In Finnish terms, then, family daycare is one part of the daycare system for providing publicly funded care while parents work.

Although municipalities were required to provide publicly funded child care beginning in 1973, not all parents had an entitlement to a space in publicly funded child care until more than 20 years later. One reason was that municipalities did not have adequate funds to organize and offer daycare places for all children. If there were not any vacant places in publicly funded daycare centers or in family daycare, parents had to organize daycare in a private setting. The 1996 new act on daycare changed this, entitling all parents with children below the school entering age (7 years) to have a place for their children in municipal and public daycare. Since 1997 it has also been possible for families to receive economic support from the municipality to arrange private daycare for their children if they prefer. In addition, parents with children below the age of 3 were entitled to an allowance if they decided to care for their infants and toddlers themselves.

Parents in the lower-income brackets have especially taken advantage of the home care allowance and stayed at home to take care of their children. The basic, general allowance paid by the state averages about 250 euros a month for the first child. In addition to this, the state pays an additional home care allowance (maximum about 170 euros), the amount of which varies according to the income of the family. Furthermore, there is a special stay-at-home allowance (about 170 euros for children under 2 years of age) paid by an increasing number of municipalities. The home care allowance does not fully compensate for lost income, but it gives parents the option to take care of their children themselves. The allowances are paid only to the parent who stays at home. It can be the mother or father. The state allowances continue until the child is 3 years old. Moreover, if there are several children in the family, every one of them below 3 years of age adds slightly to the sum of allowances.

Over the last 5 years, the percentage of Finnish children in some form of daycare has remained constant at 51.2% (public and private), with wide variations between various regions of the country and, especially, between urban and rural areas. About 47.7% of the children between 0 and six years of age are in public daycare, while 3.5% attend private daycare provisions with public support. The figures for full-time and part-time (< 5 hours) daycare are 36% and 12%, respectively. Of children younger than three years of age, 22% are in public daycare including daycare centers, family daycare, or group home daycare. By the age of 6, however, 90% are enrolled in a official preschool program (Sosiaali- ja terveysministeriö, 2002; Stakes, 2003).

The main purposes of Finnish daycare have always been to provide high quality care and education and to assist families with their daily lives. Early childhood educators in Finland are particularly concerned with children's general well-being. Unlike early education in many parts of the world (Ben-Peretz, 1996; Hargreaves, 1994; Hargreaves & Tucker, 1991), Finnish child daycare and early childhood education focus more on care, upbringing and general development than on early "academic" outcomes, such as recognition of letters and numbers.

According to Puroila (2002), Finnish preschool teachers focus especially on the quality of their actions and interactions with children in their care. They think about relationship building—relationships between themselves and the children and relationships between the children and their peers. Preschool teachers focus on children's basic physical care, as well as their emotional and social needs. These stands are in stark contrast to the goals of early childhood education in some parts of the world where the emphasis is on lesson planning and academic outcomes for preschool children. Finish researchers (Anttonen & Sipilä, 1994; Estola, 2003; Julkunen, 1991; Juujärvi, 2003; Sarvimäki & Stenbock-Hult, 1996) have revealed that preschool teachers focus on caring as actions and interactions, as relationships between people and as a phenomenon.

## SHARING OF EDUCATIONAL RESPONSIBILITIES BETWEEN HOME AND DAYCARE

As the Act on Children's Day Care (Laki lasten päivähoidosta, 1973) took effect, critical educational discussions ensued about the relationship between the responsibilities of daycare and the family for children's upbringing. The effect of a rapidly changing modern society upon children's upbringing within the family became a hot topic, fueled also by reforms throughout the 1980s in public policies relating to children and their upbringing, including the Comprehensive School Act (Peruskoululaki, 1983), the Child Welfare Act (Lastensuojelulaki, 1983), and the Act on Child Care and the Right to Meet Children (Laki lasten huollosta ja tapaamisoikeudesta, 1983). For example, the Child Welfare Act defined the child's right to special protection and all-around care, to a safe and inspiring environment, and to balanced and versatile early childhood experiences. Within the context of these new rights, then, what was to be the role of the daycare center and what was to be the role of the family in the child's upbringing?

The justification for adding educational goals to daycare policies was that daycare was supposed to be consistent with and supportive of upbringing provided by parents at home. Parents were considered to be primarily responsible for their children's upbringing and development in spite of the fact that children spent many hours each week away from their parents in daycare. Furthermore, parents were to be kept informed about the education their child received in daycare. Parents were to be able to make sure that the daycare was sufficiently versatile and that it contributed to the child's development. Versatility meant providing periods of play for the children, both guided and free, as well as games and developmental and creative activities indoors and outdoors.

This debate about the roles and responsibilities of parents and daycare for the upbringing of children brought pressure for reform, especially with regard to articulation of specific educational goals for daycare as expressed in the Amendment to the Act on Children's Day Care (Muutos lakiin lasten päivähoidosta, 1983). Committee Report (Komiteamietintö, 1980). With this amendment, the duty of daycare was to support parents' goals for the upbringing of their children. Together with homes, the amendment required daycare to (1) promote balanced social and emotional development of children's personalities; (2) support children's aesthetic, intellectual, ethical, and religious upbringing; and (3) foster their potentials for learning throughout early childhood. For its part, education in daycare was to offer the child safe and warm human relationships, activities supporting each child's development in a variety of ways, and a favorable environment in which to grow up in harmony with each child's background and abilities. Furthermore, daycare was to support children's growing understanding that they share responsibility for the well-being of the groups to which they belong and that they can participate in maintaining peace and in caring for the environment. Daycare was to include religious education that was respectful of each family's moral and ethical convictions. Religion was seen to be part of Finnish heritage and celebrating religious festivals was considered important; but religious instruction was viewed as cultural rather than theological in daycare. The instruction of religion was clearly the parents' duty.

The educational goals for daycare, as presented in various official documents, are similar to the stated goals of the comprehensive school (i.e., compulsory education, grades 1–2) in that both focus on cognitive, ethical, social, religious, and aesthetic aims. However, official goals for daycare and comprehensive school differ in significant ways. For instance, goals for comprehensive school typically focus on desired outcomes, such as specific knowledge or skills that children should acquire in school, while daycare goals focus on children's experiences and internal processes rather than external outcomes. Daycare goals focus on what the teachers should do in the course of their daily interactions with children, while comprehensive school goals focus on what the student must be able to do in specified content and study areas.

## DAYCARE EXTENDS INTO AN INTEGRATED AND VERSATILE EARLY CHILDHOOD EDUCATION SERVICE

At the beginning of this new millennium, Finland established an integrated system for child care, early education, social service, and family support, which combine to form the basic and integrated system for early childhood education service and support form for families, as illustrated in Figure 6.1.

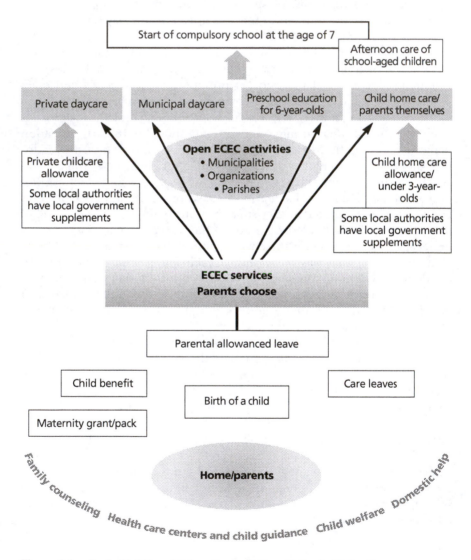

Figure 6.1.   Early Childhood Education and Care Policy in Finland.

The underlying values in Finnish approaches to the Finnish Early Childhood Education and Care policy system (ECEC) and Early Childhood Education (ECE) derive from international agreements on children's rights, national acts and decrees, and other local guidelines for early childhood education. The aims of early childhood education are rooted in Finnish history and culture, as well in national traditions in education and also European pedagogical heritage.

Finnish ECE emphasizes respect for each child's individuality and the chance for each child to develop as a unique person. Finnish early educators also guide children in the development of social and interactive skills, encouraging them to pay attention to other people's needs and interests, *to care about* others, and to have a positive attitude toward other people, other cultures, and different environments. The purpose of gradually providing opportunities for increased independence is to enable all children to take care of themselves as "becoming adults," to be capable of making responsible decisions, to participate productively in society as an active citizen, and to take care of other people who will need his help.

The new ECEC system responds to (1) the child's right to early childhood education, (2) parents' right to a daycare place or other care allowances for their child, and (3) demands for educational cooperation between professional educators and parents with regard to the education of young children in daycare, preschool, and school. The integrated system provides coordinated services through health care centers, daycare centers, preschools, and comprehensive schools. Health care centers offer help to families in issues of children's physical health. For example, nurses in health care centers follow children's physical development, assist families in the prevention of children's sicknesses, support and promote children's health, and take care of vaccinating children.

In spite of mandated cooperation between home and school on behalf of the child's education and development, however, parents maintain ultimate rights and responsibilities for the education of their children (Opetushallitus, 2000; Sosiaali- ja terveysministeriö, 2002; Stakes, 2003). This means that parents are interested in their children's growth, guide their children's behavior, and set secure limits of behavior for them. Parents also bear responsibility for the upbringing decisions made in the family.

In the last few years, several additional ECE policy documents have been issued. For instance, the first national guidelines for early childhood education were published in 2002 (Sosiaali- ja terveysministeriö, 2002). These guidelines state, for instance, that early childhood education and care are part of lifelong learning. Care, education, and teaching should form a seamless whole, which flexibly supports the individual development of each child. There is a special emphasis on treating children as equal individuals. The guidelines steer the development of early childhood education programs at the municipal level, establishing quality expectations and general perimeters for curriculum.

In Finland the curriculum in early childhood and preschool is defined broadly and it comprises the general aims of education and learning; the conceptual framework of education; learning and the learning environment; a detailed description of content aims; evaluation; cooperation with parents and with the staff involved in the welfare of children/pupils; and descriptions and principles of teaching pupils with another linguistic or cultural background, or needing special support.

Other important documents have also influenced the direction and development of early childhood services. These include the Principles for the Curriculum in Early Childhood Education (Stakes, 2003), the Principles for the Curriculum in Preschool (Opetushallitus, 2000), and the Principles for Basic Education (Opetushallitus, 2003). Each document contributes to ECE in complementary ways. For example, the Principles for the Curriculum in Preschool guide the development of local preschool curricula and specify quality criteria that are to be addressed. According to these documents, the term "early childhood education" refers to the educational service as educational interactions, experiences in children's lives to promote balanced growth, development, and learning, and to pedagogical decisions. Early childhood education is viewed as one important and meaningful part of children's lifelong learning.

According to all official documents, the starting point for early childhood education is a view of the child as a human being whose growth, development, and learning happens in formal and informal ways in different environments. This shared view about the appropriate starting point for early education is based on comprehensive, multidisciplinary knowledge and research about children, as well as on contemporary knowledge and research about learning theories, early childhood pedagogy, and Finnish cultural tradition (Opetushallitus, 2000; Stakes, 2003). In the documents, children are viewed as the builders of their own lives and experiences. Children have to be listened to on issues involving them and they have to be treated as equal persons. Each child learns as she or he takes part in various everyday activities, play, and learning situations, alone and together with other children.

Preschool is implemented in accordance with the Basic Education Act (Perusopetuslaki, 1998). Nationally, preschools operate under the authority and supervision of the National Board of Education. However, responsibility for providing preschools, as well as their administration and pedagogical oversight, rests with each municipality. A goal of preschool as an integral feature of Finnish early childhood education is to provide appropriate learning experiences for children in the year prior to the entry into school. For instance, preschool typically includes learning sessions guided by the teacher, acquisition of information and problem solving, as well as free play and games in interaction with adults and other children. The work in preschool is based on different play forms and activities in concert with the child's stage of development. Crucial content areas in preschool are language and interaction, understanding mathematical concepts and phenomena, environment and nature, physical and motor development, and art and culture, as well as ethics and view of life. In contrast to this, the activities of small children in daycare are holistic, flexible, and take place in the context of playing.

In preschool, the year before entry into primary school, the purpose of the teacher's work is to support the child's learning and to promote each child's readiness to enter school. The aims of preschool education are determined by each child's possibilities and abilities to develop and learn, as well as by the needs of society. Preschool aims at strengthening the children's positive self-image and abilities to learn. Children need to adopt basic knowledge, preparedness, and skills on the basis of their age and abilities. They have to learn to understand the significance of the peer group in learning. Children need to practice the rules of social life, including what their society regards as the significance of good manners in everyday life (Niikko & Havu-Nuutinen, 2004).

## IMPLEMENTING EARLY CHILDHOOD EDUCATION IN A DAYCARE SETTING

The national documents of ECE (Sosiaali- ja terveysministeriö, 2002; Stakes, 2003) include consideration of both content and pedagogical topics. The curricular content and emphasis of ECE programs vary with the age of the children and their situations. In general, the younger the children, the greater the proportion of interaction between children and adults that takes place *while providing care and caring*. For instance, with infants, preschool teachers, and assistants (usually assistant nurses or child minders) interact with children while changing their diapers and feeding or comforting them. These interactions and situations are considered educational and instructive. The preschool teacher or the assistant sometimes initiates and sometimes follows the baby's lead in games like peek-a-boo or pat-a-cake.

The preschool teacher or assistant purposefully elaborates on the baby's efforts to communicate. For instance, when the baby attempts to retrieve a toy just out of reach, the preschool teacher or assistant might say, "You are reaching for the ball. I am getting the ball for you now" to narrate the situation. These situations involve education, instruction, and guidance, all of which contribute to the child's general well-being, development, and learning. In early childhood education, *good care and caring* are the basis of all activities and behavior. With their basic needs well satisfied, children can take interest in other children, the environment, and activities available to them by the teacher's design or their own invention.

The content and pedagogy of early childhood education, in a very general way, arise from the European and Finnish tradition of early childhood education, not academic disciplines like mathematics, science, history and civics, aesthetics, ethics, and religion (Hänninen & Valli, 1986; Stakes, 2003). At the early childhood level, disciplinary boundaries, often obvious in school subjects, disappear as children explore the world around them. Unlike school children who might study math at 10:30 and history at 11:30, the infant, toddler, or preschooler constructs knowledge across disciplinary boundaries in different activities and play.

The national curriculum policy also stresses that young children acquire capabilities as they gradually familiarize themselves and gain understanding of the diverse phenomena of the world around them. However, disciplinary orientations give the educator a framework within which to look for, adapt, and offer experiences, situations, and environments so children's growth and development can proceed. In primary school (grades 1 and 2) school subjects are typically organized around traditional academic disciplines (Opetushallitus, 2000).

Language is regarded as a part of all the disciplinary orientations and the most important area of thinking and expression. Children are encouraged to use good and precise language (Stakes, 2003). Early childhood educators encourage children to tell about their own feelings, opinions, and thoughts in various everyday situations. Children are offered opportunities to describe their observations and express their conclusions orally in both learning and play situations. Fairytales, stories, poems, and nursery rhymes are read or told to children. Also children are encouraged to produce stories and fairytales in cooperation with other children. Children are taught to learn to listen to other people.

According to Finnish policy guidelines and contemporary pedagogical thought, the content to be learned in early childhood education should be approached in an integrative and unifying manner, with adults always bearing in mind the child's viewpoint, existing strengths and capabilities, and current interests. Play and everyday activities, both indoors and outdoors, hold an honored position in Finnish ECE. Children play for the sake of playing because play gives them deep satisfaction and joy. Finnish preschool teachers also view movement as central to children's well-being and healthy development. Movement is a natural way for children to get to know themselves, other people, and their environments.

Exploration and wonder of new things are regarded as inherent qualities of young children. When exploring, children satisfy their curiosity and feel that they are part of the community and the world around them (Niikko & Havu-Nuutinen, 2004; Sosiaali- ja terveysministeri, 2002; Stakes, 2003). This understanding of children's natural curiosity and urge to explore leads Finnish preschool teachers to guide children to make observations and to explore their environment indoors as well as outdoors. As children explore using all their senses, teachers, too, engage all their senses to observe the children and quantify or describe what they are doing. Teachers write down anecdotal notes, later categorizing them as, for example, illustrations of social or language development or acquisition of a new math concept. Teachers use their observations of children's free play and sensory exploration of their indoor and outdoor environments as inspiration for class activities and projects.

The policy guidelines acknowledge that children learn through play and because playing is often a social act, the peer group has a remarkable influence on both the process and content of play across the early childhood years (Stakes, 2003). As children reach preschool in the year prior to their entry into compulsory school, their teachers recognize the contributions of spontaneous play, as well as play-like activities designed by the teacher to promote the development of academic skills. In addition, daily movement activities and experiences are viewed as the foundation for the child's well-being and healthy growth.

As a whole, the official documents of ECE offer the framework for young children's development and learning and also for the work of preschool teachers and their assistants. The documents focus on individual children and their interests. The preschool teacher's role is to plan and construct everyday activities and different learning environments for children. Unlike elementary school, preschool teachers use subject matter content areas only as frameworks and orientations, not as the basis for instruction.

## COOPERATION BETWEEN HOME, DAYCARE, AND PRESCHOOL

Among the central goals of early childhood education in Finland is the establishment of ongoing collaboration between educators and families. Although all official documents suggest that parents and professional educators must share responsibility for children's upbringing and education, these documents also firmly establish that parents are the child's first and most important teachers. Therefore, educators in daycare and preschool should both respect and reflect each family's values and goals for their children.

In reality, however, many points of agreement and many obstacles lie along the road to building productive cooperation between professional educators and parents throughout the course of the early years. Several studies have established general agreement among parents and early childhood educators about their respective roles and responsibilities. For instance, the majority of parents and staff in some studies agreed that the daycare center was responsible for both care and education of children (Niikko & Havu-Nuutinen, 2004; Reuna, 1999; Seppälä, 2000). In addition, a survey by Reuna (1999) found that the majority of both parents and ECE staff were opposed, for example, to giving more responsibility for education to the daycare center. However, other studies have noted important areas of disagreement between professional educators and parents. For instance, Seppälä (2000) found vast disagreements between preschool teachers and parents about the division of responsibilities. Most of the parents in the study believed that responsibilities were appropriately divided. Parents emphasized the primary responsibility of homes and parents for educating young children. They believed that the major role of professional preschool teachers was to lend parents support in their efforts to educate their own children.

The majority of ECE professionals in the study held the opposite view that too much responsibility for early education rests on the shoulders of professional educators. They suggested that this imbalance resulted from growing demands on parents from the workplace, increases in working hours, and general uncertainty among parents about how to effectively educate their young children.

Seppälä (2000) found that parents and teachers differed in their views about what they should be teaching children. Parents stressed their own role in teaching social and ethical skills. For them their most important task was to teach their children to differentiate right from wrong. On the other hand, professional educators emphasized their role in teaching basic cognitive skills.

With regard to each group's opinions about the other group's teaching responsibilities, Seppälä (2000) noted both areas of agreement and disagreement. Parents believed that the professionals bear primary responsibility for teaching children to read and do sums, for arousing children's desire to learn, and for encouraging them to get along with different kinds of people. Some of these goals identified by parents were in line with teachers' views that teachers' primary responsibilities lay in the area of teaching basic cognitive skills. From the perspective of the professional educators, the most important task for parents was to give children a feeling of security. Parents seemed to take this for granted, however, and emphasized instead their role in teaching social and ethical skills.

It is interesting to speculate about the finding that parents took for granted their role in helping children feel safe and secure, while teachers noted this as the most important task of the parents. The finding seems to imply that, while parents view security development as a given, teachers view it as an area in need of greater attention and deeper understanding by parents. In spite of these differences, however, several studies have found that both parents and professional educators consider cooperation between home, daycare, and preschool important (Niikko & Havu-Nuutinen, 2004; Seppälä, 2000), though those groups sometimes agreed and sometimes differed on the specifics. In general, preschool teachers emphasized the importance of cooperation more than parents did. Interestingly, though, the younger the parents, the more importance they attached to cooperation between preschool teachers and themselves. Perhaps this finding reflected preschool teachers' views that younger parents tended to recognize their lack of experience, while older parents tended to rely less on the preschool because they believed themselves to be more experienced and had greater confidence in their parenting abilities. Maybe it is true that younger parents need generally more support and help from other people than do older parents. Parents and professional educators held rather similar views on preconditions and hindrances to establishing and maintaining cooperation between home and school.

In the opinion of both the groups, the cornerstone of successful home–daycare and home–preschool cooperation was what they referred to as functional cooperation, including listening to one another, engaging in discussions as equal participants, meeting together, providing information to one another, and expressing hopes about the child to one another. Other dimensions of functional cooperation included providing constructive feedback to one another in several forms, such as having the courage to take up problem issues with one another as they arise rather than letting them fester unspoken and unaddressed. Parents and teachers identified several other key ingredients of successful cooperation between home and daycare/preschool, including mutual openness, honesty and trust, shared ground rules, and respect for differing opinions. Two additional criteria emerged as well: peacefulness and tranquility were considered keys to successful cooperation. Furthermore, parents emphasized the significance of professional qualifications, permanence of staff, and adequate resources in the daycare and preschool sites.

Among the roadblocks to cooperation noted by parents and teachers were, for example, lack of commitment or effort toward cooperation; inadequate skills for interpersonal communication and cooperation; and prejudice or predetermined negative attitudes of one group toward the other. Parents and professional educators also recognized differences in their educational views. For instance, differences in their views on rules of behavior and accounting for each child's individual needs were considered hindrances to mutual cooperation (Niikko, 2004a; Niikko & Havu-Nuutinen, 2004; Seppälä, 2000).

## EARLY CHILDHOOD EDUCATION PERSONNEL
## AND DAILY WORK

Early childhood education provides socially and economically necessary services for the care, education (upbringing), and instruction (teaching) of the youngest citizens of Finland. Both parents and professional educators are widely viewed as having significant influence upon developmental and educational outcomes for the country's children. Finnish people believe that, by developing trusting and mutually respectful relationships with their parents and their teachers, children will have a strong foundation for optimal development, growth, and learning to learn throughout life's course.

In Finland, teachers who work in daycare, preschool, or primary school (grades 1–6) have different qualifications and duties (Asetus sosiaalihuollon ammatillisen henkilöstön kelpoisuusehdoista, 1992; Asetus kasvatustieteellisen alan tutkinnoista ja opettajankoulutuksesta, 1995; Perusopetusasetus, 1998). Preschool teachers and leaders of daycare centers are required to have a bachelor's degree (3 years at the university) in the discipline. Also qualified for these positions are social educators who have a degree from a polytechnic institute (3 years of study), with a minimum of 55 credits in early childhood education.

In the daycare center, preschool teachers are responsible for upbringing, care, teaching, planning, and evaluation in their classrooms. Moreover, their duties involve cooperation with parents, colleagues in the field, school teachers, public health nurses, and family care minders. In addition to these tasks, the leader's duties also include responsibility for general administration, development, and overall activities, as well as internal and external cooperation of the entire daycare center. In daycare centers with more than 100 children, the leader is not assigned to any group of children. According to the Act on Children's Day Care (Laki lasten päivähoidosta, 1973), the leader in these larger centers concentrates on the administration, management, and pedagogical leadership of the daycare center.

Assistants (assistant nurses or child minders), who work in support positions in the daycare center or preschool, have a diploma (study time, 3 years) from an institute of health or from a vocational school. Assistants work together with preschool teachers, participating in upbringing, caring, and teaching, as well as planning and evaluation. Prior to employment, family daycare minders must have passed a childcare course that requires a few weeks of study. A family daycare minder works as an independent municipal employee, usually in her own home, and she is responsible for pedagogical activities, providing meals, and cooperating with parents and the daycare center.

Preschool teachers are required to have a university degree with a specialization in preschool teaching. Primary school teachers (grades 1–6) are also qualified to teach at preschool. The duties of a preschool teacher include education (upbringing), planning and carrying out teaching, evaluation, and developing preschool curriculum, as well as cooperation with parents, daycare center, and primary school. Primary school teachers (grades 1–6) need to have a master's degree from a university.

Group size in Finnish daycare centers is set by national policy relating to the ages of the children. In full-time daycare centers, for every four children younger than 3 years of age and every seven children between the ages of 3 and 6, there must be at least one qualified preschool teacher and two assistants (assistant nurses or child minders) meeting the requirements of the Act on Children's Day Care (Laki Lasten päivähoidosta,1973, 1990) and in the Basic Education Decree (Perusopetusasetus, 1998). In part-time daycare for children from 3 to 6, and in preschool for 6-year-olds with daily attendance not exceeding 5 hours, the corresponding ratio is one preschool teacher and one assistant for 13 children.

Both private and municipally funded family daycare is regulated by the Decree on Children's Day Care. In daycare centers and family daycare settings, the majority of the teaching personnel are classified as preschool teachers and assistants (assistant nurses or child minders). The early childhood workforce in Finland is overwhelmingly female: only 4% of the employees are men (Ministry of Social Affairs and Health, 2000).

Since 1990, municipalities have had more authority to establish guidelines and standards for daycare centers and family daycare settings. Therefore, adult:child ratios, group sizes, adult qualifications, educational backgrounds, pedagogy, and teaching may vary from one municipality to another. Changing guidelines and the diversity of pathways into early childhood education have brought educational heterogeneity to the field and even to individual child care centers and preschools.

When staff members are likely to have different backgrounds, they may be especially well suited to assume different roles in the center. For instance, preschool teachers' expertise and educational background are in the field of pedagogy and teaching, whereas the expertise of assistants and daycare minders is more in the arena of social care and support (Välimäki, 1998; Karila & Nummenmaa, 2001). In practice, preschool teachers have the highest status in early childhood settings and they have a privileged position in comparison to the others. Preschool teachers have traditionally had responsibility for pedagogy and its development in early childhood settings.

The academic and professional background of preschool teachers can be traced back to the earliest days of early childhood education in Finland. Even today, preparation of preschool teachers emphasizes traditional philosophical and pedagogical perspectives and values. However, in recent years, early childhood research and educational science have started to play an increasingly important role in the education of prospective pre-school teachers. University students in the preschool teacher education departments are introduced to contemporary scientific thinking, research methods, and professional development as it supports and challenges tra-ditional ECE beliefs and practices.

Care is an essential dimension of ECE work, especially in daycare centers and family daycare settings, where emphasis is placed on promoting chil-dren's physical growth and health. In basic care settings, typical tasks include attending to children at meals, allowing children to play outdoors, toileting, washing, looking after cleanness, and the afternoon rest. The smaller the child, the more hours each day are spent on basic care (Hujala, Puroila, Par-rila-Haapakoski, & Nivala, 1998; Karila & Nummenmaa, 2001; Puroila, 2002). Tasks associated with basic caring are typically assigned to assistants rather than to preschool teachers, whose expertise lies more in the pedagog-ical and instructional realm (Niikko, 2005). Puroila's (2002) study on day-care center employees indicated that all professions considered children's well-being to be the most important factor in early childhood education. Unfortunately, though, the study did not clarify what participants meant by the term "well-being" or whether persons in different professional positions tended to have different views on the meaning of the term.

As noted above, the roles and responsibilities of various personnel in childcare settings have often been defined on the basis of their educational backgrounds as preschool teachers, assistants, or family child minders. However, a trend toward multidisciplinary professionalism has gained ground in recent years. In many forward-looking centers, the personnel for pedagogy and instruction and the personnel for care and caring are now forming multiprofessional communities of educators. These developments in professional practices result from a variety of interrelated factors, includ-ing changes within society, at work and in families, as well as in the need to address unexpected symptoms in children, policy mandates controlling group sizes and adult:child ratios, and frequent turnover of ECE staff (Bardy, Salmi, & Heino 2001; Jaakkola & Säntti, 2000; Karila & Nummen-maa, 2001).

Studies indicating disturbing changes in Finnish children, such as an increasing percentage of children who are insecure (Kekkonen, 2000; Laine & Neitola, 2002; Niikko & Havu-Nuutinen, 2004), have given rise to the multiprofessional approach. Among the symptoms of this insecurity evident in daycare and preschool settings are children's restlessness, increased need for physical contact with an adult, difficulty in accepting limits, bullying, and aggressiveness. The hope is that a multidisciplinary approach, where preschool teachers and assistants together share responsi-bility for all aspects of daily life in daycare and preschool settings, will lead to positive integration of experiences for children. Together these professionals will be able to attend, in a coordinated and integrated way, to children's general well-being and their social, emotional, and academic needs, as well as to developing cooperation with parents.

To implement more integrated and better coordinated early childhood education services, then, there is a need to move from the individual work of the past toward cooperation between professions and toward adopting a more comprehensive view of each professional's role as an educator (as preschool teacher, assistant, and primary teacher), in which personnel in each professional position share in the process of educating children (Hujala et al., 1998; Karila & Nummenmaa, 2001). All professional educators are supposed to have a holistic view of the child (Niikko, 2004b ; Sosiaali- ja terveysministeriö, 2002; Stakes, 2003). What is also necessary is to develop pedagogical awareness, which is said to be less structured in Finland than elsewhere (Huttunen, 1996).

Challenges to shift pedagogical practice from adult-centered to child-centered work require that professional educators adopt new strategies. A few studies on work practices in daycare centers and preschool have reported that what professional educators say differs from what they actually do in everyday practice (Huttunen, 1989; Niikko & Havu-Nuutinen, 2004; Poikonen, 2003). For example, early childhood educators typically reported that they acted in a child-centered way or that the starting point for their work was the child. However, observations of their everyday practices indicated that the way they worked with children remained, to a great extent, adult-centered. The primary function of early educators was to arrange activities for children to do individually or in groups.

The child-centered model emphasizes interacting with the child as an individual and as a subject. This means that the child interacts consciously and in a goal-oriented way with adults and other children. All children are treated as equals. They are listened to and take part in making decisions that concern then and, apart from this, their views are taken into account according to their age and stage of development. Child-centered work also emphasizes the role of the peer group as a contributor to each child's learning and development. In child-centered work, the teacher functions as a resource for the children's activities, but not always as the initiator and organizer of these activities. The adult tries to accurately interpret the children's actions and intentions and to interact with them throughout the day to foster coherence for each of them (Karila & Nummenmaa, 2001).

Furthermore, child-centered work emphasizes the *context* of growth, development, and learning. Here children's development, growth, and learning are to be seen from the viewpoint of their everyday life, including children's experiences at home and in the center, as well as children's experiences with adults and children in the community and the broader society. These contexts are not separate. Rather, they all interact with one another and with the developing child (Hujala et al., 1998; Pyykkö-Salpa-kivi-Vuorio, 1985; Ruoppila, 1984). Therefore, professional educators must pay attention to all of the contexts in which children live.

To transform this idealistic view on child-centeredness into reality, professional educators must first reassess their own pedagogical work, starting with everyday activities. Professional educators must be able to go beyond the context of the daycare center when analyzing their own work as educators, professionals, and teachers. Educators must really and truly involve children as equal partners in generating ideas for activities, as well as in planning and implementing these activities. Educators must see the difference between what they consider to be important to children and what children themselves consider important. Moreover, professional educators must also see each situation from the children's point of view and think of what children want to do and learn.

## CONCLUSION

The significance and responsibilities of daycare within Finnish society have changed dramatically in the past 30 years. Many developments in Finland mirror those in other Nordic countries in such arenas as daycare as social service, the structure of daycare provisions, the principle of integrated service, curriculum development, in-service training, cooperation between professionals and parents, and distribution of work responsibilities among professionals with different backgrounds. Developments in Finland also mirror those in other Nordic countries with regard to changes in philosophy, practical pedagogy, orientation toward child-centeredness, and the creation of umbrella entities responsible for various aspects of children's care, caring, education (upbringing), and instruction (teaching).

Introduction of the coined term "educare" is but one manifestation of efforts to coordinate, rather than separate, educational and caregiving aspects of professional work in early childhood settings. Although these trends are evident throughout the Nordic region, each Nordic country has, of course, implemented change in its own way (Alvestad, 2001; Broström, 2003; Johansson, 2003; Karlsson Lohmander & Pramling Samuelsson, 2003). For example, both Sweden and Finland have grappled with early childhood curriculum and cooperation issues. Finland focused especially on developing preschool programs for 6-year-olds, curricula, and principles for ECE pedagogy, while Sweden established an early childhood curriculum emphasizing academic and cognitive aspects for children beginning at age 3 (Alvestad, 2001). As another example, Norway has placed more emphasis on methods in its curriculum reforms (Johansson, 2003), while Finland has focused more on goals and content.

In Finnish daycare, the focal issue has been the confrontation between the public and the private, that is, the confrontation between the state and the family. The importance of childhood and, very recently, the relationship of education (upbringing) and instruction (teaching) have received considerable attention. Additional issues include the interests of the family as reflected in social policy, the interests of labor as reflected in educational policy, and the employment of women. In the earliest days of the development of early childhood education in Finland, the role of the state was to set a policy to be followed in detail by municipalities as they implemented various daycare provisions. Today, however, the state's primary role is to provide guidance, facilitate evaluation, and provide partial funding for childcare provisions as the municipalities see fit to develop them. In short, daycare is a statutory service, subsidized by the state that municipalities are obliged to arrange but that remains voluntary for children and families.

From the very beginning, Finnish daycare has been viewed as a *social care service* for families. The most basic task of daycare has been to respond to the childcare needs of Finnish families and to help them with their daily lives. Today, daycare is one of the services provided by Finland's modern welfare state. Daycare has gradually grown into a universal social and educational service for all children and families. As a social service, daycare is part of educational and family counseling, child protection, home care, and health service.

Originally, daycare provisions arose to address economic realities in a rapidly post-industrializing and changing nation. Parents needed to work. Working parents needed care for their children. The language of early regulations and policies focused on adults and their needs, not on children and their well-being and their good life. The child was regarded more as an object of care, education, and instruction than as an active participant in it. Over time, however, the child has become the centerpiece of childcare as it is described in official documents. Research shows that practitioners desire gradually to change their rhetoric, and, to a somewhat lesser extent, to modify their daily practice in the direction of more child-centeredness. In official pedagogical documents, children are increasingly seen as active participants in the settings where they find themselves— home, school, and community. They are more and more thought of as active and capable learners, not as an age or a stage or a number to be counted in adult:child ratios or group sizes.

Over the course of recent decades, the social care task of daycare has acquired a new educational dimension. This tendency has been visible in Norway, too (Johansson, 2003). In Finland in the 1980s, as a result of a political compromise, educational reforms attempted to harmonize the relationship between families and daycare provisions. Early childhood education became an umbrella term for all educational, social, and childcare services to children below school-start age. The underlying idea was to achieve consensus between professional educators and parents through their interactions and cooperative efforts. The reforms emphasized the primary role of parents as educators of their own children. While there is widespread acclamation of this principle, there is also widespread disagreement about how much responsibility early childhood professionals bear for the upbringing of Finnish children.

At the beginning of the new millennium, daycare services grew into *universal early childhood education services,* the primary task of which is to support the child's holistic growth, development, and learning and to support parents in their roles as educators. From the point of view of those providing ECE services, parents have both the right and the duty to raise their children; but when children are in daycare or preschool, the professional educators share these responsibilities with parents. The new unified-services approach means that various childhood services, including health care center, daycare, preschool, and primary school, are now integrated into a carefully sequenced and articulated whole.

In Finland, the goal is to create a seamless whole from the three levels of early childhood education: (1) services for children between birth and 6 years, (2) preschool services for children in the year prior to their school-start, and (3) the continuity from preschool to compulsory school. Guiding principles and curricula have been designed to facilitate children's movement from one stage to the next as an uninterrupted sequence.

Although the four dimensions—well-being, "all-around care," caring, and care—are visible in Finnish daycare, it is, however, care that has received the primary emphasis (Niikko, 2005). The same phenomenon seems to be true in Denmark (Broström, 2003). Care was and still is determined by the children's age and physical needs. In other words, the smaller the child, the more attention is paid to care. Those employed in early childhood settings are to have appropriate qualifications for their duties in care and education (Asetus sosiaalihuollon ammatillisen henkilöstön kelpoisuusehdoista, 1992).

Just as these four dimensions of care have long been central in Finnish approaches to early childhood education, so too the division of responsibility and the division of labor among professional positions have long-standing history in Finland. Care and caring have historically been the responsibility of the less educated members of the staff, such as assistants (assistant nurses or child minders), while tasks associated with teaching and learning have been the purview of the more educated preschool teachers. In Finland and in Sweden where similar divisions of labor have long existed (Karlsson Lohmander & Pramling Samuelsson, 2003), differences in assigned duties arose from a variety of historical, political, educational, and attitudinal factors in ECE rather than from real attention to children and their needs. Recent years, though, have witnessed a trend toward greater interdisciplinarity in the assignment of duties within childcare settings and, hence, a greater sharing of roles and responsibilities among staff members with diverse educational and experiential backgrounds.

Current changes in society, working life, and families, along with results from recent pedagogical studies, are central topics of discussion in contemporary Finnish daycare settings. Although care, education, and instruction form one entity in educare thinking, learning is nevertheless considered the domain of the compulsory school, rather than daycare or preschool. Educare has been more about separating care and education than about unifying them. This may have been due to the long-established practices, such as occupational diversification and consequent separation of duties, as well as to differences among various early childhood professionals in their appreciation for care and education. It is said that educare thinking has slowed down the development of preschool. The educare concept is mainly used by researchers and shunned by people working in the field. Given the many and various ways in which the term is used, its meaning remains unclear.

At the moment, one of the major tasks in Finnish early childhood education is to develop better cooperation between parents and early childhood educators and to involve parents in more meaningful ways in decision making in daycare, preschool, and primary school. Professional educators will increasingly have to listen to parents' views about educational issues and to share responsibility for care, education, and instruction with parents. Professional educators must learn to regard parents as resources for educational work, not just as users of care services. Modern views assert that early childhood education is basically a joint communal activity in which professional educators, parents, and other related people contribute to the ultimate outcome—what is best for children and their future life.

## REFERENCES

Alestalo, M. (1986). *Structural change, classes and state: Finland in a historical and comparative perspective. Research group for comparative sociology* (Research reports 13). Helsinki: University of Helsinki.

Alasuutari, M. 2003. *Kuka lasta kasvattaa* [Who brings up the child]. Helsinki: Gaudeamus.

Anttonen, A., & Sipilä, J. (1994). Viisi sosiaalipalvelumallia: Eurooppalaisten hyvinvointivaltioiden vertailua sosiaalipalvelujen näkökulmasta [Five models of social service: Comparing European welfare states from the point of view of social services]. *Janus*, 3, 226–248.

*Asetus kasvatustieteellisen alan tutkinnoista ja opettajankoulutuksesta. Nr. 576/1995* [Decree in education and teacher education. No 576/1995].

*Asetus sosiaalihuollon ammatillisen henkilöstön kelpoisuusehdoista. Nr 804/1992* [Decree on the professional qualifications of social welfare personnel. No 804/1992].

Alvestad, M. (2001). *Den komplekse planlegginga: Forskolelaerarar om pedagogisk planlegging og praksis* [Complex planning: Pre-school teachers on pedagogical planning; in Swedish]. Göteborg: Acta universitatis Gothoburgensis.

Bardy, M., Salmi, M., & Heino, T. (2001). *Mikä lapsiamme uhkaa?* [What threatens our children?] (Report 263). Helsinki: Stakes.

Ben-Peretz, M. (1996). 'Women as teachers: Teachers as women'. In I. F. Goodson & A. Hargreaves (Eds.), *Teachers' professional lives* (pp. 178–186). London: Falmer Press.

Bronfenbrenner, U. (1979). *The ecology of human development.* Cambridge, MA: Harward University Press.

Broström, S. (2003). Unity of care, teaching and upbringing—A theoretical contribution towards a new paradigm in early childhood education. In M. Karlsson Lohmander (Ed.), *Researching early childhood: Care, play and learning curricula for early childhood education* (pp. 21–38). Sweden: Göteborg University, Early Childhood Research and Development Centre.

Estola, E. (2003). *In the language of the mother—re-storying the relational moral in teachers' stories.* Finland: University of Oulu.

Hargreaves, A. (1994). *Changing teachers, changing times: Teachers' work and culture in the postmodern age.* London: Cassell Wellington House.

Hargreaves, A., & Tucker, E. (1991). Teaching and guilt: Exploring the feelings of teaching. *Teaching and Teacher Education,* 7, 491–505.

Havu, S. 2000. *Changes in children's conceptions through social interaction in pre-school science education* (Publications in Education 60). Finland: University of Joensuu.

Hujala, E., Puroila, A-M., Parrila-Haapakoski, S., & Nivala, V. (1998). *Päivähoidosta varhaiskasvatukseen* [From daycare to early childhood education]. Jyväskylä: Gummerus.

Huttunen, E. (1984). *Perheen ja päivähoidon yhteistyö kasvatuksen ja lapsen kehityksen tukijana* [Cooperation between the family and daycare and how it supports education and the child's development] (Publications in Education 2). Finland: University of Joensuu.

Huttunen, E. (1989). *Päivähoidon toimiva arki. Varhaiskasvatuksen käytäntöjen kehittäminen* [Everyday life in daycare: Developing the practices of early childhood education]. Jyväskylä: Gummerus.

Huttunen, E. (1996). Day care in the USA, Russia and Finland: Views from parents, teachers and directors. *European Early Childhood Education Research Journal,* 4, 33–47.

Hänninen, S.-L., & Valli, S. 1986. *Suomen lastentarhatyön ja varhaiskasvatuksen historia* [The history of Finnish kindergarten and early childhood education]. Helsinki: Otava.

Jaakkola, R., & Säntti, R. (2000). *Uusperheiden lapset ja vanhemmat. Perheiden rakenne, toiminta ja talous* [Children and parents of new families. Families'struture, action and economy] (Report 174). Helsinki: National Research Institute of Legal Policy.

Johansson, J.-E. (2003). The Norwegian early child education and care curriculum—Background and comments. In M. Karsson Lohmander (Ed.), *Researching early childhood, care, play and learning: Curricula for early childhood education* (pp. 83–107). Sweden: Göteborg University. Early Childhood Research and development Centre.

Julkunen, R. (1991). Hoiva ja professionalismi [Caring and professionalism]. *Sosiologia*, *2*, 75–83.

Juujärvi, S. (2003). *The ethic of care and its development: A longitudinal study among practical nursing, Bachelor-degree social work and law enforcement students* (Department of Social Psychology Studies 8). Helsinki: University of Helsinki.

Karila, K., & Nummenmaa, A.-R. (2001). *Matkalla moniammatillisuuteen. Kuvauskohteena päiväkoti* [Towards multiprofessionalism as exemplified by the daycare centre]. Juva: Wsoy.

Karlsson Lohmander, M., & Pramling Samuelsson, I. (2003). Is it possible to integrate care, play and learning in early childhood education? In M. Karsson Lohmander (Ed.), *Researching early childhood: Care, play and learning curricula for early childhood education* (pp. 95–110). Sweden: Göteborg University. Early Childhood Research and development Centre.

Kekkonen, M. (2000). *Perusturvallisuus päiväkodiss.* [Basic security in the kindergarten]. Helsinki: Union of Health Care and Social Professionals.

*Komiteamietintö. 1980:31* [Committee Report 1980:31]. Helsinki: They.

Kortteinen, M. (1982). *Lähiö. Tutkimus elämäntapojen muutoksest* [The housing estate: A study on changes in the way of life]. Keuruu: Otava.

Laine, K., & Neitola, M. (2002). *Lasten syrjäytyminen päiväkodin vertaisryhmästä* [Exclusion of children from their peer group in kindergarten]. Turku: Suomen Kasvatustieteellinen seura.

*Laki lasten huollosta ja tapaamisoikeudesta. Nr. 361/1983* [Act on Child Care and the Right to Meet One's Children No 361/1983].

Laki lasten päivähoidosta Nr. 36/1973. Nr. 451/1990 [Act on Children's Day Care No 361/1973, No 451/1990].

*Lastensuojelulaki Nr. 683/1983* [Child Welfare Act No 683/1983].

Ministry of Social Affairs and Health (2000a). *Early childhood education and care policy in Finland. Background report prepared for the OECD. Thematic review of early childhood education and care policy.* Helsinki: Ministry of Social Affairs and Health.

Ministry of Social Affairs and Health (2000b). *Early childhood education and care policy in Finland. Report 21.* Retrieved December 21, 2004, from http://pre20031103 .stm.fi/english/pao/publicat/pacontents52.html

*Muutos lakiin lasten päivähoidosta Nr 304/1983* [Amendment to the act on children's day care 304/1983]

Niikko, A. (2003). *Lastentarhanopettajat tulevina kasvattajina* [Preschool teacher students as future educators] (Research Reports of the Faculty of Education 84). Finland: University of Joensuu.

Niikko, A. (2004a). Education—a joint task for parents, preschool teachers and kindergarten student teachers. *International Journal of Early Years Education*, *12*, 260–274.

Niikko, A. (2004b). Varhaiskasvatuksen ydintä etsimässä. [Looking for the core of early childhood education]. In J. Enkenberg, E. Savolainen, & P. Väisänen (Eds.), *Tutkiva opettajankoulutus—taitava opettaja [Studying teacher education—skilfull teacher]* (pp. 222–234). Joensuu: University Press.

Niikko, A. (2005). *Suorittavasta hoidosta eettiseen huolenpitopedagogiikan toteuttamiseen* [From routine mechanical care to implementing ethical pedagogy of care] (Research Reports for the Faculty of Education 94]. Finland: University of Joensuu.

Niikko, A., & Havu-Nuutinen, S. (2004). *Esiopetuksen laatu. Liperin kunnan esiopetuksen arviointi 2002–2003* [Quality of pre-school education. An evaluation of pre-school education in the municipality of Liperi 2002–2003]. Joensuu: Yliopistopaino.

Opetushallitus (2000). *Esiopetuksen opetussuunnitelman perusteet* [The principles for the curriculum in preschool]. Helsinki: Opetushallitus.

Opetushallitus (2003). *Peruskoulun opetussuunnitelman perusteet* [The principles for the curriculum in primary school]. Helsinki: Opetushallitus.

Puroila, A.-M. (2002). *Kohtaamisia päiväkotiarjessa—kehysanalyyttinen näkökulma varhaiskasvatustyöhön* [Everyday encounters in daycare centers—a frame analysis of early childhood work]. Oulu: University Press.

*Peruskoululaki Nr. 476/1983* [Comprehensive School Act. No 476/1983].

*Perusopetuslaki Nr. 628/1998* [Basic Education Act. No 628/1998].

*Perusopetusasetus Nr. 986/1998* [Basic Education Decree. No 986/1998].

Poikonen, P.L. (2003).*"Opetussuunnitelma on sitä elämää." Päiväkotihenkilöstö opetussuunnitelman kehittäjän.* ["The curriculum is part of our daily life." Daycare-cum-primary school community as a curriculum developer] (Studies in Education, Psychology and Social Research 230). Finland: University of Jyväskylä.

Pyykkö-Salpakivi-Vuorio, A. (1985). *Päivähoidon kasvatustoiminta* [Pedagogy of daycare]. Rauma: Kirjayhtymä.

Reuna, V. 1999. *Perhebarometri 1999. Vanhemmuutta toteuttamassa* [Family barometer 1999. Being a parent]. Helsinki: Väestöliitto.

Rinn, R., & Jauhiainen, A. (1989). *Kulutus, professionaalistuminen ja valtio. Julkisen sektorin koulutettujen reproduktioammattikuntien muodostuminen Suomessa* [Consumption, professionalism and the state: Emergence of educated professions of reproduction in the public sector in Finland]. Turun yliopisto. Kasvatustieteiden tiedekunta, A:128. Finland: University of Turku.

Ruoppila, I. (1984). Varhaiskasvatus elämänkaaritutkimuksen valossa [Early childhood education in the light of life curve research]. In M. Ojala (Ed.), *Early childhood education research in Finland* (pp. 239–261). Helsinki: Lastensuojelun Keskusliitto.

Sarvimäki, A., & Stenbock-Hult, B. 1996. *Hoito, huolenpito ja opetus* [Care, all round care and teaching]. Porvoo: Wsoy.

Seppälä, N. (2000). *Yhteispelillä lapsen parhaaksi. Perhebarometri 2000* [With cooperation for the best of the child. Family barometer 2000]. Helsinki: Väestöliitto.

Sosiaali- ja terveysministeriö (2002.) *Varhaiskasvatuksen valtakunnalliset linjaukset* [National policy definition on early childhood education and care]. Sosiaali- ja terveysministeriön julkaisuja 9. Finland. Ministry of Social Affairs and Health.

Stakes (2003). *Varhaiskasvatussuunnitelman perusteet* [Principles of early childhood education plan]. Saarijärvi: Gummerus.

Stakes (2000). *Lapset päivähoidossa 1997-*2003 [Children in daycare 1997-2003] Retrieved December 21, 2004, from http:// stakes.fi/varttua/tyopouta/tilastoja/paivahoito_tilasto.pdf

Tilastokeskus (2004). *Miehet ja naiset tilastoina* [Men and women as statistics]. Retrieved December 21, 2004, from http://www.stat.fi/tk/he/tasaarvo.html

Välimäki, A.-L. 1998. *Päivittäin. Lasten (päivä)hoitojärjestelyn muotoutuminen varhaiskasvun ympäristönä suomalaisessa yhteiskunnassa 1800- ja 1900-luvulla* [Every day. The evolution of the children's (day)-care system as an environment for early growth in Finnish society in the 19th and 20th centuries]. Acta Universitatis Ouluensis. E 31. Oulun: University of Oulun.

CHAPTER 7

# BETWEEN TWO CONTINENTS, BETWEEN TWO TRADITIONS

## Education and Care in Icelandic Preschools

**Johanna Einarsdottir**
*Iceland University of Education*

Early childhood education in Iceland can be traced to the beginning of urbanization in the 1920s, when the Women's Alliance in Reykjavík opened the first full-time daycare center for poor children. In 1940 a new part-time program, called playschool, emerged in Iceland. Daycare centers were full-time programs and limited their enrollment to priority groups, such as children from poor or single-parent homes, while playschools were half-day programs open to everyone. The Women's Alliance continued to provide playschools and daycare centers for the next 30 years until, in 1973, both were integrated under the Ministry of Education. This represented an important shift. The care and education of children prior to compulsory school was no longer viewed as social policy geared especially toward poor children. Preschool, regardless of whether it was full or part time, was now

*Nordic Childhoods and Early Education*, pages 159–182
Copyright © 2006 by Information Age Publishing
All rights of reproduction in any form reserved.

a part of the nation's education policy (Lög um hlutdeild ríkisins í byggingu og rekstri dagvistunarheimila. Nr. 43/1973).

The concepts of daycare centers and playschools were used for early childhood education programs in Iceland until 1991. Since then the term *playschool* has been used for all early education programs for children up to 6 years old prior to the age of compulsory education (Lög um leikskóla. Nr. 48/1991). In 1994 playschool education became by law the first level of schooling in Iceland, although it was neither compulsory nor free of charge (Lög um leikskóla. Nr. 78/1994). Although the term *playschool* (leikskóli) is used throughout Iceland to this day, I will use the term *preschool* in this chapter for the sake of consistency with other chapters.

Preschools in Iceland today are intended for children under 6 years old or until they go to primary school in the fall of the year in which they turn 6 (Lög um leikskóla no. 78/1994). Most children start preschool when they are 2 or 3 years old. Approximately 94% of children age 3–5, 90% of two-year-olds, and 27% of children younger than 2 years of age attended preschools in 2004 (Hagstofa Íslands, 2005). Attendance rates have been rising in recent years primarily because most mothers are in the workforce, but also because of the increasing recognition of preschool as an important part of children's lives.

Local authorities supervise the building and operation of most preschools and bear the expenses involved. Parents' contributions cover roughly 30% of operation costs, except for the oldest children for whom preschool is, in most municipalities, free of charge for 4 hours a day. Icelandic preschools today vary in size, from one-classroom preschools with only a few children to a six-classroom preschool with 180 children. However, most preschools range from 40–90 children, with approximately 20 in each classroom. The children are sometimes grouped by chronological age, but in other instances, there are mixed-age groups, with, for example, 3-, 4-, and 5-year-olds together in groups, or 2- and 3-year-olds may be placed in one group, while 4- and 5-year-olds are in another group. Children can attend preschool from 4 to a maximum of 9 hours a day. The teacher:child ratio varies by age in accordance with legislation, from 1:5 for the youngest children rising to 1:10 for the oldest children (Reglugerð um starfsemi leikskóla, Nr. 225/1995; Reglugerð Nr. 642/2002 um breytingu á reglugerð um starfsemi leikskóla Nr. 225/1995). The Ministry of Education formulates an educational policy for the preschools and publishes the *Preschool National Curriculum Guidelines* (Ministry of Education, 1999).

As indicated by the name "playschool," free play occupies a central and honored role in Icelandic preschool programs. However, some observers have noted recent incursions by more structure and formal instruction. In addition, politicians place growing demands on preschool to include more academic subjects. While this observation alarms early childhood educators, the phenomenon cannot yet be described as a trend or pattern.

Another serious threat to Iceland's preschool system today is the lack of qualified preschool teachers. In 2004, only 28% of the educational personnel in preschools were certified preschool teachers (Hagstofa Íslands, 2005). In practice, this means that the most educated preschool teachers are in administrative positions, while the least educated staff members work with the children.

Iceland's geographic location has played a significant role in virtually all aspects of life, including the development of early education policy and practice. Located in the Atlantic Ocean midway between Europe and America, Iceland is distanced from most of the other Nordic countries, including, Norway, Sweden, Finland, and Denmark. While Iceland remains fundamentally Nordic in many respects, cultural influences from both North America and Europe are evident. Waves of contemporary educational thought wash ashore from both continents as well.

In this chapter I describe and analyze early childhood education in Iceland. I describe the various contexts in which early childhood education occurs today, including the broad cultural context, as well as the educational context, including the foundations of early childhood education, the laws, and the national curriculum. Additionally, I examine both distinct features and current dilemmas facing the Icelandic preschool.

## CONTEXT

Researchers have pointed out that a variety of contexts affect school practices, including both curriculum and pedagogy (Bloch, 1987; Bresler, 1998; Goffin, 1989; Goldstein, 1997). Graue and Walsh (1998) defined context as a "culturally and historically situated place and time, a specific here and now" (p. 9) and they maintained that children and early childhood education are never untouched by these contexts. Alexander (2000) observed that schools and classrooms are microcultures in their own right and that they combine the messages and requirements from the larger culture, while adding some of their own. Results from a recent study on preschool teachers in Iceland showed the influence of different contexts on the curriculum, the teaching methods, and the preschool teachers' beliefs and goals. The following interrelated and overlapping contexts influenced each other: the culture of the preschool; the educational context, which overlapped with the preschool context; and the cultural context of Iceland, which influenced the values manifested in the other contexts (Einarsdottir, 2002).

## Cultural Context

Spodek and Saracho (1996) observed that as various early childhood programs have evolved around the world, they have been both modified by and adapted to prevailing cultural beliefs. Spodek (1991) suggested that the content of all education is culturally defined, traditionally in terms of how each society defines the ideals of truth, virtue, and beauty. Therefore, the specific cultural content of preschools in one society will not be found in the curriculum of preschools in other societies.

Other authors have suggested that cultural beliefs and values affect teachers' view of children and their own pedagogical practice. For example, Bruner (1986) proposed that culture is central in shaping human life and the human mind. He used the term *folk psychology* for the underlying beliefs in a culture about human tendencies and beliefs about how our own mind and the minds of others work. Bruner and Olson (1996) suggested that teachers' folk psychology is reflected in their teaching. That is, the beliefs and values of the culture affect the beliefs and values of the individual and those, in turn, affect the curriculum and the teacher's methods. Thus, teachers' folk pedagogy reflects their folk psychology.

Cultural psychologists have identified significant variations in childhood worlds across human populations, as well as differing beliefs about childrearing and interpersonal relationships (Kagitchibasi, 1996; Kitayama & Markus, 1999; Shweder et al., 1998). These culture-specific differences in childrearing practices and believes, in turn, influence, both directly and indirectly, various aspects of children's lives in each culture. For instance, studies on early childhood teachers in different cultures have shown that early childhood programs have their roots in cultural beliefs and the values of the larger culture (Carlson, 1997; Cuffaro, 1997; Einarsdottir, 1998, 2002; Lee & Walsh, 2001; Tobin, Wu, & Davidson, 1989; Wollons, 2000). This influence of culture, both present and historical, can be seen in numerous aspects of contemporary childhood and early childhood education in Iceland.

The Icelandic culture can be traced back to the 9th century when a group of independent people left Norway to escape the oppressive dominance of King Harald the Fair-Haired, who unified Norway, and the heavy taxation he forced upon his subjects. They sailed westward on the Atlantic Ocean for about 600 miles and settled on a geographically isolated island where it seemed almost impossible to live because of the cold climate and harsh nature, including volcanic eruptions and drift ice.

The first settlers in Iceland were farmers, fishing was a sideline, and the country was predominantly rural until the beginning of the 20th century. Children had responsibilities to contribute to the work of the family, but they were also allowed to play freely in nature. The industrial revolution arrived late in Iceland, and the changes it created were unusually sharp and sudden as the society was transformed from predominantly rural to urban and industrialized in only a few decades. Reykjavík became the only city and people moved there from the farms. As Reykjavík grew rapidly, proper housing was in short supply and many people lived in poverty.

The economy changed dramatically in a very short time. Iceland, one of the poorest nations in Europe in the beginning of the 20th century, rapidly became one of the highest ranked nations in prosperity and standard of living (Ólafsson, 1996). Currently, more than 90% of Iceland's people live in urban areas, with approximately 62% of the population in the Reykjavík metropolitan area, an urban setting with most of the advantages and disadvantages of modern urban life (Reykjavíkurborg, 2002).

Assessment of one's own culture can be problematic due to the potential for oversimplification and generalization. Still, one could expect to find broad agreement, by Icelanders and others who know us well, that Icelanders typically are quite proud of their country, especially the bounty and beauty of its nature. Icelanders highly value the ancient culture, the sagas, the language, and the literary heritage. As one of the world's least populated and geographically most distinctive countries, we are also proud of our economic success and welfare system.

According to a European value survey, Icelanders form strong bonds to their land, stronger than other Europeans (Halman, 2001). Among the apparent characteristics of the modern Icelandic society are an individualist approach to life, as well as openness to modern ways of life and technical advances. In many commentaries, Icelanders are depicted as particularly independent, freedom-loving individualists (Lacy, 1998; Ólafsson, 1989). Foreigners living and conducting research in Iceland have, however, noticed that, for Icelanders, maintaining individuality also means taking responsibility (Cuffaro, 1997; Lacy, 1998).

Recent surveys of the values of life in modern societies (Halman, 2001; Jónsson & Ólafsson, 1991), revealed ways in which Icelanders are both similar to and different from people in the other Nordic countries. Often these differences were a matter of degree, rather than radical disparity. Survey participants were asked to choose among values that emphasized individual freedom, on one hand, and equality, on the other hand. Unlike people from other Nordic countries, Icelanders rated equality slightly higher than individual freedom. In spite of this, however, Icelanders were much more in favor of competition and private enterprise rather than public enterprise in the workforce than were respondents from other Nordic nations. Icelanders also had a stronger belief that hard work leads to success.

Historically, Icelandic children have enjoyed a great deal of freedom and have often been left to their own devices throughout much of the day.

School-age children were frequently left unsupervised during the day; and from a young age, children have taken care of their younger siblings. Likewise, children have been allowed to play freely outdoors for hours without adult guidance. Research has shown that Icelanders value children's freedom, and believe that freedom to play and explore the environment without adult supervision is an essential aspect of growing up (Kristjánsson, 1991). Compared to the other Nordic countries, Icelandic children enjoy more freedom from an early age (Kristinsdóttir, 2000); and according to the European value study, Icelanders place more emphasis on teaching children the value of both hard work and independence (Halman, 2001).

In spite of Icelanders' long history of giving children freedom to play unsupervised and explore their natural environments on their own, both parents and educators today express some concern over these cultural traditions. On one hand, they want Icelandic children to be able to play and explore freely in their daily activities; but on the other hand, they worry that they are leaving the children with too little supervision. Concerned Icelanders say that Icelanders today still do not know how to live in a city. They claim that they raise their children as though they were still living on farms, but without the adults' supervision that was provided when the parents' work was in the home and the farmland immediately around it.

## Educational Context

Rapid urbanization in the first decades of the 20th century changed the living conditions of Icelandic children dramatically and created the need for out-of-home care. The aim of the first daycare centers was to provide shelter, warmth, and wholesome nourishment for poor children to ensure their health and hygiene (Barnavinafélagið Sumargjöf, 1974). Children in these daycare centers typically were cared for by personnel with no professional background. Prior to 1946, when the Pedagogical College was established, only four women had received some training in working with preschool children (Einarsdottir, 2004a). The establishment of the Pedagogical College marked the beginning of professionalization for both preschool teachers and preschool teacher educators.

*Foundations of Early Childhood Education.* When daycare centers and playschools were first established in Iceland, various types of early childhood programs had already evolved throughout the world. In the earliest days, Icelandic preschool philosophy and practice were influenced by Nordic traditions, British ideas, and American theory and practice. Unlike preschool movements in many parts of the Western world at that time, Froebel's German kindergarten model had little influence, in spite of its influence in the other Nordic countries (Haug, 1993; Honkavaara, 1998;

Johansson, 1998; Lenz Taguchi & Munkammar, 2003; Lund, 1998). Froebel's "gifts" and "occupations" were, for example, rarely used in Icelandic preschools. Instead, Iceland looked to other philosophies for inspiration. For instance, the first specially designed building for a daycare center, built in 1931, was designed after the British nursery school model, as a result of a London visit by Steingrímur Arason, an influential Icelandic educator. He found the nursery school model, with the emphasis on fresh air and nutrition, appropriate for the deprived Icelandic children who attended daycare centers (Sigurðardóttir, 1998, 1999).

Valborg Sigurðardóttir, the pioneer in the field of Icelandic early childhood education and the first director of the Pedagogical College, completed her master's degree in education and child psychology in the United States in 1945. There, she became familiar with the leading theories of the day and introduced some of them into Icelandic practice when she returned to her homeland. Child development theories, especially Gesell's maturationist theory, dominated the Icelandic preschool movement in its infancy. Hence, when the Pedagogical College was established, the curriculum strongly reflected American traditions and trends, as well as Nordic ideas and practices. The Social Pedagogical Seminar in Stockholm, where child development theories were in the foreground, also served as a model (Einarsdottir, 2004a).

Hence, during the first years of preschool in Iceland, theory and practice represented an amalgam of British and American ideas within the context of decidedly Nordic cultural influence. In 1950 the Preschool Teachers Union was founded and and became a part of the Nordic Preschool Teachers Association and emphasized cooperation with them. Thus, Nordic influence on the Icelandic preschool has evolved and has become more evident throughout the years. In the 1970s, Jean Piaget's theory of intellectual development came to prominence in many parts of the world, including the Nordic countries. The curriculum at the College of Preschool Teachers incorporated Piaget's theories, thereby influencing future generations of Icelandic early childhood educators. The influence of Piaget's theories was very much evident in the first Educational Plan for preschools published in 1985 (Ministry of Education, 1985).

*Current Influences.*   In increasing numbers through the years Icelanders have pursued graduate studies abroad. Early childhood educators often receive their further education in other Nordic countries, as well as in Britain and the United States. As a result, contemporary Icelandic philosophy and practice bear noticeable stamps from both continents, Europe and North America. In fact, many innovations and foreign influences in Iceland can be traced directly to a particular Icelander's graduate study abroad. For example, Caroline Pratt's unit blocks came to Iceland through New York and were introduced in an in-service course in 1991. Since then, preschool education programs have offered a course in block building as unit blocks have joined other standard classroom materials in Icelandic preschools. During the 1980s the High/Scope approach, created in America, found its way into Icelandic preschool practice (Hohmann, Banet, & Weikart, 1979). Although Icelandic early educators did not adopt all of High/Scope's features, they did incorporate one of its central requirements: that children be offered meaningful choices about what they want to do and how they want to do it, within a structured framework established by the teacher. Traces of High/Scope can still be seen in today's Icelandic preschools, especially in the ways teachers offer children choices about which activities they prefer.

In 1993, the idea of emerging literacy through play was introduced in two preschools (Einarsdottir, 1996, 2000). Previously, the Icelandic preschool environment did not include much print or other literacy-development material, except for children's literature. Through teacher development and in-service education programs, practices associated with emerging literacy through play have spread to many preschools. Today, one can see play activities that incorporate early literacy experiences. For example, preschool teachers regularly encourage children to use letters and printed materials in their play.

Italy's Reggio Emilia approach came to Iceland through Sweden. In recent years, groups of early childhood educators have visited Reggio Emilia, and, as a result, many preschools are adopting ideas from Reggio Emilia, especially the emphasis on art and documentation of children's activities. The Project approach, coming directly from Lilian Katz at the University of Illinois, is now a part of the preschool teacher education curriculum and is increasingly being used in Icelandic preschools. While the Montessori method featuring structured material and activities has never taken root in Iceland, three preschools have implemented Steiner's pedagogical ideas. Among the elements of the Steiner's Waldorf approach these preschools have adapted are the emphasis on natural play materials, emotions, and rhythm.

Preschools in Iceland, then, typically include eclectic practices that have been brought to Iceland's shores from abroad for nearly seven decades, often by a few Icelandic educators who were introduced to new ideas through study abroad. Early childhood educators have chosen from these ideas what they find fitting with their own ideas about what is good for children and what should be emphasized in preschool education. The strong Icelandic notion that children should have a great deal of freedom may explain why preschool teachers were attracted to child choice in High/Scope and specific aspects of Waldorf's approach rather than to the more structured Montessori method. However, in spite of these many and varied foreign influences, Icelandic preschools retain characteristically Nordic qualities. These qualities may, indeed, provide a philosophical and methodological foundation that enables Iceland's early educators to weave coherent early childhood practices from a cloth of many different colors.

*Laws and National Curriculum.*  The activity of the charitable women who fed and sheltered poor children in the 1920s has now evolved into the first level of schooling in Iceland. The Preschool Teacher's Union views the opportunity to attend preschool as a basic human right for all children. The union argues that the first priority of local municipalities should be to ensure that there are enough preschool spaces for all children to attend (Félag íslenskra leikskólakennara, 2000).

Icelandic preschool education laws state the following overarching aim: that children should be provided with emotional and physical care so they can enjoy their childhood. Preschools should support children's overall development, as well as their broad-mindedness and tolerance. Christian values should be inspired. In addition, preschool should lay the foundation for children to be independent, active, and responsible participants in a democratic society (Lög um leikskóla Nr. 78/1994, article 2). These aims are reflected in the *National Curriculum Guidelines* and in the policy of the Preschool Teacher's Union. The education of preschool teachers also builds on the law of preschool education and the *National Curriculum.*

The current *National Curriculum* was published in 1999 by the Ministry of Education and is a policy-setting guideline for pedagogical work in preschools. It is meant to provide a flexible framework, not specific content, for preschools throughout Iceland. According to the *Curriculum,* preschool education should encourage the development of the whole child and emphasize creative activities, such as art, drama, and music. According to the *Curriculum,* play is the foundation for children's learning and development, and should therefore be the central and predominant feature of children's preschool experience. In addition, the *Curriculum* underscores the following themes: movement, the cultivation of the native language, creative arts, music, nature and the environment, and culture and the society. These themes fuse and are integrated with other basic activities such as play, daily care, and life learning skills. The *Curriculum* also stresses the importance of life skills. Among the essential life skills to be experienced directly in preschool are those associated with participation in a democratic society. Icelandic children should play an active role in making plans for their school day, making decisions, and evaluating situations as they arise. Life skills also encompass social competencies, such as following rules, resolving disputes peacefully, and respecting the rights of others. The *Curriculum* also emphasizes the learning that takes place during routine activities, such as meal times, where children practice manners, conventions, and social skills. Based on the broad guidelines in the *Curriculum,* each preschool develops its own educational plan. One preschool may, for instance, put special emphasis on music this year, while another preschool might emphasize nature or the environment.

## FEATURES AND DILEMMAS IN ICELANDIC PRESCHOOLS

During the last decade, I have conducted several studies on the pedagogical practices of Icelandic preschools (Einarsdottir, 1998, 2002, 2003, 2004b). Below I present an overview of findings from these studies, with the aim of describing characteristics and dilemmas facing the Icelandic preschool today. The purpose of the first study (Einarsdottir, 1998) was several fold: to learn about the role of educational personnel in children's dramatic play, to investigate how early childhood teachers intervened or participated in children's dramatic play, and to understand practitioners' attitudes and opinions concerning children's dramatic play, as well as their views of their own roles and functions in relation to dramatic play. The second study (Einarsdottir, 2002) investigated, through participant observation and interviews, the working methods of two Icelandic preschool teachers, their beliefs about early childhood education, and the goals of their program. Using focus groups consisting of early childhood educators, the purpose of the third study (Einarsdottir, 2003) was to investigate how Icelandic preschool teachers, especially those with extensive academic and professional preparation, view early childhood education and the role of the preschool teacher. The most recent study was a qualitative study describing in detail the pedagogy and beliefs of two preschool teachers (Einarsdottir, 2004).

Findings from these studies, taken together, reveal both general characteristics and contemporary dilemmas facing Icelandic preschools. For instance, results indicate that a large proportion of a typical Icelandic preschool day is devoted to free play and free choice, that is, activities that the children choose themselves. The school day is typically divided into four kinds of activities: (1) activities that are planned and chosen by the children, such as free play, outside or inside play, and free choice; (2) activities preplanned by the teachers for small groups of children; (3) group time, where the whole group is together, for example, singing, listening to a story, doing a calendar, or sharing information; and (4) routine activities including lunch and rest.

Findings also reveal several trends and patterns in the daily schedules. Icelandic children typically have breakfast and a free play period when they arrive at the preschool in the morning. A typical morning at an Icelandic preschool might reveal some children sitting quietly looking at books, other children making a mad dash to join a group of friends in a chase game, and still others sitting at a table drawing. Breakfast is available for those children who want to eat and have not had breakfast at home. Breakfast usually consists of bread and butter, cheese, cereal, milk, and cod liver oil.

After breakfast in most daycare centers, one group of children has choice time and outdoor play, while the other group engages in group work for about one hour. Group work might include art or construction projects, for example. The children who play outside typically come inside about 45 minutes before lunch because it may take them quite a while to take off layers of clothing in the clothing room, which is a part of most Icelandic preschool buildings. Once they have shed all the outdoor clothes, they gather with their classmates for group time, where they typically sing songs or hear stories. The preschool kitchen staff prepares lunch and serves it family style. The children take turns setting the tables in the classrooms. After lunch they have rest time. The youngest children sleep but the older ones are allowed to read quietly. After lunch and rest, the children who were in group work in the morning go outdoors for play and choice time, while the children who were outside in the morning remain inside for group work. Children play outdoors in every type of weather for 1–4 hours daily. After snack time in the afternoon, there is usually another choice time, and the day ends with story reading and free play. Thus, more than 50% of the day is spent playing and participating in child-initiated activities. Approximately $3\frac{1}{2}$ hours a day is devoted to routine activities and group time where the whole class is together. Only a small part of the day is devoted to preplanned activities or group work.

## Freedom and Control

Findings from the two ethnographic studies show that Icelandic preschools emphasize outdoor and indoor play in their day-to-day practice (Einarsdottir, 2002, 2004b). The four preschool teachers who were observed created a supportive environment for play by providing ample space, time, materials, and equipment. However, the teachers played somewhat different roles during children's free play. Two of the teachers were physically present when the children played and were actively involved with the children. When explaining the reason behind the tendency to be actively involved in children's play, one teacher explained that the educational personnel in her preschool have agreed that it is important to be present when the children are playing in order to observe and follow the development of their play, to prevent noise and bad manners, and also to intervene if the play is going nowhere or in the wrong direction.

In the other two classrooms, the children were allowed to play alone in closed rooms adjacent to the main classrooms. While the children were

playing, preschool teachers communicated with other adults and prepared materials for teacher-initiated activities or for the children to use
during choice time. They did not typically interact with the children during play unless the children asked for their help or invited them into the
play. Like the more involved teachers, these teachers explained their
"hands-off" approach in terms of what they believed best served the children's development. They explained that it is important for children to
have freedom to play undisturbed by adults as long as the play is going
well. One of them said:

> I think that we should be present but not too much in the play. Let them play
> on their own account, but always be there in proximity, stay in the main
> room, and be able to go into the small room.... If there is some abnormal
> noise from the room, some disagreement that we can hear that they cannot
> resolve, then we intervene. However, we do not intervene right away when we
> see that two children disagree. First we look and listen, and if we see that they
> cannot handle it, we intervene. Also when we notice that the children are not
> engaged in the play; for example, if someone is always coming out of the
> room complaining about something, then we go in and discuss with them.
> Also when some individuals have chosen to be in there that we know have
> had problems playing together, we keep an eye on the group. So it depends
> on the individuals playing how much we leave them by themselves.

All of the preschool teachers explained that the children should be
allowed to be free from adult involvement and interference when they are
playing outside. The educational personnel most frequently stick together
sitting on benches by the building or standing together in groups when
they are on the playground, leaving the children to themselves unless they
need some assistance.

Findings from the study on the role of Icelandic preschool teachers in
children's play (Einarsdottir, 1998) are consistent with results from the ethnographic studies. Results from the observations of adults' roles in children's play showed that, in some settings, the teachers were present when
the children were playing; but in other preschools, they were not and the
children were often left to play by themselves. The results also indicated
that Icelandic preschool practitioners have a rather passive or reserved role
in children's play and that they are reluctant to participate in the play
unless the initiative comes from the children. The observations revealed
that adults' participation in children's play was infrequent. Even so, when
the participants were asked in a survey about the teacher's role in children's play, they answered that they should prepare the play and have
influence on the play. Thus, there seemed to be some inconsistency
between the observed teacher behavior and their survey answers. Perhaps
the personnel reported what they thought they *should be* doing on the sur-

vey, but behaved quite differently in actuality, following instead their beliefs and traditions in the field.

Participants in the focus-group study (Einarsdottir, 2003) discussed the role of the preschool teachers in children's learning, as well as their interactions with the children. The study included four homogenous groups. One group included only preschool teachers; another group included only preschool directors; the third group included preschool consultants; and the fourth included only preschool teacher educators. The groups agreed on numerous fundamental early childhood practices, such as the importance of play. However, some interesting differences of opinion also came to light. For instance, preschool teachers and most of the preschool directors criticized the practice of allowing children to play without adults present. Among the reasons they cited in their criticism of unsupervised play was that children often enact difficult and confusing experiences during play. Therefore, an adult should be present to assist them so the play is meaningful. They also mentioned the danger of mobbing when no adults are present and observed that if someone gets hurt, the staff would have problems explaining to parents what had happened. One of the preschool teachers said: "Of course you should not live life expecting the worst things to happen. That is just boring and unexciting. But it has shaped my view that things have happened in closed rooms. You know, I am just afraid."

Concern about parents becoming upset when children get hurt is a rather new phenomenon in Icelandic preschools. In the past, most parents and early educators simply accepted that children sometimes get hurt when they play and take risks as they try new things. Perhaps Iceland has been influenced by North American trends, which we would previously have viewed as *overconcern* about children's safety.

Other participants revealed a different perspective, mentioning the importance of the children having a space of their own. Children should have places where they are trusted to play and be on their own. For instance, one of the preschool directors who received her education in Denmark said:

> The situation in my preschool is that we have one excellent playroom where three children can play together. We control which children are in there together and there are closed doors, and they enjoy it.... They are always happy in there and find it just fantastic to be allowed to be in there by themselves. And like I say, we trust them and give them much responsibility.

The preschool consultants talked about the advantages and disadvantages of adult participation and intervention in children's play. They noted that in recent years early educators have been encouraged to participate, whereas in the old days preschool personnel just walked around to check on the children occasionally. The preschool consultants were in general agreement that there is a fine line between supporting children's play through active involvement and interfering. These consultants noted that preschool teachers should carefully assess whether they are hindering the children's independence and initiative or supporting the children as they explore the world through their play.

Preschool consultants and preschool teacher educators also discussed the importance of having faith in the children's competence and trusting them, while still being emotionally and physically available to them. They felt that children should generally be trusted to play alone, but they should know that the educational personnel are in the vicinity ready to assist and support them if they ask for it. This approach leaves it up to the children to request adult participation or assistance and represents still another dimension of trusting the children's competence.

Taken together, these studies reveal dichotomies of opinion and practice in Iceland. These differences of opinion once again point to the various sources of influence upon early education in Iceland, including the United States and Europe, especially the Nordic countries. What should the early childhood teacher's role be during children's play? How closely should children be monitored? Under what circumstances and in which ways should teachers become involved in children's play? Consistent with their counterparts in other Nordic countries (Åm, 1984; Ivarson, 1996; Knudsdottir-Olfosson, 1991; Lindqvist, 1995), some Icelandic preschool teachers in the present studies believed that children should be allowed to play on their own without adult intervention. These early childhood educators emphasized trusting the children and giving them freedom and responsibility, while others focused on finding ways to guide children to ensure that their play is safe and productive. The latter perspective is more consistent with views expressed by American teachers, who emphasize the importance of providing children with variety and choice for play that is carefully supervised by adults (Carlson, 1997; Kontos, 1999; Tobin et al., 1989).

Icelandic preschools have strong roots in the Nordic preschool tradition, which builds on a romantic view of children (Haug, 1993; Honkavaara, 1998; Johansson, 1998; Lenz Taguchi & Munkammar, 2003; Lund, 1998). In this view, children should be happy and free; they should learn from experiencing the environment directly, including the inevitable bumps and bruises that come from playing freely without intrusive adult supervision. These views are consistent with the Icelandic culture's conventional beliefs about children and childrearing, where freedom is seen as an intrinsic right of childhood. However, increasingly, these fundamental Nordic beliefs are being scrutinized from a more international perspective, where adults are expected to be in more control of children's lives, and where children's freedom is restricted in the name of keeping them safe from dangers, real and imagined. For example, children are now required to wear helmets when riding bikes; there is now stricter inspection of playground equipment; and both parental and public discussion reveals concerns that Icelandic children are left too much to take care of themselves and that schools and society in general lack discipline.

## Teaching and Caregiving

As in the other Nordic countries, Icelandic early educators distinguish between caregiving and teaching (Karlsson Lohmander, 2003). The concept of caregiving, well explained by Leawitt (1994), emphasizes the nature of interactions between the child and the caregiver. Although the term *caregiving* is sometimes used in America and elsewhere to refer to basic custodial care, caregiving in the Nordic sense is far from a minimum standards notion (Broström & Wagner, 2003). The Nordic concept of caregiving of course includes physical caretaking, but it also requires mutual regard, warmth, and a genuine sense of shared personal and emotional involvement between the child and the adult. The Nordic concept of teaching, on the other hand, refers to transmission of knowledge from the adult to the child, or in a more contemporary pedagogical sense, to the adult's designing experiences through which the child will gain knowledge through active involvement. One Icelandic preschool director described the role of the preschool in this way:

> We can never look away from our role as caregivers. We have such young children and they need this warmth, care, and safety in their environment to be able to strengthen and develop. And then there is, of course, education and upbringing, to transmit knowledge and educate. Strengthen them socially and their self-images so they can use what the environment has to offer.

Like those in other Nordic countries, Icelandic preschools have traditionally emphasized caregiving over teaching. This was evident from the beginning, when Iceland's first preschools, funded by a charitable organization, were established for children with evident social needs. Their main purpose was to provide poor children with warmth from caring adults, wholesome nutrition, hygiene, and opportunities to play outside in the fresh air.

Today, nutrition and outdoor play remain important aspects of preschool life, as indicated by their inclusion in the *National Curriculum.* My ethnographic studies (Einarsdottir, 2002, 2004b) confirmed that nutrition and outdoor play actually are central to the preschool experience in Iceland. The preschools I studied emphasized meal times and nutrition, and the preschool teachers frequently talked with the children about the importance of healthy food. Free play in the outdoors also remains a mainstay of Icelandic preschool practice. Children typically play freely on the playground once or twice during the day, usually for 1–2-hour periods regardless of the weather. Preschool teachers explained that outdoor play is an important outlet for children's energy. One of the teachers said: "I am in favor of outdoor play.... It is our fault if the children do not get enough movement. On the playground the children run, climb, and exercise the most. They also feel better after they have been outdoors, they eat better, and they rest better."

Another consistent theme among the participating preschool teachers was the importance of children's happiness. For Icelandic preschool teachers, happiness means that children participate enthusiastically in activities; choose their playmates; eat well; express their emotions freely, laughing or crying as the situation dictates to them; and enjoy friendships with the educational personnel. The preschool teachers also emphasized the development of social skills, especially those that lead to satisfying interpersonal relationships. Their goal is for children to learn to live in harmony with others, showing respect and consideration for each other, recognizing the feelings of others, feeling empathy for others, and learning to get along well with each other. These same themes also appear in Icelandic preschool laws, including the *National Curriculum*. In addition, recent research has shown that Icelandic parents also value social interaction and relationship-building as the main reasons for having their children attend preschool (Forskot, 1998).

The term *teaching* is relatively new in the Icelandic preschool context. While preschools have historically existed to provide caregiving, the last decade has witnessed an evolution toward viewing preschools as educational institutions. While caregivers were previously called *fóstrur* (nannies), the term *leikskólakennari* (playschool teacher) is used to describe early educators who are now required to have a university degree. Early childhood discourse now includes both traditional terms and concepts and more recent developments, leading to interesting dilemmas and contradictions that are currently being discussed and debated in Iceland (e.g., Dýrfjörð, 2001).

Although Icelandic preschools today may be viewed by some as shifting from an emphasis on caregiving to an emphasis on teaching and learning, not all preschool personnel are flowing with this tide. For instance, one of the teachers explained that the concept of "teaching" as opposed to "caregiving" is alien to her. She stated that she has never used the term *teaching* to describe her work. When questioned further, she stated that all good interactions between adults and children in preschool settings may actually involve some aspects of teaching and learning, indicating that the terms may not be as distinguishable from one another in actual practices as they are in the early childhood discourse. However, another preschool teacher said that she is quite comfortable with the term *teaching*: "I am teaching the children all the time, from the time I sit down with them at the breakfast table…. Teaching includes answering questions and talking…. I teach them most indirectly through daily routine, group work, and group time."

The participants in the focus group study (Einarsdottir, 2003) discussed that preschool teachers today experience certain dilemmas with regard to contemporary terms and concepts. They indicated that Icelandic pre-school teachers are not used to, and perhaps not comfortable with, the term *teaching*. They did not, however, reach consensus concerning whether they should be using the term "teaching" or not. One preschool consultant expressed the view that the preschool teachers were using the concept because they felt they *should* use it, not because they have made the shift in paradigm from caregiver to teacher. She commented:

> This is not a concept that we used to use, and we are not using it today, but we have been told at some point to use this concept. It sounds better…. We knew of course what we were doing in the preschool, but we had difficulties in connecting it to teaching…. I am sure that a large group of preschool teachers does not want to use this concept, although they do it because it sounds good.

Others mentioned that preschool teachers had to get used to the teach-ing concept. This adjustment would require them to redefine the concept and look at its meaning more broadly than just as direct instruction. The participants in the focus groups agreed that teaching and caregiving are intertwined. Some expressed the view that caregiving should come first because children must be comfortable and happy in preschool before they can learn anything. "Respect and loving care always come first," one of the preschool directors commented.

The group of preschool teacher educators who participated in the focus group study did not deny the role of preschool teachers as caregivers, pro-viding intimate relationships with the children, but they also emphasized the importance of discussing and redefining concepts such as teaching and caregiving.

According to law, the Icelandic preschool is now an educational institu-tion. Preschool teachers are, however, not all comfortable using school-like terms such as *teaching*. Many of them associate the term *teaching* with teacher-directed instruction on academic subjects. By objecting to terms like teaching, they are not saying that they do not want children to learn anything or that they do not help the children learn. The difference is that they see themselves doing this informally rather than through didactic instruction.

Although the distinction between the terms *care, education, teaching*, and *upbringing* may seem more semantic than real in everyday practice, the fact remains that, like early educators in the other Nordic countries, Icelandic preschool teachers and teacher educators continue to discuss and debate these terms and the relative worth of each in today's preschools. Nordic scholars have argued in favor of merging the terms *teaching, education*, and *care*. Broström (2003) built on Nygren's (1991) ideas and presented a frame that unites care, education, and teaching. He described three dimensions of care. The first he called *need-care*, referring to the child's basic needs for security, safety, and attachment. The preschool teacher provides need-care through a warm and empathic relationship with the children. Brostöm called the second category *upbringing-care*, referring to teacher behaviors that support children in their acquisition of societal norms and values. He labeled the third category *teaching-care*, referring to teacher behaviors that support children in their construction of knowledge and skills. Broström's last dimension of care is in concert with Lisa Goldstein's (1999) ideas on the resemblance between Vygotsky's zone of proximal development and Nel Noddings's description of caring. Goldstein argued that Noddings's work and Vygotsky's work share essential understandings of the contours of the relationship between teacher and learner. These ideas are new in the Icelandic preschool context but may prove useful in the struggle to combine care, education, and teaching.

## REFLECTIONS

The ideas that lie behind the first preschools in Iceland were similar to those of the other Nordic countries, reflective of the spirit of the times and in concert with knowledge about child development and early education available at that time. Preschools were social welfare institutions that emphasized children's happiness, play, and social development through caregiving (Barnavinafélagið Sumargjöf, 1974; Lenz Taguchi & Munkammar, 2003). Icelandic early educators talked about the "whole child" and acknowledged the importance of all domains of development, including emotional, social, cognitive, language, and motor areas. Icelandic early educators generally shared a firm belief that children develop from within, given the right "caregiving" conditions, including sufficient freedom from overcontrol by adults. This was a romantic view of children and childhood. Terms like *knowledge, teaching*, and *learning* were not used in the preschool context because these concepts belonged to the realm of formal education. Caregivers purposefully created preschools with a homelike atmosphere where children were provided with warmth, wholesome nutrition, and hygiene and the opportunity to play. The central ingredient required for a successful preschool, a place where children could happily develop from within, was warm, caring, almost familial relationships between adults and children. These ideas reflected the philosophy of the British nursery schools, child psychology theories of the times, and to a lesser extent Froebel's ideology, emphasizing growth and development evolving from within as a result of children's innate capacities, nurtured by caregivers.

In 1994 preschools officially became the first level of schooling, though neither mandatory nor fully funded by the state. This shift in public policy came in the wake of new views about children and childhood, often inspired by new ideas from North America. Many of these new ideas were inconsistent with traditional Icelandic views about children and childhood, as well as about the structure and content of early childhood education. As a result, the last decade has witnessed considerable friction between traditional Icelandic early childhood practices and new ideas washing ashore from abroad.

Icelandic preschool teachers seem to be divided into several camps regarding the proper role of the preschool. One camp, the most traditional, emphasizes the preschool years as the golden age of free play and development. Consequently, the role of the preschool is to provide care, as well as emotional and social support. Another camp emphasizes preschool as the first level of formal education, where adults are teachers (not caregivers), whose job is to ensure that children learn what they need to learn even at this tender age. Still another camp argues that caregiving and teaching are mutually inclusive concepts, both necessary to ensure high-quality experience and outcomes for Icelandic children prior to their entrance into formal schooling at age 6.

This struggle between traditional Icelandic philosophy and practice, on the one hand, and contemporary ideas from abroad, on the other, is not surprising, given Iceland's location in the Atlantic, midway between North America and Europe. Even with its isolated location, Iceland is now increasingly touched by the tides of globalization. Technology, travel, and widespread use of English as a common language blur national boundaries, as do such collectives as the European Union. It is not surprising, then, that pedagogical practices at the preschool level also come under the influence of both local tradition and increasing globalization. Many Icelanders pursue their graduate studies abroad. The number of textbooks in Icelandic is limited, so students of early childhood education study the contemporary literature in the field from other Nordic countries and the United States. With increasing regularity, international influences confront conventional Icelandic beliefs about children, childrearing, and education of young children.

As Bruner (1986, 1996) and others have suggested, cultural beliefs find their way into all social institutions, including preschools. Philosophical and pedagogical tensions in today's Icelandic preschool mirror emerging questions in society as a whole about children, their upbringing, and their early education. The conventional Icelandic view that children should be independent and free to play and explore the environment now comes under fire from those who argue that children need closer supervision and/or earlier academic instruction.

This friction in today's Icelandic preschool can be regarded as a conflict between traditional cultural views and newer international trends. Icelandic early childhood education has been influenced by ideologies, programs, and trends from the other Nordic countries, as well as from other parts of Europe and the United States. Icelanders modify these ideas as they hit our shores, sometimes adapting them to fit our existing cultural beliefs, sometimes adapting our beliefs to fit the new ideas, and sometimes struggling to create a balance. Will Icelandic early educators integrate their old ideas with newer views to create a hybrid? Will new ideas triumph over traditional views? Will Icelandic preschoolers continue to spend more than 50% of their time in free play, often without much adult supervision, or will they spend more and more time receiving teacher-directed instruction? Will Icelandic preschool teachers truly accept the challenge to merge caregiving and teaching and become co-constructors of knowledge with the children whose lives they influence daily? No one yet knows how this story will end.

## REFERENCES

Alexander, R. (2000). *Culture and pedagogy: International comparisons in primary education.* Oxford, UK: Blackwell.

Åm, E. (1989). *Lek i barnehagen, de voksnes rolle* [Play in the preschools, the role of the adults]. Oslo: Universitetsforlaget.

Barnavinafélagið Sumargjöf (1974). *Barnavinafélagið Sumargjöf 50 ára.* Reykjavík: Author.

Bloch, M. N. (1987). Becoming scientific and professional: An historical perspective on the aims and effects of early education. In T. S. Popkewitz (Ed.), *The formation of school subjects* (pp. 3–20). New York: Falmer Press.

Bresler, L. (1998). The genre of school music and its shaping by meso, micro, and macro contexts. *Research Studies in Music Education, 11,* 2–18.

Broström, S. (2003). Unity of care, teaching and upbringing: A theoretical contribution towards a new paradigm in early childhood education. In M. Karlsson Lohmander (Ed.), *Researching early childhood: Care, play and learning curricula for early childhood education* (pp. 21–38). Göteborg: Göteborg University.

Broström, S., & Wagner, J. T. (2003). Transitions in context: Models, practicalities and problems. In S. Broström & J. T. Wagner (Eds.), *Early childhood education in five Nordic countries: Perspectives on the transition from preschool to school* (pp. 27–36). Århus, Denmark: Systime.

Bruner, J. (1986). *Actual minds, possible words.* Cambridge, MA: Harvard University Press.

Bruner, J. (1996). *The culture of education.* Cambridge, MA: Harvard University Press.

Bruner, J. S., & Olson, D. R. (1996). Folk psychology and folk pedagogy. In D. R. Olson & N. Torrance (Eds.), *The handbook of education and human development: New models of learning, teaching and schooling* (pp. 9–27). Cambridge, UK: Blackwell.

Carlson, H. (1997). Early childhood education in societal context: Teachers in three countries speak about early childhood education. *Early Education and Development, 8*(2), 169–186.

Cuffaro, H. K. (1997, October). *A teacher's journey from theory to philosophy.* Paper presented at the Reconceptualizing Early Childhood Education conference, Changing Visions in a Postmodern World, Teachers College Columbia University, New York.

Dýrfjörð, K. (2001). Umönnun eða skólun: Hvort er mikilvægara í leikskóla? [Caregiving or education: What is more important in preschool?]. *Reggio fréttir, 2*(3), 3–10.

Einarsdottir, J. (1996). Dramatic play and print. *Childhood Education, 72*(6), 352–357.

Einarsdottir, J. (1998). The role of adults in children's dramatic play in Icelandic preschools. *European Early Childhood Education Research Journal, 6*(6), 87–106.

Einarsdottir, J. (2000). Incorporating literacy resources into the play curriculum of two Icelandic playschools. In J. Christies & K. Roskos (Eds.), *Play and literacy in early childhood: Research from multiple perspectives* (pp. 77–90). Mahwah, NJ: Erlbaum.

Einarsdottir, J. (2002). Tradition and trends: Practices and beliefs of two Icelandic preschool teachers. *International Journal of Educational Policy, Research, and Practice, 3*(3), 47–68.

Einarsdottir, J. (2003). The role of playschools and playschool teachers: Icelandic playschool educators' discourses. *Early Years: An International Journal of Research and Development, 23*(2), 103–116.

Einarsdottir, J. (2004a). "Það var lítill skilningur á því að það þyrfti að kenna stúlkum að passa börn." Valborg Sigurðardóttir fyrrverandi skólastjóri. [There was little understanding of the need to teaching young women to take care of children." Valborg Sigurðardóttir former principal]. In B. Hansen, J. Einarsdottir, & Ó. H. Jóhannsson (Eds.), *Brautryðjendur í uppeldis og menntamálum* [Pioneers in education] (pp. 143–160). Reykjavík: Rannsóknarstofnun KHÍ.

Einarsdottir, J. (2004b). Tvær stefnur—tvenns konar hefðir í kennslu yngri barna. [Two ideologies—two traditions in teaching of young children]. *Uppeldi og menntun: Tímarit Kennaraháskóla Íslands, 14,* 57–77.

Félag íslenskra leikskólakennara. (2000). *Leikskólastefna Félags íslenskra leikskólakennara* [The Preschool teacher's union policy]. Reykjavík: Félag íslenskra leikskólakennara.

Forskot (1998). *Dagvist barna. Foreldrakönnun. Júní–ágúst 1998* [Reykjavík Preschools. Parent survey. June–August 1998]. Reykjavík: Dagvist barna.

Goffin, S. G. (1989). Developing a research agenda for early childhood education: What can be learned from the research on teaching? *Early Childhood Research Quarterly, 4*(2), 187–204.

Goldstein, L., S. (1997). Between a rock and a hard place in the primary grades: The challenge of providing developmentally appropriate early childhood education in an elementary school setting. *Early Childhood Research Quarterly, 12,* 3–27.

Goldstein, L., S. (1999). The relational zone: The role of caring relationships in the co-construction of mind. *American Educational Research Journal, 36*(3), 647–673.

Graue, E. M., & Walsh, D. J. (1998). *Studying children in context: Theories, methods, and ethics.* Thousand Oaks, CA: Sage.

Hagstofa Íslands (2005). *Landshagir 2005* [Iceland statistics 2005]. Reykjavík: Hagstofa Íslands.

Halman, L. (2001). *The European values study: A third wave. Source book of the 1999/2000 European values study surveys.* Netherlands: EVS, WORC, Tilburg University.

Haug, P. (1993). *Den nordiske barnehagemodellen, særpreg og* kvalitet [The Nordic preschool model, characteristics and quality]. Volda: Möreforskning.

Hohman, M., Banet, B., & Weikart, D. (1979). *Young children in action: A manual for preschool educators: The cognitively oriented preschool curriculum.* Ypsilanti, MI: High/Scope Press.

Honkavaara, P. (1998). Anniversaries in the Finnish kindergarten system how and why the system was created. *International Journal of Early Childhood, 30*(1), 7–9.

Ivarson, P. M. (1996). *"Fri lek" i förskolan—barn och vuxna tillsammans eller var för sig* ["Free play" in the preschool-children and adults together or separated]. Uppsala: University of Uppsala.

Johansson, J.-E. (1998). *Barnomsorgen och lärarutbildningen: En analys av metodikäment utbildningen av förskollärare och fritidspedagoger* [Child-care and teacher education]. Göteborg: Göteborgs Universitet.

Jónsson, F. H., & Ólafsson, S. (1991). *Úr lífsgildakönnun 1990: Lífsskoðun í nútímalegum þjóðfélögum* [From life values survey 1990: Life values in modern societies]. Reykjavík: Social Science Research Institute.

Kagitcibasi, C. (1996). *Family and human development across cultures: A view from the other side.* Hillsdale, NJ: Erlbaum.

Karlsson Lohmander, M. (Ed.). (2003). *Researching early childhood: Care, play and learning curricula for early childhood education.* Göteborg: Göteborg University.

Kitayama, S., & Markus, H. R. (1999). The pursuit of happiness and the realization of sympathy: Cultural patterns of self, social relations, and well-being. In E. Diener & E. Suh (Eds.), *Subjective well-being across cultures.* Cambridge, MA: MIT Press.

Knudsdottir-Olofsson, B. (1991). *Varför leker inte barnen?* [Why do the children not play?]. Stockholm: HLS.

Kontos, S. (1999). Preschool teachers' talk, roles, and activity settings during free play. *Early Childhood Research Quarterly, 14*(3), 363–382.

Kristinsdóttir, G. (2000). Tíu ára börn standa vel að vígi: Athugun á færni, áhyggjum og lausnum barna [Ten year olds are doing well: Study on children's worries and solutions]. *Uppeldi og menntun: Tímarit Kennaraháskóla Íslands, 9,* 77–94.

Kristjánsson, B. (1991). Barnolyckor i ett kulturellt sammanhang. Islandska barns vardagsliv och öden studie baserad på två tidligare undersökingar [Accidents on children in cultural context]. *Nordisk Psycology, 42,* 199–218.

Lacy, T. G. (1998). *Ring of seasons: Iceland, its culture & history.* Ann Arbor: Univerisity of Michigan Press.

Leawitt, R. L. (1994). *Power and emotion in infant-toddler day care.* Albany: State University of New York Press.

Lee, K., & Walsh, D. J. (2001 (April). *The self and curriculum in American early schooling: Four early childhood teachers' folk pedagogy.* Paper presented at the annual conference of the American Educational Research Association, Seattle, WA.

Lenz Taguchi, H., & Munkammar, I. (2003). *Consolidating governmental early childhood education and care services under the Ministry of Education and Science: A Swedish case study.* Paris: UNESCO.

Lindqvist, G. (1996). *Lekens möjligheter* [The possibilities of play]. Lund: Studentlitteratur.

Lund, S. G. (1998). Facts and figures about early childhood and youth education in Denmark. *International Journal of Early Childhood, 30*(1), 1–6.

*Lög um hlutdeild ríkisins í byggingu og rekstri dagvistunarheimila. Nr. 29/1973* [Laws on the state participation in building and running of day care centers. No. 29/ 1973].

*Lög um leikskóla. Nr. 48/1991* [Law on preschools. No 48/1991].

*Lög um leikskóla. Nr. 78/1994* [Law on preschools. No 78/1994].

Ministry of Education (1985). *Uppeldisáætlun fyrir dagvistarheimili. Markmið og leiðir* [Educational plan for day-care centers]. Reykjavík: Author.

Ministry of Education (1999). *Aðalnámskrá leikskóla* [National curriculum for preschools]. Reykjavík: Author.

Nygren, P. (1991). Virksomhetsteori og barnevernsarbeid [Activity theory and child care work]. In H. Brock (Ed.), *Virksomhetsteorien. En innföring og eksempler* (pp. 159–196). Oslo: Falken Forlag.

Ólafsson, S. (1989). *The making of the Icelandic welfare state. A Scandinavian comparison.* Reykjavík: Social Science Research Institute.

Ólafsson, S. (1996). *Hugarfar og hagvöxtur* [Values and economic growth]. Reykjavík: University of Iceland.

*Reglugerð Nr. 642/2002 um breyting á reglugerð um starfsemi leikskóla Nr. 225/1995* [Regulation No. 642/2002 about changes on regulation No. 225/1995].

*Reglugerð um starfsemi leikskóla, Nr. 225/1995* [Regulation on playschools, No. 225/ 1995].

Reykjavíkurborg (2002). *Síðustu tölur frá Reykjavík 2002* [Latest numbers from Reykjavík]. Retrieved February 16, 2004, from http://www.reykjavik.is/displayer .asp?cat_id=597

Shweder, R. A., Goodnow, J., Hatano, G., LeVine, R., Markus, H., & Miller, P. (1998). The cultural psychology of development: One mind, many mentalities. In W. Damon (Ed.), *Handbook of child psychology* (Vol. 1, pp. 865–937). New York: Wiley.

Sigurðardóttir, V. (1998). *Fósturskóli Íslands: Afmælisrit í tilefni 50 ára afmæli skólans 1996* [Iceland College of Preschool Teachers]. Reykjavík: Gott mál.

Sigurðardóttir, V. (1999). Brautryðjandinn Margaret McMillan (1860–1931): Málsvari barna [The pioneer Margaret McMillan (1860–1931): Children's advocate]. In H. S. Kjartansson, H. Ragnarsdóttir, K. Indriðadóttir, & Ó. Proppé (Eds.), *Steinar í vörðu. Afmælisrit helgað Þuríði Kristjánsdóttur, sjötugri* (pp. 91–105). Reykjavík: Rannsóknarstofnun KHÍ.

Spodek, B. (1991). Early childhood curriculum and cultural definitions of knowledge. In B. Spodek & O. N. Saracho (Eds.), *Yearbook in early childhood education: Issues in early childhood education* (pp. 1–20). New York: Teachers College.

Spodek, B., & Saracho, O. N. (1996). Culture and the early childhood curriculum. *Early Child Development and Care, 23,* 1–13.

Tobin, J., Wu, D., & Davidson, D. (1989). *Preschool in three cultures: Japan, China and the United States.* New Haven, CT: Yale University Press.

Wollons, R. (2000). *Kindergarten and cultures: The global diffusion on the idea.* New Haven, CT: Yale University Press.

CHAPTER 8

# LEARNING AND DEVELOPMENT IN PLAY

**Pentti Hakkarainen**
*University of Oulo*

The true power and potential of play in the lives of young children often become lost amid discussions of its role in "real learning" at school or the largely intuitive argument that play *always* promotes development. The goal of this chapter is to offer a reinterpretation of the significance of play in early childhood education, using the Finnish context as an example. The chapter begins with a description of the status of play in the three Finnish guidelines for the ages 0–8 years, as well as an overview of various definitions of play and approaches to play research. Next, I introduce a narrative approach as an alternative way to interpret learning through play, incorporating illustrative examples from three narrative learning environments: the Fifth Dimension, learning literacy in play, and the joint play world of adults and children. These environments are part of an experimental research program in which we have systematically varied the form and content of narratives. Simply put, we define a "narrative approach" as any activity based on make-believe in any form, including, for example, stories, pictures, music, and movement. We propose that the developmental

potential of play should be reevaluated and our model of vertically integrated ECE helps to solve some basic contradictions in the Finnish educational system with regard to the role and power of play.

## NORDIC PERSPECTIVES ON PLAY IN ECE

Throughout the Nordic countries, play enjoys an especially privileged status in early childhood education programs (ECE). Official ECE documents
in Denmark, Finland, Iceland, Sweden, and Norway reflect the rarified status of play. For example, the Finnish document guiding planning ECE programs (National Curriculum Guidelines on Early Childhood Education
and Care in Finland, 2003, p.19) defines the status of play:

> Children play for the sake of playing, and at best, play can give them deep
> satisfaction. Although children do not play in order to learn, they learn
> through play. Play is rather an attitude than an activity of a certain kind, and
> the same activity may signify play for one child but not for another. As play-
> ing is social by nature, peer groups have a significant effect on the way the
> playing situation develops....
>
> Children use everything they see, hear, and experience as elements in their
> play. When they play, they imitate and create new things. They pick up things
> that are meaningful for them from the sphere of both the real world and that
> of fantasy and fiction, translating them into the language of play. All that is
> visible in the play is meaningful to the child, but not all that is meaningful to
> the child is visible in the play. (p. 19)

Official documents in other Nordic countries also speak to the importance and centrality of play. For instance, Sweden school authorities
describe the status of play this way: "Play has always been central to Swedish
child care. Nowadays it is even included in the national curriculum for
compulsory schools. Playing games helps the child to understand the world
around it, to develop its imagination and creative powers and to learn to
cooperate with others. Play is at the heart of public care activities in Sweden" (The Swedish School System, 2005). In Norway official documents
also reify the value of play even beyond ECE, calling for play as a part of
children's daily experience through the first four grades in elementary
school.

This high regard for play evidenced in these official documents is based
on the supposition that play promotes children's psychological development
and learning. However, definitions of play vary considerably and research
provides little evidence of the positive developmental effects of play.

## DEFINITIONS OF PLAY AND PLAY RESEARCH

The majority of play research has focused on one question: What actually is play? Many researchers have tried to define play or articulate its characteristics. For instance, Hughes (1998) listed the following characteristics and benefits:

> Play has five essential characteristics. It is intrinsically motivated, freely chosen, pleasurable, non-literal, and actively engaged in by participants. Early theories of play emphasized its biological and genetic elements...while contemporary theories stress the emotional, intellectual, and social benefits of play. (p. 25)

However, it is far more difficult to investigate how play develops over time or to identify those qualities of play that actually promote children's development. Answers to these questions depend very much on the theoretical frame of various play studies. We can roughly divide theoretical frames into two main types: one-level play frames and multilevel frames. One-level frames focus only on the play behaviors themselves, that is, on what the children say and do. Multilevel frames take the sociocultural context of the play into account. Multilevel frames look at development as parallel to historical changes (Scribner, 1985). According to this view, play development consists of individual, local, societal, and global changes. For example, El'konin (2005) demonstrated using anthropological and historical data that the change in children's status in society has changed their play. Interestingly, such nested changes in play force us to change our understanding of what is internal and external in play.

The puzzling relationship between internal and external aspects of play creates problems for defining it as a factor in development. Play is an intrinsically motivated process, with results and developmental effects that are not immediately visible. Researchers have addressed this problem somewhat by focusing on different aspects of learning in play situations, as illustrated in the following quote in which the authors focus on the value of play in social cognition and self-identity development:

> The merit of play is that it assists children in exploring and understanding various roles and interaction patterns, thereby supporting their understanding of their social world and facilitating their efforts to build a realistic sense of self. Play seems to serve as an information-seeking process for the children and as a means to interact with their environment. In addition, play helps children learn how to learn. (Saracho & Spodek, 1998, pp. 8–9)

Multilevel frames define play as a conglomerate of different activities or contexts. For instance, some argue that play has both a meta-level and an actual level (Bateson, 1972). Others describe play as the syncretistic proto-type of aesthetic creativity from which different forms of aesthetic creation are differentiated (Lindqvist, 1995; Vygotsky, 1987). In other words, play, based on aesthetic reactions, is nearer to experiences in artistic self-expression than to cognitive/academic learning. Others have written that play is a specific type of activity driven by the contradiction between sense and meaning (El'konin, 1999; Hakkarainen, 1999).[1] These frames emphasize the specific holistic, contextual, multilevel nature of play.

In reality, though, play is dialectical; it includes many contradictory elements and conflicting forces. For example, a child may strive for a high social position in a play group while, at the same time, needing to cooperate with play partners on equal footing so the play can proceed. Another interesting contradiction in play is that young children often need to act like an adult. The challenge is to reveal the inherent contradictions in play, as well as the connection between these contradictions and developmental outcomes for children's overall development and learning.

## THE FINNISH ECE CONTEXT

Early childhood services for 0–8-year-olds in Finland are community-based and divided into three steps: (1) daycare centers or coordinated family day care for children between birth and 5 years of age, (2) kindergarten class for 6-year-olds, and (3) elementary grades in school (1–2). Traditionally the Department of Social Welfare and the Department of Education at the community level have shared or divided responsibility for arranging child-care services in the Finnish municipalities. Kindergarten class could be located in a school or in a daycare center depending on municipal decision. However, educational reforms beginning at the turn of the new millennium, especially the transfer of authority for daycare from the Department of Social Services to the Department of Education in 35% of the municipalities, have resulted in greater integration of care and education in Finland. The trend toward integrating care and education is evident in new program documents from day care through preschool and elementary school.

In the new system, various public laws and three official documents regulate early childhood education in Finland. These documents are the national curriculum guidelines on early childhood education and care (September 2003), the national curriculum guidelines on kindergarten education (August 2000), and the national curriculum guidelines on elementary school education, grades 1–2 (September 2004). These guidelines outline a unified structure for municipal plans and describe a constructivist learning concept to be implemented at all levels. The unified structure refers to the normative identical content of curricula at all three levels. This identical content should support seamless passage from preschool to kindergarten to primary grades and further on. The requirement for a constructivist learning approach is grounded in the theories of Piaget. According to the official documents, play should have a central role in day-care and playful learning should be a fundamental aspect of kindergarten curricula. However, in the primary grade document, subject matter learning, rather than play or playful learning, takes the central role.

A stated goal of recent reforms in the Finnish educational system was to improve continuity of programs and services throughout the early childhood period. Since August 2001, all communities have been required to offer kindergarten, designed as a transition between the playful preschool curriculum and the subject matter–focused elementary school. All children have a right to attend a kindergarten class free of charge even though attendance is noncompulsory. More than 90% of all 6-year-old children attend a kindergarten class. Although the reforms and official documents address continuity problems structurally, continuity remains problematic at the level of actual practice. There are many plausible explanations for this lack of coordination and continuity between daycare, kindergarten, and elementary school, not the least of which are differences in perspectives on the role and value of play, both in the language of the official documents and at the service-delivery level.

In Scandinavian early childhood education a central concept is children's "free play," which means child-initiated play. However, numerous studies have suggested that free play is less central in Finnish daycare practice than one might expect, based on the language in the official documents and the rhetoric of early childhood educators. For instance, data from informal investigations I have carried out with students in advanced education courses raise questions about the nature and extent of play activities in actual practice. During our observations, we defined play as an activity including elements of make-believe. Our observations indicated daily time for play was rarely more than 1 to 2 hours out of an 8–10-hour day and that playtime was typically distributed through the day according to a schedule determined by the teacher rather than the children's interests. The remaining hours in day care were typically divided between routines (toileting, snack, lunch, nap) and teacher-initiated activities, such as circle time for singing and hearing stories; table activities, such as drawing or tracing letters; or outdoor activities, such as nature walks and field trips.

Further analysis of the official ECE documents provides clues about this disconnect between official language and actual daily practice. Authors of the Finnish ECE documents had little knowledge of the real developmental potential of play. Notably lacking in the documents is a thorough analysis of the nature of learning through play. The inclusion of subject matter guidelines for preschool programs serving children between birth and 5 years of age strongly indicates the authors' orientation toward "academic learning" over play. To the extent that play is valued at all, it is for its role (or *possible role*, according to the documents) in cognitive development. However, the authors do not offer an analysis or explanation of the developmental transition from play for the sake of play itself to playful learning. The documents recommend preschool and kindergarten activities such as play sessions, oral storytelling, reading of books, dramatizing stories, and children's storytelling; but the documents do not connect such activities with child development or the benefits of narrative learning, defined as children's creative experimentation within a narrative frame. These shortcomings in the documents and their likely consequences in daily practice motivated Finnish school authorities to develop separate nationwide creativity programs. These programs are now coordinated under the auspices of the National Board of Education for children between the ages of 6 and 16. The goal is to learn about school-initiated creativity programs and best practices in order to develop national programs.

## PLAY AND LEARNING

Several challenges lie in the path toward true understanding of the strong and inextricable link between play and learning. At the most basic level, these challenges arise from variations and inconsistencies in defining play, as well as in perspectives about what constitutes play versus learning. (Note: Even the typical term "play versus learning" reflects the challenges at hand.) For example, we see a clear conceptual dichotomy between play and learning among first-year students in the teacher education program at the University of Oulu in Finland. These students distinguish between play and learning in much the same way as did the authors of the Finnish ECE documents and in a way that is consistent with discourse in elementary and secondary education. According to this view, play happens in "teaching situations," where the goal is acquisition of knowledge, as defined by the teacher. To the contrary, according to this prevalent view, no one is trying to teach anyone anything during children's free play. Playing is a general developmental characteristic of children, then, not an opportunity for learning.

An essential difference between play and learning, according to this perspective, is the unit of analysis. Learning is typically understood as an individual process, while play is a collective phenomenon. When our first-year students discuss play, they suggest that teachers identify learning outcomes or goals for their students relating directly to specific and explicit content. In kindergarten and school settings, teacher education program students say, teachers can quantify learning by determining how much each child has learned in terms of specific content knowledge or skill development.

Like the Finnish documents, ECE documents in several Nordic countries emphasize the role of play in developing learning potential and readiness for academic learning. These statements become problematic in practice, however, as it is often difficult, if not impossible, to show precise outcomes from play activities, especially a direct line from play to quantifiable results in terms of content knowledge and skill. It is even difficult to measure the effects of play upon children's learning potential or readiness for academic learning because educators tend to use the same instruments for assessing potential and readiness as for measuring gains in content knowledge and skills.

Both in terms of theory and practice, confusion abounds around the concept of learning potential. According to Illyenkov (1991), for example, the term has three different and overlapping meanings:

1. Implemented ability to carry out certain actions or operations at the present moment,
2. A pure potential, possibility to acquire schemes of these actions and to learn to carry out actions applying them.
3. An individual disposition toward some domain of activity (math, music, etc.) as equivalent to endowment, ability, and its degree in an individual person.

Illyenkov further noted that potentials are developed and realized fragmentarily and that only few individuals attain the highest possible level of general abilities (e.g., thinking or creative imagination). Illyenkov argued that educational systems, then, actively produce differences in potentials.

In spite of the lack of a universal definition of play or research data supporting claims of its value, many researchers, theorists, teacher educators, and practitioners share my view that play is a producer of potentials (Broström, 1999; Davydov & Kudryavtsev, 1997; Pramling, 1994; Van Oers, 2003). This strong belief is typically grounded in years of experimental education with children, as well as observations of children in a variety of settings, including those where play is central and those where it is peripheral.

I now discuss the concept of play as a producer of potentials. Its value as a producer of potentials does not lie in concrete, measurable results, such as school knowledge and skills. Rather, its value lies in its inherent ability to open the door for children to have new, child-friendly experiences and new, child-friendly contacts with their surrounding world. Play is inextricably connected with learning, even academic learning, because it increases children's opportunities to actively produce and experiment with new hypotheses. Piaget (1946/1972) used the term "active learning" in this connection. According to Piaget, a child's active experimentation during play exceeds his or her present level of mastery in the areas associated with the play. For example, a child's experimentation with large and small blocks, square and round blocks, green and blue blocks, exceeds her mastery of categorization with regard to size, shape, and color. An adult can support the child's learning by creating new situations and environments for exploration, experimentation with new attributes, and creating and solving problems.

From the institutional point of view, then, play is an effective tool for attaining formal learning goals, such as, in the example above, skills in categorizing, differentiating shapes, and naming colors. However, play is not just a vehicle for cognitive development and learning. Its potential is far greater. From the important perspective of children's own culture, or subculture, the essential feature of play is that it brings with it the opportunity to do something together. This is a powerful reward for children, who do not share adults' goal orientation or utilitarian points of view. They do not think consciously about their own learning or social development while they are playing. Rather, as Corsaro (1997) pointed out, this difference in adult's and children's ways of looking at play explains why adults do not understand children's tendency to repeat simple play behaviors and dramatic episodes, such as building a block tower and knocking it down or pretend cooking, over and over, a cake to be served to peers sitting at a nearby table.

One plausible explanation for these differing interpretations is that it is much easier for adults to see the external, material features in play than it is to recognize and understand children's ideas, sense, and meaning. In evaluating the developmental impact of play, the most popular criteria are realism of actions, technical mastery, mastery of knowledge, and thinking skills, not such factors as imagination, motivation, or emotional "perezhivanie,"[2] or expression of one's emotional life through play. Sutton-Smith (1995) wrote that the importance of play lies not at all in the development of academic skills, as is often asserted, but rather in other functions. "Play is best understood in terms of the quality of the individual subjective experience that it affords" (p. 288).

When children construct play situations and roles, they do not aim, consciously, to develop social relationships, learn the social skills of the adult world, or master knowledge and skills in a content area. Instead, the object of learning, or the learning outcome, is mediated through the play process itself. As children play, they freely cross the disciplinary, subject matter boundaries created by adults. From the children's perspective, these boundaries do not even exist. The only limit is the child's own imagination. For example, while pretending to drive a car by simply moving an imaginary steering wheel, the child has no realistic intention to move from one location to another or expectation that he will, in fact, wind up in his imaginary destination, if indeed he has one. The child is not setting out to gain skills that will eventually be useful for driving a real car. The purpose of the play, though the child is probably unaware of his purpose as he plays, is to explore and represent his idea of driving, its sense from his own experience and point of view. This is why young children so often use only symbolic action to represent an imagined situation, such as, in this example, the child's turning of an imaginary steering wheel to represent driving. Play is based on imagination. Play activates the imagination and trains it. Play creates opportunities for the imagination to see things that are not visible to those who are not engaged in play. A special feature of play is that nothing really changes objectively as in work processes. Changes take place on an imaginary level. Properties of things are separated and transferred to other contexts in imagination. The child's emotional involvement accompanies these changes.

Many theorists believe that play has a close connection with the development of emotions and motives, providing a means for children to express, explore, and elaborate them. Fein (1981) claimed that the child imitates need states rather than real experienced needs. For example, a child pretending to sleep may not be at all tired and may not want to fall asleep. When a child pretends to cook a meal and eat it, he may or may not be hungry. By pretending to sleep or eat when he is not immediately experiencing sleepiness or hunger, the child plays out an imaginary need state. Play, then, gives children a stage for experimenting with sense making, emotional experiences, imaginary need states, and motivations.

Emotional experiences and motives expressed, elaborated, modified, or extended through play serve as mediating factors in a child's relationship to reality and to his own affective states. Play does not produce knowledge within the child or tools and techniques for mastering reality or for distinguishing fantasy from reality. Rather, play encourages mental flexibility, or the ability to change one's approach in real situations, which can be exhibited later in life. For example, pretending to play school prepares the child in some ways to adopt the pupil role when he goes to school.

From the child's perspective, play has no utilitarian function. Incentives and motives arise from the process of playing itself, as a result of intellectual challenges, imagination, fantasy, and emotional experience. Children see no need to produce anything material or have a concrete result. The goal is to perform an adopted role and the result of play depends on the success of role performance. The play process, in and of itself, is important then, because it is a usually pleasurable experience that creates new opportunities, adds new dimensions to children's existing experiences and emotions, creates mental flexibility, and promotes further exploration of the environment.

It is often difficult for adults to think about playtime as a learning situation because play may not leave visible, material results. The process of play, playing itself, fascinates children. It captivates individuals involved in the play. Children typically experience play as a pleasurable and desirable activity, which they favor over other kinds of activity. However, for all its benefits from the perspective of the players themselves, adults often have difficulty in discerning learning processes or outcomes in play. Gadamer (1975, p. 93) described this aspect of play: "The movement which is play has no goal which brings it to an end; rather it renews itself in constant repetition.... The actual subject of play is obviously not the subjectivity of an individual who among other activities also plays, but instead the play itself."

From the prevalent adult perspective about what constitutes real learning, pretend play would be, at best, a strange learning situation. Donaldson (1993, p. 69) captured the paradoxical aspect of learning in play in her description of a typical adult's point of view that playing children are involved in "the apparently pointless activity of treating things as what they are not." She referred to three characteristics in children's use of objects during pretend play: (1) children use physically present objects to stand for, or serve as, other objects that are not present (a block becomes a telephone); (2) children attribute properties to objects that these objects do not actually possess (a toy car can fly); and (3) children create totally imaginary objects where, in reality, only empty space exists (children step over a pretend dog lying in front of a pretend fireplace in the dramatic play corner at the preschool).

Donaldson (1993) further points out that learning is not simply the acquisition of facts from people and experiences in a child's surrounding environment. Instead, Donaldson described a new and evolving mode of the mind, the "construct mode," which must be fed by deliberate, constructive acts of imagination. This deliberate, constructive use of imagination, feeding the new and evolving "construct mode," then, is a primary function of pretend play, in Donaldson's view. She describes the construct mode as follows: "Instead of here/now or there/then the mind will next begin to concern itself with a locus conceived as somewhere/sometime or anywhere/anytime. Thus in the construct mode we are no longer restricted to a consideration of episodes in our own experience—or even those we heard about from others. We start to be actively and consciously concerned about the general nature of things" (Donaldson, 1993, p. 80). Donaldson's construct mode nicely emphasizes the beginning of creative imagination in play.

Vygotsky presented a similar perspective on learning among young children in his analysis of the relationship between children's aesthetic creativity and play. Vygotsky (1987, p. 249) believed that playful learning takes place in a paradoxical form of "impossibilities" and that "these impossibilities would be dangerous for the children if they hide genuine and real mutual relations between ideas and objects. But they are not hiding anything, but, on the contrary, reveal color and underline. They strengthen (and do not weaken) the perception of reality in children."

Some people believe that play is the poor cousin of real learning because play, by its very nature, often involves a distortion of reality, at least a distortion of adults' perceptions of reality. Instead, play is a key factor in the development of the learner. According to Vygotsky, Donaldson, and Bateson (mentioned at the beginning of the chapter), then, the benefits of play in learning do not relate to mastering content or content-related skills, but rather to the development of more general and generalizable cognitive abilities, including the ability to learn how to learn and the ability to distinguish fantasy from reality.

The role of play in learning and development depends on the type of play and its pedagogical use. At the kindergarten level in Finland, for instance, we see a continuum of adult participation in children's play and use of play as a teaching tool:

1. Children engage in independent pretend role-play and adults participate only indirectly. For example, children have a shopping play in the play corner and adults are drinking coffee in the kitchen. Adults have collected props and play materials for shopping play; children asked to have permission to take them and start playing.

2. To promote the development of children's skills, knowledge, and personal traits, adults introduce new elements into children's play episodes as opportunities present themselves without breaking or derailing the mode or direction of the play. For example, Van Oers (1996) describes children's shoe store play, in which adults looked for teaching opportunities by asking questions, such as how can you be sure what kind of shoes are inside each box without opening the boxes? In this case children had to invent a system of symbols to denote the kind, size, and color of each pair before they mastered writing skills. In this play children were challenged to learn semiotic function they had not mastered before.

3. Teachers frequently and purposefully use play as a didactic method to promote specific learning outcomes in classroom settings. The third approach actually has little resemblance to authentic play because teachers are simply capitalizing on children's inclination to play as a way to involve them (perhaps even trick them) into content learning (Hakkarainen, 2002). As an example of this, a teacher might create a dice game to get children to practice adding numbers so they will know how many hops their piece can make on a game

board. This teacher sees no intrinsic value in playing the game; rather, it serves only as an enticement to practice an academic skill.

## NARRATIVE LEARNING

Typical methods for assessing learning outcomes in school settings do not reveal the true potential of play in the development of learning. However, developmental psychology provides several alternatives for capturing play-based learning and development. Among these alternatives is the narrative method or approach. The prototype of narrative learning is a story. Dewey described the power of a story in learning:

> Much assistance in the selection of appropriate material may be derived by considering the eagerness and closeness of observation that attend the following of a story or drama. Alertness of observation is at height whenever there is plot interest. Why? The balanced combination of the old and new, of the familiar and the unexpected... alternatives are suggested, but are left ambiguous, so that our whole being questions: What happened next? Which way did things turn out? (1910/1933, p. 253)

Bruner (1986, 1990, 1996) viewed a narrative as a condensation of life and endowed upon the story a special status as the unit of analysis for psychological development. For him, narrative was a symbolic schema through which a child interprets the world. Narratives describe and organize the world in which the child lives and acts. This function covers both the inner and the outer world. Narratives and narrative learning live very close to an individual child's personal experiences and sense making and it is through analysis of their play and narratives that adults can gain insight into their world, including their academic development and learning.

Egan (1986, 2005) proposed "the story form model" for curriculum design. A starting point of any story is a contradiction or opposite. The story of "Cinderella," for example, is about tension between good and bad; all features of the characters and all actions in the plot relate to this tension. Similarly, according to Egan, human efforts to discover the structure, sense, and meaning of phenomena and our narratives about this discovery all involve contradictions and tensions of one sort or another.

Fairy tales promote the same aspects of learning as does pretend play. El'koninova (1999, p. 183) described the psychological nature of classical fairytales as follows: "What the fairy tale prescribes in full aesthetic form are models of motives of moral behavior rather than models or specific ways to realize those motives, i.e., how to apply or measure up to them. The unselfish desire of the main character in a fairy tale to rectify a misfortune that has befallen others or him is realized not so much by the main character, but by the magical forces. The main character is rather passive in pursuing the aspiration to accomplish an altruistic deed; but he is active in one thing: he wants to help the victim of the misfortune; he resolves to offer his assistance; and he assumes responsibility for the actions entailed by his acceptance to accomplish such a mission. The main character in a fairy tale himself takes the decision to act nobly. We find a good illustration of this in the Brothers Grimm fairytales, "Twelve Brothers" or "Rapunzel."

According to El'koninova (1999), the secret charm of classical fairytales lies in our emotional identification with the story's main character:

> A model of the initiative behavior (sense of an action) is singled out by the child not through mental inferences and the operations of thought, but through a direct emotional relation to the main character, through participation in the events in the story. In assisting the hero, a child wants to do together with the main character what an ideal fairy tale world expects from the main character, and experiences with him all the trials he must undergo to prove his intentions. But to acquire the "experience" of this sense creating behavior, the child must participate in a story's events from the beginning to end and stay immersed in the make-believe world through all the events in the story. (p. 187)

Make-believe used in play may not aim at probing the sense of an action and emotional identification with the make-believe characters as fairytales do. However, there are many parallels between pretend play and fairytales. For instance, children often experiment with similar frames, involving ideal moral behavior, for example, during pretend play.

Although we can find many parallels between pretend play and fairytales, we can also find differences. For example, a fairytale constructs spatial boundaries in a specific way: "The world of a story is divided into two semantically opposite, nonintersecting spaces. A clear dividing line in the form of river, field, fence, or hearth separates the two spaces from one another. The boundary between the spaces always belongs to only one of the spaces, not both at the same time: for example, the door of a house belongs to inner space. The characters living in this space cannot change their surroundings. Only the main character can cross the boundary between the spaces and move from one to another" (Propp, 2000, p. 185). In pretend play, on the other hand, a door can become a window in the flash of an imagination or a river can become a landing strip or a sleeping dog can disappear all together.

In the next sections, I describe three environments, all part of an experimental research project, using different forms of the narrative approach as an alternative way to interpret learning through play.

## THE NARRATIVE LEARNING ENVIRONMENT OF THE FIFTH DIMENSION

The learning environment called "The Fifth Dimension"[3] actively uses elements of narrative learning. The Fifth Dimension, called 5th D, is a computer-supported learning environment developed by Michael Cole at the University of California, San Diego. The activity framework in 5th D combines fantasy journeys with challenging problem solving. Children participate in the journey by moving through mazes in a series of computer games. Task cards guide problem solving. Behind the whole system, there is the mysterious, invisible Wizard. He or she answers children's letters and notes and helps them in navigating through their mazes. The driving purpose behind the 5th D environment is to promote the creation of children's subcultures. Activities should be meaningful and joyful; but, at the same time, they should be intellectually challenging and enhance overall development.

Adults bring some elements of a classic story to the 5th D environment. For example, magical forces, typically in fairytales, are represented by the invisible Wizard, who donated the environment to the children and communicates with them through e-mail. Activities are organized using a journey metaphor; on their "journey" children meet challenges and problems. This "journey" is symbolically described with a scale model of a maze, where progress is only possible after the child solves a problem encountered in each room along the maze.

The first versions of the 5th D environments were organized for children who had lost their motivation for learning in the classroom setting. Cole and his colleagues tried to capitalize on children's motivation to play games and use this motivation for educational purposes. Meaningful and enjoyable 5th D activities had the hidden agenda of improving the children's basic academic skills—an endeavor in which their schools had failed them. To emphasize the difference between school and the 5th D environment, 5th D activities were offered as after-school activities and arranged as clubs (Cole, 1996).

Activity in the 5th D environment has a different structure compared to school settings. For instance, children play computer and board games. They draw, read stories, and interact with other children using telecommunication. Separate activities are connected to one another by a make-believe world, using the metaphor of a journey symbolized through the maze. Task cards guide problem solving at each stop along the maze. Curricular content is embedded in games and other activities. Subject matter may include communication skills, math, social studies, health, science, technology, and the arts, all with an emphasis on problem solving. Children participate in the activities individually and in groups. Their initiative and participation in the peer community is an important element of 5th D activities. Another characteristic of 5th D environments is that there is no position of strong adult authority.

The 5th D program has been implemented in many countries across the world, including Finland, the United States, Spain, Sweden, and Denmark. Finland has three 5th D programs, located in Hyvinkaa, Kajaani, and Rauma. Different 5th D environments found various ways to eliminate the authority position of adults. Although adults are typically present for safety and supervision, the children themselves decide where their journey will start, how to proceed from one activity to the other, and with whom they want to play. Each child is free to pursue his or her own individual goals and interests. Adults do not present tasks connected with the games in the maze; rather, tasks emerge naturally from the 5th D play-world. Children decide for themselves which tasks to choose and which strategies to use to complete their tasks. The 5th D environment radically changes the traditional question–answer scheme of communication between teachers and children (Mehan, 1979).

The Wizard is the creator and custodian of the 5th D but no one has seen him or her. Compared to typical classrooms, 5th D environments dramatically change power relationships between adults and children. The Wizard plays an important part in the elimination of adult authority positions in 5th D environments. Adults who help the children with 5th D activities are cast in the role of the Wizard's helpers. They are mediators between the Wizard and the children, but they are not authority figures or decision makers in the same sense as the classroom teacher.

Various other characteristics of the 5th D environment contribute to this special atmosphere for learning. Narrative content is present in the frame story of the Wizard, as well as in the games and the imaginary journey through the mazes (Nicolopoulou & Cole, 1993). But the narrative setting also includes the challenge of solving realistic problems connected with language, math, and other school subjects. This unusual combination of narrative and problem solving is quite different from typical school lessons.

Our own experimental study of narrative learning in the 5th D environment started in 1996 with children from 5 to 8 years of age (Hakkarainen, 2004). The first two versions of the 5th D learning environment were constructed following the original model. Adults prepared the environment, decided the size of the maze, and collected the games and other materials. The children got a message from the Wizard ("Velho" in Finnish), which included the blueprint of the maze. The children started by constructing the scale model of the maze. Task cards and the maze included instructions for what the children should do to learn. In the first version children transferred the problem-solving tasks into the "maze" play and in the second version they needed adult help for problem solving (Jutila & Niemela, 2000). However, our research team discovered that the task cards did not fit with the game narrative, including the Wizard and an imaginary journey through the maze.

On the basis of field notes and videotaped activities, we asked whether organized activities with task cards were appropriate for the youngest children in the 5th D program, the 5- and 6-year-olds. The children who participated in the first version of the program lost interest in the tasks after only a few sessions. Instead, they launched their own play of "the maze" in an adjacent room. They transformed cognitive tasks on the cards into "traps" situated in a play maze they constructed on their own. The traps were surprises or exciting challenges the children adopted from different sources, including familiar TV shows, videos, or books. In most cases, players got "trapped" when an object fell down and blocked their way or a secret door suddenly opened in the imaginary wall.

The maze enactment arose from a suggestion by the Wizard's helper and the presentation of big wooden building blocks to children. One of the boys initiated this play line involving traps after complaining: "No one listens to my ideas." An adult then encouraged him to build a maze the way he liked. When the child created a trap, the adult asked if the Wizard had proposed the addition of traps. The child denied this and explained the differences between the 5th D maze and the maze he was constructing from blocks. The trap idea attracted other children to his maze. At times all the children participated in the trap play and ignored the activities presented on the task cards.

As indicated by the following transcribed dialog, the children elaborated on the trap idea as they jointly constructed the block maze.

> Antti: Mikko, place more traps!
> Mikko: I have more than 10 already.
> Antti: More obstacles!
> Mikko: Done already. Want to see one? If someone goes this way, this falls down and I'll push one more.
> Mikko: By the way, I am the boss in this maze. Remember that!
>
> ———
>
> [Kaisa walks by]
> Kaisa: May I guess what these are?
> Mikko: What?
> Kaisa: Those traps.
> Mikko: Guess!
> Kaisa: This is one.
> Mikko: Right-o! Remember it, Kaisa. Don't fall down over here!

> [The block maze is built on the floor of the e-mail room. Children could walk through the maze or move toy animals in it. The problem was that the loosely structured maze could easily tumble. Mikko gave the following advice to the others.]

Mikko: Wait, don't move! You have to go through the whole maze!

Mikko: I have something to say! Don't move! Wait!

Adult: Wait! Mikko has something to say!

Mikko: If you get into a trap, you have to wait until I come and save you. I'll remove the fallen trap and animals. OK, you can move now.

Why was the trap maze more attractive to the children than the original 5th D mazes? This was partly due to the nature of the tasks on the cards and the games used in the early version, which merely transformed paper and pencil school tasks onto a computer screen. These simple cognitive tasks did not make sense to the youngest children, who had just started school or were getting ready for compulsory school. The essence of the maze was the surprise one might meet at any turn. The maze was not a technical construction project, but, rather, the embodiment of the sense of the maze using wooden blocks.

The second version had the same basic idea as the first one. Tasks were revised and included more kindergarten activities as the children came from kindergarten class. The Wizard was introduced for the children, as the nephew of Troll children knew earlier. The Wizard invited the children to participate in a test in order to become Wizard's helpers. The narrative content of the second version turned the maze into exciting play. Children started to decorate the maze they had just constructed on the Wizard's initiative. But the decoration was, at the same time, story making. When an adult asked what the children were doing, they did not hear the questions: "We cannot hear you. We are working on this." One of the few answers was, "We want to make it more exciting!" As a result, the maze was a collection of children's own short stories. The stories can be read in the decorations as can be heard in the children's explanations, as illustrated below:

> [A boy presented the decorated maze to an adult. One trap room constructed of stones was designed to fall down when someone entered the room. The boy presented his own construction.]

Pasi: This is what I have done. It is Witch Mountain.

Adult: What happens in the mountain?

Pasi: A witch lives there.

> [Places a self-made witch puppet on the mountain]
> Adult: Yes.
> Pasi: I made it by myself.
> Adult: There she rests. Is she friendly or something?
> Pasi: Friendly.
> Adult: Or scary?
> Pasi: Scary! She catches. If you are not silent when entering the room, she may catch you.

In the first two versions of 5th D, the maze and the tasks were, from the children's perspective, two separate realities. However, in the maze the children themselves constructed at the Wizard's suggestion, children traveled through a maze composed of their own challenging stories. In these two versions there were two sets of tasks: problem-solving tasks from the Wizard and children's story-based tasks or challenges. As the children worked on the second maze, the Wizard made another suggestion—that they construct adventures for each room by working together in pairs. The Wizard sent the following task by e-mail, which an adult read to a pair of girls:

> Adult: This is the message the Wizard sent: construct three towers of blocks. The yellow one is higher than the red one. The red one is lower than the blue and the blue is higher than the yellow. When you have solved the problem send me a picture of it in a letter. Good luck!

One of the main challenges in narrative learning is ambiguity or uncertainty about the learning task. Do the children really understand the directions? A goal of our study was to investigate how changes in narrative content changed children's interpretation of the problem situation. We found four transitions in the dialogue between two girls, age 6:3 and 6:6, and an adult on the tower problem relayed from the Wizard.

> 1. *Transition from individual building to cooperation.*
> Minna: My tower is so little. Kirsi has one so big [whining voice] [The girls quarrel over the blocks]
> Adult: What's that? You are a pair. Hey! [Minna takes blocks from Kirsi's tower and Kirsi takes them back]
> Kirsi: No, you can't take, but Minna took from my tower.
> Minna: We must work together. Let's place these first. [Takes blocks from Kirsi's hands and makes a yellow tower]
> 2. *Transition to joint trial-and-error attempt.*
> Kirsi: I'll construct the red tower.
> Minna: These go like this and then you add one.

Kirsi:  I'll take the red one and you take the blue.

Minna:  You have to take away from that.

Kirsi:  Give one to me!

Minna:  Still more away. Now we have it!

3. *Mixing colors.*

Minna:  There's not enough of those…. Too little blocks [Smacks her lips and looks keenly at the adult]

Adult:  What can you do in such a situation?

Kirsi:  Me know. Put those blocks here and then one more from the yellow [Gives advice to Minna]
Now we have it?

Adult:  How do you know what color that tower is? [Shows the mixed color tower]

Minna:  This is blue because there are mostly blue blocks.
[The girls take the extra blocks away]

4. *Solving the block tower problem.*

Minna:  What then?

Kirsi:  Wait a minute! Let's put one block here and then we take one away from this one.

Minna:  Not correct. This should be higher than the red one.

Kirsi:  Should the red one be higher or this one?

Adult:  Did it say that you have to use all the blocks?

Kirsi:  Now I know!
[Makes the yellow tower lower]

Minna:  The blue one was higher.
[The girls solve the problem by checking each color in turns]

Kirsi:  Now.
[The adult reads the task once more and the girls check the towers]

The problem-solving situation started with a conflict when the girls quarreled about who could play with the blocks. The adult reminded them that they should solve the problem together. After this the work proceeded as a genuine joint process, but the solution was reached only after the adult's hint that all the blocks were not necessary.

The role of the Wizard in this example was not far from the role of an ordinary teacher, who gives the tasks, encourages the children to attack the problem, and checks whether the solution is correct. The difference is that the Wizard was a virtual teacher and the adult represented him in the immediate problem-solving situation.

Based on our observations of the two first versions of 5th D, we concluded that kindergarten children need a stronger narrative framework if we wanted the program to work well for such young children. Adult-defined challenges on the task cards did not make sense to the children. By strengthening the narrative and situating the tasks firmly within the context of the story, we expected to increase children's understanding of the tasks as well as their interest in sustained participation. We moved step-by-step in our experimental work to narrative learning environments called "play world." At first maze and task cards were eliminated and problems were presented inside the narratives. Some dramatized stories did not include any formulated problems to be solved. But the stories conveyed a strong moral message, which influenced children's free play after story presentation. Systematic construction of play world requires adult participation after story presentation (Hakkarainen, 2004).

A thematic play world lasting several months is constructed by adults and children together using stories, folk tales, music, lights, dramatizations, visual aesthetics, pretending, role characters (presented by adults), scenery settings, etc. Themes are selected by picking out some central themes from folk tales or stories, which are important in children's general psychological development (e.g., fears, acceptance of differences, lying, etc.). The basic problem connected with each theme is handled from different points of view during successive sessions of joint activities in a play world.

The problems connected with themes of play worlds are not ordinary well-defined problems. They are focused on the exploration of sense. Play worlds present problems as riddles of sense and meaning, which presuppose creative solutions. Adults organize play world activities, but adults' participation should follow the aesthetic logic of play activity. Problems met in a narrative environment are not well defined. Problems have several levels and can be interpreted in different ways.

In addition to 5th D, our research project also involved analysis of the Learning Literacy in Play project described in the next section.

## LEARNING LITERACY IN PLAY

The project started as ongoing experimental work in literacy development using the narrative approach. Two master's degree students developed the Learning Literacy in Play environment at the Kajaani Department of Teacher Education. The basic philosophy was developed in El'konin's work in the 1960s and Zuckerman continued it. Vygotsky (1991) formulated the dilemma first as a question: Why are children not able to profit from their mastery of oral language when they start to write and read? When they start to read and write their mastery is on the level of 2-year-olds, while their oral language is consistent with their chronological age. El'konin (1999) developed modeling tools, which enhance transition from oral to written language. Zuckerman (1997) used these tools in the narrative world of sounds developed for 4- to 5-year-old children.

In our experimental work three successive narrative learning environments are constructed using the theoretical model: the adventure of forest animals in the world of Finnish sounds, the adventure of animals in the world of letters and writing, and the adventure of researchers in the world of grammar. All these adventures create an alternative learning environment compared to preschool and school activities.

A basic concept in the creation of alternative learning environments, such as 5th D and Learning Literacy in Play, is that such settings should differ from ordinary classrooms in significant ways, that children's experiences and ways of participating will differ from those in classrooms, and that the learning process will proceed differently as well. The following excerpt is from a pizzeria play involving a group of 6-year-old kindergarten children (Vähänen & Yrttiaho, 2000, pp. 42–55). Three girls initiated the play, which later included as many as 16 children.

> [The play started from the discussion between three girls]
> Selja: What shall we begin? Let's play, okay?
> Henna: Don't know.
> Noora: Let's play with Barbie dolls. We can get more from the small children.
> Selja: We have enough.
> Henna: I have it! What about a pizzeria?
> Noora: Don't know.
> Selja: Let's have a pizzeria.

After a moment of negotiation, the girls decided on a name for the pizzeria and wrote it on a piece of paper:

> Noora: What's the name of the pizzeria?
> Selja: Let's see. Maybe just "Pizzeria Toukovakka" (Spring crop)
> Henna: Is it Mac? (MacDonald's)
> Mary: Or Hessburger?[4] It is Hessburger.
> Noora: Yep.
> [The girls wrote the name "Hessburger" on a big piece of paper and discussed what letters are needed.]

In planning the play children used their own real-world experiences as much as possible. The children requested a folder for a menu. They decreed that orders should be written down on a small pad. For writing they needed ballpoint pens. They tested different colors and models. They dressed the table with a tablecloth and a vase filled with flowers. All waiters wore similar vests with floral decorations. They had a water bucket and a sponge for wiping the table. They found a real cash register in an adjacent room and requested a paper ribbon. The children required a spike for the receipts. The children even constructed a credit card machine near the cash register for customers who wanted to pay with plastic.

Launching the play required reorganizing the space to accommodate the pizzeria and the addition of materials not typically found in this environment, such as the cash register and the receipt spike.

The children had to negotiate with the adults throughout the pizzeria play. The children created the pizzeria in a small upstairs room with a loft. The loft served well as the restaurant kitchen because it included a play stove and kitchen utensils. However, the children wanted a table downstairs to create the dining area.

> Henna: We need a table.
> Selja: Could we take the dinotable? [A table used in the dinosaur play]
> [Asks permission from an adult]
> Selja: How can we place this table here? Can we move the clothes rack?
> Noora: For sure, let's move the whole rack to the corridor.
> [In order to write menus and take orders children needed writing utensils and pictures of various foods from magazines. They compared, ordered, and classified materials when drawing up the list.]
> Selja: [to an adult] Can we have pads for taking orders? We need paper for writing the menu. [Has a folder in her hand]
> Henna: How many menus do we need?
> Noora: Let's make two or three.
> Henna: We can cut a picture from the magazine and then write.
> Selja: Yep!
> Henna: I'll do desserts. [Writes while talking]
> Selja: I'll do food. [Writes something]
> Four more children become interested in writing lists. Mary, Tanja, Antti, and Jani joined in to plan what to put on the menu and organize the play.
> Mary: We need a cash register and money.

[Selja and Henna fetched the old cash register and asked to have a real paper ribbon for it. They did not find play money and Noora proposed to make cash cards. Selja said that a spike was necessary for keeping the receipts in order. Mary asked an adult to make a holder for the receipts. She came holding a block of wood with a spike in her hands. The other children made a device for processing credit cards by cutting a whole in a cardboard box.]

> Within the framework of the plot created jointly by the children, they were able to agree on and organize play projecting into future time. There were no major conflicts and everyone was enthusiastic about each new turn as the story developed through creation of the setting (the pizzeria) and the organization of props. The planning of the play offered the children an opportunity to be involved in joint child-initiated activity. Outside such a strong play frame, cooperation between so many children would be impossible and would result in unsolved conflicts. Here, though, the play process proceeded smoothly. When somebody proposed a turn of events, the new proposal supported the previous one and added a new dimension to it. (Vähänen & Yrttiaho, 2000, p. 55)

In support of one another's ideas, the children incorporated writing and reading into the play frame. All initiatives came from children themselves and emerged within the play situation, not from separate learning tasks, as illustrated by the excerpt below:

> Henna:  Do we need more than this paper? I'll write here "apple."
> How is it written? Is this correct?
> Selja:  Vegetarian pizza starts with a "V."
> Antti:  Then "e."
> Henna:  Selja, what am I writing?
> Selja:  Probably "lettuce" because you have "le" here.
> Antti:  Here we have fruit.
> [Shows pictures in a magazine]
> Henna:  Cut them out for me.

As the children were writing their lists, other uninvited children came along. They also began to work on the lists. No one was excluded because the children who initiated the pizzeria realized that much work remained to be done.

> [Mary and Tanya follow what is going on]
> Selja:  What would this be?
> Mary:  Write "meat pastry."
> [Selja wrote]
> Henna:  Shall I write the drinks here?
> Mary:  I could help you do it.
> Selja:  Shall we start with Mary?
> Henna:  Don't know.

In this play situation, reading and writing became shared tasks, not solitary, individual tasks as they often are in ordinary classroom situations. While none of the children in this play episode were fluent readers or writers, they were able to extend and exceed their individual mastery levels by working cooperatively. All children made mistakes in spelling, but the onlookers offered sometimes-helpful suggestions. Each child's learning was promoted, at least in small steps toward mastery, as one read or wrote and the other reflected and commented. In the course of the play, the roles changed, with readers becoming responders and writers becoming readers as the situation and their play roles dictated.

> [Mary writes down an order from Arttu, Salla follows.]
> Arttu: I'll have an ice-lolly.
> Mary: Fizzy, fizzy, ice, fizzy ice.
> Arttu: Strawjuice[5] then.
> Salla: "Saw"! It reads, "saw" here!
> [Mary does not say anything, adds letters, and stops writing. Next she takes an order from Keela]
> Keela: This lady would have…. Where is strawjuice?
> Mary. On this page are the strawjuices. "Saw."
> Salla: "Saw"! Again it reads, "saw"!
> [Mary stares at Salla, makes a smacking sound with her lips, and writes down the missing letters.
> Mary has to rewrite the order from Arttu, because she has lost the paper.]
> Arttu: One ice-lolly and a strawjuice.
> [Mary writes strawjuice and spells out the letters]
> Mary: Now it is correct.
> Salla: Hmm.

Mary did not comment on Salla's corrections. Instead, she added letters. She was obviously irritated, but acted according to her role in the pizzeria play, possibly because breaking her role to make remarks to Salla outside the play would probably have led to open conflict. The third time Mary checked her own writing carefully and emphasized that now it was correct. This provides a good illustration of the specific nature of a play frame. Role actions are based on imagination and the creation of a mutually created storyline, but relationships and emotions connected with these actions may be genuine. In the following excerpt Mary accepts comments from Keela, who is much younger than she.

> Mary: What is your name?
> Keela: Keela.
> [Mary writes Kela]

> Keela: Look! A letter is missing! K-e-e-l-a.
> [Keela shows her "teller card"].
> Mary: Yep, right.
> [Mary adds an e]

"The kitchen team" in this play has to be able to read, because they have written orders from the "waiters." Mirja was not able to read, but the others helped her. When Henna came with her "orders," she helped with the reading. Mary, in the role of a waiter, helped Mirja prepare the food.

> Mary: Hi Mirjaaa! Have you prepared the food? Okay. Wait a moment, I'll go to help. Mirja, now I'll come to help you!
> [Mirja has collected orders on the spike. Mary takes one and reads]
> Mary: Ice-lolly. Strawjuice.
> Mirja: Strawjuice.
> Mary: You try, too.
> Mirja: Don't know really. You read it and I will prepare.
> [Mirja puts on a tray items that Mary reads from the slips of paper]
> Mary: That's all!
> Mary: Take them out!
> Mirja: To whom?
> Mary: K-e-e-l-a, to Keela. [Spells out the letters]
> [Mary helps Mirja with the orders and supports her reading]
> Mary: Mirja! Arttu's order!
> [Mirja takes the note and Mary reads aloud to Mirja]
> Mary: Now you can do it yourself.
> Mirja: Yep!
> [Mirja goes to "the kitchen" and calls for Mary. Mary did not react, so Mirja comes and whispers into her ear]
> Mary: Why not?
> Mirja: That's why.
> Mary: Let's go, we two and read them together.

Earlier Mirja was not interested in reading and writing, but the situation changed radically after this play. She started actively to practice these skills and learned reading in 2 months with peer assistance. Her role in the play was of great help to her because she was shy and often retired from situations in which she felt unsure.

In their play frames, children jointly construct a shared zone of proximal development, to use Vygotsky's term. None of the players has all of the knowledge or skills needed to enact the play, so they help one another in turns. Even in situations with an adult, children often provide the scaffolding themselves, as illustrated in the next passage:

> Antti:  [to an adult] I am writing a shopping list, can you help?
> Adult:  What do you want to write?
> Antti:  Soft drink and ice cream.
> Adult:  What letter does soft drink begin with?
> Antti:  Sssoft drink. (Exaggerating the beginning "s" sound)
> Mary:  It is "s."
> Antti:  What does it look like?
>         [Mary shows and continues her work on writing the menu.]
> Antti:  What is the last letter in "ice cream"?
> Mary:  Mmm.
> Antti:  It's ready now.

In this episode the adult withdrew when he saw that Mary was able to help Antti. The play frame created natural situations for peer scaffolding for learning concrete skills. These skills, then, became an integral part of an authentic play context, not a separate learning task, as is often the case in school.

Written language had a central role in the pizzeria episodes. The play context and experience offered an excellent environment for making sense of reading and writing. The children diligently compared written letters and sound forms because texts were important in their play. They observed independently that speech can be transformed into written text and written notes can be used in a meaningful way. Written language was an important tool in this play activity, as it often does when children initiate play episodes. The question of how to write words correctly appears again and again as children construct stories and play frames together.

The learning environment described above differs from typical Finnish kindergarten and elementary school practice where reading and writing are taught as basic skills. In school, teachers focus on the mastery of technical reading and writing skills. Much less attention is paid to sense-making in typical classrooms than in a child-initiated play setting like the one cited above.

Even in child-initiated play settings, however, adults can gently guide play toward desired learning activities and they can create the need for specific kinds of learning by influencing the structure or the content of the play. The goal is to make learning an integral part of the play structure itself, rather than something separate and compartmentalized, as it often is in school. For instance, in a play environment similar to the one with the pizzeria (Hall, 1994), children were told that it is possible to use different symbols and shorthand writing for taking orders from restaurant patrons. Messages are still understandable. When the children realized that they could write understandable messages in a shorter time with the shorthand, they began to use that method consistently.[6]

We can see, then, how both 5th D and Literacy Learning through Play create learning environments where play and narrative learning are central. Next I briefly describe the third narrative learning environment in our experimental study, in which adults and children together created a shared world of play.

## Play-Worlds as a Challenge for Self-Change

Children's independent free play is a central ideal in Scandinavian early childhood education, even if this ideal is not always realized in daily practice. However, some educational goals require adult participation rather than independent free play. In spite of continuing debates about the appropriate balance between freedom and adult guidance during play, the Finnish daycare system has experimented with different approaches to adult participation in children's play. For example, direct play teaching was used in "didactic plays." Teachers created play corners in daycare centers throughout Finland, hoping to stimulate children's peer play (e.g., play store, home, doctor's visit, party). And, in some places, teachers supported children's free play as the cornerstone of their daily daycare experience. However, in most situations, adults were organizers, supporters, and regulators of children's play, but they did not participate actively in the play (Hakkarainen, 1990, 1999).

Lindqvist (1996) proposed a radically different approach in her play-world concept. She suggested that adults and children should jointly develop challenging play-worlds following the aesthetic form of play. The approach is based on Vygotsky's theoretical idea of the aesthetic nature of play. Vygotsky argued that all forms of children's art share common roots. "This syncretism points to the common root that unites all different branches of children's art. This common root is the child's play, which serves as the preparatory stage for his artistic creation" (Vygotsky, 2004, p. 67). According to this view, then, play has a special role in the development of artistic creativity and imagination. In practical work teachers can capitalize on the syncretistic, or unifying, nature of play, using literature, drama, dance, paintings, and other art forms to inspire play and, conversely, using play to inspire further creative and imaginative self-expression through various art forms and media.

Proponents of the joint approach suggest that adults and children construct shared play-worlds around some important and central theme in children's lives, such as their children's fears, moral dilemmas, the interest in the tensions between good and evil. Usually teachers initiate the creation of a play-world by telling a good story or tale. For example, a teacher might read a story about Moomin trolls and then work together with the children to develop a play on this topic. As the play evolves, both children and teachers may introduce new elements. For instance, teachers might help children elaborate on the theme by enacting a specific role or scene. Together children and teachers might construct props and scenery or agree jointly to imagine particular settings and props.

One of the play-worlds in Lindqvist's (1995) developmental work was called "Alone in the Big Wide World." The starting point was the basic goal of Scandinavian early education, "to create the atmosphere of safety in children's lives." A demanding task for educators is determining how to address children's fears as they try to create and maintain safe environments for them. A potential risk in dramatizing children's fears, for example, is that the environment will seem unsafe to the children, even though the goal of such play is to give concrete faces to different fears and, thereby, help children develop psychological tools for dealing with their fears when they arise in the real world. Lindqvist addressed the dilemma by clearly differentiating between "horror" and "terror." Horror can arise from a concrete danger, which, in turn, provides the opportunity for children to handle the fear constructively. On the other hand, terror includes undefined, abstract fear, which cannot be met constructively.

A good, multilayered text can provide a beginning point for developing different meanings and orientations in children's play activity. Adults and children together step into the text and start to jointly create a shared imaginary world. An important character of texts used for this purpose is their dramatic quality and challenging plot. The text should be open to several viable interpretations. Usually, texts like this were written for both adults and children. Examples include *Winnie the Pooh*, *Alice in Wonderland*, or *Moomin Troll*.

Our research documented that adults and children can indeed construct shared play-worlds based on such texts. For example, adults may take on the role of one of the story characters and, in this role, they visit the children in an everyday environment, such as their classroom. Such dramatizations appear to make adult participation in play worlds easier for both adults and children. Role characters and their dialogue with children help the use of imagination. A role character is a mediator between the literary world and everyday reality and can enhance adults' possibility to develop children's play and imagination.

Physical changes in the environment help to turn an ordinary setting into another world. This can be a joint project of adults and children. Adults can use artistic methods of theater purposefully to create live experiences in an imaginary world. All methods of aesthetic expression can be combined in the creation of play-worlds. These methods include dramatic scenes, music, dance, painting, storytelling, and the like.

Since 1996 joint construction of play-worlds has been part of our experimental work to vertically integrate groups for children between the ages of 4 and 8. The use of play-worlds is also a familiar approach in integrated educational work in multiage grouping. These groups bring together children from day care, kindergarten (6 years old), and elementary school (first and second graders). Approximately 70–80% of the time, these children work in one big multiage group. During the remainder of their time in school, they work in smaller, age-segregated groups. Shared play-worlds make it possible for all children in these broad age groups to participate equally in learning experiences. The following section includes a description of the construction process in a recent project based on the text by famous Swedish writer Astrid Lindgren. The play-world was based on her novel *Ronya, the Robber's Daughter* and was carried out during the spring term of 2003.

When constructing shared play-worlds with children, teachers should have clear educational goals as a framework. These goals guide them in selecting an appropriate text to launch the play-world. In this case, the teacher's educational goal was to develop the feeling of togetherness in the children's group and, thereby, enhance individual children's social skills. Within the group of 26 children, 10 had diagnosed special needs. Some were hyperactive and unable to concentrate. Others were developing normally, but were timid and shy. The theme started before Christmas vacation in 2002. Teachers read Astrid Lindgren's book, *Ronya, the Robber's Daughter* to the children in parts during December and the children wrote diaries reflecting on the story or made drawings. The children saw the same adventure on video just before the break.

When they returned to school in January, teachers initiated a discussion about the most exciting characters in the story. The children said they would like to construct a play-world based on the story. The adults responded to the children's proposal. One morning a troll girl, "Inka," (one of the adults) appeared in the class and invited the children to help the trolls build a new cave because the old one was destroyed. The children's building project produced five different caves for the trolls. The adults carefully observed the children's independent activity in the cave construction process.

The children themselves came to the same conclusion as adults: the play-world of trolls is not possible without clear rules. This problem was attacked indirectly. "Inka" appeared when the children were playing trolls and told them that, in the old troll community, they used to have a village elder to settle disputes. But there was no longer such an elder in the community, so a new solution was needed. The children suggested elections like the parliamentary elections a couple of months earlier. The elected elder was a boy from the second grade with special needs. He organized the preparation of rules for the play community.

The roles enacted by the adults were adapted to meet the children's needs and interests. A shy and timid adult troll, "Ines," did not dare enter the children's play-world. She just handed a message from "Inka" and waited for the children's reactions. She especially attracted shy girls in the group and her growing initiative encouraged the children.

Adults also created a different figure in the hyperactive troll "Mirkku." She wanted to be kind, but she disturbed, and sometimes destroyed, the others' activities. The presence of this character turned some children, especially those who were diagnosed with hyperactivity and behavior problems, wild. We videotaped Mirkku's visit and then showed the tape to the children afterward. This viewing session raised questions about how the rules of the troll community could be made more effective. The elected elder formulated the conclusion: "If someone does not follow the rules, he or she should write on the wall of the cave: I WILL NEVER DO IT AGAIN." All children accepted the rule, made it their own, and followed it in all later sessions without adults' control.

The modification of adult roles aimed at group effects. A shy-person role provided a model for timid girls on how to overcome their shyness and participate in the joint play-world activity. The hyperactive troll "Mirkku" was more problematic because the children readily recognized that Mirkku was like one particular boy in the classroom. This raised the question: Should adults offer the children negative models of behavior through role enactment? In this case, the shared experience of seeing an adult imitate the behavior of some children, reviewing the videotape and engaging in discussion about the situation led to some positive psychological outcomes. The children started to discuss quite seriously the conditions under which they would let "Mirkku" visit their play-world again and what rules she would have to follow. Joint decision upon the rules in the group had visible effects on hyperactive boys. The rules were meant for "Mirkku," but as a matter of fact the children made the rules for themselves. Each member of the group was not just individually responsible for his or her behavior, but the whole group bore collective responsibility. These observations led to a students' project, in which the problems of children with ADHD diagnosis were attacked using joint narratives and play-world construction.

The most visible changes at the individual level took place in the school life of the "village elder" during the play-world project. The boy was in the second grade during the project. He participated in three earlier play-world projects with this group of children. Each narrative environment had obvious effects on his life situation. In the beginning, at age 4, he had quite serious neurological learning problems, visited a therapist weekly, and needed a personal aid in all group activities. The position of village elder in the fourth play-world project gave him the challenge of taking personal responsibility for the social order of the whole play community. By this time, he no longer needed constant adult help. In his role as village elder, he turned not to adults, but rather to his peers when he needed guidance and support to resolve disputes in the community. His improved social position within the peer group seemed to inspire changes in his views on learning as well. For instance, while he earlier had great difficult with math, he now joined his peers in saying "math is cool."

Each of the three narrative learning environments in our study, 5th D, Literacy Learning through Play, and Joint Play-Worlds, demonstrated the potential of narrative-based play as an alternative approach to learning in the early childhood years. Both 5th D and Joint Play-World projects used narrative-based approaches to meet the needs of children from relatively wide age spans.

## The Potential of Narrative Learning in Child Development

Vygotsky claimed that play always creates the zone of proximal development (ZPD). What did he mean by this, especially given that much of his discussion about ZPD was intertwined with direct instruction, not play?

Pretend role-play includes several factors requiring understanding of another person's position and point of view. It is quite interesting to compare the relationship between the same two children in their everyday interactions and in their play. Taking the other person's perspective may actually be easier in play than in everyday situations. In role relationships two or more children need to coordinate their actions with the actions of others. They need to understand differences in the person's actual positions and the positions he takes in character. The use of objects in play further reinforces perspective taking. For example, if the child playing the role of doctor uses a small stick as a syringe, the child playing the role of patient must understand the "doctor's" actions and play along or the episode will be disrupted. Children often have to understand a peer's use of an object without direct conversation. This requires attention to nonverbal clues and in-character actions of the other child.

Certain features of play, such as using one object to represent another, are widely accepted as indicators of general psychological development. But from the perspective of psychological development, the easiness of substituting a model or symbol for an object is not the main feature of play. More essential is why children make substitutions. Is their perception distorted? We can easily find out by asking them that children are able to understand the real meaning of objects and phenomena, but meaning making is not guiding their actions. Children give another sense for the whole situation and objects, using them in a "wrong" way. This tension between meaning making and sense making is the driving force of development in play. Play operations can be real and derived from the meaning of objects, but the sense of the situation varies depending on play plot and other factors. The sense of play may be preserved even if realization differs.

Role actions and relationships are closely connected to the development of children's self-picture. Here, the direct connection between the individual and his or her play actions disappears. The play role mediates this relationship or even substitutes for the real subject (acting person). A child playing "bunny" is "me-bunny" carrying out bunny-like actions. Through roles a child identifies with other humans, but has the awareness that an ordinary child, himself, is playing the role. This is a case of double subject, which helps the child to gradually find his or her real self.

Play actions draw away from real person and real subject, but paradoxically this makes the child more conscious about his or her possibility to decide on play actions. The child starts to understand himself as the subject of emotional experience, "perezhivanie." Researchers have designed experimental studies to examine the relationship between the level of pretend role-play (independent elaboration of roles, the level of role performance) and self-picture (stability, consciousness of self-image) experimentally. This work suggests a direct relationship between these factors. For example, systematic development of pretend roles with weak players (2–6 months) has visible effects on their play skills and self-picture (El'konin, 1989).

Developmental effects of play, as described above, are still isolated phenomena. We have the challenge to explain more comprehensive and holistic characteristics of development connected with play, as Vygotsky sketched in his general approach. El'konin (1978/1999) identified four broad domains of development in which the developmental potential of play is essential: (1) needs and motivation, (2) overcoming cognitive egocentrism, (3) internal actions, and (4) volitional features of the child's actions.

According to El'konin, essential changes take place in the development of a child's motivation under the influence of play. At first an adult and adult's actions provide a model for the child's actions. The child wants to act like the adult at the stage of object play. The next step in motivational development is based on a new type of relationship with cultural surroundings. This relationship is emotionally colored and establishes new sense and meanings for playing with objects. For example, a child's play with a doll changes from the most basic forms, simply manipulating the doll, to more elaborate forms including emotional and cultural content, such as reenacting the relationship between mother and child when the mother is trying to get the child to mind and culturally specific childrearing rituals.

El'konin (1978/1999) thought that condensation and shortening of play actions is a clear indication that the child has observed human relationships and has experienced indirectly their emotional tenor. This is why the child at first understands only the emotional significance of adult actions toward others and thinks that this is the basis of all relationships between adults. For example, when a small child sees his or her parents quarreling, the child reacts to the emotional state of the mother without understanding the quarrel as a phenomenon or its reasons.

But a child's emotional identification with adults does not change him or her into an adult. The child clearly understands even when he enacts an adult role in play that he is, in reality, still a small child. The child is emotionally oriented to the sense or underlying meaning of adults' activity, but he realizes his position as a child in the adult world. This contradiction produces a need for being like adults, which is possible in the imagined situations of pretend play. From the perspective of play's developmental potential, then, we can see that play promotes new motivations, including the motivation to be like, or pretend to be like, adults in play. Emotionally colored immediate wishes are transformed into more general conscious intentions. In this case, a small child's wish to be like an adult transformed into general, intrinsic motivation to grow up and become more adult. Residing in this wish is the need to learn the knowledge and skills required of adults.

Development of play and internalized actions go hand in hand. Play actions rest less and less on substituting objects as children mature. At the beginning, play actions are detailed, and concrete objects are necessary for them. Later, merely naming an object can substitute it, as, for example, when a child in the shopping play pays by putting her hand in the pocket, takes imaginary money, and says, "Here you are." As children grow, play actions are shortened and often take the form of symbolic gestures complementing talk. For example, while a younger child would feed a puppet with a real spoon, an older child might just do a slight indicatory movement toward the mouth of the puppet. Play actions are in the no man's land between external and internal actions when they are carried out as suggestive external actions, as would be the case when two boys were playing traveling to the mountains by going around the space of our play club and holding in their hands imaginary bags full of equipment. In this case, play action was no longer external, but not yet completely internal either.

We may say that play creates the opportunity to transform external action into internal action, which is supported by speech. In this sense, play creates the zone of proximal development of internal actions. We can suppose, then, that play creates connections between phenomena and objects that are otherwise not possible. For example, two boys were constructing a steering device for a rocket and combined different parts from an old television set and an old clock in order to create an image of mechanical transmission. This may have important effects on learning and problem solving outside the play situation, since, for example, it may inspire reflection and critical thinking. El'konin (2005) proposed that play develops general mechanisms of thinking.

Play guides children's activity in a way, which is important in volitional regulation of action. Among young children role-play typically evolves hidden rules, but as children grow older, play activity is gradually governed by more open rules, as was the case in the troll play-world described earlier. Vygotsky (1966/1977) emphasized that in role-play the child has to consistently and continuously repress immediate impulses in order to act according to the role taken. For Vygotsky this was a basic feature of play, which supported his assertion that play always creates the zone of proximal development. For El'konin, the child's voluntary acceptance of a role behavior model and the act of comparing real actions with the role model's actions constituted the core of volitional development through play. For example, a child may take on the role of a shy troll and then compare his everyday actions in the same situations.

Zaporozhets's (1986) experimental work demonstrates the importance of play in the development of will and volition. In general, movements are the domains of activity where children consciously start to train volitional actions, as is the case, for example, when young children first try to catch a ball or hit a ball with a bat. In sports situations, the play frame and the quality of required movements changed over time. In more formal dramatized situations, such as plays to be produced for an audience, children prepared more carefully and concentrated intensively than they did in spontaneous dramas, such as cooking dinner in the house corner. In any type of play, though, the child carried out a double task: performing a role (in sports, staged dramatizations, spontaneous dramas) and, simultaneously, controlling his or her own behavior. The standard model for the role taken by the child guides activity and is the criterion upon which actions are judged. This duality is the basis for reflection. In play there is not yet conscious will and control based on it. But the child's affective relationship to a play activity includes all elements of intentional action.

## DISCUSSION

There is a clear structural similarity between play and narratives. Bruner (1996) even claimed that narrative is a structural unit of child development through which the child interprets the world. He wrote about the "narrative construal of reality." Donaldson (1993) talked about "narrative mode" as a developmental stage in a child's life. Narrative and story mediate and create sense and meaning in a child's life. Glaubman, Kashi, and Koresh (2001) claimed that we should adopt a narrative approach to pretend play. Each theorist desired to create a more comprehensive way to understand and explain learning and development.

Learning in play cannot be evaluated or developed with the same methods as in school. Instead, new approaches, like narrative learning, are necessary to develop play, as well as the potential benefits of play for children. Narrative learning is a holistic learning concept combining emotional, volitional, and cognitive aspects of learning. The starting point in narrative learning is not cognitive skills or subject matter, but, rather, sense making at both individual and cultural levels. This orientation gives learning greater developmental potential. Long ago, Dewey (1910/1933) recognized this potential and proposed the use of stories in school instruction.

Play can be used to enable children to make more sense of their lives. Children try to create their own fantasy world when they move in and out of their real and pretend situations. Children create their own versions of an event, real or imagined. This sense making was the key to the development of consciousness in Vygotsky's theory of mind.

But how can play and narrative learning be used for sense making in everyday ECE practice? Our research program started from simple observations about Finnish school practice. Curious and eager first graders lost their internal motivation for learning motivation in 3–4 years. Play makes sense to children because they themselves create both the play and the sense, but school learning seldom makes sense to children. The experimental material above describes our attempts to create sense in learning situations and to document internal potentials of play and narratives.

Narratives were used for sense making first in traditional problem-solving situations (tower building problem). We then moved to the learning of basic skills in the children's play environment (maze play, pizzeria play) and in the last example (play world of trolls) to an illustration of dynamic assessment through play (Lidz & Gindis, 2003). Play-world was based on the assessment of developmental needs in the group, and the role figures were shaped according to these needs.

The empirical evidence from our study demonstrates how narratives and play change the learning process. But these changes in the learning process focus primarily on the development of psychological functions or problem solving rather than on broader developmental outcomes.

Yet we still need to know more about the developmental potential of play and how to capitalize on it in early childhood education. Vygotsky's and El'konin's theoretical approaches advanced knowledge about general qualities of play to a greater extent than have practical experiments. The potential of play lies in sense making and its connection to the development of human consciousness. Both Vygotsky and El'konin drew a clear distinction between meaning and sense making. For them, play was the activity in which children experiment with sense making, using culturally defined meanings as tools. Learning in play necessarily involves sense making. Therefore, play has great developmental potential and, as Vygotsky argued, creates the zone of proximal development. Sense making within the ZPD can be readily observed as children make choices in cooperation with peers during play.

What does the narrative learning approach require of teachers? How does using the narrative approach change a teacher's daily work? What new challenges does it pose? The Scandinavian free play tradition proposes that children should be left by themselves in fluent play situations and school tradition emphasize teacher's all-knowing authority. It has been quite difficult to understand the importance of the children's point of view and construct child-centered learning situations. The teacher should let children develop their own ideas. The construction of a child-centered learning situation presupposes that teachers have skills of carrying out different roles, dramatization, storytelling, and understanding the developmental dynamics of play and narrative learning.

In our research program, we have studied narrative learning and the use of play-worlds in vertically integrated child groups including children between the ages of 4 and 8 in two Finnish cities. The research focused on the role of narrative learning in the "crisis" developmental period of 5–7 years.[7] The main problem is how narrative learning experience helps children to overcome developmental challenges and create a sustainable motivational basis for school learning (Hakkarainen, 2002).

In our field studies focusing on vertical integration of age groups, we have combined three separate curriculum guidelines (day care, kindergarten, and elementary grades) into one developmental program. However, we did not change the structure of the curriculum, but we selected activities using their developmental impact as the major criterion. We emphasized personality development more than learning of concrete basic skills or content orientation as the Finnish guidelines do. We transformed the constructive learning approach in the national guidelines into narrative learning methods. We viewed the development of learning potential as a part of lifelong learning in our program. The Finnish guidelines, stressing school readiness, take a shorter developmental perspective than our perspective on lifelong learning.

The present Finnish educational system produces contradictory results. We have gained top results in international comparative studies of school achievement among 14-year-olds in main school subjects (OECD, 2002). But, at the same time, 20–30% of Finnish school children have learning difficulties and many more are not content with school. Simultaneous with the new curriculum guidelines, the National Board of Education has launched a national project on developing children's creativity at school. Separate and often contradictory projects, like the content-focused curriculum guideline alongside the national creativity project, will not solve problems in the Finnish educational system. Rather, we propose that a more holistic narrative learning approach in early education would capitalize on and promote children's developmental potential, thereby creating a more realistic solution.

## NOTES

1. The original Russian terms "smysl" and "znacenie" are difficult to translate into English. The scope and content of "sense making" and "meaning making" are broader in Russian. They are often translated with the terms "personal significance" and "meaning." But their difference is essential in Russian play theory where "as if" acting is based on "sense making" and not "meaning making." In order to make this difference we use the terms "sense," "sense-field," "personal sense," and "cultural sense," although they are not an exact counterpart of Russian terms.

2. "Perezhivanie" means to "live through emotions." The Russian term is often not translated into English.

3. The term was adopted from Vygotsky's fellow researcher, A.N. Leontiev, to denote the psychological development of consciousness and sense making.

4. A Finnish chain of hamburger restaurants.

5. Makes a new word by combining juice and straw.

6. In our example, children used the Finnish language where written and spoken language are very close. Transformation of oral language into a written form is easier than in English.

7. Vygotsky called this period "the crisis of the seventh year."

## REFERENCES

Bateson, G. (1972). *Steps to the ecology of mind*. New York: Ballantine Books.

Broström, S. (1999). Drama games with 6-year-old children: Possibilities and limitations. In Y. Engeström, R. Miettinen, & R. -L. Punamäki (Eds.), *Perspectives on activity theory* (pp. 250–263). New York: Cambridge University Press.

Bruner, J. (1986). *Actual minds, possible worlds*. Cambridge, MA: Harvard University Press.

Bruner, J. (1990). *Acts of meaning*. Cambridge, MA: Harvard University Press.

Bruner, J. (1996). *The culture of education*. Cambridge, MA: Harvard University Press.

Cole, M. (1996). *Cultural psychology*. Cambridge, MA: Harvard University Press.

Corsaro, W. A. (1997). *The sociology of childhood*. Thousand Oaks, CA: Pine Forge Press.

Davydov, V. V., & Kudryavtsev, V. T. (1997). Razvivayushie obucenie. Teoreticeskaya osnova perekhoda ot doshkol'nogo do shkol'nogo obuceniya. [Developing education: Theoretical basis of transition from preschool to school]. *Voprosy psikhologii, 43*(1), 3–18.

Dewey, J. (1933). *How we think.* Boston: Henry Holt. (Original work published 1910).

Donaldson, M. (1993). *Human minds.* London: Allen Lane Penguin Press.

Egan, K. (1986). *Teaching as story-telling.* Chicago: University of Chicago Press.

Egan, K. (2005). *An imaginative approach to teaching.* San Francisco: Jossey-Bass.

El'konin, D. B. (1989). *Izbrannye psikhologicheskie trudy. Tom 1* [Collected psychological works, Vol. 1]. Moscow: Pedagogika.

El'konin, D. B. (1999). *Psikhologiya igry* [The psychology of play] (2nd ed.). Moscow: Vlados. (Original work published 1978).

El'konin, D. B. (2005). The psychology of play. *Journal of Russian and East European Psychology, 43,* 1–2.

El'koninova, L. I. (1999). Predmetnost detskoi igry v kontekste ponimaniya igrovogo i skazochnogo prostranstva – vremeni [The object-orientation of child play in the context of understanding of space-time in play and stories]. *Mir Psikhologii, 4,* 181–192.

Fein, G. G. (1981). Pretend play in childhood: An integrative review. *Child Development, 52,* 1095–1118.

Gadamer, H. (1975). *Truth and method.* New York: Seabury Press.

Glaubman, R., Kashi, G., & Koresh, R. (2001). Facilitating the narrative quality of sociodramatic play. In A. Göncu & E. L. Klein (Eds.), *Children in play, story, and school* (pp.132–157). New York: Guilford Press.

Hakkarainen, P. (1990). *Motivaatio, leikki ja toiminnan kohteellisuus* [Motivation, play and object-orientation of activity]. Helsinki: Orienta Konsultit.

Hakkarainen, P. (1999). Play and motivation. In Y. Engeström, R. Miettinen, & R.-L. Punamäki (Eds.), *Perspectives on activity theory* (pp. 231–249). New York: Cambridge University Press.

Hakkarainen, P. (2002). *Kehittävä esiopetus ja oppiminen,* [Developmental teaching and learning in early childhood]. Jyväskylä, Finland: PS-kustannus.

Hakkarainen, P. (2004). Narrative learning in the Fifth Dimension. *Outlines, 4*(1), 5–20.

Hall, N. (1994). Play, literacy and the role of the teacher. In J. R. Moyles (Ed.), *The excellence of play* (pp. 113–124). Buckingham, UK: Open University Press.

Hughes, F. P. (1998). *Children, play, and development.* Needham Heights, MA: Allyn &Bacon.

Illyenkov, E. V. (1991). *Filosofija i kul'tura* [Philosophy and culture]. Moscow: Politizdat.

Jutila, V., & Niemelä, M. (2000). *Velhon jäljissä labyrinttimatkalla.* [Following the steps of the wizard in maze-journey]. Kajaani: Oulun yliopiston Kajaanin opettajankoulutusyksikön julkaisuja Sarja C 7.

Lidz, C., & Gindis, B. (2003). Dynamic assessment of evolving cognitive functions in children. In A. Kozulin, B. Gindis, V. Ageyev, & S. Miller (Eds.), *Vygotsky's educational theory in cultural context* (pp. 99–118). New York: Cambridge University Press.

Lindqvist, G. (1995). *The aesthetics of play: A didactic study of play and culture in preschools.* Stockholm: Almqvist & Wiksell.

Lindqvist, G. (1996). *Lekens möjligheter.* [The possibilities of play]. Lund, Sweden: Studentlitteratur.

Mehan, H. (1979). *Learning lessons.* Cambridge, UK: Cambridge University Press.

National curriculum guidelines on early childhood education and care in Finland (2003). Retrieved May 24, 2005, from http://www.stakes.fi/varttua/english/curriculum.htm

Nicolopoulou, A., & Cole, M. (1993). Generation and transmission of shared knowledge in the culture of collaborative learning: The Fifth Dimension, its play-world, and its institutional contexts. In E. A. Forman & C. A. Stone (Eds.), *Contexts for learning: Socio-cultural dynamics in children's development* (pp. 283–314). New York: Oxford University Press.

Piaget, J. (1972). *Play, dreams and imitation in childhood* (C. Gattegno & F. M. Hodgson, Trans.). London: Routledge & Kegan Paul. (Original work published 1946)

OECD (2002). *First results from the OECD programme for international student assessment.* Retrieved May 24, 2005, from http://www.pisa.oecd.org/document/55/

Pramling, I. (1994). *Kunnandets grunder* [The basics of mastery] (Göteborg Studies in Educational Sciences 94). Göteorg: Acta universitatis Gothenburgensis.

Propp, V. (2000). *Russkaya skazka* [The Russian fairytale]. Moscow: Labirint.

Saracho, O. N., & Spodek, B. (Eds.). (1998). *Multiple perspectives on play in early childhood education.* Albany: State University of New York Press.

Scribner, S. (1985). Vygotsky's uses of history. In J. V. Wertsch (Ed.), *Culture, communication and cognition: Vygotskian perspectives* (pp. 119–145). New York: Cambridge University Press.

Sutton-Smith, B. (1995). Conclusions: The persuasive rhetorics of play. In A. D. Pellegrini (Ed.), *The future of play theory* (pp. 275–295). Albany: State University of New York Press.

The Swedish school system: Childcare in Sweden (2005). Retrieved May 24, 2005, from http://www.skolverket.se/sb/d/354/a/944#paragraphAnchor0

Van Oers, B. (1996). Are you sure? The promotion of mathematical thinking in young children. *European Early Childhood Education Research Journal, 4*(1), 71–89.

Van Oers, B. (2003). *Narratives of childhood: Theoretical and practical explorations for the innovation of early childhood education.* Amsterdam: VU University Press.

Vygotsky, L. S. (1977). Play and its role in the mental development of the child. In M. Cole (Ed.), *Soviet developmental psychology,* (pp. 76–99) (C. Mulholland, Trans.). White Plains, NY: M. E. Sharpe. (Original work published 1933/1966)

Vygotsky, L. S. (1978). *Mind in society* (A. Kozulin, Trans.). Cambridge, MA: Harvard University Press.

Vygotsky, L. S. (1987). *Psikhologiya iskusstva* [The psychology of art]. Moscow: Pedagogika. (Original work published 1965)

Vygotsky, L. S. (1991) *Pedagogiceskaya psikhologiya* [Pedagogical psychology]. Moscow: Pedagogika.

Vygotsky, L. S. (2004). Imagination and creativity in childhood. *Journal of Russian and East European Psychology, 42*(1), 7–97. (Original work published 1930)

Vähänen, L., & Yrttiaho A. (2000). *Mitä kuusivuotiaat oppivat omaehtoisessa luovassa leikissä?* [What six-year-olds learn in free creative play?]. Unpublished master's thesis, Oulu University, Kajaani Department of Teacher Education, Finland.

Zaporozhets, A. V. (1986). *Izbrannye psikhologicheskie trudy. Tom 1* [Collected psychological works, Vol. 1]. Moscow: Pedagogika.

Zuckerman, G. (1997). The transition from preschool to school activity: A Vygotskian perspective. *Tijdschrift voor Ontwikkelingspsychologie, 2,* 87–102.

CHAPTER 9

# CHILDREN'S PERSPECTIVES ON THEIR CHILDHOOD EXPERIENCES

**Stig Broström**
*The Danish University of Education*

Educators, researchers, and the general public in modern societies view schools as a major cultural influence on children. In most countries, a primary function of school, at all levels, is to socialize and educate students so they will be able to function well in a given society. From this widely accepted perspective, children become *objects* that can be formed by society and culture, as represented largely by their teachers. Over the last 100 years, however, progressive educators, such as John Dewey (1960), Cèlestin Freinet (Beattie, 2002), A. S. Neill (1962), and, in Denmark for example, C.C. Kragh-Müller (1963), have challenged this view of children as objects to be molded by teachers who represent the larger social and cultural context. Instead, progressive educators have argued that children are active participants in and constructors of their own development and learning. Therefore, they argue, children's own perspectives must be integrated into all aspects of educational planning and implementation.

*Nordic Childhoods and Early Education*, pages 223–255

In spite of progressive educators´ efforts to promote the notion of *child as active participant*, however, the idea has not been broadly accepted or applied in compulsory school, except in rarified settings, such as experimental schools. The idea has been somewhat more widely accepted at the preschool level, especially in the Nordic countries, where early educators sometimes implement practices reflecting the *child as active participant* concept. During the 1960s and 1970s in Denmark, for instance, some preschools promoted an anti-authoritarian, child-centered approach (some say *extremely* child-centered approach), often with decidedly Marxist leanings. In recent years, a more moderate version of the child-as-active-participant view has prevailed at the preschool level, at least in the rhetoric of early education and often in practice as well. These changes are in keeping with other emerging perspectives accompanying the shift from modern to postmodern life in the world's increasingly globalized societies.

## THE PARTICIPATING CHILD, THE COMPETENT CHILD

The emergence of modernity, as characterized by Giddens (1990), for example, brings new possibilities for realizing progressive educators' ideas from the previous century, namely, seeing children not as objects, but rather as participants and subjects with their own rights and responsibilities. Societal changes during the last two or three decades have paved the way for the emergence of a new type of childhood, characterized first of all by individualization and the idea of self-formation (in Danish, *selvdannelse*), often extended to include children's responsibility for their own learning (Bjørgen, 1991). This modern theoretical perspective focuses on children's existing and emerging competencies, rather than on adult-like qualities they still lack. The model is generative rather than deficit-based.

Thus, step by step, as modern societies have changed with respect to their views about the children's *place*, educators' views about children and childhood have also changed. Both literally and figuratively, children in modern and postmodern societies are now to be heard and seen. Their rights are to be taken seriously and protected. For example, in Norway, Sweden, and Iceland, children have their own official ombudsman, while Denmark has established a similar, but less influential *Børneråd*, or advisory board. These official advocates are charged with ensuring that children's voices are not only heard, but also correctly understood within the larger society.

Most important for the protection and promotion of children was the creation of the *United Nations Convention of the Rights of the Child* (1989). This landmark legislation delineated rights for children and expressed vision and hope for children the world over. Related to the theme of valuing children's perspectives, the Convention specifies four fundamental and universal rights for children: (1) the right to survive; (2) the right to develop to the fullest; (3) the right to protection from harmful influences, abuse, and exploitation; and (4) the right to participate fully in family, cultural, and social life. It is the right to develop to the fullest and the right to participate fully that are most closely aligned with postmodern notions of self-formation and of children as subjects, not objects, as well as the theoretical perspective that children are active participants in their own development and constructors or co-constructors of their own knowledge.

Even in the articulation of these fundamental rights, though, lies tension between children's rights to protection and to participation. In many, if not most, countries children's rights to protection have been reified extensively through public policy and law, while their participation rights have been largely ignored (Srgitta, 1993). Evidently, then, it seems to have been easier to protect children than to listen to them or to liberate them.

However, as postmodern views about children and childhood have emerged, and with further impetus from ratification of the Conventions by all nations around the world, with the notable exception of the United States and Sudan, societal agents, such as educators, politicians, and parents, have been forced to grapple with the inherent contradictions between protection and participation, with the ultimate goal of finding an appropriate balance. Among the talking points in this debate, for example, is children's right to protection from sexual predators versus their right to sexual expression. Another example is the tension between children's right to freedom and independence versus their need for protective supervision (or, at least what adults perceive to be their need for protective supervision).

The Nordic countries quickly and enthusiastically ratified the Convention in the first years of the 1990s, creating an historic milestone in the recognition of children as fully vested "human beings" with rights nearly equivalent to those of adults (Verhellen, 1994). Of course, however, some age-related limits remain on children's rights to full participation in democratic society, as, for example, with the minimum-age requirements for voting and driving.

General changes in society and strong political support for children's rights have coupled with postmodern views and theories on childhood, establishing a new understanding of what children's lives should be like. Taken together, these changes have created a climate where progressive educators' ideas from the previous century can take root. For example, in the Nordic countries prior to the postmodern period, development and learning were generally viewed as distinct from one another. Development involved the nearly automatic emergence of inner qualities or competences, while learning involved the teacher's direct influence on the child to transmit knowledge and skills. However, with the dawn of postmodern views and theories came the new realization that learning and development are integrated and dynamically interactive. This new understanding has paved the way for significant changes in both the theory and practice of early childhood education.

In the following section, I present three interrelated theoretical frameworks, which, in some respects, can be seen as a context for growing interest in children's perspectives in education and research. These three frameworks are (1) childhood sociology, (2) childhood psychology, and (3) children as participants, a more general perspective seen in various disciplines and approaches to research. Actually a fourth dimension might also be added, namely childhood philosophy. Today parents and teachers, as well as public discourse, give space to young children's personal reflections and thoughts, accepting, to greater and lesser extents, children as constructors of their own philosophies of life. However, the fourth framework will not be discussed extensively in this chapter.

In the Nordic countries, the three frameworks are often discussed as if they were something brand new. However, these theoretical perspectives are incorporated, sometimes implicitly and sometimes explicitly, in existing theories, which, interestingly, the three new theoretical approaches criticize. In short, the three approaches present interconnected arguments. For instance, childhood sociology refutes existing (old) knowledge about children and argues for the fact that children create their own life in a specific context of history and circumstances. Similarly, childhood psychology refutes "old" psychological ideas, especially developmental psychology. In contrast with developmental psychology, at least in its most traditional articulations, the new approach "childhood psychology," at least in its most extreme articulations, claims that children do not need to go through socialization because they are born as competent persons.

The third perspective, "children as participants," refers to a general view, taking shape in many different disciplines and theories, wherein children are consistently viewed as active members of their own culture and society, with both the right and the capacity to influence their own lives. In short, children are seen as active participants in a democratic society and, therefore, as active "democrats" (a translation into English of a term frequently used in Denmark).

## Childhood Sociology

Numerous sociologists have described changes in various aspects of childhood's structure and content in modern societies (Brannen & O'Brien, 1995; Corsaro, 1997; Honing, 1999; James, Jenks & Prout, 1998;

Qvortrup, Bardy, Srgitta, & Wintersberger, 1994). These emerging sociological perspectives provide one important context for growing interest in
children's perspectives in education and educational research, as well as
for increasing recognition of children's roles and value in modern society.
The importance of children's views and voices has become a central theme
in recent childhood sociology. In recent years these themes have also
appeared with increasing regularity in related disciplines, such as psychology and education. Inspired by the new childhood sociology, numerous
research studies have investigated children's perspectives on a wide range
of topics.

Childhood sociology generally looks at childhood as a social construction and, with that, questions two traditional points of view: (1) the traditional developmental psychological perspective that children develop from
one separate and distinct stage to another (e.g., Piaget, 1952), and (2) the
idea of primary and secondary socialization, with primary socialization taking place in the home with the family and secondary socialization occur-
ring later when children move out into the broader community of
preschool and neighborhood. Contemporary childhood sociology challenges the assumption that social and societal conditions dominate the
child's socialization (James et al., 1998). Instead, proponents of the new
childhood paradigm argue for the study of childhood, children's relations,
and children's culture in their own right, rather than as a consequence of
external social forces and influences. Proponents of this perspective see
children as whole and complete persons with their own status, needs, and
rights, and not as incomplete versions of the adults they will become. Thus
they do not see children as incompetent human beings who have to go
through a primary socialization to establish a fundamental trust or secure
attachment before they can meet the outer world with new peers and
adults. They are competent and ready to participate in social life, so to say,
as newborns. This point of view matches the realities of modern life in
many parts of the world. In Denmark, for example, most children between
1 and 6 years of age already spend many hours in daycare in the company
of peers and adults other than their parents. In short, children are social
agents who create their own life, just as adults do, within a specific context
of history and circumstances.

Within childhood sociology, researchers typically work from one of two
distinctively different perspectives: constructivism or realism. Researchers
using constructivism as a theoretical frame focus on the universe of meanings that provide a context for children, whom they view as research
objects (Jenks, 1996). For example, in a recent Danish study (Rasmussen &
Smidt, 2003), researchers asked young children to take photographs of
places in the neighborhood that they found interesting. Through reflection on the photos as well as the children's stories and arguments for tak-

ing these particular pictures, the researchers constructed a universe of meanings. For example, the children took photos of dens and lairs they had built in the loft of a home and outside in a tree. They also took photos of a shack they had constructed. Researchers interpreted the photos and children's comments about them as illustrating children's need to create their own world separated from the adults.

To study children and how they live, researchers who use a realistic theoretical framework may take a micro-oriented, subjective approach as described in Rasmussen and Smidt's (2003) study above and in numerous other studies as well (Corsaro, 1997; James & Prout, 1990; Tiller, 1998), or a macro-oriented, structural, objectivistic approach (Qvortrup, 1999; Qvortrup et al., 1994). As a further example of the micro-oriented approach, Corsaro (1997) observed a few children around the preschool sandbox and described their play, conversations, and arguments in great detail. In stark contrast to Corsaro's micro-approach, Qvortrup (1999) used a macro-oriented approach to investigate children's perceptions and understanding of their own lives by studying quantitative data and narrative descriptions of several historical periods, including modern times.

The field of childhood sociology holds considerable promise as a framework for further study of children and childhood, including research on education and care.

## Childhood Psychology

Another important context for growing interest in children's perspectives in education and educational research, as well as for increasing recognition of children's roles and value in modern society, is the shift from developmental psychology to *childhood psychology* (Sommer, 2003a, 2003b, 2003c). A major attribute of this shift is that the subdiscipline called developmental psychology, which focused primarily on change over time in various domains, including intellectual, social, emotional, physical, linguistic, and ethical, has now become childhood psychology. Some critics argued that developmental psychology focused on a "what the child is becoming" or "what the child is lacking at this age" approach. Childhood psychology, on the other hand, focuses on characteristics and attributes of children in all domains from an additive rather than a deficit perspective. In short, childhood psychology does not view newborn children either as isolated from the surrounding world or born relatively unskilled; but, on the contrary, childhood psychology operates from the perspective that children are born with internal communicative competences and an interdependent mind (i.e., they have an awareness of being dependent on others and of others' being dependent on them). Thus, the phrase "the competent child" has gained wide acceptance and cache. For example, Trevarthen presents this perspective:

> The image of the biological newborn needing "socialization" to become a person does not apply when attention turns to evidence for complex psychological expressions in the response of contented healthy newborns to people who take them as persons with intentions and feelings of companionship, and who feel pleasure when the infant responds. (1998, p. 16)

This new idea of the competent child derives from a number of observational studies of infants, including, for example, the Blank-face Study (Murra & Trevarthen, 1985). According to a systematic plan, researchers interrupted infants' interactions with their mothers. Researchers then videotaped and analyzed each child's reaction to this interruption. Through this process, researchers were able to describe well-defined social-emotional reactions on the part of the infants. In another study, Melzoff and Moore (1998) used a phenomenological perspective to examine the nonverbal infant's universe of experiences. For example, researchers interpreted their observations of very young infants' body languages as expressions of the babies' need for social interaction. Similarly, from the perspectives of *psychoanalytic and developmental psychology,* Daniel Stern (1998) described, often in poetic language, infants' experience of themselves and their surroundings. For instance, Stern interpreted infants' experiences and emotions in various types of interactions where their parents expressed differing attachment, nearness, and absence behaviors. Thus, both the research methods and the results of the research (i.e., findings documenting children's competence) argue in favor of taking a children's perspective.

In recent years, then, research methods taking children's perspectives have contributed significantly to psychological literature on childhood. Findings from such research and from research using more traditional methods increasingly demonstrate that children exhibit competence from the moment of birth onward. Therefore, it is clear that childhood psychology, like childhood sociology, holds considerable potential as a framework for the study of children and childhood in the postmodern world.

## The Child as Active Participant

The emerging sociological and psychological perspectives, described above, provide important contexts for growing interest in children's perspectives in education and educational research, as well as for increasing general recognition of children's roles and value in modern society.

Embedded in childhood sociology and childhood psychology and also standing on its own feet as a theoretical frame is the third prospective, children as active participants, emphasizing children as subjects, not objects, and social agents (Jensen & Schnack, 1997; Jørgensen & Kampmann, 2000). The third approach both reflects and contributes to changing perspectives on the nature of childhood and children themselves, especially with regard to children's competence as active participants in their own development and important contributors to society. Modern perspectives on childhood, coupled with growing faith in children's competence and views of children as "human beings" rather than "human becomings" (Qvortrup et al., 1994), taken together, create potential and pathways for children to participate in society with a status that is roughly equivalent to the status of adults.

## INFLUENCE OF POSTMODERN FRAMEWORKS ON EARLY CHILDHOOD EDUCATION

Under influence from progressivism, in particular, and postmodernism, in general, preschools and schools have implemented important educational changes. Recent decades have witnessed a shift in educational discourse from "how to teach children something identified as important by adults" to "how to create learning environments in which children are subjects, not objects, who actively participate and utilize their own competence and agency." Here at least two important dimensions must be mentioned: (1) children's active role in their own learning process (i.e., that they learn through their own activity, not through the teacher's presentation of knowledge); and (2) the influence of Nordic notions about children's democracy upon teaching.

In early childhood education in the Nordic countries, focus has shifted from the notion of "cooperation with the children"—where teachers seek children's cooperation (rather than simply their compliance) in activities and experiences the adults have designed—to a situation where children actually influence and participate in planning of the educational process (Pramling Samuelsson & Sheridan, 2003). For example, the Swedish preschool curriculum articulates a democratic approach in early education: "Children develop their ability to express their own thinking and understanding and thus they can influence their own situation" (Utbildningsdepartementet, 1998, p. 14). In Denmark ideals about egalitarianism, emancipation, and participation in a "lived" democracy are firmly entrenched in preschool discourse and daily practice (Broström, 2003, p. 43). Reflecting the Danish perspective on the importance of democracy in the daily lives of children, the *Act on the Folkeskole* states that the school shall prepare the pupils for active participation, joint responsibility, and rights and duties in a society based on freedom and democracy. Teaching practices and daily school life must therefore build on intellectual freedom, equality, and democracy (Undervisningsministeriet, 1995). Therefore, it is not sufficient for preschools and schools to *prepare* children to participate in democratic society when they become adults; rather, preschools and schools must themselves *be* democracies.

The ideal of childhood emancipation is also animated here. In order for children to participate in and contribute to a democracy as children, they must be emancipated, or free from too much adult control and supervision. This Nordic ideal is in tune with rights expressed in the *Convention on the Rights of the Child.*

This view of children as co-constructors, along with adults and peers, of knowledge and as individuals who construct their own understanding of the world demands that educators also recognize children's competence as agents, active participants, in their own learning processes. This idea originates from constructivist theory, which focuses on the individual child's construction and learning, and also from theories of social constructionism, which gives more due to learning as a result of social interaction in a specific context.

Piaget (1929) and others, including Glaserfeld (1995), build on the theory of constructivism, looking at children as active subjects who create or construct their own world. Because children want to understand their world, they experiment with their surroundings through hands-on exploration and associated mental activity, and, thereby, construct meaning. For example, a group of 4-year-old children in a preschool wondered aloud why they were simultaneously able to observe both the moon and the sun. Before the preschool teacher got a chance to respond, a little girl constructed her own explanation: "Of course the reason is that the infants are ready to take a nap now, so they need the moon; and we older children are ready to play now, so we need the sun." In this way, the children invent their world. From the constructivist perspective, then, it is preferable to give children the opportunity to construct their own meanings, even when those meanings will later be modified, as in the above example, than to simply transmit the adult's knowledge to them. The adult's role is transformed from transmitter to co-constructor, one who, together with the children, helps them solve problems and construct their own understandings.

This freedom to be active in the environment, constructing and co-constructing knowledge, is in concert with Nordic ideas about egalitarianism, emancipation, and democracy. The preschool or school operates as a democracy. Children are more equal with adults than they are in autocratic or authoritarian systems. They are emancipated or free of overcontrol and oversupervision by adults. "For instance, children in Nordic preschools are routinely allowed (probably encouraged) to do things that children in American preschools are forbidden to do. In Denmark, for example, preschool children routinely climb trees, carry stacks of porcelain dishes, cut apples with sharp knives, use saws and drills for woodworking, and play in 'pillow rooms' that are off-limits to adults" (Wagner, 2003, p. 21).

The Nordic view of children as active participants who should have significant influence on their environments does not end at the school gate. Rather, children are viewed as an important part of societal life in a democracy. Children are not spectators but active participants and contributors. Obviously, they do not participate equally in everything all the time; but they are always involved, at least in principle. For example, in an area of Copenhagen experiencing vandalism and violence, instead of punishing children and young adolescents thought to be involved, authorities gave the children a few workmen's huts and invited them to work together with some social pedagogues to build their own drop-in center.[1] By providing the children with the materials and the support they needed to build a drop-in center, local authorities demonstrated that they viewed the children as active, thinking, responsible subjects, rather than as objects in the political process. Because Nordic children are given the opportunity to participate actively in a democratic society from their earliest years, they develop what has been identified as "action competence" (Jensen & Schnack, 1997). This means they develop competencies that enable them to participate even more actively and to contribute even more significantly as they gain further experience. They do not have to wait until some magical age, such as 18, to begin to participate actively in society or to contribute to its development. As a consequence, it is not unusual in Denmark for children to fight for their rights. For example, a group of children recently fought successfully for an area in their neighborhood where they could gather, listen to music, and skateboard. However, having such an ability to raise their voices in society does not seem to spoil them. Rather, it may make them more concerned for the plight of others. For instance, we often see children working together with adults to collect clothes or toys for children in developing countries or for children in war-torn areas.

These three theoretical frameworks—childhood sociology, childhood psychology, and children as active participants—coupled with new societal foundations have given rise to new approaches in early childhood education and educational research, both of which evidence a growing tendency to stress children's perspectives.

## CHILDREN'S PERSPECTIVES

The three approaches—childhood sociology, child psychology, and children as active participants—both individually and collectively reflect growing interest in what I call here "the children's perspective," an umbrella term incorporating a variety of interrelated concepts and philosophical stances. In the early childhood literature, we sometimes see wording that appears at first glance to be more exact, such as "child perspective" or "perspective of the child" or "children's perspectives." For example, the term, "children's perspectives," by its very linguistic construction, acknowledges that children have a perspective, that this perspective may differ decidedly from adults' perspectives, and that children may have differing perspectives one from another. As further examples, some writers might say that the child ombudsman takes "*a child perspective*," but then use the term "*child's perspective*" (with an apostrophe) to describe situations in which children themselves take a more active role as participants in education or in research. However, discrete distinctions between the terms are the exception rather than the rule in recent literature. Some writers fail to define the terms clearly. Others use the terms interchangeably or to represent overlapping concepts.

The fundamental concept underlying the "children's perspective" orientation is that children are competent, have rights, and should be viewed as contributing members of a democratic society. Children are not preparing to be competent or to earn rights or to contribute. They *already are* capable of active participation and competent use of their rights and agency.

The children's perspective concept incorporates general societal views on children and on child-related policies, as well as educators' and researchers' views on children and childhood and, most importantly, children's own views. However, when educators and researchers talk about the children's perspective, they likely refer to one of two different orientations toward the concept: (1) they may focus their attention on the ways in which adults look at children and reflect on what they, as adults, perceive to be the children's perspectives; or (2) they may focus on how children look at their own world, their conditions, and themselves (Qvarsell, 2003). Thus, the concept "children's perspective" encompasses how adults and society try to understand children's lives, as well as how children themselves experience and describe their lives. However, even the children's own descriptions come to light through an adult filter, since it is adults who "translate" information provided by the children in public discussions as well as in scholarly debates.

During the last three decades, many different points of view have emerged in the Nordic countries during these public discussions and scholarly debates about the children's perspective. From societal, theoretical, and research perspectives, the issues are complex and touch on such matters as how parents should raise their children in a postmodern era, which rights children should have, and the extent to which children should approach equality with adults and be emancipated. In the early 1990s a number of researchers articulated a definition that captured the essential multisidedness of the concept. For example, the Swedish researcher Kerstin Strandell (1997) defined the children's perspective this way: "It deals with both taking children's standpoint and listening to children from their position as children, and as an adult, imagining how children think in an effort to reduce the distance between the generations, which can hinder communication" (p. 19, author's translation). Thus, children's perspective must ultimately be defined as the adult's attempt to understand, often through imagination, the thoughts and views children have of their own life.

On a cultural-political level the Danish *Børneråd*, the governmental advisory board overseeing matters relating to children, has actively sought out the child's perspective by establishing a panel, made up of 60 fifth-grade classes with 1,225 children. In the period from 1998 to 2000, these children directly informed the *Børneråd* about their experiences, meanings, and suggestions concerning topics related to children's everyday life (Hviid, 2000a). In 1999 thousands of children wrote letters to the Minister for Social Affairs telling her their views on issues that bothered them (Heering, 1994). Children often described their family problems. For example, many children expressed their concerns about their parents' divorce and the appearance of a new stepmother or stepfather. Other children wrote about feeling victimized and lonely. The Børneråd and the Minister corresponded with the children, hopefully giving them assurances that their voices had been heard. Further assurance that their voices had been heard could be seen in the fact that the Børneråd implemented initiatives to reduce victimization in school. These initiatives have had a practical effect on children's life at school.

These two examples, the children's panel and the children's letter-writing campaign, represent children's active involvement in a lived democracy. The response of the Børneråd and the Minister for Social Affairs reflect the extent to which children's active participation is truly valued and respected.

A child's perspective is also clearly visible in other aspects of political and social life in the Nordic countries. In Denmark, for example, courts typically listen to children's voices about where they wish to live if their divorcing parents cannot come to a suitable agreement. Children's interests are also taken into account in cases where one parent dies. Here part of the inheritance goes to the surviving spouse and part to the children.

Each child's portion is frozen in a public trustee's office until the child turns 18 years of age.

In education a children's perspective is evident when the teachers' investigations and documentation of how children think and feel form the primary basis for their instructional decision making.

Early on Jean Piaget showed an interest in understanding children's perspectives. For instance, in *The Child's Conception of the World* (Piaget, 1929), he described specific characteristics of children's thinking at different ages. Continuing this line of inquiry, and further inspired by a phenomenological perspective, Swedish researcher Ingrid Pramling (Pramling, 1983; Pramling Samuelsson & Sheridan, 2003) uses interviews and conversations with children to illuminate a children's perspective as a foundation for both research and practical classroom work for the early years. Taking the child's perspective in educational settings means creating daily teaching practices that are in concert with children's ways of thinking and communicating. In research the phenomenological approach highlights the child's perspective and actively involves the child as an informant. This approach is powerful in Swedish early childhood education and research, and is clearly included in the Swedish curriculum for preschool as well.

## Children's Perspective in Early Childhood Education

Taking in and making use of children's knowledge and background in planning and implementing educational practice is a well-known tool. Curriculum theories often refer to children's knowledge and background as "participant conditions." Thus, in the field of curriculum theory, we see a movement away from teacher-initiated and teacher-directed teaching, what we might call a Tyler-inspired understanding of curriculum (Tyler, 1949), toward a dynamic curriculum model (Print, 1993) or a practice-based model (e.g., Skilbeck, 1976). Tyler, who has greatly influenced curricular thinking in Denmark, proposed that the teacher should decide ahead of time what the aims and content of instruction should be. Furthermore, Tyler demanded that educational objectives should guide the teacher's decision making about what kinds of experiences children need.

Taking a different tack, proponents of the dynamic model argue for reflecting the reality of curriculum development in educational organization. For example, Stenhouse (1975) created a process-oriented curriculum, claiming that all factors in the current situation have to be taken into consideration. From this perspective, educational practice is viewed as a creative and unpredictable process characterized by time and place, as well as children's backgrounds and current situations. Furthermore, educational practice, in reality, is also under both direct and indirect influence from a large number of outside factors, such as class size, numbers of teachers, and special needs of children within the group. This dynamic, process-oriented model requires the preschool teachers to continuously investigate and reflect on their own practice and avoid mechanical use of a fixed curriculum. The teacher's role is to interpret a given curriculum, if one exists, from a children's perspective and then to co-construct daily learning experiences with the children. The teacher continuously has to do "situation analysis," using the children's current emotions and understandings as the starting point for the next steps in the educational process. In other words, children's perspective is an integrated part of the curriculum.

For example, the Reggio Emilia approach illustrates how a documented knowledge of children's previous experiences and life experiences, referred to in Italy as the children's "track," can influence educational planning (Canevaro, 1988; Cecchin & Larsen, 2002). In the Reggio Emilia approach, teachers consistently begin their planning and focus their reflection on the children's perspective, focusing on their knowledge of the particular children in their group, their interests, attitudes, friendships, home conditions, and outside influences.

However, according to the *United Nations Convention on Children's Rights* (1989), children should have more than an indirect influence on educational planning and practice via the preschool teacher's interpretation of children's interests and current conditions. The Convention emphasizes that children have the right to express their own views, to be listened to, and to be actively involved in decisions that affect them. In other words, it is imperative that children have opportunities to practice the principles of democracy throughout their early childhood years.

In concert with the children's perspective stated in the Convention, the Swedish curriculum (Ministry of Education and Science in Sweden, 1998) states that children should participate and cooperate in educational decision making. The purpose is to give children the opportunity to promote their own learning and, at the same time, participate in democracy. The law (1998, pp. 16–17) mentions that preschools should ensure that children develop the ability to:

1. Express their thoughts and views, and thus have the opportunity to influence their own situation.
2. Accept responsibility for their own actions and for the environment of the preschool.
3. Understand and act in accordance with democratic principles by participating in different kinds of cooperation and decision making.

Critics argue forcefully that these aims are too ambitious. They claim that children shouldn't have rights until they are capable of exercising responsibility and competent decision making. Of course, neither the Conventions nor the Swedish State Curriculum argue for involving children in problem solving or decision making that is beyond their comprehension and their competence; but the underlying issue is that they should be able to participate actively in decisions that affect them, to the extent that they are able, so that their competence and abilities continue to develop and blossom.

To deal with children's perspective in education is to give children voice, to listen to them, and help them realize their ideas and perspectives. The starting point, at the preschool level, is for adults to listen to them carefully and take them seriously on matters that they are competent to discuss and decide. Based on this understanding, I present some Nordic examples of social and educational approaches where a child's perspective has been taken into consideration.

In 1989 the Norwegian Council for Cultural Affairs established a project called "Try Yourself" in which children age 7 to 14 were invited to become autonomous actors in public arenas to create and implement their own leisure-time activities without adult intervention (Kjørholt, 2001). From school and other institutions, the children obtained a simple application form on which they explained their ideas for leisure-time activities and indicated what kind of support they would need to implement their plans (Kjørholt, 2001). During a 3-year period, nearly 1,700 children expressed their ideas and got support to carry them through. In many local areas, children created "children's culture houses," where they could meet on their own premises and be together and play in their own way. Besides supporting children's own culture, the project also generated new knowledge about modern childhood: "Children are no longer out in their local environment. They do not climb trees any more, and they do not construct huts in the treetops" (Kjørholt, 2001, p. 71), as indicated by the fact that most of their proposals were for indoor spaces. This represented a transition from traditional outdoor activities during leisure time in a Nordic country to a preference for indoor activity. Actually, the project was intended as a tool for protecting and revitalizing the traditional childhood defined as nature, outdoor life, and play, which did not turn out to be in concert with the children's interests as expressed in their proposals.

The Nordic child culture project, *The Storyride Project* (Broström, 2002; Riihelä, 2003), provides another example of the children's perspective. During a 3-year period in the mid-1990s, numerous preschool teachers and researchers from several Nordic countries participated in this project, where children were "given the word," as Nordic people say. This means that children were the primary speakers, the ones who did the talking and the telling. Teachers then helped them to act as their own agents, as subjects rather than objects, to increase their opportunities for constructing their own culture and telling their own stories.

In this project, children took center stage as agents who actively produced knowledge and fantasy. The project demonstrated that children can and do act as their own agents and construct a culture of their own. They are not, as some would argue, merely passive recipients or consumers of a constant stream of incoming information. However, Riihelä (1996) warns that children may become more and more users of child culture as created for them by others (e.g., commercial companies that create fantasies for children and companies that create animated video games) rather than producers of their own culture in spite of their capacities to do so. Therefore, modern education must conscientiously and consistently take the child perspective into consideration so children can exercise their existing and emerging capacities.

In the project the children told their own stories. The preschool teacher wrote the stories down word for word and then read them aloud. The child who created the story either accepted it or corrected it as the teacher read. Sometimes the children made drawings to accompany their stories or wrote the story themselves using their own writing—called "play writing" in Denmark. Finally, the children and adults packed the stories and took them to the post office to mail them to children in their "friendship preschool," an exchange institution in their own country or in another Nordic country. The "friendship preschool" mailed stories as well.

All told, the children generated about 4,000 stories and among these, about 500 were Danish. As an example, a 5-year-old girl constructed the following story with dramatic episodes and a hero as problem solver: "Once there was a wolf, he lived far off from his Mum, and then the Dad arrived, then they returned to the Mum. Now it is over." In this short story, the little girl built upon her previous experience with tales, demonstrating that she has learned to use conventions of structuring a story with a beginning, middle, and end. She also used this story to grapple with a problem, or at least a challenge, in her own life, namely separation from her mother. Through storytelling, play, and drawing, children are given a chance to express themselves and, at the same time, to influence their surroundings and strengthen their identity.

Incorporating a children's perspective into the educational process is, in some respects, related to a child-centered understanding, as well as to both constructivism and constructionism. The shift in curriculum theory from objectives and content as the starting point toward a central focus on learning as the child's subjective construction raises new questions for early childhood educators and places new demands upon the preschool teacher's role. For instance, under the new approach, preschool teachers must be prepared to follow children's leads as they construct their own understandings. This requires teachers to "think on their feet" rather than follow a preplanned agenda for accomplishing learning goals the adults established in advance. An activity in the sandbox, which the teacher originally imagined as a construction activity, may turn, at the children's inspiration and direction, to a scientific inquiry about bugs or an investigation of differences between wet sand and dry sand. Such an educational approach is more challenging for teachers than simply following step by step a plan they created in advance. Following the children's leads requires that teachers be able to identify the academic content as it emerges along the way. In the sand box example, for instance, the teacher must be prepared to "think on her feet" to follow the children as they divert their discussion from construction to bugs.

However, despite the appeal of these notions about letting children follow their own leads and inspirations, James and colleagues (1998) are among those who warn against problems that may arise if we overly cultivate the approach. They describe the "tribal child" that may result from an exaggeration of children's cultural codes and competences, and an idealization of childhood as a totally isolated and autonomous universe without any likeness or relationship to the adult's world. To avoid such an isolation from the adult's world, the teacher must consciously reflect on the relationship between a child's perspective and an adult perspective, and consequently create a curriculum that integrates them both.

## Children's Perspective in Early Childhood Research

In contemporary Nordic society, education, and research, children's voices are heard and their actions are seen to a far greater extent than in the past. However, this new phenomenon is not yet universal or even widespread. Even if these are only baby steps, they represent fundamental and radical changes in childhood and childhood research during recent decades.

In the 1970s early childhood research, children and childhood were more or less invisible, often hidden beneath mountains of quantitative data and statistics (Alanen, 1992; Andenæs, 1991). However, Bronfenbrenner's (1979) arguments for gathering data from natural settings paved the way for new research strategies in which children were seen as actors in their own lives, shaping their own daily experiences. For example, American researcher Barrie Thorne stated: "Kids are competent social actors who take an active role in shaping their daily experiences. I want to sustain an attitude of respectful discovery, to uncover and document kids' points of view and meanings" (1993, p. 12).

Thorne's idea to "uncover kid's points of view and meaning" was parallel to what happened in Nordic early childhood research in the early 1980s, strongly swayed by such international influences as, for example, Atkinson and Hammersley's (1983) ethnographical methods, and William Corsaro's (1981) ethnographical studies on children's friendships. This trend in Nordic research was characterized by early efforts to take children's perspectives. Influenced by ethnographical and cultural analytical approaches in other parts of the world, the trend to take children's perspective became more prevalent in Nordic research during the 1980s. Early on, Norwegian researchers provided leadership in designing and implementing studies featuring the children's perspectives (Jørgensen & Kampmann, 2000). For example, Norwegian researcher Per Olav Tiller (1984, 1988, 1998) strongly influenced the emerging definition and concept of taking children's perspectives. Swedish researchers also contributed to these efforts. For instance, Berglund (1985) argued in favor of ethnographical studies and articulated characteristics of high-quality ethnographic work. He stated, for example, that ethnographic research occurs in natural settings and situations; it has an phenomenological orientation because its goal is to study children's intentions, thoughts, emotions, and behaviors; it emphasizes context; it is holistic; and, finally, it is multimodal because it makes use of many different data collection methods. To further this ethnographical approach, Swedish researchers Ehn and Löfgren (1982) contributed theoretical reflections and methods concerning data collection through observation and participation and also concerning forms of analysis through a study of everyday life in preschool (Ehn, 1983).

To take a child perspective, phenomenological researchers gather data on children's experiences, thinking, and acting through participant observations, videotapes, and interviews (Pramling Samuelsson & Lindahl, 1999) because "children's possibilities to constitute knowledge in a specific learning situation depend on the ability of grown ups to start from the way children see, think and understand the world around them" (Pramling Samuelsson & Sheridan, 2003, p. 121).

The shift during the 1980s from a positivistic research paradigm toward a phenomenological/ethnographical approach emphasizing qualitative research methods also resulted in a dramatic increase in the use of children as informants. A characteristic of the ethnographic work is that it recognizes informants, in this case children, as experts on the subject of their own lives. American ethnographer Jim Thomas defined the researcher's task as one of raising the child's "voice to speak to an audience on behalf of their subjects as a means of empowering them by giving more authority to the subject's voice" (1993, p. 4). This trend brought with it many new possibilities and many new challenges in childhood research and its applications.

## CHILDREN AS INFORMANTS IN CHILDHOOD RESEARCH

Having children as informants creates countless possibilities in childhood research and enables investigators to pursue a plethora of new research questions. Having children as informants has the potential to uncover different dimensions of knowledge about children and their lives. However, isolated knowledge from individual studies using children as informants is not adequate. First, it is unclear how researchers can and should establish reliability for children's statements gathered through ethnographic methodology. How reliable is an individual child's telling? How well does the researcher capture, understand the nuances, and build a reliable picture based on the child's telling? Can we generalize anything beyond this child and this particular situation? Finally, the use of children as informants raises an important ethical question: If we truly respect children and childhood, when and to what extent is it in children's best interest for them, knowingly or unknowingly, to help adults uncover details of their everyday life and secret spaces?

In the Nordic countries, research aimed at describing and understanding the world, or worlds, of children, including their thinking, emotions, motives, and meanings, became more common at the beginning of the 1980s. In the early stages of this work, Nordic researchers gathered data through observations of children in natural settings, where they produce and organize their own lives, actions, and relationships. Around the middle of the 1980s, a breakthrough in research came as investigators began to make more extensive use of informal conversations and formal interviews with children as a means of capturing and understanding their world. In addition, a softening of "either/or" thinking about qualitative versus quantitative research during the 1990s opened many new possibilities for childhood research in the Nordic countries.

However, in spite of this softening of boundaries between qualitative and quantitative work, quantitative methods remained more prevalent in the field of school research, while qualitative research remained dominant in early childhood educational research.

Although quantitative methods dominated in early childhood studies throughout this period, some researchers (e.g., Christensen, 2000) also used quantitative methods. In fact, children under age 18 were more often used as informants in quantitative than qualitative studies. A systematic review of Scandinavian childhood research literature between 1985 and 2000 revealed 117 publications in which children under 18 years of age were informants. Most of the studies were survey investigations using quantitative methods, especially questionnaires (Andersen & Ottosen, 2002). Of the 117 reports, articles, and books, 77 were published in Norway, 30 in Denmark, 5 in Sweden, and 1in Finland. Five were published jointly by two or more Nordic countries. Because researchers have greater access to children in schools than in many other settings, much of the Nordic childhood research focuses on school-age children. However, many questions have arisen about researchers' continuing use of questionnaire instruments for data gathering. For example, a Danish study on children as informants in a number of questionnaire-based projects concluded that, in general, 7- to 9-year-olds typically did not adequately understand and respond to questionnaire items (Andersen & Kjærulf, 2003). Obviously, children who cannot yet read and write cannot complete questionnaires. Therefore, most qualitative research taking the perspective of children under the age of 7 has relied on observation and interview techniques. Because observation and interviews have been and still are the dominant methods in early childhood education research, I discuss these methods further in the following sections.

## Participant Observation Methods

Most research in early childhood settings relies on observation, with varying degrees of researcher participation, as the primary data-gathering strategy. Often researchers practice open and active participant observations (Junker, 1960; LeCompte & Preissle, 1993). As they collect data, researchers also become actively engaged in supporting children in their daily activities. Thus, the role of the participant-observer as a researcher and the purpose of the study must be well known to the children, the parents, and the teachers. Adler and Adler (1987) define such a role as an active partnership: "Researchers who adapt active membership roles do more than participate in social activities of group members; they take part in core activities of the group. In so doing, they generally assume functional, not solely research or social roles, in their settings."

During the last two decades, numerous Nordic researchers have used participant-observation. As just two examples, Swedish researchers Fine and Sandstrom (1988) became participant-observers in their investigation of quality in children's lives, as did Åm (1989), a Norwegian researcher, who studied play as a vehicle through which children produce culture.

However, the full and equal participant-observer role is only one approach along a spectrum that also includes participant-as-observer, observer-as-participant, and observer-only (Junker, 1960), all of which give the researcher greater distance and space to record data and reflect upon it immediately than does the full participant-observer approach. Some researchers argue that gaining distance and space from full involvement in children's activities makes it possible to record long, coherent, and detailed descriptions, including direct quotes of the children's verbal expressions.

To meet the demands and opportunities of the moment, some researchers move freely along the spectrum, sometimes participating actively while observing and sometimes observing from a distance. The more peripheral role may enable a researcher to seek an insider's perspective on the children, their relationships, and their activities without the distractions of simultaneous participation. In fact, some researchers argue that peripheral membership is the best way to acquire such an insight through direct, first-hand experience (Adler & Adler, 1987). Hutchby and Moran-Ellis (1997) also describe the merits of this peripheral membership, which they call "the detached observer" (p. 10), because it enables researchers to focus on children's communication and interactions.

A number of Nordic studies have employed this peripheral membership or detached observer approach. For example, in a study on children's friendships, Broström (1999) maintained considerable distance from the children and did not interact with them at all. In a period of 2 hours, the researcher recorded target children's interaction with peers, as well as their actions and verbal expressions. Using preestablished definitions of social competence and friendship as the basis for observation sampling units, as well as for later analysis and interpretation, the researcher focused on characteristics such as proximity, intimacy, positive emotions, and exhibiting qualities of "we-ness." The goal was to address these research questions: How can an interaction between two children be understood? Do we see signals showing positive emotions, we-ness, and intimacy? Among the findings of this study were that all observed children were involved in a shared life with peers and that most experienced being friends with at least one peer.

In the previous example, the researcher began with a predetermined definition of children's friendship, and, for that reason, his observations were focused on preestablished behaviors and qualities of children's interactions and friendships. However, many researchers take a more open, less focused, approach, at least in the beginning stages of their research. During this initial phase, many researchers avoid recording any data at all, since they fear that what they see, find valuable or interesting, and, hence record will merely be a reproduction of their already-existing understandings of children and childhood. Before recording data, then, these researchers attempt to fully immerse themselves in the setting and to clear away any preconceived or stereotypical thinking. However, others, including Ehn (1983), argue that researchers should think of preschool settings as strange and exotic because it is much easier to recognize new patterns in settings we consider unfamiliar than in settings we consider well understood and familiar.

Danish researcher Mariane Hedegaard (1990) argued that adult researchers can take a child perspective most adequately and effectively when they focus their observations on children's intentions, interactions, conflicts, and capacities. Focusing on *intentions,* researchers describe the child's initiatives, attempts at contact, and understanding of demands from their surroundings. Focusing on *interactions,* researchers describe who approaches the child and how this happens, how the child approaches other children and adults, and how the resulting shared experiences and interactions emerge. To focus on the child's *conflicts,* researchers describe how the child handles verbal and physical disagreements. And, finally, focusing on the child's *capacity,* researchers describe the child's efforts to acquire new competencies, skills, and knowledge—in other words, what the child struggles with in order to appropriate new norms, skills, and knowledge (Hedegaard, 1990).

A number of Danish researchers have found that they can observe within these goal-directed and focused parameters and still find room to uncover quite new dimensions and patterns in children's interactions. For example, using the methods and definitions Hedegaard articulated, a study of quality in children's lives (Berg, Broström, Hännikäinen, Rubinstein Reich, & Thyssen, 1996; Broström & Thyssen, 1996) identified several patterns of interaction between 4-year-old children in numerous Danish, Swedish, and Finnish preschools. For example, researchers identified a frequent pattern in which two or more children directed their activity toward the same object, such as a toy. The researchers called this pattern *shared activity* and explained that shared activity typically involved dialogue and other forms of communication about the object and the activity. Researchers noted that, when children were involved in shared activities, their relationship with one another was often symmetrical, that is an equal, *person–person relationship.* Researchers also noted another dimension of shared activity, which they called *creative participation.* Here, researchers noted that children often created something—a block structure, a collage, or even new words set to a well-known tune while jumping together on a sofa—during shared activities.

Researchers also noted other shared activity patterns. For example, sometimes one child was more eager and enterprising than other children. When one child initiated a shared activity or changed an ongoing shared activity, appealing to other children to participate, researchers used the term *initiating participation.* When a child expressed his or her leadership role in demanding or dominating ways, researchers used the term *initiating, directing participation.* In this case, the dominated child did not act as an equal participant because he or she only carried out the ideas of the child exhibiting initiating, directing participation. Researchers identified the dominated child's pattern as *performing, submissive participation.*

## Interview Methods with Children as Informants

Although observation methods, with various levels of researcher participation, are a fundamental tool for investigating the children's perspective
in Nordic early childhood research, the predominant data-gathering
method using children as informants is the interview, ranging in design
from the informal conversational interview to the formal, structured interview. In the late 1980s several publications on child interviews contributed
to a more systematic use of children as informants in Nordic research
(Enggaard, 1984; Lindh-Munter, 1989). The trend was further promoted
by publication of several handbooks on interviewing techniques for the
growing numbers of preschool teachers who were becoming involved in
developmental research (Doverborg-Österberg & Pramling, 1988; Løkken
& Søbstad, 1998).

Numerous researchers have described different forms of interviews
including structured, semi-structured, unstructured, and "open-ended."
Many investigators, including, for example, Pellegrini (1996) and Enggaard (1984), view the open interview as the most helpful for generating
data on the children's perspective. However, researchers have also noted
various problems with interviewing young children, both in terms of
research methodology and in terms of impact on the children themselves.
For instance, using children as informants in interviews often requires
props and supporting activities, such as the use of photographs or stories.
Furthermore, it is often difficult to get children to participate willingly in
interviews, but research ethics forbid coercion or unnecessary deception.
In addition, the question of validity frequently arises. Do the interview
questions really address the research questions under study? Are they likely
to yield useful research data? Both Piaget's child interview method, often
replicated or adapted in contemporary research, and modern interview
theory focus on the validity question. Researchers have also debated the
advantages and disadvantages of interviewing children individually versus
in pairs or groups, both in terms of data yield and impact on the children
as informants (Enggaard, 1984; Kvale, 1996; Mishler, 1996). For instance,
Enggaard (1984) recommended that interviewing children in pairs or
groups gives them a feeling of safety and security when they are in the role
of informant, knowingly or unknowingly.

Danish researcher Steinar Kvale's (1996) theory and methodology
regarding child interviews are among the most influential and frequently
used. Kvale's approach is based on phenomenological and hermeneutical
perspectives. Here the researcher carries through an ongoing analysis and
interpretation of the data, confronting both parts and whole in order to
end up with a valid interpretation. In hermeneutical analysis, researchers
organize the data in sequences and from here they construct a meaningful

interpretation, which is expressed in a "good Gestalt." This figure (Gestalt) is then confronted with each sequence (part) in order to evaluate the interpretation. Such a dialectical confrontation of parts and whole is, so to say, endless, but it will stop when the researcher believes the interpretation is valid. This approach raises questions about how interview data should be analyzed and interpreted. In recent years, the Nordic countries have witnessed an enormous increase in the number in interview studies attempting to describe children's views on a variety of topics relating to the educational system. For example, Pramling Samuelsson and Sheridan (2001) investigated the nature and extent of children's participation in and influence on their preschool settings. As mentioned earlier, participation and influence are important goals in the Swedish preschool curriculum.

In this study, researchers interviewed 39 5-year-old children in their preschools for 15 to 30 minutes. They used the word "deciding" in their interview questions because this word is more familiar to children than the word "influence." Researchers used a structured interview technique, asking all the children the same basic questions: (1) What would you like to do in preschool if you could decide yourself? (2) Do your teachers know what you like to do most of all? (3) How do you make decisions about what to do at school? (4) Who decides what to do in preschool? (5) What can you decide together with the teacher? (6) What can you decide by yourself? (7) Where can you decide most, in preschool or at home?

Researchers divided the forth question, into three parts, asking in questions 4, 5, and 6 what children can decide for themselves, what they can decide jointly with the teachers, and what the teachers decide in the preschool. When asked about what the teacher decides, the children who were informants in this study were absolutely sure that the teacher decides more or less everything that goes on in the preschool. For example, "She decides everything" was a typical response. Thus, the children often experienced the teacher's decisions as overriding what they themselves wanted to do (Pramling Samuelsson and Sheridan, 2001), as illustrated by the following excerpt from an interview, beginning with a follow-up question posed by the interviewer to gather more information about children's thinking:

Interviewer (I): Yes, do you usually draw here during the day?
　　　　　　　I: Mm, can you draw when you feel that you want to go and draw?
　　Child (C): No, not often but sometimes.
　　　　　　　I: How come?
　　　　　　　C: Because it is the teachers who decide.
　　　　　　　I: Do they decide when the children can draw?
　　　　　　　C: No, but they decide if we have to do something else and then I can't draw.

This dialogue is typical and represents the children's general view on their lack of opportunity to make decisions or influence the course of their daily lives in preschool. In this example, then, researchers gained new insights by collecting and analyzing data from the children's perspective, leading to the conclusion, which may well startle and upset preschool teachers, that preschool practice is not in accordance with the official aims of early education in Sweden calling for active participation by the children in decision making, including strong and meaningful influence over the course of daily life and activity in the preschool setting.

Similarly, a Danish interview study of preschool children's expectations about school (Broström, 2003, 2000) uncovered hidden negative dimensions of which the teachers were unaware. Several months before they entered *bornehaveklasse*, the Danish equivalent to kindergarten in the United States, a noncompulsory but widely available class, often located in a primary school building, 375 6-year-olds were asked two questions: "What do you think you will *do* in kindergarten? " and "What do you think you will *learn* in kindergarten?" A large and unexpected number of these children expressed some form of insecurity and nervousness about entering kindergarten. For instance, 24% expected to have a teacher who would command children to sit still and be quiet. The researcher found it particularly troubling that 5% of the children expected their school to be an *authoritarian* place in which the teacher would scold and have power and, worse, wield this power by hitting children. The following interview excerpt from a boy 6.9 years of age illustrates an informant's skepticism about an upcoming school experience, similar to the anxiety found among 24% of the children, as well as the belief that school would be an authoritarian place, as found among 5% of the participants:

> I: What do you think you will do in kindergarten class?
> C: I have no idea. Play. I do not look forward to school. I will not go there.
> I: What do you think you will learn in kindergarten class?
> C: I will learn to read and write "Daniel" [his own name]. I need to be nice and do what the teacher says. Walk to the playground when the teacher tells me. Also learn to draw pictures.

Like 5% of the children in the sample, a boy, 6.5 years of age, characterized school as an authoritarian place where the teacher would command the children:

> I: What do you think you will do in kindergarten class?
> C: Music, homework, and play outside.
> I: What do you think you will learn in kindergarten class?

> C:  Draw correctly, do homework correctly, play correctly, play outside in a good manner, eat correctly, learn to play with toys correctly. You will be scolded if you do not play correctly. If people do not like to play with me, you have to play by yourself. You will get a smack from the teacher.

The examples above were from boys. Interestingly, it was predominantly the boys who expressed concern that school would be an authoritarian place where children would be required to sit still, be quiet, and follow the teacher's orders. It should be noted that adults have long been forbidden by law from hitting children in Denmark, making the children's expressed concerns about being hit by teachers all the more fascinating.

Early childhood researchers often hope that their work will have meaningful, real-world applications. In the case of this study, knowledge of children's preexisting views and expectations about kindergarten may help their teachers welcome them more warmly and empathically so as to liberate them from a false (hopefully) understanding of school.

## CHILDREN AS RESEARCHERS

Just as there is a trend in the postmodern world toward engaging children as active participants in their own education, so too a trend toward engaging children in research on childhood may be on the horizon. To date, adults have designed and conducted virtually all research about children. This gives rise to a contradiction. On the one hand, researchers aim to uncover dimensions in children's lives, thereby objectifying them, making them into "the exotic other" to be studied and analyzed. On the other hand, researchers are increasingly interested in taking children's perspectives and involving them in the research process to minimize their objectification. Most often, however, children only participate in research in the role of persons who are comfortable being interesting in the researcher's eyes and willing to be studied. However, a few pioneering research projects have succeeded in involving children in a meaningful role as co-researchers. For example, Danish researchers Rasmussen and Smidt (2003) carried out a project on children's use of their neighborhood. The study explored the idea that children not only should be heard in the planning of their neighborhoods, but also that they should participate in the actual decision-making process. As a group of international researchers argued, "an understanding of how children experience and construct a sense of place is a foundation for engaging children in changing such place" (Christensen & O'Brien, 2003, p. 1).

In their study, Rasmussen and Smidt (2003) viewed children not only as neighborhood change agents but also as researchers who collect data, which might become the basis for decision making and important change. The participating children selected and photographed the places they loved in their neighborhoods. They presented their photographs and accompanying narratives to the researchers, who then interviewed them about their views on their neighborhoods. Researchers interpreted children's data collection and presentation as representing their need to create their own world separated from the adults. As they published the results of their study, the researchers acknowledged their hope that their findings would enable children to have more freedom and opportunities for self-organization in their preschools and schools.

Another Danish researcher, Pernille Hviid (1999), investigated 6- to 9-year-old children's views about how they spent their leisure time in their after-school programs. In this study, the children served as researchers (Hviid, 2000b). They conducted interviews with friends about life in the after-school program. They created the interview questions themselves, generating quite a different list of questions than Hviid herself had envisioned. The children decided whom to interview and handled the tape recorder and other logistics. The children generated quite different data than would have been collected had an adult constructed the interview and, therefore, produced new knowledge from the children's perspective. Among the findings of the study was that children characterized a good life in leisure time as being engaged in interesting activities, as well as having the opportunity for social interactions. The worst thing at the leisure-time center was to be excluded, to be outside the social life. As a 9-year-old girl said, "You are standing here and feel lonely."

Although at first it may seem meaningful and democratic to involve children in a role as co-researchers, this new practice also raises ethical questions. For example, children may not fully realize how much will be required of them when they first agree to take the role of co-researchers in a study (e.g., Putman, Liss, & Landsverk, 1994). In addition, having children as co-researchers may inadvertently compromise other children's right to refuse to participate, since children may find it more difficult to refuse to answer questions from a peer than from an unfamiliar adult researcher.

## IN CHILDREN'S BEST INTEREST...

Life in modern times seems to be "normalizing" the idea of children as competent, active participants in societal life, including decision making, and the notion that children bring to the task adeqate motivation and capacity to participate meaningfully and productively. Much more than in previous generations, parents and teachers expect children from an early age to raise their voices and express their views. Even in preschool (in principle, at least), children participate in the planning of their education. Increasingly, children have become involved in research, often now taking the role of informants and, rarely, the role of co-researchers. More and more, then, parents, teachers, and researchers act in accordance with *United Nations Convention of the Rights of the Child*, stressing the concept and value of children's participation in society as fully vested persons, with many of the same rights as adults. However, while we can certainly celebrate "progress," we should not go too far down this path without considerable reflection and analysis. Early childhood researchers must continue to discuss ethical dimensions of our work (Alderson, 1995; *Children & Society*, 1996). There is no definitive answer to the question of the balance between protection and participation for children. Hence, it is incumbent upon early childhood researchers, teachers, policymakers, and parents to raise and examine these questions again and again.

Educators and researchers often try to establish trust and intimacy with children so we can observe them more closely and enter their world to become more a part of their lives, their thoughts, and their feelings. To be ethical, adults must enter a child's world with respect, humility, and caution. Perhaps this respect, humility, and caution should lead us to take a step back, rather than a step forward, in our work with children, creating greater distance between ourselves and the children we hope to understand more fully. Surely, our right to exciting new data and new insights about teaching are no more important than the children's right to privacy and protection. Perhaps it would benefit children, in some cases at least, to be left alone or protected from well-meaning adults who want to study them, lobby for them, and enhance their opportunities for participation.

## NOTES

1.   Social pedagogues are persons who have been especially trained to work with children in after-school, recreational, and preschool settings. They have a background that might compare to a combined education as an early childhood teacher or a social worker in the United States.

## REFERENCES

Alder, P., & Alder, P. (1987). *Membership in field research*. Newbury Park, CA: Sage.
Alanen, L. (1992). *Modern childhood? Exploring the 'child question' in sociology* (Research report no. 50). Jyväskyla: University of Jyväskyla, Institute for Education.

Alderson, P. (1995). *Listening to children: Children ethics and social research*. Barnardos: Barkingside.

Åm, E. (1989). *På jakt etter barnperspektivet* [Search for the child's perspective]. Oslo: Universitetsforlaget.

Andenæs, A. (1991). Fra undersøgelsesobjekt til medforsker? Livsformsintervju med 4-5 åringer. [From object to co-researcher: Interviews with 4-5 years old children]. *Nordisk Psykologi, 43*(4), 274–292.

Andersen, D., & Kjærulff, A. (2003). *Hvad kan børn svare på? Om børn som respondenter i kvalitative spørgeskemaundersøgelser* [Children as respondents in qualitative research]. Copenhagen: Socialforskningsinstituttet.

Andersen, G., & Ottosen, M.H. (Eds.). (2002). *Børn som respondenter: Om børns medvirken i survey* [Children as respondents: Children's participation in survey]. Copenhagen: Socialforskningsinstituttet.

Atkinson, P., & Hammersley, M. (1983). *Ethnography: Principles in practice.* London: Tavistock.

Berglund, G. W. (1985). *Den etnografiska ansatsen: Ett aktuelt inslag i pedagogisk forskning* [Ethnographical approach]. Uppsala: Pedagogiska institutionen, Uppsala Universitet.

Beattie, N. (2002). *The Freinet movements of France, Italy and Germany, 1900–2000: Versions of educational progressivism* (Mellen Studies in Education, Vol. 74). New York: Edwin Mellen Press.

Berg, M., Broström, S., Hännikäinen, M., Rubenstein Reich, L., & Thyssen, S. (1996). The child's perspective: An extended view of what constitutes quality. In F. Laevers (Ed.), *The child's involvement. Report from the Collaborative CIDREE Project on Early Childhood Research, Part 2* (pp. 34–41). Edingburgh: CIDREE Scottish Consultative Council on the Curriculum.

Bjørgen, I. A. (1991). *Ansvar for egen læring: Den professionelle elev og student* [Responsibility for own learning]. Trondheim: Tapir.

Brannen, J., & O'Brien, M. (1995). Review easy childhood and sociological gaze: paradigm and paradoxes. *Sociology, 29*(4), 729–737.

Bronfenbrenner, U. (1979). *The ecology of human development: Experiments by nature and design.* Cambridge, MA: Harvard University Press.

Broström, S. (1999). Friendship among five-year-old children in iindergarten. In H. Vejleskov (Ed.), *Interaction and competence. Report of the CIDREE Collaborative Project on Early Childhood Education* (pp. 21–29). Edinburgh: CIDREE Scottish Consultative Council on the Curriculum.

Broström, S. (2000). *Børns forventninger til skolen og indfrielsen af disse* [Children's expectation to school and fulfilment]. Copenhagen: Danish University of Education.

Broström, S. (2002). Children tell stories. *European Early Childhood Education Research Journal, 10*(1), 85–97.

Broström, S. (2003). Transition from kindergarten to School in Denmark: Building Bridges. In S. Broström, & J. T. Wagner (Eds.), *Early childhood education in five Nordic countries: Perspectives on the transition from preschool to school* (pp. 39–75). Århus: Systime Academic.

Broström, S., & Thyssen, S. (1996). *Kvalitet i barnets liv i daginstitutionen: Et finsk, svensk, dansk forskningsprojekt* [Quality in children's life]. Copenhagen: Danmarks Pædagogiske Institut.

Canevaro, A. (1988) Una struttura di connessione narrativa. In *Una scola une sfondo*. Milano: Nicola.

Cecchin, D., & Larsen, I. S. (2002). *Pædagogiske forbindelse: Kontinuitet mellem børnehave, skole og fritidsordninger* [Educational relations: Continuity between preschool, school and after school]. Copenhagen: BUPL.

*Children & Society*. (1996). Special issue on ethics of social research with children. *Children & Society, 10*, 2.

Christensen, E. (2000). *Det 3-årige barn* [The 3-years old child] (Report no. 3 fra forløbsundersøgelsen af børn født i 1995). Socialforskningsinstituttet 00:01. Copenhagen: Socialforskningsinstituttet.

Christensen, P., & O'Brien, M. (Eds.). (2003). *Children in the city: Home, neighborhood and community*. London: Routledge Falmer.

Corsaro, W.A. (1981). Entering the child's world: Research strategies for field entry and data collection in a preschool setting. In J. Green & C. Wallat (Eds.), *Ethnography and language in educational settings* (pp. 117–146). Norwood, NJ: Ablex.

Corsaro, W.A. (1985). *Friendship and peer culture in the early years*. Norwood, NJ: Ablex.

Corsaro, W.A. (1997). *The sociology of childhood*. Thousand Oaks, CA: Pine Forge Press.

Dewey, J. (1960). *Democracy and education: An introduction to the philosophy of education*. New York: MacMillan.

Doverborg-Österberg, E., & Pramling, I. (1988). *Om at forstå børns tanker—og om at samtale med børn* [Understanding children's thoughts]. Vejen: Åløkke.

Ehn, B. (1983). *Skal vi leke tiger?* [Shall we play tiger?]. Lund: Liber.

Ehn, B., & Löfgren, O. (1982). *Kulturanalys* [Culture analysis]. Klippan: Gleerups förlag.

Enggaard, J. (1984). Interview-studie af børns selvforståelse [Interview-study of children's understanding of themselves]. *Tidsskrift for NFPF, 3–4*, 37–44.

Fine, G. A., & Sandstrom, K. L. (1988). *Children: Participant observation with minors*. London: Sage.

Giddens, A. (1990). *The consequences of modernity*. Cornwall, UK: Polity Press.

Glaserfeld, E. von. (1995). A constructivist approach to teaching. In L. P. Steffe & J. Gale (Eds.), *Constructivism in education* (pp. 3–15). Hillsdale, NJ: Erlbaum.

Hedegaard, M. (1990). *Beskrivelse af børn* [Description of children]. Århus: Århus Universitetsforlag.

Heering, K. (1994). *Sæt ord på dit liv: Breve fra børn til Socialministeren* [Describe your life. Letters from children to the minister of Social Affairs]. Børnerådet og Socialministeriets informations og konsulentvirksomhed. Copenhagen: SIKON.

Honing, M. S. (1999). *Entwurf einer Theorie der Kindheit*. Frankfurt am Main: Suhrkamp.

Hutchby, I., & Moran-Ellis, J. (1997). Children's social competence. In I. Hutchby & J. Moran-Ellis (Eds.), *Children and social competence: Arenas of action* (pp. 7–26). London: Falmer Press.

Hviid, P. (1999). *Til lykke: Børneliv i SFO og skole* [Congratulations: Children's life in after school and school]. Copenhagen: Danmarks Pædagogiske Institut.

Hviid, P. (2000a). *Børnepanel: På sporet af 5. klasse* [Children's panel: Following grade 5]. Copenhagen: Børnerådet.

Hviid, P. (2000b). Metodiske overvejelser: Forskning med børn, der deltager [Methodological reflections: Research with children as participants]. In P. S. Jørgensen & J. Kampmann, *Børn som informanter* [Children as informants] (pp. 55–69). Copenhagen: Børnerådet.

James, A., Jenks, C., & Prout, A. (1998). *Theorizing childhood.* Cambridge, UK: Polity Press.

James, A., & Prout, A. (Eds.). (1990) *Constructing and reconstructing childhood: Contemporary issues in the sociological study of childhood.* London: Falmer Press.

Jenks, C. (1996). *Childhood.* London: Routledge.

Jensen, B. B., & Schnack, K. (1997). The action competence approach in environment education. *Environment Education Research, 3*(2), 163–178.

Junker, B (1960). *Field work.* Chicago: University of Chicago Press.

Jørgensen, P. S., & Kampmann, J. (Eds.). (2000). *Børn som informanter* [Children as informants]. Copenhagen: Børnerådet.

Kjørholt, T. (2001). The participating child: A vital pillar in this century? *Nordisk Pedagogik, 21*(2), 65–81.

Kragh-Müller, C.C. (1963). *I morgen er for sent* [Tomorrow is too late]. Copenhagen: Rhodos.

Kvale, S. (1996). *Interviews.* London: Sage.

LeCompte, M., & Preissle, J. (1993). *Ethnography and qualitative design in educational research.* London: Academic Press.

Lindh-Munther, A. (Ed.). (1989). *Barnintervjun som forskningsmetod* [Child interview as research method] (Centrum för barnkunskap, Report om barn, no. 1). Uppsala: Uppsala Universitetet.

Løkken, G., & Søbstad, F. (1998). *Observation og interview i børnehaven* [Observation and interview in preschool]. Copenhagen: Munksgaard.

Melzoff, & Moore. (1998). Infant intersubjectivity: Broadening the dialogue to include imitation, identity and intention. In I. S. Bråten (Ed.), *Intersubjective communication and emotion in early ontogeny.* Cambridge, UK: Cambridge University Press.

Ministry of Education and Science in Sweden (1998). *Curriculum for pre-school.* Stockholm: Frizes.

Mishler, E. G. (1996). *Research interviewing: Context and narrative.* Cambridge, MA: Harvard University Press.

Murra, J. & Trevarthen, C. (1985). Emotional regulation of interactions between two-month-olds and their mothers. In T. M. Field & N. A. Fox (Eds.). *Social perception in infants* (pp. 177–197). Norwood, NJ: Ablex.

Neill, A. S. (1962). *Summerhill: A radical approach to education.* London: Victor Gollancz.

Pellegrini, A. D. (1996). *Observing children in their natural world: A methodological primer.* Hillsdale, NJ: Erlbaum.

Piaget, J. (1929). *The child's conception of the world.* London: Kegan Paul.

Piaget, J. (1952). *The origins of intelligence in children*. New York: International University Press.

Pramling, I. (1983). *The child's conception of learning*. Göteborg: Acta Universatis Gothoburgensis.

Pramling Samuelsson, I., & Lindahl, M. (1999). *Att förstå det lille barns wärld med videoens hjälp* [To understand young children's world by use of video observations]. Stockholm: Liber.

Pramling Samulsson, I., & Sheridan, S. (2001). Children's conceptions of participation and influence in pre-school: A perspective on pedagogical quality. *Contemporary Issues in Early Childhood, 2*(2), 169–194.

Pramling Samulsson, I., & Sheridan, S. (2003). Delagtighet som värdering och pedagogic. [Participation as evaluation]. In *Pedagogik och Forskning i Sverige. Barns perspektiv och barnperspektiv, 8,* 70–84. Göteborg Universitet.

Print, M. (1993). *Curriculum development and design*. Australia: Allen & Unwin.

Putnam, F. W., Liss, M., & Landsverk, J. (1996) Ethical issues in maltreatment research with children and adolescents. In K. Hoagwood, P. S. Jensen, & C. B. Fisher (Eds.), *Ethical issues in mental health research with children and adolescents* (pp. 113–132). Mahwah, NJ: Erlbaum.

Qvarsell, B. (2003). Barns perspektiv och mänskliga rättigheter: Godhetsmaximering eller kunskabsbilding? [Child's perspective and human rights]. In E. Johansson & I. Pramling Samuelsson (Eds.), *Pædagogisk forskning i Sverige. "Barns perspektiv och barnperspektiv"* [Educational research in Sweden. Child's perspective and child perspective] (Vol. 8, pp. 1–2, 101–113). Göteborg Universitet.

Qvortrup, J. (1999). Barndom og samfund. In P. Jørgensen Schultz & L. Dencik (Eds.), *Børn og familie i det postmoderne samfund.* [Child and family in post modernism]. Copenhagen: Hans Reitzel.

Qvortrup, J., Bardy, M., Srgitta, G., & Wintersberger, H. (Eds.). (1994). *Childhood matters: Social theory, practice and politics*. Aldershot, UK: Avebury.

Rasmussen, K., & Smidt, S. (2003). Children in their neighbourhood: The neighbourhood in the children. In P. Christensen & M. O'Brien (Eds.), *Children in the city: Home, neighbourhood and community* (pp. 82–100). London: Routledge-Falmer.

Riihelä, M. (1996). *How we deal with children's questions? Semantic aspects of encounters between children and professionals in child institutions*. Helsinki: Stakes. Saarijävi, Gummerus Kirjapainooy.

Riihelä, M. (Ed.). (2003). *Barnens Sagobroar i Norden. Pohjolan lasten satusiltoja* [Children's telling bridges]. Jyväskylä: Stakes, Nordiska Kulturfonden.

Skilbeck, M. (1976). *School-based curriculum development and teacher education*. Mimeograph. OECD.

Sommer, D. (2003a). *Barndomspsykologi: Udvikling i en senmoderne verden* [Childhood psychology in a modern world]. Copenhagen: Hans Reitzel.

Sommer, D. (2003b). *Barndomspsykologiske facetter* [Dimensions of childhood psychology]. Århus: Systime Academic.

Sommer, D. (2003c). Børnesyn i udviklingspsykologien. Er et børneperspektiv muligt? [View on children in developmental psychology. Is a child perspective possible?]. In E. Johansson & I. Pramling Samuelsson (Eds.), *Pædagogisk forskn-*

*ing i Sverige. "Barns perspektiv och barnperspektiv"* [Educational research in Sweden. Child's perspective and child perspective] (pp. 85–100). Göteborg: Göteborg Universitet

Srgitta, G. (1993). Provision: Limits and possibilities. In P.L. Heiliö. E. Lauronen & M. Bardy (Eds.), *Politics of childhood and children at risk: Provision-protection-participation* (Eurosocial Report 45, pp. 35–47). Vienna: European Center.

Stenhouse, L. (1975). *An introduction to curriculum research and development.* London: Heinemann Educational Books.

Stern, D. (1998). *The interpersonal world of the infant: A view from psychoanalysis and developmental psychology.* London: Karnac Books.

Strandell, K. (1997). *Jeg är glad att jag gick på dagis: Fyrti ungdomar ser tilbaka på sin uppväkst* [I am happy for my days in preschool]. Stockholm: HLS Förlag.

Thomas, J. (1993). *Doing citical ehnography.* London: Sage.

Thorne, B. (1993). *Girls and boys in school.* Buckingham, UK: Open University Press.

Tiller, P. O. (1998). *Hverandre: En bok om barneforskning.* [A book on child research]. Oslo: Gyldendal norsk forlag.

Tiller, P. O. (1988). Barn som sagkyndige informanter [Children as competent informants]. In M. K. Jensen (Ed.), *Interview med børn* [Interview with children] (pp. 41–72). Copenhagen: Socialforskningsinstituttet.

Tiller, P. O. (1984). Barns ytringsfrihed og bruk av barn som informanter [Children's freedom of expression, and children as informants]. *Barn, 4,* 26–34.

Trevarthen, C. (1998). The concept and foundation of infant inter-subjectivity. In S. Bråten (Ed.), *Intersubjective communication and emotion in early ontogeny.* Cambridge, UK: Cambridge University Press.

Tylor, R. W. (1949). *Basic principles of curriculum and instruction.* Chicago: University of Chicago Press.

Undervisningsministeriet (1995). *Lov om Folkeskolen* [Act on the folkeskole]. Copenhagen. (English version: www.uvm.dk/cgi/printpage/pf.cgi).

United Nations (1989). *Conventions of the rights of the child.* Retrieved November 2004, from www.CRIN.org

Utbildningsdepartementet (1998). *Läroplan för förskolan* [Curriculum for pre-schools]. Stockholm: Fritzes.

Verhellen, E. (1994). *Convention of the rights of the child.* Leven: Verhellen & Garant.

Wagner, J. T. (2003). Introduction: International perspectives and Nordic contributions. In S. Broström & J. T. Wagner (Eds.), *Early childhood education in five Nordic countries: Perspectives on the transition from preschool to school* (pp.11–25). Århus: Systime Academic.

# CHAPTER 10

# RECONCEPTUALIZING EARLY CHILDHOOD EDUCATION

## Challenging Taken-for-Granted Ideas

**Hillevi Lenz Taguchi**
*Stockholm Institute of Education*

We must begin *wherever we are*…in the text where we already believe ourselves to be. (Derrida, 1976, p.162)

### "WHAT DO YOU DO AFTER YOU'VE MET POSTSTRUCTURALISM?"

In 1995 Jeanette Rhedding-Jones published an article titled *"What Do You Do after You've Met Poststructuralism?"* In this chapter I want to show how a poststructuralist-inspired, theoretically multidimensional, and inclusionary approach to learning theories and the practices that arise from them challenge the still-prevalent modernist idea of articulating one grand learning theory for postmodern education.

*Nordic Childhoods and Early Education*, pages 257–287

## Poststructural Theory and Its "Linguistic Turn"

Poststructural theory, as in *after (post)* structuralism, took a decidedly linguistic turn away from the idea of uncovering essential and fundamentally unchangeable human traits as mental or societal structures, suggesting instead that anything we think we know about ourselves or the world is simply constructed and formulated meanings in different forms of human expressions and languaging. Nothing can be understood in any kind of way, without being given a meaning; that is, without being *languaged* ("textualized").

Even the shapes and functions of the body have adapted to the meanings we have given them in specific cultures and contexts (Butler, 1993). The body *is* materialized meanings, as is femininity, masculinity, sexuality, childhood, and, for that matter, all forms of pedagogical practice. This illustrates a refusal to polarize and separate what is an unconditional and unchangeable nature, and our meaning-making/knowledge of it. Therefore, poststructuralism aims to dissolve one of the most fundamental Western bipolar logics: the subject–object bipolarity.

Poststructuralism is also a move away from 20th century dominant constructivist learning theory, in education as in other social sciences. Instead of a separate subject making meaning of the object, as in constructivist theory, the subject–object dichotomy is dissolved and everything is materialized meaning and meaning materialized. It becomes impossible to clearly separate what is the object in itself and what is our materialized, textualized meaning-making of it. Such poststructuralist epistemological reasoning makes sense when we consider that the same object or phenomena is understood differently in different meaning-making contexts within cultures and even more so between different cultural contexts. Thereby, as the French philosopher Derrida (1976) has stated, everything is *"text."* This shift is what is more commonly understood as "the linguistic turn."

## Swedish Early Childhood Education: The Reggio Inspiration

In this chapter I try to give an answer to Jeanette Rhedding-Jones's question in relation to what has happened in parts of Swedish early childhood education, commonly dedicated to what has been called the "Reggio Emilia inspiration" (Dahlberg, Moss, & Pence, 1999). This approach to teaching and learning reflects new theories of learning and knowledge that emerged after the linguistic turn in poststructural theory in the humanities, social, and educational sciences (Davies, 1997; Dickens & Fontana, 1994; Silverman, 1993; Steier, 1991; Uscher & Edwards, 1994).

The Swedish State Early Childhood Curriculum, published in 1998 (Lpfö-98), calls for a constructivist approach, but also includes ideas about cooperative learning, thus transgressing into a more poststructural way of understanding knowledge and learning. ECE practitioners inspired by the preschool practice in the Italian city of Reggio Emilia have successfully animated constructivist theory in their daily practice, with a view of children as investigators of the world and constructors of their own knowledge (e.g., Bruner, 1996; Gardner, 1985; Marton & Booth, 1997; Pramling Samuelsson & Asplund, 2003; Säljö, 2000). But they have also challenged themselves toward a practice that makes sense only with the help of poststructural discourse of materialized meaning-making, *as well as* with a view of the child as a co-constructor of culture and knowledge (Dahlberg et al., 1999; Lenz Taguchi, 2000; Lind, 2004; Project Zero & Reggio Children, 2001).

Since the first municipal preschools were built at the end of World War II, early childhood practitioners in the northern Italian city of Reggio Emilia have undertaken a political quest by making the children's understandings and meaning-making of the world around them visible to the local community, with the help of what is usually conceptualized as pedagogical documentation. But the documentation is not used just to make the children visible and their voices hearable in a political sense, but also to enforce the cooperative, meaning-making processes in groups of children, their parents, and early childhood teachers.[1] These practitioners would, however, not "confess" to any specific learning theory, but rather to a careful selection of "excellence" from a multitude of theories representing many different disciplines, as well as artistic and poetic languaging and imagery that cannot be scientifically classified. This can be theorized as an inclusionary approach in line with poststructural theory (Lenz Taguchi, 2003, 2004; Rinaldi, 2001) and constitutes a movement into a use of pedagogical documentation as a tool for what I have called the "practice of an ethic of resistance" (Lenz Taguchi, 2000, 2003, 2004).

## An Ethic of Resistance: Deconstructing What We Already "Know"

An ethic of resistance refers to conscious acts of thinking deeply about the assumptions and taken-for-granted notions we bring with us (often without awareness) as we engage in our daily work with children. As we practice an ethic of resistance, we deconstruct, or take apart, what we "know to be true," to reflect on it, analyze it, criticize it, and resist its seductive powers arising from its familiarity.

But this deconstruction also has an ethical dimension. Once we have deconstructed our assumptions, thought critically about them, resisted them, and come to different understandings, we often face professional decisions with an inextricable ethical component. Once I revisit and revise what I "know" about how children think and learn, or about what approach I should use to help them grow, then I may be ethically obliged to change what I actually do with them. Based on my new understandings, I cannot ethically continue with my old practices. And neither can I stop with my new understandings. I am ethically obligated to continue to examine my practices, always looking for better ways to "do good" for these particular children with whom I am working.

To be able to do deconstructional work in an ethic of resistance, we need documents to work with. The concept of pedagogical documentation refers to any kind of document from pedagogical practice—anything from a videotaped sequence, photographs, taped conversations between children investigating something, notes or observations from children's work, to the materialized and explorative thinking of the children manifested as drawings or constructions in different materials such as clay, trash materials, or sand. From a pedagogical perspective, documentation is not simply to capture or make visible a memory from the past (retrospective), but rather, to enable us to analyze and deconstruct, and to be able to make choices for possible learning processes tomorrow (prospective). These documents, then, become active "agents" in planning new learning challenges and preconditions for further cooperative and investigative work and play among the children.

Working deconstructively with documentation means that we can analyze how children and we ourselves, as early childhood educators, understand what is taking place, or, as I would say in a poststructural discourse, what discursively informs the children, as well as the preschool teachers. This way of deconstructively *reading the text* of the documents helps us make visible or, so to speak, tell the story of teachers' daily practice, which, in turn, provides a concrete starting point for thinking deeply about these practices and their philosophical or theoretical underpinnings. To be able to change and develop practice as an ethical learning environment for all children we must, as Jacques Derrida stated in the quote above, "*begin wherever we are... * in the text where we already believe ourselves to be" (1976, p. 162).

Simply put, preschool teachers participating in reconceptualizing early childhood education in Sweden are actively engaged in displacing "teaching truths" in favor of teaching more ethically and in a displaced sense more "truthfully." In this chapter I illustrate this reconceptualization concretely through examples from two preschools in the Stockholm area. I will not provide theoretical overview of major aspects of reconceptualizations in ECE after the linguistic turn; but rather, I will show what such reconceptualizations can be all about in everyday preschool practice. In the first example, I illustrate the practice of an ethic of resistance, with a focus on the processes of the preschool teachers themselves. In the second example, I will spotlight children's learning processes.

## Draw a Map of Who You Want to Change Places With

The preschool in the first example is located in a suburb south of Stockholm in a middle-class area. The preschool serves about 38 children age 1–5, with about 16 children in the younger group (1- and 2-year-olds), and about 22 children in the older group (3- to 5-year-olds). About three full-time preschool teachers, called pedagogues in Sweden, work with each group, taking turns eight hours each, between 7:00 AM and 6:00 PM Monday through Friday. The following example from this preschool illustrates how teachers reconstructed their practice.

At this preschool, a group of 10 five-year-olds ate lunch each day at a certain table, always seated in the same places. The table was located in the art studio area, where other children were also engaged in a project designed to help them develop spatial knowledge and orientation within their immediate everyday surroundings. Some children were seated on the floor, drawing maps to show their routes to the preschool from home. Other children were drawing maps to a hidden treasure—freshly baked cinnamon rolls—in the park adjacent to the preschool. Over a period of several days, two of the 5-year-old girls repeatedly asked if it were possible for them to change places at the lunch table. The preschool teachers decided to incorporate this request into the ongoing spatial orientation project by adding a map-drawing task. The children immediately agreed to the new assignment responding to the teacher's request: "Please draw a map to the person you want to change places with. Don't tell anyone who it is while you are working, so we can guess later" (Lenz Taguchi, 1997). The children engaged in the task, some with ease, getting started right away and finishing quickly. Others put more time and energy into the task, thinking long and hard or adding more detail into their drawings. However, all of the children ultimately produced a drawing and showed great interest in how seating at the table would eventually turn out. The session was documented with videotaping and photographs of the drawings.

Later the children met in even smaller groups of three to four children to read each others' maps and discuss various possible interpretations of the maps. In these meetings the children debated and cooperatively reflected upon concepts like "opposite from me" in relation to "on the opposite side of the table," as well as on graphical symbols like arrows and lines and how they should be interpreted in this context. The result of these meetings was that children expanded their knowledge of how a map can be made and what it communicates to others, which inspired them to more map-drawing. The children changed places at the lunch table after long debates on how to satisfy everyone's wishes, which wasn't possible without compromises among the children.

## Multiple "Readings" of the Children's Map-Drawings

The teachers analyzed the map-drawings in four different ways. (In poststructural discourse, I would refer to these ways of analyzing as four different "readings" of the map-drawings.) Directly after the assignment, the teachers discussed how the children reacted to the assignment and the kinds of maps they created. Their goal was to use this analysis as a foundation for planning the next day's activities, especially to find ways to make the task more interesting and more challenging for the children. Later, the teachers continued to analyze this assignment in collaboration with me, as a researcher, and other colleagues at the site, ultimately engaging in four separate *readings* or analyses of the first day's documentation. Importantly, the teachers began *where they were* in their thinking and pedagogical practice, trying to make visible and understand what came to their minds and what they valued in the children's drawings, illustrating the crucial message in Jacques Derrida's quotation at the beginning of this chapter: "*begin wherever we are...*"

Derrida makes this statement in relation to the process, or, as I would rather talk about it, the simultaneous practical and theoretical *movement* of poststructuralist deconstruction, which has been an important inspiration for the use of documentation as a pedagogical analysis tool. By documenting their ongoing instructional practice, especially during children's investigative group work, calling for cooperative meaning-making, teachers make visible the children's learning processes and strategies, as well as their own teaching strategies and practices as they interact with, listen to, and observe the children.

It is important to note that documentation work is, at once, practical and theoretical. It both inspires and requires reflection, movement, and change. In our attempts to make meaning of what we see in any piece of documented practice, whether it be a drawing, a photograph of a child's cardboard construction, a videotaped play sequence, dialogue, or problem solving, we need to account for the notions, beliefs, values, ideas, and practices that discursively inform the children, as well as the preschool teachers themselves, that is, the tools for thinking and performing we have access to through our previous and ongoing "discursive inscriptions," in poststructural discourse, or what we usually refer to as *previous experience*. This is a process of thinking deeply and critically about staging, arranging, doing, and analyzing our own pedagogical performances. We do multiple *readings*, or repeated analyses, trying to understand the same situation in many ways, in an effort to more thoroughly understand what we see and hear from multiple perspectives.

Multiple readings protect us from the taken-for-granted, which typically constitutes a major portion of our first reading or analysis. Here is what I did and said. Here is what the children did and said. This reflects what I am familiar with, what I know to be "true" and "right." With each iteration, though, multiple readings increase opportunities for resistance, our own resistance to the status quo in our instructional practice. "Resistance" is here *not* about opposing or simply replacing one understanding with another, which is then later abandoned. It is *not* about clinging on to particular forms of knowledge through a mistaken belief that they are the only true ones. Rather, it is about a continuous process of displacement and transgression from *within* what we already think and do; from *"where we are,"* to quote Derrida, from the understandings we have now. Such resistance is an act of ethics. Elisabeth Adams St. Pierre has written about such an ethic in the following way: *"(It) explodes anew in every circumstance, demands a specific re-inscription, and hounds praxis unmercifully"* (1997, p. 176; see also Lenz Taguchi, 2000).

In addition, multiple readings of documentation help teachers "resist" shallow evaluations of children's work, inspiring instead deeper and more thoughtful analysis of children's work, both as process and as product. This thought-filled analysis helps teachers make ethical choices about what they will do next to challenge the children appropriately to further their learning. Multiple readings help teachers think carefully about preconditions for learning for groups of children, as well as for the individuals who make up these groups. How much time will be required? What kinds of spaces? What materials? What kind of challenging questions? Multiple readings of pedagogical documentation involve a process of visualizing "where we are," enabling us to formulate other possible ways of understanding teaching and practicing it.

The readings focused on only six of the ten drawings and maps produced by the children on the day of the assignment. All four of the readings described below were conducted soon after the session with the children. However, the full meanings of these readings did not emerge until later, after repeated analyses and reflection. The analyses were conducted in a floating and crisscrossing process over a period of about a month. We met formally only two times to discuss the drawings as well as other assignments in the project, but discussions and note-taking was also taking place more or less on a daily basis. Also, one of the preschool teachers (Hjelm, 2001) investigated two of the readings by examining texts on constructivist thinking about children's map-drawings (Marton & Booth,

1997), and social-constructionist thinking about what a map is (Wood, 1992), which added extensively to the ongoing discussions and readings.

The readings were iterative and reiterative, each reading influenced by the last and influencing the next, as is the process with deconstructive discourse among teachers and their colleagues. However, I present them below as if they were separate to make them more accessible and palpable to readers who were not part of the process. It is important to understand that these readings were done cooperatively, that is, they are the result of a cooperative process, so we have no interest in showing who eventually came up with which reading. However, I will sometimes quote one person to show how we used documentation of our own discussions to make visible the taken-for-granted notions in our thinking and, thereby, help us with further *readings* (analysis). (To comply with standards of ethical research and to assist readers, we have replaced the children's real names with more English-sounding names below.)

## A Developmental Psychological Reading

After the trading places assignment, the teachers and I spread the children's drawings out on a large table. What immediately came to mind as we tried to make meaning of the drawings were questions from developmental psychological discourse. In extensive research developmental psychological discourse has been singled out as the dominant discourse, or even what Michel Foucault and researchers following him would call the "regime of knowledge," within Swedish ECE practices (Burman, 1994; Dahlberg et al., 1999; Foucault, 1998; Hultqvist, 1990; Lenz Taguchi, 2000; Nordin-Hultman, 2004). Borrowing words from the feminist poststructural philosopher Butler, I would say that developmental psychological concepts are the tools that lie most readily at hand in the toolbox for our meaning-making when we try to understand children's work (Butler, 1993). For example, one teacher was fascinated that a couple of children had made drawings from above (Michael's aerial view of the table, Figure 10.2) and from above with a profile of himself (Nick's drawing, Figure 10.1). She commented that it would be difficult for a child, or even an adult, to draw a room from above as if the person drawing was not present in the scene. She claimed that these drawings were, in a sense, "weird," and "it is unnatural for children to draw from above because they are never above anything" (Lenz Taguchi, 1997). The teacher's comment revealed that she probably took for granted the Piagetian notion that children are egocentric, which, from the perspective of developmental psychology, means that children's behaviors must be viewed as coming from their own self-oriented perspective. From this Piagetian view of the child, the teacher believed that it would therefore be *unnatural* for a child to draw a map as if he or she were a bird flying above the table because this would not be part of the child's own experience. From this view of children as egocentric and unable to imagine anything from a perspective other than their own, drawing an aerial view, like Michael did, would be as unnatural as a child's drawing himself in profile, as Nick did, rather than a full frontal view. Another preschool teacher also revealed that she took the tenant of the egocentric child for granted when she asked, "When did humans actually invent this idea of drawing from above in this unnatural way?" (Lenz Taguchi, 1997).

Thinking in line with and thus using the discursive tool of psychological discourse meant that the early childhood teacher thought it unnatural for Nick to draw himself in a profile, since the discourse informed her that the child is limited by his experience of seeing his full face in a mirror and, therefore, he would be unable to draw a profile of himself. Nick started off by drawing himself in a seemingly perfect profile (see Figure 10.1), and then drew the table and the other children from behind or with faces toward the spectator. The psychological *reading* of Nick's drawing is revealed in one of the preschool teacher's comments stating that he "lifts himself out of the picture and takes the perspective of the spectator" (Lenz Taguchi, 1997).

We asked ourselves why Michael and Nick would actually be able to draw an "unnatural" aerial view and why Nick was able to draw himself in profile. One preschool teacher explained that these particular children were able to do this because they had been drawing much more than other children since a very young age. Here, without realizing it at the time, the preschool teachers switched to a discourse of graphical competence, which can be seen in the *semiotic reading*, further elaborated below. From this perspective, these were simply skilled and artistic children with extensive drawing experience.

Figure 10.1.   Nick's drawing

In such a reading these children had discovered the "unnatural" ways of drawing as an adult or an artistic performance, rather than drawing "naturally from within," as a child is supposed to do, according to the developmental psychological discourse. This way of explaining or justifying Michael's and Nick's "unnatural" drawings as "skilled" showed that the preschool teachers tried to fit this "unnaturalness" into the discourse of "the natural" by saying that the children had not simply developed skill through training, but also from unusual talents "by nature," that is, a talent given and expressed "from within," which is in line with, rather than in resistance to, a dominant psychological reading.

The graphical reading, then, was enmeshed within the discursive regime of psychological discourse in preschool teachers' thinking. So, even if it could be argued that the preschool teachers were initially doing *multiple* readings, when talking both of the egocentric child and graphical skills, it was not done as a deconstructive "resistance" reading. It was only later that true deconstructive talks began as teachers examined the two readings side by side and came to understand the two readings as different and equally important in understanding what each child had done and why. At this later time the reading of graphical skills was done in terms of resistance against the psychological reading, in an attempt to displace and reduce the strength and "naturalness" in that reading.

Another example of us reading from the psychological discourse of the egocentric child occurred when we tried to read Vanessa's drawing (Figure 10.3). Some teachers understood her drawing, simply showing the face of the friend with whom she wanted to change places, as "proof" of the idea of the egocentric child. Reading from a discourse of the egocentric child, Vanessa's drawing was considered natural (i.e., in line with the discourse most readily at hand), whereas, as pointed out above, drawing from above (an aerial view), or drawing oneself in profile, was considered unnatural in relation to the discursive regime of psychological discourse, or natural only in terms of being a result of inborn talent.

As I will argue later in this chapter, a deconstructive process requires simultaneous displacements, not only of taken-for-granted understandings, but also of how these readings are valued in an ethical sense. The teachers involved in this project and I, as researcher and part of the group, did not enter the realm of deconstructive resistive practice until we encountered Vanessa's and Margaret's drawings (Figure 10.4), which we viewed as problematic and lacking in several important ways, in spite of the naturalness we assigned to them. Our discussions took us into the next reading, *a constructivist reading*, where through extensive conversation about our disappointment in these drawings and our inability to value them as highly as the others, we began to make displacements. These displacements brought us to new ways of understanding and valuing the drawings in a decidedly nonhierarchical way. Only then did it become possible for us to make a conscious choice to value the two girls' drawings on an equal plane with the drawings of what we had understood as their more "talented" class-mates, Michael and Nick, in terms of the lessons each drawing held about the children's learning processes.

## Displacing a Psychological Reading

When choosing to work with an assignment such as the spatial orienta-tion project, preschool teachers as well as researchers are led by uncon-scious expectations and notions about the subject/content, in this case, about what a map is. These notions and expectations are tied to sometimes different and/or contradictory discourses that inform us about how to make meaning of what we see and hear, as well as how to value what we see and hear. In the initial conversation between the three preschool teachers and me, it became obvious that all four of us valued the drawings in similar hierarchical ways. We all had similar views about which drawings repre-sented "talent" and which were lacking. We also shared similar ideas about the characteristics of a map.

Hence, we all thought that the two boys who had made drawings with a perspective from above (e.g., Michael, Figure 10.2), or almost from above with the profiles (e.g., Nick, Figure 10.1), had actually done maps, whereas the girls (Vanessa, Margaret, Julie, and Ann, Figures 10.3, 10.4, 10.5, and 10.6) and the remaining four boys had coped with the assignment in vari-ous ways. We saw Vanessa's drawing (Figure 10.3) and Margaret's drawings (Figure 10.4) as problematic and lacking as adequate responses to the question the teachers had put forward to the children. We questioned

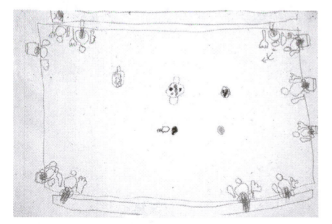

Figure 10.2.   Michael's drawing.

whether the children would be able to use these drawings as maps in the upcoming session, for which we sketched out a scenario where the children could read each others' maps, trying to figure out who wanted to change places with whom. We asked ourselves if such a request of the children to read each others' maps would be ethically right, given the circumstances and readings at hand, where the lack of "map qualities" in some of the drawings seemed so obvious to us.

Importantly the questions related to the lack of "map quality" imply a dominant idea of what a map should look like. This idea contradicts the dominant expectations of what children's drawings are all about, from within an understanding of developmental psychology in the previous reading. So, on the one hand, the preschool teachers did *not* expect the children to draw maps that looked like maps, with a perspective from above, but, on the other hand, the assignment itself *required* exactly that "unnatural" skill from the children. Since the preschool teachers had not discussed their expectations and notions on map drawing beforehand, this had to be done later in the deconstructive talk that followed. This talk started by going back to the scene of the assignment by looking at the videotape. After a couple of minutes of watching the video, an obvious reading of the situation was evident. Many of the drawings could easily be understood as a completely adequate answer to the very question posed: "Please draw a map to the person you want to change places with. Don't tell anyone who it is while you are working, so we can guess later" (Lenz Taguchi, 1997). Below is Vanessa's obvious answer to this question (Figure 10.3). She wrote the name of the boy she wanted to change places with "as a whisper beside his ear, since we mustn't tell anybody who we want to change places with" (Lenz Taguchi, 1997).

Figure 10.3.   Vanessa's drawing.

As the teachers and I looked at the video, many things became visible, or clear, to us for the first time. We now had a better picture of the task from the children's perspective. What did "draw a map" mean to the children? Which part of the task was most salient to them, deciding whom they wanted to change places with, keeping the secret, or drawing a map? These questions, which arose from our viewing of the videotape, enabled us to rethink the values we used to decide which responses were adequate, which were highly artistic, and which were lacking in some way. Perhaps the children's drawings should not be viewed or evaluated as maps, but rather as responses to a question put before them in a context that did not signal any certain expectation of what a map should look like.

Armed with these new insights about the demands of the task, as seen from the children's perspective, it became easier to start reading against the grain, in "resistance" to our taken-for-granted notions about maps and about how children should respond to the task teachers had given them (Davies, 2000). One preschool teacher described a previous experience where she and her colleagues had developed a series of activities to help children gain spatial orientation skills in the woods, where they frequently played. This teacher insisted that children understood that it wasn't possible to make a map of the forest, the hill, and the lake from an egocentric viewpoint if they wanted another child to be able to follow their maps to locate a hidden treasure. She suggested that, in their daily lives, children typically encounter all sorts of maps, such as maps of the city, the subway system, and the ski slopes. Another preschool teacher then suggested that children also have extensive everyday experience with overhead perspectives, as, for example, when they build castles from blocks or sand and play with dolls or cars in these constructions on the floor or in sandboxes.

By thinking about children's previous experiences with maps and overhead perspectives, we were able to take another step toward displacing their original taken-for-granted ideas about how the children should have responded to the assignment. Now the discussion moved toward ways to successfully help children develop map-drawing competencies to represent their understandings of spatial relations. Perhaps we could build upon what they learned during an earlier spatial orientation assignment showing the way to school. We thought about ways to help the children reconstruct their maps of the route from home to school. As an alternative we considered making an overhead projection to help children recall their previous mapping experiences. This exploration of alternatives represented yet another small step forward in displacing dearly held ideas we had previously taken for granted.

## A Constructivist Reading

To further investigate how to understand what some of us thought a map should look like, one of the preschool teachers did further investigations on children's map drawing (Hjelm, 1999). She came back to us with a constructivist reading inspired by the constructivist researchers Ference Marton and Shirley Booth (1997). According to these researchers, a map must include, at least to some degree, both logical and spatial correspondence. Children typically develop logical correspondence first and spatial correspondence later. Logical correspondence means that all the objects in the mapped area must be present in the drawing. The larger the number of objects, the higher the degree of logical correspondence required. Spatial correspondence refers to the map drawer's awareness of the relative space between the objects in the drawing, and how this corresponds to reality. The higher degree of spatial correspondence, the more the map represents actual spatial relationships in the real world.

Logical and spatial correspondence are not fully developed until school age at the earliest (i.e., about the age of 7). According to Marton and Booth (1997), a drawing that has neither logical nor spatial correspondence is not a map. Applying this definition, then, the teachers could see that Vanessa's and Margaret's drawings did not qualify as maps, and Julie's and Ann's drawings included little evidence of logical or spatial correspondence. However, both Michael's and Nick's drawings had a very high degree of logical and spatial correspondence.

In accordance with constructivist thinking, the interest of the teacher would now be to challenge the children to reach the goal of correct map-drawing skill, in line with constructivist knowledge on how children develop this skill. Children who showed evidence of neither logical nor spatial correspondence should be challenged to become aware of what logical correspondence means before spatial correspondence, since this is in line with how map-drawing skills generally develop. Children who showed awareness of logical correspondence should be challenged further with this, as well as becoming aware of spatial correspondence. However, since the children were only 5 years old, there was no need to challenge these children toward an awareness of spatial correspondence, since this normally might not be achieved due to the children's young age (Marton & Booth, 1997; Hjelm, 1999).

## Displacements of the Constructivist Reading

Displacing our dominant developmental psychoanalytical notions about children's drawings with a constructivist reading did, however, not lead to consensus on how to proceed with the project. One of the preschool teachers argued that focusing on map qualities as defined by Marton and Booth demonstrated that teachers still valued the qualities of Michael's and Nick's maps more than the maps of the other children, who had used different, perhaps highly inventive, strategies to represent their thinking. Many of the children's maps were still considered lacking, especially the girls' drawings. Another problem was that the teachers themselves had been unclear about the demands of the task when they asked the children to do maps. Neither the children nor the teachers and myself had a shared idea of what a map could or should be within the context of this assignment. In other words, it didn't seem fair to the children to stay with a constructivist reading. It seemed necessary to do more and other readings of the drawings to be able to sort out where we were in this project and what new steps and challenges to pursue.

In addition to this, and perhaps more importantly, we began to ask ourselves about the process of using multiple readings as a tool for pedagogical analysis from an ethical point of view. Our discussions repeatedly evolved into a search for "excuses" to value all children's work, even if it did not include characteristics of a map. This aspect of our conversation represented an ethical struggle, in which the value of content knowledge and skill (in this case, how to draw a conventional map) was pitted against our desire to be equitable in valuing children's work. Also, we noticed a disturbing gender factor at play in both our psychological and our constructivist readings of the drawings. It was clearly boys who managed to draw maps that we prized most highly, either in terms of a naturally inborn talent or a highly developed technical skill using logical and spatial correspondence. The girls' drawings were clearly and typically relational (faces, chairs with hearts), or simply plain and uncomplicated compared to the boys' drawings.

Once we realized the value-based and gender-based biases in our earlier discussions, we also felt ethically compelled to make additional readings, now with our heightened awareness of equity, including gender equity, as an issue. Could it be possible, from such an ethical standpoint in relation to valuing the children's work, not just to challenge the other children in the direction of Michael's and Nick's techniques, but also to challenge these two boys to explore other means of expression and communication as the girls had done?

In relation to a constructivist reading, then, we realized that we did not want to confine our thinking about the children's work by focusing exclusively on pre-established conventions of map construction, such as logical and spatial correspondence or aerial perspective. We realized that we wanted to include aspects of equity in our further analyses. Two of the children (boys) obviously employed these conventions to a greater degree than did the other children, but did this mean that these boys necessarily learned more from the task or had more important ideas to share than their peers who represented their thinking in other ways?

## A Social Constructivist Reading

Consciously trying to think differently than from within the dominant psychological and the almost-as-dominant constructivist discourses, the preschool teachers now started to think in a kind of reverse logic. If a map-drawing is not about logical and spatial correspondence, as in the constructivist reading, or limited by children's egocentric thinking, as in the developmental psychological reading, how can we understand what map drawing might be? Shifting into reverse to think about what something is not is an important practice in the deconstructive "resistance" process, and refers to the practice of *"sous rature,"* translated as "under erasure" (Derrida, 1976). French philosopher Jacques Derrida, cited at the beginning of this chapter, conceptualized deconstruction as a movement from *within* the notions and discourses that inscribe our thinking. Putting a reading, concept, or understanding "under erasure" means that we cross it out, not to erase it forever, but to temporarily reverse and displace our understandings. The crossed-out word remains legible/readable, because we need and value it, but crossed out because we need to displace our taken-for-granted understanding in order to become more ethical listeners, thinkers, and practitioners (Derrida, 1976; Lather, 1995, 1997; Lenz Taguchi, 2000, 2003).

So, what other understandings of the children's work were possible? The preschool teachers initially tried to think about the purpose behind the drawings. What purpose did the children have in mind when they made the drawings? Did their drawings fulfill their goals? If we think of the general idea of a map, as well as these children's drawings, as a construction of the social world as each child experiences it, we begin to see each child's drawing as an expression of that child's understanding of the task and of map construction. The drawings had a purpose and a specific function: to convey certain information (Hjelm, 1999; Wood, 1992). With such a reading, we discovered another meaning in Vanessa's, Margaret's, Ann's, and Julie's drawings. In the drawing below, Juliet gave very clear and specific details about where she sat at the table, beside her two best friends, and whom she wanted to change places with at the other corner across the table (Figure 10.4).

In the session where the children read each other's drawings, all of the children easily read the girls' drawings, with the exception of a few difficult concepts that Ann's drawing evoked (discussed below). For example, every-

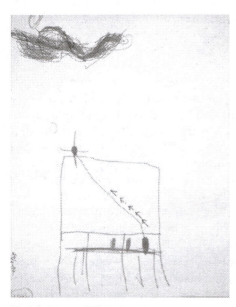

Figure 10.4.   Julie's drawing.

one knew that Margaret was in love with Michael, so everyone quickly recognized exactly which children were represented by the two chairs with
hearts over them. (See Figure 10.5.) And Vanessa's drawing was just as easy
to read with the name of the boy she wanted to change places with written
beside his ear (Figure 10.3).

During this session, teachers and children discussed various ways of
responding to the assignment, as well as various ways to read the drawings.
From the children's perspective, all drawings were adequate and functional
in relation to the purpose of the assignment. These discussions of different
drawing strategies inspired the children to attempt to draw different kinds
of maps to fulfill the purposes they learned from one another or new ideas
and purposes of maps they invented while playing. The children's interest
in map-drawing continued and became a part of this particular classroom's
culture during the next couple of years, even though the older children
went on to school and younger children started. Map-drawing became a
heritage from this 6-month project that left traces in both the environment
and in the skills of this particular group of children.

This social constructivist reading of the drawings gave new meaning and
made the girls' drawings more highly valued in the eyes of the preschool
teachers. This new attitude toward the children's work was then transmitted to the children during subsequent activities, where the drawings were
used as a starting point for discussing the readability. Such covert transmis-

sion of attitude and value helped the children value each others' drawings in a more equal manner, not thinking that one drawing was necessarily better than the other, but simply fulfilling the purpose of the map-drawing task in different ways.

Adults "hidden agendas" arising from dominant discourses that inform teachers' thinking and doing exude a powerful, palpable presence in every classroom. Children are sensitive and skillful readers of these adult agendas (Davies, 2003). In this case, children surely read the teachers' hidden agendas (preexisting, taken-for-granted notions) about the qualities of good and bad maps. Armed with new insights arising from their social constructivist readings, the teachers were now in a position to examine their "hidden agendas" openly and critically, with a view toward changing their everyday practice in ways that would welcome the children's perspectives on an assignment, as well as various appropriate and meaningful options for completing the task satisfactorily.

Here again, the ethical dimension of resistance to taken-for-granted ideas becomes apparent. By making our taken-for-granted notions visible to ourselves and one another during these deconstructive talks, we became able to displace them, making room for multiple ways of thinking, understanding, and doing—both for ourselves and for the children. However, I am not arguing here that a larger number of readings necessarily results in more opportunities for making more ethical choices. Rather, I want to point out that dominant discourses exclude other understandings, and that more than one or two readings makes possible displacements of taken-for-granted ways of valuing the children's strategies. In addition, more than one or two readings may make more ethical choices possible as we "problematize" our ways of understanding and valuing what the children have done.

This reasoning can be understood with other words, namely that making excluded or absent understandings visible doesn't necessarily mean that a truer or more virtuous choice can be made. If this were so, we would be able to develop a finite list of readings, which would inevitably enable us to identify an objective, universally acceptable, "most ethical" approach. (For more on this, see ethical particularism in Kihlbom, 2002.) However, a single, universally acceptable, "most ethical" choice is not possible. Therefore, all we can realistically hold ourselves accountable for are these: (1) trying to make visible the conditions and readings we believe ourselves to have (what we view as natural and taken-for-granted); (2) when possible, trying to make supplementary readings with the help of other theories, thereby making visible the absences and exclusions in our immediate taken-for-granted reading; (3) consciously trying to problematize what we take for granted and resist the understandings that dominate our thinking and are most available to us; and, lastly, (4) making new choices, some of a more unconscious kind revealed in our attitudes toward the children and their work, and others, very conscious and driven by our sense of responsibility to our new understandings of ourselves, our work, and the children. Hopefully we will be able to perceive those different choices as more ethically framed and considered options, and, from that perspective, select the best choice in relation to the circumstances and context for the children and ourselves as their teachers.

## A Semiotic Reading

I will finish this example by offering a fourth, quite simplified reading, which I have, in a perhaps inadequately shallow sense, called a *semiotic reading*. Such a reading takes into account our understandings of the children's use of different kinds of signs and symbols as they worked on the changing places assignment. In Swedish ECE practice, children's drawings have been seen as expressions of the child's inner psychological and cognitive development through essentialist and universal stages (Lind & Åsén, 1999).

Because of this widely held view that drawings represent a child's inner self, framed and limited by the developmental stage the child is in, questioning the qualities of small children's drawings and paintings is often still seen as taboo. According to this line of thinking, the quality of the work will naturally improve as the child matures mentally, psychologically, and physiologically.

However, a semiotic reading situates the drawings within a cultural, rather than an intrapsychic or developmental, context. From the semiotic perspective, we began to think of the drawings as expressions of culturally and socially specific ways of using signs and symbols to communicate meaning. From the drawings we could see which signs and symbols the children had already "taken up" from the various contexts of their lives. These expressions can be taught and practiced within culture, independent of the child's "natural development." According to the social constructivist reading, then, drawing is a means of achieving a purpose (Lind & Åsén, 1999). The cultural signs learned are tools in these expressions, as in Margaret's drawing, using two different signs to tell everyone she wanted to change places with the person she was in love with (Figure 10.5). According to this reading, children can improve their competence in graphic expression by practicing, as in the previous example of both Micheal and Nick.

In investigative projects that involve drawings and paintings, it is crucial for teachers to analyze the graphic aspects of the children's experience. However, not all subject matter lends itself well to drawing and painting as a primary means of investigation and exploration. Even if drawing can be

Figure 10.5.   Margaret's drawing.

understood as a way of thinking using hand, pen, and paper, giving another dimension to the child's understanding of the subject, some subjects are perhaps better thought of and explored through other means of expression, such as bodily movements, dramatizations, construction in all different kinds of materials, sound, voice, or photographs. We must beware of the temptation to equate children's drawings and paintings with the totality of what they know on any given subject. For some children drawing is a good way of thinking and theorizing, but for others using their bodies, building, or thinking aloud are better ways.

We must deconstruct how we value children's ways of learning, as well as their ways of expressing what they are learning. We must think about the conditions that invite children to use a multitude of ways to express their knowledge, their thoughts, and their questions. Lastly, when adding new ways of making meaning and expressing knowledge, we must guard against favoring certain expressions we personally like over others, thus normalizing those we prefer while dismissing other expressions that might actually constitute a better way of meaning-making for certain children in a specific context (Lenz Taguchi, 2000).

## Conceptualizations and Meaning-Making through the Body and the Documents

In this part of the chapter I offer two brief examples of deconstructional learning processes carried out by the children themselves. I start with the reading of Ann's drawing discussed above, and then move to a small part of a math project.

In Ann's drawing (Figure 10.6), her purpose was to show that she wanted to change places with Margaret on the other side of the table. In the session where the children read each others' maps, the other children read Ann's map as if she wanted to change places with the child sitting directly opposite her across the table. But Ann insisted that this reading was wrong. To illustrate her thinking, she actually walked across the table to show the person she wanted to change places with. The children seemed confused, conceptually, by the difference between "sitting opposite" someone and "sitting on the opposite side of the table." Ann didn't actually sit opposite Margaret, but she did sit on the other side of the table in a more diagonal direction. The other children insisted that Ann's map didn't work if she really wants to change places with Margaret. Intense negotiation ensued among the children, punctuated with lots of walking on the table, until Ann realized that her map didn't convey her intention. The teachers did not intervene as this negotiation continued. The teachers understood the children's walking across this table, which measures two meters in width, as an important way for the children to physically understand various conceptualizations. By using their bodies and comparing this physical experience with Ann's map, the children eventually constructed a shared understanding to which they could all agree.

The point I want to make here is that the children used documentation (the drawing) as a starting point for negotiations and, eventually, common understanding. Crucial to this process is using the differences in the readings as a force in their shared learning processes. In Derridean deconstruction "the play of difference," practicing "sous rature" (under erasure) becomes a means of displacing, taking on new perspectives and making new connections, and thereby, making, what I with a poststructural discourse would call supplementary and inclusionary understandings (i.e., using many theories to

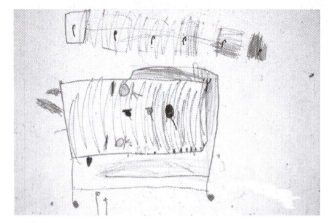

Figure 10.6.   Ann's drawing.

understand in multiple and shifting ways). Differences can be made visible by using all different kinds of expressions. In the brief example above and in the one yet to be told below, the child's own body becomes a tool for grappling with and resolving differences in terminology and conceptual understandings. This tool is often underestimated in early childhood settings.

The second example is part of a math project from another preschool that is located in a suburb west of Stockholm in a middle-class area. The preschool serves about 70 children age 1–5, with about 23 children in each of the three groups, where about three full-time preschool teachers in each group are scheduled weekdays between 7:00 AM and 6:00 PM. In the math project, children had previously been involved in a long project about birds of different kinds, and now knew a lot about birds, especially the blue tits that came to the bird feeder, in the shape of a small wooden cottage, outside of the classroom window every day thoughout the winter. As part of the bird study, the children had built a giant crow, constructing the beak and the claws in clay and wire. During these construction activities, the children frequently raised questions of size. However, their preschool teachers decided that, although size could be discussed in more general terms, actual experiences with measurement should not be the focus just then because the children were equally interested in the construction of the bird, as well as the bird's flying ability, its private and family life, and other aspects of its existence and nature.

But again and again the children brought up the question of size and measurement. One day a boy said that now he knew exactly how wide the white-tailed eagle, Sweden's largest bird, is when it flies. According to the boy, the white-tailed eagle is as wide as four 5-year-old children standing side by side with their arms stretched as far as possible. The other children immediately ran up and tried it out. The white-tailed eagle was simply huge! Figure 10.7 presents one of the spontaneous documentations of this event drawn by one of the children.

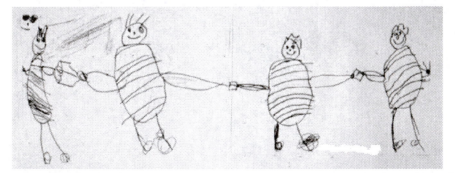

Figure 10.7.    Image of the white-tailed eagle represented by children holding hands

"How many blue tits long is the white-tailed eagle, then?" a girl asked. The children started to measure with their hands. The white-tailed eagle measured 81 blue tits! The excited children now started to measure each other. Elsa and Josephine lay down on the floor to be measured by Jonathan and Kevin. Jonathan exclaimed, "Elsa measured 11 blue tits. I measured with my index finger and thumb and pretended that it was the same size of a blue tit. But Kevin measured Josephine and she measured 27 blue tits." The children found the difference puzzling, since they could see that Elsa and Josephine are almost equal in height. One child suggested that the girls lie on the floor beside each other so they could compare. Elsa was just a little bit taller than Josephine. The following anecdote is from the children's discussions.

> Teacher: We can see that they are almost the same height, and yet there is a big difference when you counted your blue tits. Why is that?
>
> Mary: It is weird because Elsa is a little taller than Josephine.
>
> Johanna: It should have been 11 blue tits on Elsa and 10 on Josephine.
>
> Jonathan: I think Kevin took shorter steps with his fingers and that is why he got 27. I think Kevin used blue-tit babies when he measured. If you pretend that the blue tit is larger then you count fewer blue tits. When you make smaller blue tis with your fingers, there are more. When you measure smaller, there is more!
>
> Kevin: I want to try again! Last time I used small blue tits, now I will use big ones. There is a difference if you do them small or big! (Åberg & Lenz Taguchi, 2005).

The group of children reasoned that, with a "standardized" blue tit, everything could be measured. The children now negotiated further and decided that each would draw a blue tit. They would then choose the one they liked best and reproduce hundreds of copies. In choosing a blue tit to be reproduced, the children negotiated about the question from the preschool teacher about what qualities such a blue-tit must have to best serve the purpose. After thorough discussion and comparison, the unanimous choice was a blue tit in a definite side perspective with tail and beak stretched out. The children carried out this process largely on their own initiative, only supported by the teacher nearby taking notes, who offered one or two questions to help them focus. The preschool teachers helped by making the 100 copies and laminating the selected blue tit so it would be easier to use for measuring.

These children practiced what we sometimes call a "pedagogy of listening," which includes practicing asking questions, visualizing strategies and differences, and negotiating. Therefore, the children are used to carrying out such negotiation practices to the extent that they can perform them largely on their own, imitating the questions teachers have asked them, such as, "How did you think when you did this like that?" or "Explain to me what you mean when you say that" or "Please tell me how you have done this," and so forth. The children are also very aware of the documentation process, in fact, so aware that they would tell the teachers not to forget to put on the tape-recorder, switch on the camera, or take notes, if they did not themselves take care of it, by drawing, writing, and taking photographs.

From this time forward, the children measured everything with the help of blue tits. But soon another difference was made visible to the children as they cooperatively examined various documents such as drawings, photos taken by the children themselves, and notes in the large project documentation books the preschool teachers kept on the floor for everyone to add to, look at, write in, and negotiate meaning around. The children realized that if the blue tits were not put in a straight line with tail to beak, the number of blue tits would vary even though classmates were measuring the same object. Interestingly, this discovery was then used as a way to create more differences, rather than resolve them.

This bird study evolved into a year-long math project from these initial measuring investigations. This brief vignette from the large project provides an example of how difference, multiple understandings, and use of the body are central in children's learning processes. Learning resulted when their teachers made it possible for children to ask questions, theorize, try out, investigate, document, and negotiate their different understandings. When children engaged in asking questions, theorizing, trying out, investigating, documenting, and negotiating meaning, they also experienced, directly and indirectly, the ethical aspects of confronting and resolving differences. For example, these children encountered ethical issues and questions when differences in their thinking became visible to them. Instead of valuing different results as right or wrong or better or worse ways of measuring, these children were used to thinking of other ways to explain differences, as we saw in their discussion of the way results differed because some children measured with baby blue tits while other children measured with larger blue tits. This way of thinking in terms of different strategies or explanations, instead of valuing in terms of right or wrong, better or worse, is, I would say, a more ethical way of handling difference and more productive in relation to the learning involved. When difference is honored as central to the way we understand the world and each other, learning becomes cooperative meaning-making with a strong ethical dimension.

## Deconstructive Talks at the Heart of an Ethics of Deconstructive Resistance

I have elsewhere more thoroughly theorized on the practice of deconstructive talks, conceptualized as a conversation between theories of Jacques Derrida's (1976) writing "sous rature" (under erasure) and Jürgen Habermas's (1988) communicative action (Lenz Taguchi, 2000). This conversation shows that Habermasian theory of communicative action is, by itself, inadequate for the kind of negotiated learning practices important to postmodern education. Derridean deconstruction practice works as a supplement to Habermasian theory because it adds inclusionary, displacing and transgressing qualities to meaning-making as the central aspect of learning, and is not simply trying to come to what Habermas would understand as an agreed-upon truth and/or intersubjective meaning-making. Derridean deconstruction practice also adds the dimension of teacher planning with the explicit purpose of creating learning challenges for individuals and groups in cooperative learning situations. Deconstructive talk relies on difference (theorized from the Derridean concept of *différance*) in the meaning-making process, rather than, as in Habermasian theory, on identifying truth, truthfulness, and rightness in the communicated arguments. In a deconstructive talk, difference is understood as a productive force rather than as a threat to consensus or a problem to overcome (as in Habermasian theory). Deconstruction is about disruptions, destabilizations, undermining and challenging taken-for-granted notions, values, practices, and pedagogy-as-usual. The major challenge in deconstructive talks is the requirement for self-reflection—thinking about *what and why* we see, hear, and value what we see, hear, and value. For example, in the map-drawing activity, teachers engaged in deconstructive talk had to examine what discourses about children, about learning, and about map-drawing informed our ways of thinking and valuing. This reflection, then, enabled us to resist what we previously took for granted and think differently. As the feminist poststructural educational researcher Bronwyn Davies has stated, "Any reading against the grain implies a detailed knowledge of the grain itself" (2000, p.114). The more you know about how the taken-for-granted notions in your own thinking have been constructed, the easier it is to resist such taken-for-granted thinking.

An educational practice that attempts to put taken-for-granted notions under continuous deconstructive "erasure" can be conceived of in terms of a "self-wounding laboratory as we attempt to be accountable to complexity. Here, thinking the limit becomes our task" (Lather, 1995, p. 3). So, instead of emancipation from false consciousness, as in critical theory of early feminism, we continuously trouble, as Lather expresses it, and contest the things we think we cannot think without. Lather writes about a diaspora (i.e., a forced exile), forcing oneself out of one's best way of knowing (Lather, 1997). The preschool teacher (as the researcher) is thus problematized as "the one who knows" and is "placed outside of mastery and victory narratives" (Lather, 1995, p. 3). In other words, teachers problematize the usual view of themselves as someone who owns certain knowledge to be transmitted to children, and the researchers problematize the standard view that they can produce true knowledge about teaching practice. Instead both try to engage in co-constructive practices of knowledge with the children and the researched, trying, at least temporarily, to force ourselves out of the unavoidable position of power in relation to the other. In addition, both the teacher and the researcher take into account their own impact and effect on the learning process, in terms of everything from material preconditions, aspects of time, place, questions, body language, and so forth (i.e., learning and research are situated in a specific context that must be made visible and displaced *from within*). As such, Derridean deconstruction can also be understood simultaneously as a political and *feminist* movement. Hekman commented on criticisms of deconstruction as negative—destructive—in the following way, as she implied the feminist aspect of it:

> The point of Derridean deconstruction, however, is not to erase categories, but to displace the oppositions that have structured the dichotomies of Western thought. So conceived, deconstruction is not a negative project; it is not an effort to reverse binary oppositions or to replace them with a new orthodoxy. Rather it involves the displacing of the play of oppositions that has informed not only Western thought but also the inferior status of women. (1990, p. 26)

The feminist aspect concerns much more than this political aspect in the feminist poststructural theories of subjectification (Butler, 1997; Davies, 2000; Lenz Taguchi, 2004; Nordin-Hultman 2004), but I cannot discuss this here. However, this political aspect is not insignificant in relation to the obvious emancipative aspects that an ethic of resistance has on the female preschool teachers I have studied and worked with over the last 10 years (Lenz Taguchi, 2000). The deconstructive talk invites preschool teachers to a practice that attempts equality in meaning-making. By emphasizing difference, multiple readings, and equality in evaluation, the power of the *true–false* binary is undermined and sometimes dissolved.

## Transgressing into an Inclusionary Poststructural Approach

One of the major challenges in educational methods, or what we in the Nordic region call pedagogy, is the problem of its normative character and normalizing practices. One by one throughout the 20th century and continuing now into the 21st century, Nordic ECE pedagogy has been influenced by a succession of supposedly ideal normative and normalizing teaching methods and values. As these new theories come into favor, they often became reified in the state curriculum or directives from the Board of Social Affairs, which used to oversee early childhood services in preschools until ECE was integrated into the school system with the Ministry of Education as the responsible ministry in 1996.[2]

The selection of a pedagogical method is similar in many ways to the selection of a moral or ethical standpoint or action. From both an individualistic and a broader social perspective, we choose a pedagogical method in order to "do good." Critics of a poststructurally informed, deconstructive approach in ECE argue that it is too relativistic and too ambiguous. The critics argue that, by their very nature, eclectic practices are not sufficiently grounded in any one (universialist or better) theory and lack the normative qualities expected of a robust pedagogy. But, as ethical philosopher Ulrik Kihlbom wrote in his argument on the decisiveness of ethical particularism, as opposed to an universalist ethic, which rests on assumptions that virtue is a question of all or nothing, "The morally competent or virtuous person is a moral ideal, which probably no one ever fully satisfies" (2002, p. 141). An ethical particularist stance, just as a poststructuralist stance, understands moral issues to be essentially nonuniversalist, and that persons and actions must be understood contextually, the very same way multiple readings of pedagogical practice are done contextually, as shown above. We learn how to become morally competent persons within a specific social culture, although the existence of human virtuous ideals cannot be denied (Kihlbom, 2002).

In what I theorize as an ethic of resistance, such a morally virtuous human ideal is taking responsibility by acknowledging and making visible multiple ways of understanding and making meaning of a specific content or situation. The deconstructionist philosopher Jacques Derrida talks about the force of what he calls *Necessity*, which simultaneously acknowledges the necessity of human ideals as it contains the necessity of questioning them.

The consequence of this reasoning is that poststructural deconstruction is and will always be a movement *from within* the modernist vision of wanting to do, if not better, but definitely "good," where the "good" is hence negotiable and subject to a continuous state of change in time and location. Or, as Derrida explained in an interview by referring to his own practice as a philosopher, in terms of a necessary deconstructive movement from *within,* and (equally) necessary modernist desires, ideals, and visions that make us in a sense human:

> I confess that everything I oppose, so to speak, in my texts, everything that I deconstruct—presence, voice, living, and so on—is exactly what I'm after in life. I love the voice, I love presence.... So, I'm constantly denying, so to speak, in my life what I'm saying in my books or my teaching. Which doesn't mean that I don't believe what I write, but I try to understand why there is what I call Necessity, and I write this with a capital 'N' ... a Necessity which compels me to say that there is no immediate presence. (2003, p. 8)

An important aim of this chapter is, therefore, to try to challenge the modernist exclusionary idea of finding and stipulating *one* successful learning theory for postmodern education. Instead I want to suggest a poststructuralist-inspired, theoretically multidimensional and inclusionary approach to learning theories and the practices that arise from them. Such inclusions, importantly, are here done from within the discourse of the poststructural linguistic turn, and the notion of that "there is nothing outside the text ... there has never been anything but writing" (Derrida, 1976). These words refer to the notion that nothing can exist to us, and/or be understood in any kind of way, without being given a meaning (i.e., without being, in a certain understanding, *written* or *languaged*—"textualized"—text). It is from *within* this notion of cooperative constructions and formations of meanings as discourses that different aspects of learning are included in a theoretical multidimensional approach to learning.

## Inclusionary Conclusions

In the first years of the 21st century theories of knowledge and learning have shifted toward a constructivist and/or social constructivist discourse, with a dominant view of the child as a co-constructor of culture and knowledge. Constructivist and social constructivist notions clearly provide the pedagogical framework for the Swedish state curriculum, published in 1998. In this chapter I have focused on a specific, limited aspect of Swedish ECE practice, namely what is commonly referred to as Reggio Emilia-inspired. In this small corner of Swedish practice, early childhood educators have further transgressed this shift toward constructivism or social constructivism by venturing into a theoretically multidimensional and inclusionary poststructural approach to learning and daily teaching practice. I have called this a practice of an ethics of resistance. Deconstructional talks take an inclusionary approach in this practice. Many different kinds of theoretical readings and understandings are used to help both children and preschool teachers understand and value the phenomena studied in multiple ways. In addition, multiple readings also serve as a vehicle for negotiating ethically grounded choices. Thus, the ethical aspect of this practice resides in its context-sensitive particularism, as well as in its creative, imaginative way of visualizing differences, silences, what is not immediately present, or what is excluded, side by side with what is taken-for-granted and what is present or obvious to us. In this way, deconstructional resistance of the kind I have tried to illustrate in this chapter may disrupt unequal power relationships hidden in binary constructs, including adult–child, theory–practice, individualistic learning–cooperative learning, and learning–play, to name but a few of the either-or concepts that riddle educational discourse. The purpose of the ethical resistance I have been talking about is not to reverse these binaries, but rather to attempt to continuously and repeatedly dissolve and transgress them. Thus, in a definitely modernist sense, by participating in ethical resistance we attempt not only to do good, but more importantly, to do good given the particular contextual situation and the readings possible from "wherever we are ... in the text where we already believe ourselves to be" (Derrida, 1976).

## NOTES

1. Researchers from Harvard Graduate School of Education have researched on the pedagogical practice in Reggio Emilia for several years during the almost 40-year-old project Zero, which has become an institution that conducts basic research on cognition, learning, and pedagogy, with a continuing special focus on the arts. American researchers, Howard Gardner, Ben Mardell, Mara Krechevsky, and Steve Seidel, have participated in a co-production with Reggio Children published in 2001 called *Making Learning Visible: Children as Individual and Group Learners.*

2. ECE practices in Sweden have been regulated by the Social Ministry and the Board of Social Affairs up until 1996, when ECE was integrated into the school system. The first state curriculum for ECE practices was legislated in 1998. ECE is now the first part of a lifelong learning system in Sweden regulated by the Educational Ministery. (For further information on this, see Lenz Taguchi & Munkhammar, 2003.)

## REFERENCES

Åberg, A., & Lenz Taguchi, H. (2005). *Lyssnandets pedagogik: Demokrati och etik i förskolans lärande* [Pedagogy of listening: Democracy and ethics in preschool learning practice]. Stockholm: Liber.

Adams St. Pierre, E. (1997). Methodology in the fold and the irruption of transgressive data. *Qualitative Studies in Education, 10*(2), 175–189.

Bruner, J. (1996). *The culture of education.* Cambridge, MA: Harvard University Press.

Burman, E. (1994). *Deconstructing developmental psychology.* London: Routledge.

Butler, J. (1997). *The psychic life of power: Theories in subjection.* Stanford, CA: Stanford University Press.

Butler, J. (1993). *Bodies that matter: On the discursive limits of "sex."* New York: Routledge.

Dahlberg, G., Moss, P., & Pence, A. (1999). *Beyond quality in early childhood education and care: Postmodern perspectives.* London: Falmer Press.

Davies, B. (2000). *A body of writing 1990-1999.* Walnut Creek, CA: Alta Mira Press.

Davies, B. (2003). *Frogs and snails and feminist tale: Preschool children and gender.* Brisbane, Australia: Allen & Unwin.

Davies, T. (1997). *Humanism: The new critical idiom.* London: Routledge.

Derrida, J. (2003). Following theory. In M. Payne & J. Schad (Eds.), *Life after theory* (pp. 1–51). London: Continuum.

Derrida, J. (1976). *Of grammatology.* Baltimore: John Hopkins University Press.

Dickens, D. R., & Fontana, A. (Eds.). (1994). *Postmodernism and social inquiry.* London: UCL Press.

Foucault, M. (1998). *Aesthetic: The essential works* (2nd ed.). Middlesex, UK: Penguin Press.

Gardner, H. (1985). *The mind's new science: A history of the cognitive revolution.* New York: Basic Books.

Habermas, J. (1985). *The theory of communicative action, Volume 1: Reason and the rationalization of society.* Boston: Beacon Press.

Hekman, S. (1990). *Gender and knowledge: Elements of postmodern feminism.* Cambridge, UK: Polity Press.

Hjelm, S. (1999). *Förskolebarns kartritande* [Preschool children's map-drawing]. Undergraduate thesis, Pedagogiska Insitution, Stockholm University.

Hultqvist, K. (1990). *Förskolebarnet: En konstruktion för gemenskapen och den individuella frigörelsen* [The preschool child: A construction for collectiveness and individual emancipation]. Stockholm: Symposion.

Kihlbom, U. (2002). *Ethical particularism: An essay on moral reason.* Stockholm: ACTA Universtatis Miensis. Stockholm Studies in Philosohpy 23, Almqvist & Wiksell International.

Lather, P. (1997, May). *Lecture at Linköping University.*

Lather, P. (1995, November). *Troubling praxis.* Paper presented at the American Educational Studies Association Symposium: Mourning Marxism, Feminism, Poststructuralism, and Educational Praxis, Cleveland.

Lenz Taguchi, H. (1996). The field of early childhood pedagogy in Sweden: A female project of professionalization and emancipation? *Nordiske Udkast. Journal for Critical Social Science, 24*(1), 41–55.

Lenz Taguchi, H. (2000). *Emancipation och motstånd: Dokumentation och kooperativa läroprocesser i förskolan [Emancipation and resistance: Documentation and co-operative learning-processes].* Doctoral dissertation, HLS Förlag.

Lenz Taguchi, H. (2003, March). *Possibilities and difficulties in reconceptualizing preschool teacher-training in postmodern education.* Paper presented at NFPF/NERA Congress, Copenhagen.

Lenz Taguchi, H. (2004). *In på bara benet: En introduktion till feministisk Poststructuralism* [Down into bare bone: An introduction to feminist poststructuralism]. Stockholm: HLS Förlag.

Lenz Taguchi, H., & Munkhammar, I. (2003). *Consolidating governmental early childhood education and care services under the Ministry of Education and Science: A Swed-*

*ish Case Study.* Early Childhood and Family Policy Series, No 6 – 2003. Paris: UNESCO Education Sector.

Lind, U., & Åsén, G. (Eds.). (1999). *En annan skola—elevers bilder av skolan som kunskapsrum och social arena* [Another school—students' images of school as a space of knowledge and a social arena]. Stockholm: HLS Förlag.

Lpfö-98 (1998). *Läroplan för förskolan* [Curriculum for preschool]. Stockholm: Utbildningsdepartementet/Ministry of Education and Science.

Marton, F., & Booth, S. (1997). *Learning and awareness.* Mahwah, NJ: Erlbaum.

Nordin-Hultman, E. (2004). *Pedagogiska miljöer och barns subjektsskapande* [Pedagogical environment and the construction of children's subjectivity]. Stockholm: Liber.

Pramling Samuelsson, I., & Asplund, M. (2003). *Det lekande lärande barnet i en utvecklingspedagogisk teori* [The playing and learning child in a developmental pedagogical theory]. Stockholm: Liber.

Project Zero & Reggio Children (2001). *Making learning visible: Children as individual and group learners.* Italy: Municipality of Reggio Emilia.

Rhedding-Jones, J. (1995). What do you do after you've met poststructuralism? Research possibilities regarding feminism, ethnography and literacy. *Journal of Curriculum Studies, 27*(5), 479–500.

Rinaldi, C. (2001). Infant–toddler centers and preschools as places of culture. In Project Zero & Reggio Children, *Making learning visible: Children as individual and group learners* (pp.38–46). Italy: Municipality of Reggio Emilia.

Silverman, H.J. (Ed.). (1993). *Questioning foundations: Truth/subjectivity/culture: Continental philosophy V.* New York: Routledge.

Steier, F. (Ed.). (1991). *Research and reflexivity: Inquiries in social construction.* London: Sage.

Säljö, R. (2000). *Lärande i praktiken: Ett sociokulturellt perspetiv* [Learning in praxis: A sociocultural perspective]. Stockholm: Prisma.

Uscher, R., & Edwards, R. (1994). *Postmodernism and education.* London: Routledge.

Wennerberg, S. B. (2001). *Socialkonstruktivism—positioned, problem och perspektiv* [Social constructivism—positions, problems and perspectives]. Malmö: Liber.

Wood, D. (1992). *The power of maps.* New York: Guilford Press.

CHAPTER 11

# AN OUTSIDER'S PERSPECTIVE

## Childhoods and Early Education
## in the Nordic Countries

**Judith T. Wagner**
*Whittier College*

Cross-cultural study informs us through the juxtaposition of the familiar and the new, the known and the exotic. The best lessons lie in the differences. Over the last 18 years of work and study in the Nordic countries, I have collected hundreds of photographs, field notes, and mental images, each vividly illustrating an aspect of Nordic childhood that fascinates me or shocks me by its stark contrast to what I would expect at home in America. I have photos of toddlers running naked in a daycare center, climbing a rappelling wall, using a fork to eat spaghetti with some success (and some mess!), and skiing nimbly down a Norwegian mountainside. I have images of 10 toddlers, all under 3 years of age, milling about on an underground platform in their snowsuits, waiting for a train headed for the forest where their outdoor preschool is located. Their daycare teachers are nearby, but they do not hover or admonish the children to stay away from the edge, as

*Nordic Childhoods and Early Education*, pages 289–306
Copyright © 2006 by Information Age Publishing
All rights of reproduction in any form reserved.

would surely be the case if American daycare providers were to dare to take such young children to a train station, or to an outdoor preschool in the forest, for that matter.

I have photographs of preschoolers cutting apples with paring knives as they concoct a recipe for a cake, as well as pictures of 4-year-olds hanging by their knees from a tree branch high above my head, while their class-mates use a real saw and a power drill to construct a fort. Again, the grown-ups are nearby, but not hovering or orchestrating. I have memories of 4- and 5-year-olds setting tables with lace cloths, real china, crystal glasses, fresh flowers, and lighted (!) candles to celebrate the birthday of their class mascot, a well-worn stuffed bear. Some of these images are charming; oth-ers are bewildering; and still others are downright scary. They seem almost other-worldly and represent fundamental differences between typical American (*if there is such a thing*) and characteristically Nordic ideas about children, childhood, and early education.

As a researcher, teacher educator, and early childhood practitioner, I have traveled to the Nordic region more than 30 times. On three occa-sions, I have lived and worked in Denmark for extended periods, most recently in 2003. My main qualification for writing about Nordic childhood and early education is that I know firsthand how much is to be learned—about children, about life, and about ourselves—in the company of Nordic people and Nordic ideas. Although I am a passionate and tenacious stu-dent of Nordic childhoods, I remain an outsider. From this familiar and friendly outsider's perspective, I offer my views on childhood and early education in the Nordic countries. Drawing upon material presented by other authors in this book, I contrast Nordic and American perspectives when such comparisons seem instructive. I also briefly report on my most recent research in Denmark and explore related questions about the social lives of immigrant children in Nordic countries. I end with an appeal to non-Nordic readers to consider how we might find inspiration in Nordic ways for enhancing childhood within the context of our own daily realities. I am well aware that I may misunderstand or misinterpret what I see and hear in Nordic settings and that I often paint with too broad a brush in rep-resenting both American and Nordic ideals and practices, thereby glossing over important details and distinctions.

## IDEOLOGY AS A DRIVING FORCE

In Chapter 2, Kristjansson explains that, throughout the 20th century and continuing now into the 21st century, child and family policies maintain privileged, high-profile positions in Nordic societies. "It is in this macro sense that ... the Nordic societies excel; that is, in the vitality and vividness of public discourse on childhood and in the policies arising from this discourse" and, further, that "...public child-centeredness found in the Nordic countries bears witness to" the value Nordic people place on childhood.

Even after all these years of work and study in the region, Nordic ideology, policy, and practice fascinate me, startle me, and unsettle my American sensibilities, causing me to question, time and again, my basic assumptions about children and their education, as well as about the prophets (*to borrow Strand's term from Chapter 4*) whose ideas frame my research and my daily work with children. By using singular nouns—ideology, policy, and practice—I reveal my perception that marked similarities characterize child-related precepts and values in Denmark, Finland, Iceland, Norway, and Sweden, as well as the ways in which these ideals are represented in public policy and, ultimately, enacted in daily practice. However, as Kristjansson points out, singular terms sometimes capture shared characteristics of Nordicness and sometimes conceal unique features that distinguish one Nordic country from the others.

The similarities in Nordic ideology, policy, and practice beguile me and, frankly, make me envious. Americans may have a few slogans to which most of us would subscribe, such as "our children are our most precious resource" and "children are the future of our country"; but no one can legitimately proclaim a widely shared American childhood ideology that impels child and family policy or creates a realistic expectation for consistently high standards in American child care and early education. In fact, I propose that variation is the overarching characteristic of early childhood settings in America.

The ideology represented in the Nordic concept of the *good childhood* (*en god barndom* in Danish) constitutes a powerful and driving force behind both public policy and daily practice in Nordic preschools, schools and communities. Unfortunately, there is no American counterpart to the *good childhood* concept. Furthermore, this lack of a broadly shared vision of childhood *as it should be for all children* accounts, in large measure, for fundamental differences in Nordic and American pedagogical practice and contributes to marked inequalities in American provisions for children.

Many would assert that these differences in educational quality standards result primarily from dissimilarities between the American economic system and the Nordic social welfare system, especially regarding taxation levels citizens will tolerate. However, our economic systems also reflect dramatically different ideologies about the role of the national government. Ultimately, these ideological differences play out in the way children and families are treated within our societies. Nordic people readily accept the premise that government's central function is to ensure equal standards of living and a high quality of life for everyone, and, furthermore, that citizens themselves ought to share the tax burden associated with these expectations. This premise is realized through the Nordic welfare model, which provides generous child- and family-friendly benefits.

The Nordic vision of *the good childhood* frames, as foreground or background, all chapters in this book, despite their varying topics and purposes. More generally, the concept, though often unspoken, anchors much of the early childhood discourse in the Nordic countries.

## ESSENTIAL FEATURES OF THE GOOD CHILDHOOD CONCEPT AND THE IDEOLOGY IT REPRESENTS

The Nordic concept of the *good childhood* rests on these bedrock ideals as they apply to children: democracy, egalitarianism, freedom, emancipation, cooperation, and solidarity. These ideals in their Nordic expression are tightly interwoven and mutually reinforcing; together they provide both a context and an explanation for those aspects of Nordic childhood and education that seem most exotic and most enviable to outsiders like myself.

As many of the chapter authors illustrate, the Nordic notion of democracy as an essential feature of the *good childhood* requires that children experience democracy directly as an integral and consistent aspect of their daily lives at home, in school, and in their communities. Official policy documents and curriculum guidelines in the Nordic countries acknowledge a central expectation that preschools and schools will exemplify democratic principles and that children will be active participants in these democratic environments. Egalitarianism and emancipation further the exercise of democracy in Nordic ECE settings. Nordic people espouse that children and adults are equal along many planes. They enact this principle through their commitment to emancipation, that is, the notion that children should be free from excessive adult control and supervision.

These views, taken individually and together, create psychological space, openness, and respect for children's views and their right to self-determination in much greater measure than is typical in American settings. For example, children in Nordic preschools and schools typically have a particularly strong voice (*by my American calibrations*) in decisions that affect them throughout the day. They spend a great deal of time (*again by my American calibrations*) in free play, often beyond the immediate supervision of adults, running indoors and out as their interests dictate, and engaging in potentially dangerous (*to my American eyes*) activities, like those described at the beginning of this chapter, such as climbing trees or using sharp knives and adult power tools. Formal, teacher-initiated "lessons," in the American sense, are the exception rather than the rule. Lessons seem to emerge by spontaneous combustion, rather than from advanced instructional planning, as children and adults engage together in informal conversations, typically led by the children, energized by their immediate play activities and the interests that arise during free exploration of their indoor and outdoor environments. Einarsdottir, Hakkarainen, and other chapter authors explain the Nordic concept of free play as play that is free from excessive adult control, oversupervision, and interference. This definition is quite different from the American notion of free play, a term that typically means that adults have specified a brief time, say 15 to 30 minutes, in the pre-established daily schedule when children *are allowed* to do what they want to do, often *if* they have finished the tasks the adults have given them. In many settings, especially in the kindergarten and primary grades, children earn the right to play on Friday afternoons if they behave nicely and complete their work on Monday through Thursday.

Among the most concrete manifestations of the emancipation principle in Nordic early childhood settings are kids-only rooms where adults may not trespass. In Denmark, for instance, these "pillow rooms" provide both physical space and tacit approval for pillow fights and other rough-and-tumble play beyond the watchful eyes of teachers. Pillow rooms require adults to believe that children benefit from rough play and, possibly, from opportunities to resolve conflict that will likely emerge as children have pillow fights. Danish teachers would say this represents the ideal of emancipation. However, in virtually every U.S. state, preschool and daycare licensing regulations would prohibit spaces where children cannot be readily seen and supervised by adults. Beneath these differences in Nordic and American practices lie fundamental differences in expectations about children's behavior and beliefs about their competence.

Democracy, egalitarianism, freedom, emancipation, cooperation, and solidarity collectively create the *good childhood* at both individual and group levels in Nordic early childhood settings. The ideals of democracy, egalitarianism, freedom, and emancipation empower *individual* children in a preschool or school context. Democracy ensures that children have a voice; egalitarianism ensures that children's voices have influence; freedom expands their horizons and the sphere of their influence; and emancipation gives them room to explore their options, energized by youthful inquisitiveness and passion for learning, largely uncompromised by adult authority and supervision.

But these ideals are only part of the *good childhood* story. The ideal of cooperation requires compromise and shared responsibility and, therefore, speaks more to the *individual in relation to the group.* Cooperation, compromise, and shared responsibility are clearly valued for their own sake in Nordic childhood settings and also because they represent requisite orientations for success in Nordic societies that function largely through consensus. Some Nordic scholars in this book also include solidarity among the essential elements of the *good childhood.* Solidarity instills a sense of belonging to a society with a shared history, tradition, language, and cultural practices. I will return to the concept of solidarity in later discussions about children's behavior in early childhood settings and about immigrant children's access to the *good childhood*.

The ideals of democracy, egalitarianism, emancipation, and cooperation create a context for far more equal adult–child relationships than those that are typically viewed as normative in America, where power and privilege accompany both adult and teacher status. In American ECE contexts, *responsible* adults are expected to set clear boundaries for children *in their charge* and to institute consequences (no doubt experienced as punishment by children) when children cross these boundaries. (The American phrase *in their charge* reveals a philosophical and legal orientation light years from the Nordic concept of emancipation.) All too often, in my view, American early childhood and elementary teachers spend their days as the boundary police, harping on the rules, watching for infractions, and meting out penalties. As Brostrøm and other chapter authors explain, adults in Nordic settings consciously avoid setting boundaries for behavior and exerting adult authority unless it is absolutely necessary, seeking instead to *cooperate with children* rather than to control them. I have rarely seen Nordic preschool or school teachers wield their adult power or their authority as teachers in ways that probably would be viewed as acceptable, if not desirable, in American practice. The "because I said so" mentality does not exist in Nordic settings or, if it does, it is too subtle for this outsider to recognize it.

In my experience, Nordic ECE settings are active and interesting places, where adults and children interact with one another in warm, friendly, almost familial ways. Nordic preschools are unlikely to be chaotic or inhabited by wild, out-of-control children. Perhaps the freedom Nordic children experience from their earliest days, coupled with other elements of the *good childhood*, namely cooperation, consideration for the group, and the societal conventions passed along as a function of the solidarity principle, promote acceptable behavior even in the absence of strict adult supervision and control.

Although democracy is represented as a core value in general American educational discourse, references to democracy are infrequent in American ECE discourse. A key difference is that American preschools and schools are not conceptualized as democracies, but, rather, as places where students learn about democracy. It is often said that the purpose of education in America is to *prepare* children to participate in a democracy and to teach them to use freedom when they are adults. In contrast, Nordic people expect that children should experience democracy directly from their earliest days. This means, then, that Nordic children have rights and attendant freedoms that American children are only preparing to experience later in life. Numerous practical differences, large and small, arise from these divergent ideological perspectives about children's rights within a democracy and about the nature and extent of freedom that should be accorded to the youngest members of a society.

Nordic people argue that children ought to have a voice in virtually all matters that affect them, while Americans tend to hold a narrower view about the kinds of choices that are "appropriate" for young children, such as selecting their own clothing and whether they want their sandwiches cut (by an adult, of course) diagonal or straight across. As illustrated in this book, democracy and egalitarianism also frame Nordic discussions about social justice in ECE settings. Social justice themes appear far less frequently in American than Nordic early childhood discourse.

The ideals of democracy, egalitarianism, and freedom as they relate to children are conceptualized differently in American and Nordic contexts and are far less central in American discourse and practice. On the other hand, Nordic and American notions of cooperation in ECE settings are similar in many ways. However, the American perspective lacks the broader context of consensus-building that frames the Nordic discussion, possibly due to the prevailing majority-rules orientation in America. The notion of emancipation, as it is understood in the Nordic context, is virtually absent from American ECE discourse. A practice that Nordic teachers would view as consistent with emancipation ideals, American teachers would likely view as poor adult supervision. Conversely, a practice that American teachers would view as representing appropriate supervision and protection, their Nordic counterparts would likely view as oversupervision and overprotection. Similarly, the concept of solidarity, as it is understood in the Nordic context, is also missing from American ECE discourse, and largely from the general education discourse as well. In fact, the discourse of diversity is far more prevalent in America than any discourse about shared heritage, traditions, language, or cultural practice. In fact, politically liberal Americans typically view the notion of shared "American" heritage as inherently representative of European American ethnocentricism.

As Kristjansson states in Chapter 2, children's rights and well-being have long been prevalent topics in public, political, and academic discourse in the Nordic countries. The overarching principle of children's rights provides a backdrop for Nordic conceptualizations of the *good childhood* and its core ideals. For example, in Chapter 9 Brostrøm describes tensions in Nordic debates about children's rights versus their need for protection. Children's rights are consistently spoken of with greater reverence and animated in more concrete ways in the Nordic countries than in America, as best evidenced by America's unenviable position as one of only two countries in the world that have not yet signed the United Nations Convention on Children's Rights. I argue that, for the most part, children's rights are hardly on the public radar screen in America, beyond the context of political campaigns and early childhood education conferences. To the extent that they are discussed at all, Americans hold widely divergent views about which rights should be accorded to the country's youngest citizens. Philosophically and legally children are the responsibility of and, in many ways, the property of, their parents and, when their parents are not present, their teachers. From this perspective, adults have not only the legal right but also the responsibility to make decisions for children. Many modern American ideas about children can be traced to prevailing religious beliefs at the time of the country's founding, including the belief that children are inherently evil and can only be saved through a firm adult hand and ultimate acceptance of Christianity.

The ideal of the *good childhood* and all its attendant features may sound like jargon or political rhetoric to American readers, but the concept is thoroughly engrained, broadly shared, and deeply cherished in the Nordic region, where commitment to it is palpable.

## BEYOND IDEOLOGY . . . THE FACTS OF LIFE

Clearly, Nordic children are allowed, or even encouraged, to learn by doing, even when doing has some inherent risks, while American children, often, are not allowed to try. Beyond the prevalence of the *good childhood concept* in the Nordic countries and the absence of a shared ideological frame in America, how can these differences be explained? To what extent is American reluctance based on economic concerns about insurance premiums and law suits, neither of which would be likely to worry our Nordic counterparts? To what extent is it based on limitation-related theories about children's capacities at any given age and stage of development, even though we believe that we have replaced these ideas with more modern strength-based theories? To what extent is our preference for safer, more controlled, and more academic ECE activities grounded in pedagogical practices we learned through our professional training or acquired through osmosis, rather than through ongoing conscious and conscientious examination of our work, as Lenz Taguchi recommends in Chapter 10 in her description of deconstruction, multiple readings, and ethical resistance?

Why do Nordic children seem (at least to me) to be more competent than American children to climb trees without falling, use sharp knives without slicing off their fingers, and play safely near an open fire? These questions point to the importance of cultural practices and expectations as frames for our daily decisions about children. Danish children do not cut off their fingers because they are allowed to take risks and gain experience with knives, which, in turn, enables them to meet culturally situated expectations that they will be competent. American children might, indeed, cut off their fingers because they have never had the chance to use a knife before and because the psychological environment is so charged with fear that something dreadful is about to happen if a child tries something risky.

Why are Americans so fearful that something awful will happen to our children when Nordic people seem to expect happier outcomes? (My Danish colleagues tell me this is a prevailing view—*stereotype?*—about American parents and teachers.) Perhaps this question gets us back to egalitarianism as a societal ideal and socioeconomic reality. Could it be that people in a more egalitarian society are less fearful because there are fewer intergroup differences than in a society that broadly accepts as a given that some will have and others will not? Are the *have's* destined to be afraid of the *have not's?* These ideas rarely come up in public discourse except, for example, amid the hoopla surrounding a Michael Moore film or political campaign promises. Evidently American devotion to competitive capitalism is solid and, therefore, we are prepared to accept the inevitability of *have's* and *have not's*. Among the most surprising personal epiphanies arising from my experiences in the Nordic countries is how often I unconsciously accept that there will be *have's* and *have not's* in situations where my Nordic colleagues don't see such unequal results as a possibility, let alone as a given. I accept that some preschools will be excellent, most will be OK, and a few will be, well, terrible. My Nordic colleague lives by the motto that "all children should go to the same school," meaning that all schools should be of equal quality. We will visit this concept again later.

Although I am not familiar with any studies on the topic, I imagine that, if asked to describe the characteristics of a good childhood, Americans would list such fundamental things as having the basic necessities of food, clothing, and safe shelter; being cared for by a loving family; and having access to a good education. As illustrated in several chapters in this book, these fundamentals are guaranteed in the Nordic countries by the centrality of childhood issues in social and political discourse and by the strong Nordic welfare systems. The Nordic concept of the *good childhood* focuses on grander principles and ideals, rather than basic necessities for survival.

Child and family policies, including educational policies, differ dramatically across the 50 American states and even among cities within a given state. The degree and quality of policy implementation may vary markedly from location to location, even when policies are similar, due to significant differences in levels of public funding. The American public acknowledges, and perhaps even accepts as inevitable, that school and preschool quality will vary from site to site (*have's* and *have not's* again), even within the same community, while Nordic parents, educators, and policymakers expect a high-quality standard for all schools and daycare provisions across the region. This expectation of high and equal school quality is captured in the Danish saying that "all children must attend the same school." (Interestingly, however, a Danish teacher educator recently pointed out that this saying and the sentiment behind it can backfire. She noted that the "same school for all children" policy may prevent educators and policy-makers from shining the spotlight on successful innovations. Evidently, if all schools are the same, there can be no pioneers or frontrunners.)

To be sure there are general differences in American and Nordic views about what young children are capable of doing and what they should be allowed to do, as well as differences in the ways in which child-related issues are discussed, debated, and resolved. As detailed in several chapters in this book, Nordic perspectives and practices are rooted in the historical and cultural traditions of each country, as well as from the social and economic conditions that gave rise to their child care and early education move-ments. Nordic notions about childhood freedom to explore and play were already in place when child care provisions emerged in the Nordic coun-tries. Nordic parents and early childhood teachers seem to readily accept bumps and bruises as inevitable consequences of the *freedom to which chil-dren are entitled* as they exercise *their right* to play and explore, unencum-bered by oppressive or unnecessarily restrictive adult supervision and intervention. In contrast, as noted above, American early childhood educa-tors typically take a protectionist view, fearful that children will get hurt and that we will then be sued.

Even though we often intone the same authorities, such as Piaget and Vygotsky, and reference the same programmatic benchmarks, such as Reg-gio Emilia, High/Scope, or the Fifth Dimension, for example, Nordic and American early educators often have fundamentally different ideas about what is developmentally and educationally appropriate for young children. This point can be illustrated clearly by the overnight camping trips Danish children take with their teachers beginning in preschool. In spring 2003 I visited a forest near Copenhagen where teachers from eight preschools and school-entry classes (similar to the American kindergarten) had taken 80 4-year-olds on a 4-night camping excursion—no parents allowed. The teachers and children slept together in tents, showered together, and ate together. If someone were to suggest such a field trip to preschool parents at my school or, I dare say, almost any preschool in America, there would surely be an uprising. In America, preschoolers are generally viewed as too young to be away from their parents for such a long time. American teach-ers are supposed to develop caring relationships with children, but to establish a "professional distance" between themselves and the children, a distance that would be difficult to maintain on a Danish-style camping trip. The idea of teachers and children sleeping together and showering together would no doubt cause great consternation among both parents and teachers, at least in part because of pervasive and largely unfounded fears that pedophiles lurk around every corner — or almost every corner.

## DIFFERENCES IN NORDIC AND AMERICAN ECE DISCOURSE

Nordic ideology about the *good childhood*, children's rights, and consensus building and interest in maintaining rich Nordic traditions while participating in the global world provide a backdrop for contemporary Nordic ECE discourse and explain many of the differences in contemporary Nordic and American ECE discussions. In addition, the influence of postmodern philosophies and feminist theories are far more evident in and central to Nordic than American early childhood discourse. So essential and so entrenched are these influences, and the beliefs and values they inspire, that our authors often take for granted that non-Nordic readers will have what they consider to be a "basic" background and orientation.

At the risk, or perhaps with the certainty, of misrepresenting through oversimplification, I attempt to briefly identify a few of the theories and philosophies that frame, or at least influence, many of the chapters in this book. For instance, Nordic ECE discourse often includes concepts presented in Belenky, Clinchy, Goldberger, and Tarule's (1986) landmark book, *Women's Ways of Knowing: The Development of Self, Voice, and Mind,* especially as they apply to children and the professionals who care for them. For instance, Danish researchers, teacher educators, and early childhood practitioners refer directly and indirectly to "children's ways of knowing" as distinct and deserving of understanding and respect. Appreciating children's ways of knowing requires that children's active learning and ongoing construction of the self remain the centerpiece of efforts to educate them—to be understood here in Nordic, not American, terms—throughout their early years.

The influence of feminist discourse can be seen in several chapters in this book. *Structural feminist theory* highlights economic, social, and political *structures*, particularly patriarchy and capitalism, that purposefully (or otherwise) oppress women and, therefore, ultimately affect the lives of children. *Poststructural feminist theory* introduces new elements to the discussion. For instance, poststructural feminists talk about the way interrelated oppressive structures in society create *systems* of gendered inequality in privilege and power. The combined effects of these structures and systems influence identity development among women and children, as well as their ability and inclination to resist oppressive forces. Post-tructural feminists promote women's liberation and equality by focusing on strategies for navigating through or dismantling prevailing power structures. For instance, the notion of *voice*, which appears in Broström's chapter and several others, arises from feminist theory and refers not only to expressing one's perspectives, but, even more, to being listened to and taken seriously, particularly by those empowered with greater authority and resources.

The "feminine" influence in the development of early education, as noted by many of our authors, and the fact that ECE remains predominately a female domain even today, takes on considerably different meaning in the Nordic countries than in America because gender equality remains an unrealized ideal, though not a universally accepted ideal, in America. Gender equality is far more a social, political, and economic reality in the Nordic countries. Even so, as Strand notes, because ECE represents the professionalization of traditional feminine nurturing roles, the field occupies a relatively weak position compared to other fields of knowledge and scholarship. Taking up a similar theme in Chapter 3, Johansson comments on the lessening influence of traditional female voices and perspectives in early childhood teacher education, asserting that this results from usurpation by male-dominated power structures at the university level, not from advancement of post-structural feminist ideology.

From the perspective of postmodern feminist theory, in Chapter 10 Lenz Taguchi focuses on the ways in which accepted theory and practice can be maintained or, alternatively, changed through a process of active reflection, multiple "readings" (or analyses from various theoretical frameworks), deconstruction, and ethical resistance. Lenz Taguchi also describes the ways in which ECE practice has been influenced by a succession of societal orientations and pedagogical theories. For instance, Nordic preschools arose from a perceived societal need to provide substitute maternal care and home-like environments because of "disadvantaged" children's circumstances and/or labor market demands for women in the workplace. However, as the author notes, the central role of "female nurturing" in early education is today being challenged by post-structural feminist ideology and contemporary educational theory focusing on children as active investigators of the world, constructors of their own knowledge, and, essentially, creators of their own, individual "self."

Several of our authors take up the question of power relationships between adults and children and the notion that children's voices must be heard and understood. However, as Broström points out, teachers and researchers can only understand children from our more powerful positions as adults, creating a conundrum, if not a vicious circle. But the intention that relationships between children and adults should be egalitarian and democratic and the conviction that children's rights must be respected are there, centrally and deeply rooted in Nordic childhood discourse, in stark contrast to American discourse in which similar views are rare.

Nordic authors frequently speak of the child as "subject." According to Brostrøm (2003), the general idea of the child as subject is rooted in European reform education (Rosseau, Froebel, and Pestalozzi), and, more recently, in critical pedagogy, as represented by Paulo Freire in *Pedagogy of the Oppressed* (1970). The basic idea is that the child is a subject (i.e., the active one, the learner) in the mutual, interactive and complementary process of teaching and learning. According to this view, teacher and learner, through dialogue and communication, turn their attention together toward the object, or what is to be learned.

The differences in discourse noted above are clearly rooted in theory and philosophy. However, sometimes differences seem, at first, to be merely semantic. As Broström illustrates in Chapter 9 and Niikko points out in Chapter 6, ECE professionals emphasize their roles as *caregivers* rather than as teachers. To them this is more than a simple semantic difference because it represents the heart and soul of their professional practice. For example, Niikko carefully differentiates between the terms *care, caring,* and *all-round care* as fundamentally different concepts in Finnish ECE discourse. Interestingly, such distinctions may seem inconsequential to American readers, since all of these terms, as Niikko explains them, are subsumed under the general rubric of "quality," as it is defined by the National Association for the Education of Young Children, for instance. It is interesting to imagine what a conversation between a Finnish early childhood educator and her American counterpart would be like if they were to discuss care, caring, and all-round care. The Finnish early childhood educator would find the distinctions crucial to the dialogue, while the American would probably find it difficult to figure out why the difference mattered at all. In my experience, both parties would be unaware of their own cultural and linguistic frames and might come away from such a conversation with completely different ideas about what each person had said. Herein lies both the challenge and the promise of cross-cultural conversation.

## THE ROLE, VALUE, AND SURVIVAL OF EARLY CHILDHOOD EDUCATION AS A DISTINCT FIELD

Strand's chapter deals most directly with an important notion woven more discretely into other chapters, namely that preschools and schools play an important role in Nordic nation-building, construction of Nordic identity, and minimizing social differences that may arise as social welfare systems meet postmodern challenges, including the shift toward increasing ethnocultural diversity. According to Strand, the preschool is, in the Norwegian mind at least, both "the goal and the means of realizing the full potential of an ideal social democracy; a social democratic utopia." To extend

Strand's argument from Norway to the larger Nordic context, the preschool protects the *good childhood*, and further develops the welfare state. "The preschool's special characteristics encompass the children's well-being and the symbolic values of childhood, as well as consideration of the total economic and cultural capital of the nation." As several authors note, Nordic preschools are both a platform for children's ideas and a place where they can construct their own childhood cultures, in the company of adults who want to care for them without dominating them. To achieve these goals for children in early childhood settings, Nordic scholars, like Pramling Samuelson in Chapter 5, emphasize the importance of rigorous, high-quality professional preparation for preschool and primary teachers. Nordic preschool teachers typically have academic preparation similar to, if not equivalent to, the professional preparation of elementary school teachers and the compensation levels for preschool and school teachers are closer than in America. This speaks to the importance Nordic people place on early childhood experience. Throughout America, preschool teacher qualifications are significantly lower than qualifications for elementary school teachers and preschool teacher compensation typically is far less than an elementary school teacher's salary. For example, in California elementary teachers must complete a 4-year university degree plus a state-approved 1-year teaching credential program, while preschool teachers are supposed to have about three classes in child development or early education when they begin their careers. However, course requirements for preschool teachers are routinely waived because preschools and day-care centers pay such low wages that they cannot find applicants who have completed the requirements. Further complicating the matter is the fact that preschool teaching positions are often part time and offer no health or retirement benefits, so staff turnover rates tend to be high, compromising quality in preschools and daycare centers.

Given the strong value Nordic people place on childhood and early education, it seems incongruous that several authors in this book questioned whether essential qualities of Nordic childhood, including Nordic-style ECE, will survive in the face of globalization, closer contact with other countries through the European Union, and the arrival (*invasion?*) of non-Nordic ideas through mass media and immigration, as well as a push from within to make preschool and primary education more similar for a variety of sensible-sounding reasons. Most of the authors situate this survival discussion within the context of preschool teacher education. The question goes like this: Will Nordic childhood and early education survive intact if preschool teachers, who have been the protectors of all that is essentially Nordic about Nordic childhood, are educated like school teachers and expected to *teach* like teachers rather than to *care* like preschool teachers?

The consensus in our chapters seems to be YES, Nordic childhood and ECE will survive, *maybe*.

As a familiar outsider, I predict that, in the short term, moderate changes will creep in, for example, in the form of *slightly* more emphasis on lesson planning in accordance with an established curriculum; *slightly* increased attention to early academics, such as learning letters and numbers; and *slightly* less time for play in the preschool. However, in the long term, the course seems set. Nordic preschools will become more school-like as preschool teacher-preparation programs become more similar, or, as is already the case in some countries, as the two professional preparation programs combine. I predict that this will occur in accordance with the hamburger principle. Not so many years ago, there was only one American-style hamburger restaurant on Strøget, Copenhagen's famous walking street. However, today Strøget includes numerous American fast-food and clothing shops. What was, to me, inherently Danish about Strøget has vanished. When I walk down Strøget today, I feel as if I am in Los Angeles, except that more people are speaking English on Strøget.

Is this a good thing, a bad thing, or simply a thing? Do the Danes who stroll along Strøget experience these changes as something fundamental to Nordicness or something superficial? The same questions apply to ECE. What can Nordic early childhood educators sacrifice without dismantling the essential Nordicness of Nordic childhoods? Clearly, the answer does not lie in the unrealistic expectation that primary school teachers will become more like preschool teachers if their teacher-education programs are combined. Neither does the answer lie in the equally unrealistic expectation that preschool teachers' perspectives will become stronger and more influential if they collaborate with school teachers on transition programs. School teachers will not become more like preschool teachers. They will not give up *teaching* in favor of *care-giving*.

I truly wonder what we will read in a book about Nordic ECE written a decade from now.

## NEWCOMERS: THE GOOD CHILDHOOD FOR ALL?

Several authors refer to Nordic solidarity as a cornerstone ideal in the *good childhood*. Solidarity instills a sense of belonging to a society that shares history, tradition, language, and cultural practices. Therefore, preschools can be seen as psychological/sociological space and a physical place where children experience the solidarity principle firsthand, though, as Kristjansson notes in Chapter 2, its tenets might not be spoken about directly at the preschool level. As Strand noted in Chapter 4, Norwegian preschools are grounded explicitly and emphatically on traditional Norwegian values and behavioral norms, exemplifying the notion of solidarity. However, the Organization for Economic Cooperation and Development (OECD, 1999) proposed that Norwegian preschools seem unwelcoming to children with non-Nordic backgrounds and recommended more tolerant preschools reflecting traditional Norwegian values, as well as values and customs of children from other ethnocultural backgrounds. In this sense, one principle of the *good childhood*, solidarity, may be working against non-Nordic newcomers. Some authors (see, e.g., Stephens, 1995) argue that children are unwitting pawns in the politics of culture, creating situations in which ethnic identities and practices are thrust upon them as gifts that cannot be returned and must not be laid aside.

Is Nordicness a treasure to be preserved for future generations and to be shared with children from non-Nordic backgrounds who now live in Denmark, Finland, Iceland, Norway, and Sweden? Our authors, notably all Nordic except for myself, agree that Nordicness is, indeed, a treasure and a gift. But recent immigration has generated new questions about tradition and heritage. How should Nordicness be shared with newcomers? Should newcomers play a role in shaping Nordicness of the future or is that the purview of those who are ethnically Nordic? These questions underlie the decidedly nonegalitarian-sounding debates about "the immigrant problem" in contemporary public discourse in some Nordic countries.

In a recent research project, sponsored in part by the Danish Fulbright Commission, my colleagues and I (Wagner, Camparo, Tsenkova, & Camparo, 2005) studied peer relationships in 21 elementary classrooms in 10 schools in two Danish cities. We investigated whether anti-immigrant sentiments and stereotypes track into Danish school settings. Based on the vociferous nature of Danish public debate about immigrants in recent years, our predictions painted a gloomy picture of social inequality, prejudice, and exclusion, a far cry from the cherished ideals of the *good childhood*. However, our data did not support this worst-case scenario. While a majority of the children experienced many social advantages, neither minority nor majority children disliked each other at a rate greater than random chance. Minority children were more likely than majority children to cross ethnic boundaries in selecting liked classmates, but it is unclear whether this represented a healthy accommodation to social realities for minority children or a threat to their ethnic identity development. Taken together, findings from our study suggest that minority children were neither warmly welcomed nor broadly rejected by their peers from the ethnic majority group. There was some evidence of subtle prejudice and marginalization, due to majority children's favoritism toward other majority children rather than to outright discrimination against minority children. However, preliminary findings from descriptive analyses suggest several patterns of marginalization that did not reveal themselves through whole-sample quantitative analysis. For example, preliminary descriptive analysis shows that more than 75% of the classrooms we studied were without a single minority boy in the high-status popular category. What does it mean to children when members of their own group rarely achieve high social status within their classrooms?

Our conclusion is that the principle of egalitarianism was not fully realized in any of the classes we studied, but neither was bigotry running rampant there. Challenges inevitably arise when societies experience an influx of immigrants, especially when those immigrants are easily visible, as is the case with many minority groups now settling in Nordic countries. The situation in Denmark pits two aspects of the *good childhood* against one another: egalitarianism may prohibit open hostility toward minority children, while, on the other hand, solidarity may promote strong in-group favoritism among majority children. From my perspective as a familiar outsider, it seems that our research project may provide some clues about promoting intergroup harmony in Denmark. For instance, perhaps early childhood educators would be well advised to think about antibias and multicultural curricula that emphasize inclusion and fairness because these concepts are central to egalitarian and democratic principles of the *good childhood* and, more generally, they are central to the heritage instilled through the solidarity principle. Furthermore, consistent with other studies, our research points to the need for research with much younger children to determine how best to promote positive intrapersonal and intergroup relationships between minority and majority children before patterns of inclusion and exclusion become entrenched.

## CAN THE GOOD CHILDHOOD BE TRANSPLANTED?

At the campus demonstration school where I work, we have tried mightily to transplant Nordic ideas into our Southern California environment. Surprisingly, we have had more luck on the abstract, philosophical level than on the concrete level. For instance, after a study tour to Denmark, several of our teachers tried to implement some Nordic ideas, like paying closer attention to the aesthetic qualities of our classrooms by adding fresh flowers to the lunch tables and using real dishes instead of paper plates. These innovations lasted about one week. Ideas like letting children climb trees, use knives, and light candles in school were clearly out of the question due to insurance regulations and preschool licensing requirements. However, our teachers have also tried, with somewhat greater success, to hover less and intervene only when necessary, following the examples we saw in Denmark. We have even created our "Danish deck," a porch attached to the classroom for 2-year-olds. Our goal—again inspired by our observations in

Denmark—is to let children move freely between the classroom and this enclosed outdoor space without requiring a teacher to be with them. Rarely are we actually able to let the children go on the porch alone, though. After all, as Americans, the ideas of childhood emancipation are new to us. And, besides, if the children go on the porch alone, won't someone get hurt and won't our insurance rates go up and won't we be sued...?

Just thinking consciously about the *good childhood* and all that the concept entails, especially the principles of egalitarianism, schools as living democracies, and emancipation, as we have been introduced to them by our experiences in Nordic countries and our contact with Nordic visitors to our school, has given us a platform for challenging our most taken-for-granted ideas and, hopefully, for practicing ethical resistance in ways that bring some qualities of the *good childhood* to our school in Los Angeles.

## REFERENCES

Belenky, M. F., Clinchy, B. M., Goldberger, N. R., & Trarule, J. (1986). *Women's ways of knowing: The development of self, voice, and mind.* New York: Mind Books.

Brostrøm, S. (2003). Unity of care, teaching and Upbringing: A theoretical contribution towards a a new paradigm in early childhood education. In M. K. Lohmander (Ed.), *Care, play and learning curricula for early childhood education* (pp. 21–38). Göteborg: Göteborg University.

Freire, P. (1970). *Pedagogy of the oppressed.* New York: Continuum.

OECD. (1999). *Early childhood education and care policy in Norway.* OECD Country Note. June 1999. Retrieved May 2005 from http://www1.oecd.org/els/educaion/ecec/docs.htm

Stephens, S. (Ed.). (1995). *Children and the politics of culture.* Princeton, NJ: Princeton University Press.

Wagner, J. T., Camparo, L. B., Tsenkova, V, & Camparo, J. C. (2005). *Peer preferences and social status of Denmark's minority and majority children: En god barndom.* Manuscript submitted for publication.

# ABOUT THE CONTRIBUTORS

**Johanna Einarsdottir** is Associate Professor at Iceland University of Education. She received a Ph.D. in Early Childhood Education from the University of Illinois in 2000. She has extensive experience in the field of early childhood education. Dr. Einarsdottir began as a teacher of young children in 1973, and she has been involved in teacher education in Iceland since 1977. Dr. Einarsdottir's professional interests include early childhood education, early childhood teacher education, and qualitative methodology. She is currently conducting research on children's views on their preschool education, and transition and continuity in early childhood education. She has published her work in the United States and in Europe.

**Judith T. Wagner** is Professor of Child Development and Education at Whittier College in Whittier, California, where she directs the Broadoaks Children's School. She was a 2003 Fulbright Scholar in Research and Teaching in Denmark. Dr. Wagner helped create the Child Development and Diversity Program, now called Psychology and Child Development, at Denmark's International Study Program (DIS) in Copenhagen. Her research interests include Nordic perspectives on childhood and education; social relationships of minority and majority children; and the development of stereotypes, prejudice, and in-group preference in ethnoculturally diverse settings. Dr. Wagner's recent publications include *Early Childhood Education in Five Nordic Countries: Perspectives on the Transition from Preschool to School* (2003), which she coedited with Stig Broström, and an article entitled, "Fishing Naked: Nordic Early Childhood Philosophy, Policy, and Practice" in the September 2004 issue of *Young Children.*

*Nordic Childhoods and Early Education,* pages 307–310
Copyright © 2006 by Information Age Publishing
All rights of reproduction in any form reserved.

**Baldur Kristjánsson** is Associate Professor of Education and Developmental Psychology at Iceland University of Education. He received an M.A. in Clinical Child Psychology from Gothenburg University, Sweden. In 2001, he earned his Ph.D. degree in Educational Psychology from the Stockholm Institute of Education. Dr. Kristjánsson was a school psychologist in Iceland from 1984 to 1986. Between 1986 and 1990, he collaborated with Nordic child researchers on a study of social change and childhood in the five Nordic countries. From 1992 to 1994 he worked on an educational research project, where he studied the family–school relationship in nine compulsory Stockholm schools. Dr. Kristjánsson has published his research on childhood and family life in a number of Scandinavian anthologies and journals. Currently, he is doing research on Icelandic families with adopted children from Asia. His primary research interests lie in the area of child development and family life in the context of social change.

**Jan-Erik Johansson** has been Professor of Early Childhood Education at Oslo University College in Norway since 1998. He received his teacher certificate in Sweden and a Ph.D. in Education at Göteborg University, Sweden. Dr. Johansson was a teacher and researcher in the Preschool Teacher Education University in Göteborg and later at the Teacher Education University in Karlstad, Sweden. From 1983 he was at Göteborg University working with a variety of research projects. Dr. Johansson's professional interests include early childhood education and early childhood teacher education. He is currently conducting a research project on the youngest preschool children.

**Torill Strand** is Associate Professor at the University of Bergen in Norway. She was trained as a preschool teacher during the late 1970s, worked in a preschool during the 1980s, received her Cand. Ped. diploma early in the 1990s, and has been tenured at Oslo University College, the Program for Early Childhood Education for a decade. In 2000–2001 she was a Visiting Fulbright Scholar at the University of California, Berkeley. Dr. Strand's research interests include philosophy of education, sociology of knowledge, and early childhood education. She has published widely in six countries and five different languages. Her most recent publications include *Beyond What is Given as Givens: Promises and Threats of Self-Reflexive Research, Reconzeptualizing Early Childhood Education: Educating Humanity,* and *Peirce on Education: Nurturing the First Rule of Reason.*

**Ingrid Pramling Samuelsson** is Professor and Coordinator for Early Childhood Education at the Department of Education, Göteborg University, Sweden. She has a background as a preschool teacher and was awarded the first chair in early childhood education in Sweden in 1996. Dr. Pramling Samuelsson's research primarily focuses on how children create meaning and make sense of various aspects of the surrounding world in the context of preschool (daycare and kindergarten). Another research interest is teachers' professional development. She has served as a consultant to the Ministry of Education, the National Agency for Education, and the Department of Social Welfare and Health concerning questions about children. She is also president of Swedish OMEP (Organisation Mundiale pour l'Éducation Préscolaire).

**Anneli Niikko** has been Professor of Early Childhood Education in the Teacher Education Department of Savonlinna at the University of Joensuu since 1998 and is also Dean of the Faculty of Education at the University of Joensuu in Finland. She has been involved in teacher education and continuing education in Finland since 1975. Dr. Niikko was a lecturer in early childhood education at the University of Joensuu from 1975 to 1978. From 1979 to 1989 she was the superintendent of day care centers in the city of Joensuu, and from 1991 to 1995 she was a senior lecturer in Vocational Teacher Education of Polytechnic University in Jyväskylä. Dr. Niikko has worked as the Associate Professor of Education and Early Childhood Education at the University of Joensuu from 1989 to 1990 and from 1995 to 1998. Her professional and research interests include early childhood education and early childhood teacher education. Dr. Niikko is also conducting research on child-centered pedagogy, preschool education, and portfolio work in professional development of student teachers. She has published her work both in her own country and abroad.

**Pentti Hakkarainen** has been Professor of Early Childhood Education at Kajaani University Consortium, University of Oulu, Finland, since 1997. He received his master's degree and Ph.D. in Educational Sciences from the University of Jyväskylä. He was a research assistant, senior researcher, and head of the research department at the Research Institute for Pedagogical Sciences, University of Jyväskylä, from 1970–1997. During that period Dr. Hakkarainen was also visiting scholar at the Academy of Pedagogical Sciences, Moscow, from 1973 to 1975; Aarhus University, Denmark, from 1982 to 1983; and a postdoctoral fellow at the Laboratory of Comparative Human Cognition at the University of California, San Diego, from 1992 to 1993. His professional interests include research on children's play, narrative learning, and development. Dr. Hakkarainen has published his work mainly in Scandinavian countries and Europe. He is the editor of the *Journal of Russian and East European Psychology* and vice president of the International Vygotsky Society.

**Stig Broström** is Associate Professor in Early Childhood Education at the Danish University of Education in Copenhagen, where he has taught and conducted research since 1980. For nearly 35 years he has been involved in the field of early-years education, both as a preschool teacher and a preschool teacher educator. His main areas of research are related to children's life in preschool and the first years in school, with a focus on curriculum theory, children's play, social competence, and friendship. Dr. Broström's Ph.D. thesis, an ethnographic and comparative study, deals with transition issues exposed through children's social competence and learning motivation in a Danish and American classroom. Currently he is involved with a research program that focuses on the development of a curriculum for the early years.

**Hillevi Lenz Taguchi** is Assistant Professor in Education and a postdoctoral fellow at the Stockholm Institute of Education, Sweden. She graduated from Stockholm University with a dual degree, one in behavioral sciences and the other in literature. She earned her Ph.D. degree in education in 2001. She has been involved in teacher education with responsiblity for Reggio Emilia inspired teacher education, as well as gender perspectives in teacher education. Since 2004 Dr. Lenz Taguchi has been chair of the Centre of Gender in Educational Studies at the Institute of Education in Stockholm. Her current research projects focus on democracy and gender in higher education, gender pedagogy in early childhood education, and mathematics and gender identity formation between the ages of 3 and 16. The theoretical and methodological framwork is feminist poststructural. She has published in Sweden and other parts of Europe and is currently also publishing in the United States.